'The best book for many years about Shakespeare. A fascinating account of his first year at the Globe Theatre, this book puts an end to all silly, and snobbish, theories that the plays were written by anyone but a working actor-writer from Stratford-upon-Avon. This is a wonderful account of life in the theatre and of the extraordinary Elizabethan popular appetite for great plays.' John Mortimer, *Observer* (Books of the Year)

'An enthralling study of a single year in canny Shakespeare's life. Everyone interested in the relationship between Shakespeare's life and his work should read Shapiro.' Tom Paulin, *Observer* (Books of the Year)

'Fantastically gripping.' Rebecca Tyrrel, *Sunday Telegraph* (Books of the Year)

'Superbly illuminating ... As a guide in clear prose underpinned by considerable learning, worn lightly [Shapiro] deserves whoops of applause.' Sam Leith, *Spectator*

'Shapiro proves himself a painstaking historian as well as a deft critic ... Only an extraordinary scholar could illuminate Shakespeare's singular genius by demonstrating how much his work owes to Elizabethan culture and society.' *Chicago Tribune*

'Insightful and often revelatory ... *1599* widens and deepens our understanding of four seminal plays and the mind that gave them to the world.' Desmond Ryan, *Philadelphia Inquirer*

'By giving us an account of what Shakespeare must have read, heard and seen that year, Shapiro goes further than any other biographer in accounting for the relationship between those words and his life ... He gives us a Shakespeare who chronicles his age, in a biographical form that speaks clearly to our own.' Frances Wilson, *Daily Telegraph*

'James Shapiro's *1599* is a brilliantly readable and revealing narrative.' Nicholas Hytner, *Guardian*

'The ploy of concentrating on the events of a single exciting year neatly leaves out much of what can make the average cradle-to-grave life of Shakespeare seem turgid and off the point . . . and allows Shapiro to get straight to the much more interesting question, often skimped in such books, of what Shakespeare's working life, the bit that made him matter, actually consisted of from one week and month to the next.' Michael Dobson, *London Review of Books*

'William Shakespeare has been sliced this way and that – biographically, literarily, culturally, theatrically and historically. Now James Shapiro, professor of English at Columbia University, has found a new and richly yielding angle . . . By voracious reading and a sharp eye for detail, Mr Shapiro helps us hear the plays through a buzz of contemporary voices – religious, loyal, sceptical, iconoclastic, seditious.' *The Economist*

'Triumphantly puts Shakespeare in the middle of Elizabethan London.' Rosie Millard, *New Statesman* (Books of the Year)

'James Shapiro offers brilliant new readings of the writer's work and world.' Mark Lawson, *Guardian* (Books of the Year)

'Shapiro's surgical incisions into a single year, coupled with a poignant sense of social tension and injustices, show that context is all.' Cynthia L. Haven, *Washington Post*

'Looking for a hitchhiker's guide to the Shakespearean universe? Hitch a ride with James Shapiro . . . More real and revealing than the grand, breathless fictions that fill out most biographies of Shakespeare.' Gary Taylor, *Guardian*

'In a bumper year for Shakespeare studies, the palm goes to James Shapiro's *1599*. It is a refreshing change to read a book that shows how Shakespeare was shaped by what he saw . . . as well as what he read.' Jonathan Bate, *TLS* (Books of the Year)

1599

Professor James Shapiro, who teaches at Columbia University in New York, is the author of *Rival Playwrights*, *Shakespeare and the Jews*, and *Oberammergau: The Troubling Story of the World's Most Famous Passion Play*. *1599: A Year in the Life of William Shakespeare* won the Theatre Book Prize 2005 and was also winner of the BBC Four Samuel Johnson Prize for Non-Fiction 2006. James Shapiro's most recent book is *Contested Will: Who Wrote Shakespeare?*

1599
A Year in the Life of
William Shakespeare

JAMES SHAPIRO

faber and faber

First published in 2005
by Faber and Faber Limited
Bloomsbury House
74-77 Great Russell Street
London WC1B 3DA

Typeset in Caslon by Faber and Faber Limited
Printed and bound by CPI Group (UK) Ltd, Croydon, CRO 4YY

A CIP record for this book
is available from the British Library

ISBN 978-0-571-21481-5
ISBN 0-571-21481-9

FSC
www.fsc.org
MIX
Paper from
responsible sources
FSC® C013604

For Mary and Luke

Contents

List of Illustrations

PLATE SECTION

Map of Shakespeare's London
c.1599

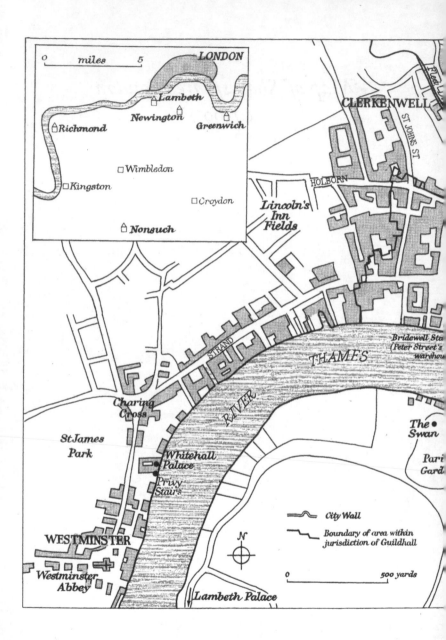

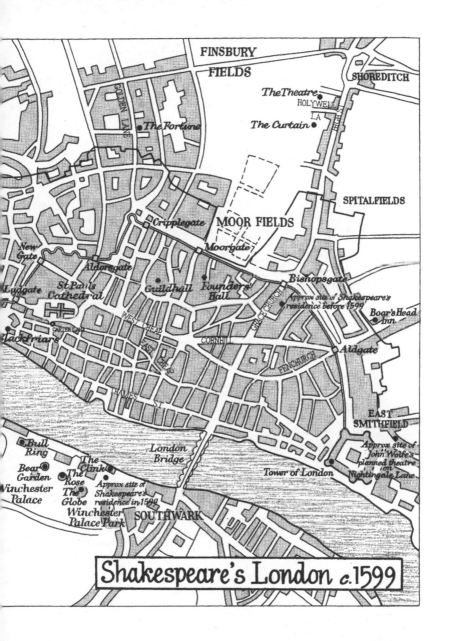

Shakespeare's London c.1599

Preface

In 1599 Elizabethans sent off an army to crush an Irish rebellion, weathered an armada threat from Spain, gambled on a fledgling East India Company and waited to see who would succeed their ageing and childless Queen. They also flocked to London's playhouses, including the newly built Globe. It was at the theatre, noted Thomas Platter, a Swiss tourist who visited England and saw plays there in 1599, that 'the English pass their time, learning at the play what is happening abroad'. England's dramatists did not disappoint, especially Shakespeare, part-owner of the Globe, whose writing this year rose to a new and extraordinary level. In the course of 1599 Shakespeare completed *Henry the Fifth*, wrote *Julius Caesar* and *As You Like It* in quick succession, then drafted *Hamlet*. This book is about both what Shakespeare achieved and what Elizabethans experienced this year. The two are nearly inextricable: it's no more possible to talk about Shakespeare's plays

Shakespeare's portrait, engraved by Martin Droeshout

independently of his age than it is to grasp what his society went through without the benefit of Shakespeare's insights. He and his fellow players truly were, in Hamlet's fine phrase, the 'abstract and brief chronicles of the time' (II, ii, 524).

The commonplace that dramatists are best understood in relation to their time would go unquestioned if the writer in question were Euripides, Ibsen or Beckett. But only recently has the tide begun to turn against a view of Shakespeare as a poet who transcends his age, who wrote, as Samuel Coleridge put it, 'exactly as if of another planet'. The impulse to lift Shakespeare out of time and place was greatly enabled by the decision of Shakespeare's first editors to present his plays out of chronological order. The First Folio of 1623 was put together by John Heminges and Henry Condell, who had worked alongside Shakespeare since the mid-1590s. Having spent most of their adult lives performing in Shakespeare's plays, they knew the sequence in which all but the earliest of them had been written. But they nonetheless decided to shoehorn them into the categories of Comedies, Histories, and Tragedies (which made for a very uncomfortable fit for 'tragedies' like *Cymbeline* and *Troilus and Cressida*). Even within these categories they ignored the order in which the plays were written, so that, for instance, the late great play *The Tempest* is the lead comedy in the First Folio.

Their decision also made the question of how Shakespeare developed as a writer much harder to answer. Over a century and a half would pass before Edmond Malone, the first scholar to tackle this question, even tried to establish the 'progress and order' of Shakespeare's plays; and to this day there is no scholarly consensus about the dates or sequence of a number of the plays, especially the early ones. Imagining Shakespeare free of time and place has made it easier to accept Ben Jonson's assertion that Shakespeare was 'not of an age, but for all time' and to forget that Jonson also called his great rival the 'Soul of the age', whose plays captivated Elizabethan playgoers. For Jonson, the two claims weren't mutually exclusive:

Shakespeare's appeal is universal precisely because he saw so deeply into the great questions of his day. Shakespeare himself certainly thought of his art in this way: the 'purpose of playing', he wrote in *Hamlet*, is to 'show . . . the very age and body of the time his form and pressure' (III, ii, 20–24).

Those who sever Shakespeare from his age do so because there is both too much and too little to know about the man and his times – too much, because the richness of Shakespeare's creative life during the quarter-century from 1588 to 1613 is impossible to contain in a single volume or a single critical intelligence. Who can claim to fathom what's at stake in every one of Shakespeare's works? Nobody, surely, has ever mastered the hundreds of chronicles, plays, poems and stories that inspired him. And the amount of information that historians have uncovered about life in Shakespeare's England is daunting. They've shown that Elizabethan culture ought to matter a great deal to us, for we've inherited its conflicting views of everything from the nature of the self and sexuality to nationhood and empire. Too little, because we don't know very much about what kind of friend or lover or person Shakespeare was. This in turn, has opened the door to those who deny that Shakespeare wrote his plays and attribute them instead to Christopher Marlowe or Francis Bacon, or the latest candidate, the Earl of Oxford. It's unfortunate, because even if we don't know much about his personality, we know a great deal about Shakespeare's career as a writer (more than enough to persuade a reasonable sceptic that he wrote his plays himself). We'd know a lot more about his life had one of the seventeenth-century antiquarians interested in Shakespeare bothered to speak with his younger daughter, Judith, who was still alive in 1662, nearly half a century after Shakespeare died in 1616. One of those antiquarians, John Ward, even made a note in his diary reminding himself to call on her in Stratford-upon-Avon, but she died shortly thereafter, and with her, a direct and intimate sense of the kind of man Shakespeare was.

At the heart of this book is the familiar desire to understand how Shakespeare became Shakespeare. The time-honoured way biographers have gone about answering this question is to locate the wellspring of Shakespeare's genius in his formative experiences. This is risky enough when writing the lives of modern authors like Virginia Woolf or Sylvia Plath, whose biographers have piles of correspondence, diaries and photographs to sift through. It's nearly impossible with Shakespeare, who left behind neither letters nor diaries. And the only two authentic portraits of Shakespeare to survive are posthumous. They depict a modestly dressed and serious man of medium build, with dark hair, full lips, large attentive eyes, a long straight nose and an unusually large forehead. But neither the engraving on the title page of the First Folio nor the funeral monument that still stands in Stratford's church – in which he looks more like an accountant than an artist – offers much of a window into Shakespeare's soul. If Shakespeare had a say in this funeral monument, he may have been responsible for its most salient feature, ensuring that he be remembered as an author: under his left hand is a sheet of paper and in his right one, poised to write, a quill. The overwhelming desire for a more expressive Shakespeare, a truer portrait of the artist, explains why paintings of impostors who more closely resemble the Shakespeare of our imagination now hang in the National Portrait Gallery and elsewhere and are the ones we find reproduced on everything from coffee mugs to editions of his works.

Biographers can only guess how Shakespeare felt about his mother, father, brothers, sisters, neighbours, friends, schoolmates or employers, or, for that matter, how and even where he spent his adolescence or the crucial 'lost years' between his departure from Stratford and his arrival in London. Those committed to discovering the adult Shakespeare's personality in his formative experiences end up hunting for hints in the plays which they then read back into what little can be surmised about his early years (and since the plays contain almost every kind of relationship and experience imaginable, this is not as hard to do as it sounds). But the plays are not two-way mirrors: while Shakespeare perfectly renders what it feels like to be in love, betrayed or crushingly disappointed, it doesn't necessarily follow, as one nineteenth-century critic put it, that he 'must have loved unhappily like Romeo, and like Hamlet not have known for a time what to get on with next'.

Circularity and arbitrariness are only part of the problem: cradle-to-grave biographers of Shakespeare tend to assume that what makes people who they are now made people who they were then. Historians of sixteenth-century England are not so sure. Because almost nobody thought to write a memoir or keep a personal diary in Shakespeare's day – revealing enough facts in themselves – we don't know whether their emotional lives were like ours. Their formative years certainly weren't. Strangers breastfed infants and babies were often swaddled for their first year. Childhood was brief and most adolescents, rich and poor, were sent from home to live and serve in other households. Plague, death in childbirth, harvest failures, and high infant-mortality rates may have diminished the intensity of family bonds. And these bonds didn't last as long: people lived, on the average, until their mid-forties (only one of Shakespeare's seven brothers and sisters made it past forty-six). Eldest sons like Shakespeare inherited all, creating friction among siblings.

Even such constants as love and marriage weren't the same. The idea of marrying for love was fairly new. Though life was shorter, most Elizabethan men and women delayed marriage until their mid-twenties (and a surprising proportion, including Shakespeare's three brothers, never married at all). Given the extremely low illegitimacy rates at the time, desire must have either been sublimated or found an outlet in non-procreative sex – perhaps both. Even the meaning of key concepts, such as what constitutes an 'individual', was different. Writers, including Shakespeare, were only beginning to speak of individuality in the modern sense of 'distinctiveness' or 'specialness', the exact opposite of what it had long meant: 'inseparability'. Given that this was an age of faith, or at the least one in which church attendance was mandatory, religion too played a greater role in shaping how life, death, and the afterlife were imagined. All this suggests that, much as we might want Shakespeare to have been like us, he wasn't. Conventional biographies of Shakespeare are necessary fictions that will always be with us – less for what they tell us about Shakespeare's life than for what they reveal about our fantasies of who we want Shakespeare to be.

I have no illusion that I can elude the dangers of circularity or arbitrariness, but I've tried my best to avoid their excesses by focusing on what can be known with greater confidence: the 'form and pressure' of the time that shaped Shakespeare's writing when he was thirty-five years old. I can't report what Shakespeare ate or drank or how he dressed, but I can establish some of the things he did this year that were crucial to his career, what he read and wrote, which actors and playwrights he worked with and what was going on around him that fuelled his imagination. Throughout, I try to be especially cautious when advancing claims about how Shakespeare might have felt – knowing that, except through the distorting lens of what he expressed through his characters or the speaker of his sonnets, we have no access to his feelings. Still, I hope to capture some of the unpredictable and contingent nature of daily life too often flattened out in historical and biographical works of greater sweep. I'm also aware that neither lives nor history come sliced in neat one-year packages (and that even the question of when the year was thought to begin and end in Tudor England isn't easily answered). Inevitably, I end up focusing more on things that can be dated, such as political and literary events, than on more gradual and less perceptible historical shifts – though, because Shakespeare's plays are remarkably alert to many of these, I do my best to attend to them as well.

I've chosen to write about 1599 not only because it was an unusually fraught and exciting year but also because, as critics have long recognized, it was a decisive one, perhaps *the* decisive one, in Shakespeare's development as a writer (and, happily, one from which a surprising amount of information about his professional life survives). My interest in this subject dates back fifteen years. At that time, though I was familiar with Shakespeare's plays and taught them regularly, I didn't know enough about the historical moment in which plays like *As You Like It* and *Hamlet* were written and which they engaged. I had no idea, for example, that England braced itself for an invasion in the summer of 1599, knew almost nothing about why English troops were fighting in Ireland, or about how rigorously the government cracked down at this time on histories, satires and sermons. I was unaware that one of the best-selling books of 1599 was '*The Passionate Pilgrim* by W. Shakespeare'. I knew less than I should have known about how Shakespeare travelled to and from Stratford or about the bookstalls and playhouses that he frequented in London (and it was only after I began working on this book that the foundations of the Globe and Rose theatres were rediscovered). I was woefully informed about the worlds lost to Shakespeare: England's recent Catholic past, the deforested landscape of his native Arden, and a rapidly fading chivalric culture. My ignorance extended beyond history. Along with other scholars, I didn't fully grasp how extensively Shakespeare revised and what these changes revealed about the kind of writer he was. And my notion of the sources of Shakespeare's inspiration was too bookish. It was one thing to know what Shakespeare was reading, another to know about what sermons he may have heard or what art he viewed in the royal palaces of Whitehall and Richmond where he regularly performed.

This work, then, grew out of frustration with how much I didn't know and frustration with scholars of all critical denominations who never quite got around to addressing the question I found most pressing: how, at age thirty-five, Shakespeare went from being an exceptionally talented writer to being one of the greatest who ever lived – put another way: how in the course of little over a year he went from writing *The Merry Wives of Windsor* to writing a play as inspired as *Hamlet*.

In search of answers I was fortunate to have access to the archives where the literary treasures of Elizabethan England have been preserved – especially the Folger Shakespeare Library in Washington, DC, the Huntington Library in San Marino, California, and the British Library (at both its old and new London addresses). Over time, I had a chance to read almost all of the books written in 1599 that Shakespeare might have owned or borrowed or come upon in London's bookstalls. My focus on a single year has also allowed me to reflect on the events of that year – recorded in contemporary letters, sermons, plays, poems, diaries, travellers' accounts, and official records – that had a bearing on Shakespeare's life and work. While I also read unpublished materials, I tried to focus on what Shakespeare's contemporaries could have put their hands on. I found myself as interested in rumours as in facts, in what Elizabethans feared or believed as much as in what historians later decided really happened. This book is the result of those labours. It has brought me closer to understanding Shakespeare, and for that alone, it has been worth it.

My hope is that the story offered in these pages can convey a sense of how deeply Shakespeare's work emerged from an engagement with his times. To arrive at that point, though, means recounting a good deal of social and political history. I've done my best to present this context briefly and accessibly, but I recognize that some may find the early chapters slow going. I beg the indulgence of those eager to learn more about how Shakespeare wrote his plays but impatient with a series of forced marches through terrain as varied as the gardens of Whitehall Palace and the bogs of Ulster. As in Shakespeare's plays, a scene or two must pass before the hero takes centre stage. And, grounded as my claims are in what scholars have uncovered, a good deal of what I make of that information remains speculative. When writing about an age that pre-dated newspapers and photographic evidence, plausibility, not certitude, is as close as one can come to what happened. Rather than awkwardly littering the pages that follow with one hedge after another – 'perhaps', 'maybe', 'it's most likely', 'probably', or the most desperate of them all, 'surely' – I'd like to offer one global qualification here: this is necessarily my reconstruction of what happened to Shakespeare in the course of this year and when I do qualify a claim it signals that the evidence is inconclusive or the argument highly speculative. Readers interested in the historical sources on which I rely will find them in the bibliographical essay at the end of the book.

The Shakespeare who emerges in these pages is less a Shakespeare in Love than a Shakespeare at Work. When the seventeenth-century biographer John Aubrey asked those who were acquainted with Shakespeare what they remembered about him, he was told that Shakespeare 'was not a company keeper', and that he 'wouldn't be debauched, and, if invited', excused himself, saying 'he was in pain'. The image of Shakespeare turning down invitations to carouse with such a lame excuse has a strong ring of truth, and the anecdote reveals as much as we are likely to learn about the value Shakespeare placed on the time he had free to write. As a resident playwright as well as actor in the Chamberlain's Men, a playing company that performed nearly year-round, most of Shakespeare's mornings were taken up with rehearsals, his afternoons with performances, and many of his evenings with company business, such as listening to freelance dramatists pitch new plays to add to the repertory. He had precious few hours late at night and early in the morning free to read and write – often by flickering candlelight and fighting fatigue. If Shakespeare was in love in 1599, it was with words. What follows, then, is a writer's life: what Shakespeare read, wrote, performed and saw published, and what was going on in England and beyond its shores that shaped plays which four hundred years later continue to influence how we make sense of the world.

The Globe

Beere bayting

Prologue

The weather in London in December 1598 had been frigid – so cold that ten days before New Year the Thames was nearly frozen over at London Bridge. It thawed just before Christmas, and hardy playgoers flocked to the outdoor Rose playhouse in Southwark in record numbers. But the weather turned freezing cold again on St John's Day, the 27th, and a great snowstorm blanketed London on 28 December.

As the snow fell, a dozen or so armed men gathered in Shoreditch, in London's northern suburbs. Instead of the clubs usually wielded in London's street brawls or apprentice riots, they carried deadly weapons – 'swords, daggers, bills, axes, and such like'. Other than the Tower of London, which housed England's arsenal, about the only places to come by some of the larger weapons were the public theatres, where they were used to give a touch of realism to staged combat. In all likelihood, these weapons were borrowed

Detail of Southwark and the Globe Theatre –
the Globe is on the left, wrongly labelled 'Beere bayting'

from the Curtain playhouse, near Finsbury Field, temporary home of the Chamberlain's Men.

The armed men didn't have far to go. Their destination was another playhouse in Shoreditch, the nearby Theatre. The Theatre, built in 1576, was London's oldest and most celebrated playhouse, nursery of the great drama of Thomas Kyd, Christopher Marlowe and Shakespeare. It was here, a few years earlier, that audiences had heard 'the Ghost who cried so miserably at the Theatre like an oyster-wife, "Hamlet, revenge!"' (not Shakespeare's play, but an earlier, now lost *Hamlet*). As the men approached the hulking building, the Theatre itself must have seemed a ghostly presence, vacant now for two years in the aftermath of a fall-out between the Chamberlain's Men and their prickly landlord, Giles Allen. Local residents, seeing the armed troupe approach, may well have been confused about what was happening during this week of holiday revels, for at the head of the group was the leading tragedian in England, the charismatic star of the Chamberlain's Men, Richard Burbage. But this was no impromptu piece of street theatre. Burbage, his older brother Cuthbert and the rest of the men bearing weapons were there in deadly earnest, about to trespass and take back what they considered rightfully theirs and, if necessary, come to blows with anyone trying to stop them.

The Chamberlain's Men were in trouble and the only way out was to get in a bit deeper. Things had begun to go wrong two years earlier, when James Burbage (Richard and Cuthbert's father and the man who had built the Theatre) had decided to build an indoor stage in the wealthy London neighbourhood of Blackfriars. The venue would have enabled his son Richard and the other shareholders of the Chamberlain's Men to act year-round for a more upmarket and better-paying clientele, providing more security than they had at the Theatre, where the lease was expiring. James Burbage had sunk the considerable sum of £600 into the venture. As the Blackfriars theatre neared completion, influential neighbours who were worried about the noise and riff-raff that the theatre might attract had succeeded in having playing banned there. James Burbage had died soon after, having also failed to renegotiate an extension on his lease at the Theatre. His sons Richard and Cuthbert had no better luck changing Giles Allen's mind. With the Burbages' capital tied up at Blackfriars and the Theatre now in Allen's hands, the Chamberlain's Men, lacking a permanent playing space, were in danger of becoming homeless.

By early December Richard Burbage had quietly approached five of his fellow actor-shareholders in the company – William Shakespeare, John Heminges, Augustine Phillips, Thomas Pope and Will Kemp – with a plan. The first thing they needed to do was find a new site for a theatre, one that was accessible to London's playgoers but outside the city limits (where playhouses weren't subject to the authority of the often hostile city fathers). Members of the company, probably Heminges and Condell, who lived in the parish of St Mary Aldermanbury, had learned that a neighbour, Sir Nicholas Brend, was looking to rent some land in Southwark. The property was a stone's throw from the Rose theatre, home of their main rivals, the Admiral's Men. The Chamberlain's Men quickly came to terms with Brend, securing an inexpensive thirty-one-year lease which was theirs from Christmas Day. The transaction was rushed and it wasn't until late February that the paperwork was completed.

They now had a building site but as yet no theatre. In the past, when they had provided a playhouse and covered the lease, the Burbages had kept the lion's share of the profits. No longer able to supply the company with a permanent home, Richard and Cuthbert Burbage made an unprecedented offer: they would secure the building materials for a new playhouse, worth roughly £700, if the five actor-shareholders would each cover ten per cent of the remaining construction costs as well as the expenses of running the theatre. The material would come from the dismantled Theatre, the pieces of its frame carefully marked and reassembled on Bankside. They'd still have to do it on the cheap: no tiles on the roof, as at the Theatre, just inexpensive (and flammable) thatch. In exchange, and for the first time in the history of the professional theatre in London, actor-sharers would be part-owners of the playhouse as well as partners in the company, the five men each receiving ten per cent of the total profits. The potential yield on their investment would be great – over £100 a year. Still, that initial investment – roughly £70 each – was considerable at a time when a freelance dramatist earned just £6 a play and a day-labourer £10 a year. The risks were also great. Few had that kind of cash on hand, which meant taking out loans at steep interest rates (the Burbages later complained that it took them years to pay off what they borrowed to cover their share). Plague might once again close the public theatres for an extended period. Fire might destroy the playhouse (as it would in 1613, when the Globe's thatch caught fire). Or the Privy Council might finally act on one of its periodic threats and close the theatres.

What made the risky plan plausible was that Richard and Cuthbert Burbage knew that their father had been astute enough to put a clause in the original lease stating that while Giles Allen owned the land, Burbage owned the theatre he built on it. But since the lease had expired, a strong case could be made that the building was no longer theirs. It was a commonplace, which Shakespeare himself had recently repeated in *The Merry Wives of Windsor*, that you're likely to lose your 'edifice' when you build 'a fair house . . . on another man's ground' (II, ii, 207–8). Allen, litigious, well connected, and brother of a former Lord Mayor, was not a man to be trifled with. But what alternative was there?

The Chamberlain's Men didn't have much time. They knew that Allen was away for the Christmas holidays at his country home in Essex. They had also heard that Allen was preparing to dismantle the building and keep its valuable timber for himself. If that happened, they'd be ruined. They certainly had to act before word of their new lease got out. They had performed before Queen Elizabeth at Whitehall Palace on 26 December (the day after their new lease went into effect) and were expected again at court on New Year's Day. Assuming that the job would probably take more than a day, they were left with a very narrow window. The snow and cold were unfortunate, and would make the work misery for the carpenters handling the frozen timber, but that couldn't be helped.

When the armed group arrived at the playhouse they set to work immediately. Even with an early start there wouldn't be much daylight; the sun had risen that morning after eight and would set before four in the afternoon. It was four days short of a full moon, but with the snow coming down there was little prospect of working by moonlight. According to evidence submitted in the heated legal battle that followed, their appearance quickly drew a crowd – friends and tenants of Allen as well as supporters of the Chamberlain's Men, including Ellen Burbage, James's feisty widow. And we can be pretty sure that the other shareholders whose livelihoods were at stake – Shakespeare, Phillips, Heminges, Kemp and Pope – were at the scene as well, among the unnamed 'diverse other persons' accompanying the Burbages.

Outmanned, a couple of Giles Allen's friends, one with power of attorney, tried to stop the trespassers – to no avail. A silk weaver named Henry Johnson demanded that they stop dismantling the playhouse, but was put off by Peter Street, the master-builder who had been brought in to supervise the job. Street explained that he was only taking the pegged vertical posts and horizontal groundsills apart in order to put them together again 'in another form' on the same site. Johnson, who was privy to the failed negotiations over the lease, probably knew better, but he backed off. By the time they were done, the workers had made a mess of the place, causing forty shillings' worth of damage.

Of all those gathered at the Theatre that day, none stood to gain or lose as much as Shakespeare. Had the escapade failed, had Allen been forewarned or had he succeeded in his subsequent court battle against the seizure, Shakespeare's alternatives would have been limited. It's hard to see how the Chamberlain's Men could have survived for long as an ensemble without a permanent playhouse – and their arrangement at the aging Curtain was only temporary. The only other available venue was the Swan theatre, built in 1595 in Paris Garden on Bankside. But the authorities had prohibited permanent playing there after 1597, following the staging of a scandalous play, *The Isle of Dogs*. Of course, Shakespeare could have continued writing plays as a freelancer, as others did, but the pay was modest. At best, he might have offered some plays as capital and joined his competitors, the Admiral's Men, as shareholder and chief dramatist, if they would have him on those terms.

Shakespeare understood that more was at stake in rescuing those old oak posts than his livelihood as a playwright. He was not simply England's most experienced living dramatist, author of (or collaborator on) roughly eighteen plays, including such favourites as *Richard the Third, Romeo and Juliet* and *The First Part of Henry the Fourth*; he also wrote for and acted alongside its most talented ensemble of players. The Chamberlain's Men had been together for five years, having emerged out of the remnants of broken and reconfigured companies, its players drawn from among the best of those who had recently performed with Sussex, Derby, Pembroke, Strange and the Queen's Men. Shakespeare himself had probably been affiliated with Pembroke's, or Strange's, perhaps both. Companies in the early 1590s formed, merged, and dissolved so rapidly, with plays migrating from one group of players to the next, that it is impossible to track Shakespeare's affiliations at this time with confidence. There were considerable advantages to a company's longevity. Since their formation in 1594 it's likely that the Chamberlain's Men had already collaborated on close to a hundred plays, almost a fifth of them Shakespeare's. When Shakespeare sat down to write a play it was with the capabilities of this accomplished group in mind. *Hamlet* would not have been the same if Shakespeare had not written the title role for Richard Burbage. Comic roles were scripted for Will Kemp's improvisational clowning. Augustine Phillips and George Bryan had been acting professionally for over a decade; Thomas Pope, who excelled at comic roles, even longer. Henry Condell, Will Sly, John Duke, John Holland and Christopher Beeston were also veteran performers and helped round out this all-star cast. The degree of trust and of mutual understanding (all the more important in a company that dispensed with a director) was extraordinary. For a dramatist – let alone a fellow player, as Shakespeare was – the break-up of such a group would have been an incalculable loss.

As darkness fell on 28 December, the old frame of the Theatre, loaded onto wagons, with horses slipping and straining from the burden of hauling the long half-ton, foot-square oak posts, began to make its way south through streets carpeted with snow. The wagons headed through Bishopsgate and south-west to Peter Street's waterfront warehouse near Bridewell Stairs, where the timber was unloaded and safely stacked and stored. The popular story of the dismantled frame being drawn across or over the Thames (which was 'nigh frozen over') to the future building site is a fantasy: it would have been too risky sledding the heavy load across thin ice and the steep tolls on London Bridge for wheelage and poundage would have been prohibitive; and had the timber been left exposed to the elements through the winter months at the marshy site of the Globe, it could have been warped beyond repair (if not subject to a counter-raid by Giles Allen's friends). Not until the foundations were ready would the frame of the Theatre be ferried across the Thames to Southwark, where by late summer, phoenix-like, it would be resurrected as the Globe.

*

On the eve of the dismantling of the Theatre, Shakespeare stood at a professional crossroads. It had been five years since he had last found himself in such a situation. At that time he was torn between pursuing a career in the theatre and one in which he sought advancement by securing aristocratic patronage through his published poetry. For a while he had done both, but the rewards of patronage (he had fulsomely dedicated two published poems, *Venus and Adonis* and *Lucrece*, to the young and charismatic Earl of Southampton) either didn't materialize or proved unsatisfying. Theatre won out, though Shakespeare kept writing sonnets, which he didn't care to publish but shared with his friends. After joining the Chamberlain's Men in 1594, Shakespeare hit his stride in the next two years with a great burst of innovative plays: *A Midsummer Night's Dream, Love's Labour's Lost, Romeo and Juliet, King John, Richard the Second, The Merchant of Venice* and *The First Part of Henry the Fourth*.

By the end of 1596, however, following one of his most successful efforts, *The First Part of Henry the Fourth*, this creative surge diminished and his range contracted. Over the next two years he seems to have only written three plays: a second part to *Henry the Fourth* and two comedies, *The Merry Wives of Windsor* and the witty *Much Ado about Nothing*. Will Kemp figured prominently in these plays as Falstaff in the two parts of *Henry the Fourth* and the *Merry Wives*, and then as the bumbling constable Dogberry in *Much Ado*. These were popular plays and Kemp a crowd-pleaser. But Shakespeare was aware that he had nearly exhausted the rich veins of romantic comedy and English history. He was restless, unsatisfied with the profitably formulaic and with styles of writing that came too easily to him, but hadn't yet figured out what new directions to take; and that depended on more than inspiration or will. Unlike his sonnet-writing, his play-writing was constrained by the needs of his fellow players as well as the expectations of audiences both at the public playhouse and at court – demands that often pulled him in opposite directions.

Shakespeare was not alone in experiencing something of a creative hiatus at this time (if three fine plays in two years can be considered a falling-off). This was not the most auspicious moment in the history of the Elizabethan stage. One could point to the relative dearth of exceptional dramatists, the pressure by authorities to curb playgoing, and the periodic closing of the theatres because of plague. During these years England also suffered terrible harvests and renewed threats of invasion from Spain. By 1597 a generation of ground-breaking playwrights – including John Lyly, Thomas Kyd, Christopher Marlowe, George Peele and Robert Greene – had passed from the scene and members of a younger generation (whose ranks included Ben Jonson, Thomas Dekker and Thomas Heywood) were only beginning to find their voices. In the course of a few short years Shakespeare had gone from 'upstart crow' (Robert Greene's jealous and belittling label) to grizzled veteran, and was virtually alone in straddling these two generations of playwrights. As an artist who thrived on rivalry and whose work is characterized by an unequalled capacity to absorb the styles and techniques of his fellow writers, Shakespeare seems to have needed competition to push him to the next level, and in 1597 and 1598 there wasn't enough of it.

The scarcity of recently staged plays on London's bookstalls was further evidence that 1597–8 were relatively lean years. Yet Londoners' craving for theatre had never been greater. In addition to the Chamberlain's Men at the Curtain and the Admiral's Men at the Rose, there were a score of itinerant companies touring through the English countryside, some no doubt performing in London while passing through town, either at inns or at the Swan. By 1600, in response to popular demand, entrepreneurs had rushed to build permanent new theatres around the city, including the Globe, the Fortune, and the Boar's Head Inn, while resident children's companies began playing at St Paul's and Blackfriars. In 1600, in an England of four million, London and its immediate environs held a population of roughly two hundred thousand. If, on any given day, two plays were staged in playhouses that held as many as two to three thousand spectators each, it's likely that with theatres even half-full, as many as three thousand or so Londoners were attending a play. Over the course of a week – conservatively assuming five days of performances each week – fifteen thousand Londoners paid to see a play. Obviously, some never went at all, or rarely, while others – including young and generally well-to-do law students at the Inns of Court – made up for that, seeing dozens of plays a year; but on average, it's likely that over a third of London's adult population saw a play every month.

Which meant that Shakespeare and his fellow dramatists were writing for the most experienced playgoers in history. Unlike modern theatres, in which actors perform the same play for weeks, months, even years, in Elizabethan playhouses the play changed daily, with resident companies introducing as many as a score of new plays annually and supplementing them with revivals of old favourites. Unsuccessful plays disappeared from the repertory after only a handful of performances. Shakespeare could count on an unusually discriminating audience, one sensitive to subtle trans-formations of popular genres like romantic comedy and revenge tragedy. But the pressure that he and his fellow playwrights were under to churn out one innovative and entertaining play after another must have proved exhausting.

It's no surprise, then, that playwriting at the close of the six-teenth century was a young man's game. None of the men who wrote plays for a living in 1599 were over forty years old. They had come from London and the countryside, from the Inns of Court, the universities, and various trades. About the only thing these writers had in common was that they were all from the middling classes. There were about fifteen of them at work in 1599 and they knew each other and each others' writing styles well: George Chapman, Henry Chettle, John Day, Thomas Dekker, Michael

Drayton, Richard Hathaway, William Haughton, Thomas Heywood, Ben Jonson, John Marston, Anthony Munday, Henry Porter, Robert Wilson and, of course, Shakespeare. Collectively this year they wrote about sixty plays, of which only a dozen or so survive, a quarter of these Shakespeare's. Their names – though not Shakespeare's – can be found in the pages of an extraordinary volume called Henslowe's *Diary*, a ledger or account book belonging to Philip Henslowe, owner of the Rose theatre, in which he recorded his business activities, mostly theatrical, from 1592 to 1609. The *Diary* is a mine of information. Henslowe's entries tell us the titles of lost plays, what playwrights were paid, and who collaborated with whom. Other entries list gate receipts, expenditures for costumes and props, and in some instances on which days particular plays were performed.

About half of all plays this year were co-authored, with two, three or more playwrights writing collaboratively, each handling the parts or scenes at which he excelled. Shakespeare co-authored several plays near the outset and end of his career, but in 1599 he wrote alone. While other playwrights had both their mornings and afternoons free to write and engage in collaborative ventures, Shakespeare's at this time were spent fulfilling his company obligations – rehearsing and performing alongside his fellow sharers, hired men and apprenticed boy actors. The only other dramatist in his situation was Thomas Heywood, who was currently under contract to act for the Admiral's Men (though he wrote for a number of companies). In a career otherwise rich in collaboration, this year Heywood also wrote alone.

A closer look at Henslowe's *Diary* also suggests that some writing teams left the services of the Admiral's Men for extended stretches and wrote for another company, almost certainly the Chamberlain's Men. For example, three of the Admiral's Men's regulars – Anthony Munday, Robert Wilson, and Richard Hathaway – mysteriously drop from Henslowe's payroll in August 1598;

and they were joined by Michael Drayton in the early winter of 1599. Not until the autumn of 1599 would they all suddenly return to the Admiral's Men with a play called *Sir John Oldcastle* – a provocative send-up of Shakespeare's controversial portrait of the Lollard martyr in his two-part *Henry the Fourth*. While records don't survive of who provided most of the twenty or so new plays that Shakespeare's company staged this year, it's likely that writers who were off Henslowe's payroll for extended periods were responsible for such Chamberlain's Men's offerings as *Owen Tudor* and *Henry Richmond*, and perhaps *A Larum for London* and *Thomas Lord Cromwell* as well. By autumn 1599, with the establishment of new playing companies at the Boar's Head Inn, Paul's, and Blackfriars, it increasingly became a seller's market: as opportunities for these freelance dramatists expanded, even more of them were drawn to writing for more than a single company.

Given the intimate working relationships between playwrights (and between playwrights and players), personality clashes were inevitable. It didn't help matters that many Elizabethan actors were skilled fencers. Just the previous September, Ben Jonson had quarrelled with Gabriel Spencer, a rising star (and shareholder) in the Admiral's Men, and, in the ensuing duel near the Curtain, killed him. Jonson, who was briefly imprisoned, only escaped hanging by reading his 'neck verse' – a legal loophole dating from medieval times whereby the literate were spared the gallows by reading from the Bible in Latin, a task easy enough for the classically trained Jonson. But he did not escape unscathed: Jonson was branded with a 'T' for Tyburn, Elizabethan London's site of execution, on his thumb. The next time he committed a felony he would hang there. Spencer was no stranger to violence, having two years earlier stabbed to death James Feake, who had come at him with a candlestick. His fatal encounter with Jonson took place the very month when Jonson's first play for the Chamberlain's Men – *Every Man In His Humour* – was performed at the Curtain.

Ironically, at the time of their quarrel Spencer was probably learning his part in Jonson's collaborative (and, in retrospect, ironically titled) play for the Admiral's Men, *Hot Anger Soon Cold*. And in June 1599 Henry Porter came to blows with fellow playwright John Day in Southwark. Day drew his rapier and killed Porter. The cause of their fight is also unknown; jurors found Day guilty of manslaughter, not murder. Day was subsequently pardoned and resumed writing for the Admiral's Men, mostly in collaboration with Dekker, Chettle and Haughton, who either accepted Day's version of the fight or put professional needs above loyalty to a former writing partner. Ben Jonson, who had also worked with Porter, was less forgiving, and classed Day among the 'rogues' and 'base fellows'.

London's civic leaders didn't share the popular enthusiasm for the rough-and-tumble world of theatre. Their view of things is offered in a petition submitted to the Privy Council in the summer of 1597 requesting that London's playhouses be closed. What was staged there, they argued, was immoral ('containing nothing but profane fables, lascivious matters, cozening devices, and scurrilous behaviours') and the audience itself a collection of misfits ('vagrant persons, masterless men, thieves, horse stealers, whore-mongerers, cozeners, coney-catchers, contrivers of treason, and other idle and dangerous persons'). But the city fathers could do little about it, since the playing companies were patronized by influential aristocrats, including members of the Privy Council (after the Queen, the most powerful political body in the realm). It must have come as something of a shock to the resident acting companies to learn at this time that the Privy Council had decided to act against them, ordering 'that not only no plays shall be used within London or about the City or in any public place during this time of summer, but that also those playhouses that are erected and built only for such purposes shall be plucked down'. If the order had been carried out it might have meant the end of the Elizabethan public theatre. The likeliest explanation – and one believed by the players themselves – is that this harsh response was prompted by the scandal created by *The Isle of Dogs*. By early October those imprisoned for their role in that play were released and the playing companies allowed to resume regular playing (except at the Swan). But the episode unnerved the playing companies, reminding them how vulnerable their situation was in London and how easily their expensive theatres could be knocked down (the Privy Council was quite explicit about the demolition order, specifying that those responsible for tearing down the theatres 'deface the same as they may not be employed again to such use'). The *Isle of Dogs* affair gives a sharp sense of the heightened sensitivity to how political topics were staged.

For Shakespeare and his fellow Chamberlain's Men, 1597–8 was not the best of times. In addition to their troubles at the Theatre and Blackfriars, they endured the deaths of James Burbage and of their patron Henry Carey, the Lord Chamberlain (whose son, George Carey, succeeded him as their patron, and later as Lord Chamberlain as well). They also lost the services of two leading players, the veteran performer and sharer George Bryan (acknowledged in the First Folio as one of the 'principal actors' in Shakespeare's plays) and Samuel Cross (whose talents were still affectionately recalled over a decade later). The rough stretch had begun a year earlier, in the summer of 1596, when an outbreak of plague had briefly closed the theatres. To earn money, Shakespeare and his fellow actors had abandoned London and taken to the road, touring through south-west England and playing before provincial audiences, with recorded stops in Faversham, Dover and Bath. For Shakespeare himself, this period would bring terrible news.

It was either while on the road or immediately upon his return from the tour that took the company to Faversham, in August 1596, that word reached Shakespeare of the death of his only son, Hamnet, who was buried in Stratford-upon-Avon on 11 August.

It could not have been easy for Anne Shakespeare to contact her itinerant husband to convey the news of Hamnet's illness and death – it would have taken a messenger from Stratford four or five days at least just to find Shakespeare – so it's unlikely that he learned of his son's demise in time to return home for his funeral. Unlike Ben Jonson, who left such a touching poem on the death of his young son and namesake Benjamin, Shakespeare left no testimonial for Hamnet. But then, unlike Jonson, Shakespeare lived at a great distance from his family, returning home infrequently. Hamnet and his twin sister Judith had been baptized on 2 February 1585, born two years after their elder sister Susanna. By the end of the 1580s Shakespeare had left his wife and three young children behind in Stratford to seek his fortune in London. He may have barely known his son, which is not to say that he did not feel his loss deeply. It may even have accounted for his diminished output in the year or so that followed. We just don't know.

The invitation to become part-owner of a new theatre on Bankside came at a critical moment in Shakespeare's career. And the venture would play a major role in the redirection of his art. The Globe offered Shakespeare a fresh start, the possibility of writing for a new set of playgoers with as yet unhardened expectations, unlike those who had been frequenting the Theatre and Curtain for so many years. Since at least 1596 – when James Burbage had tried and failed to move the company to a theatre that catered to a more privileged audience – the sharers of the Chamberlain's Men had been divided over what kind of audience they wanted to attract. Some, like the comic star Will Kemp, were deeply invested in the traditions of popular entertainment of the theatres of the northern suburbs. For other sharers – and their ranks included Shakespeare, who was most constrained by these conventions – the move to the Globe reopened the possibility of dispensing with a dependence on improvisational clowning and raucous jigs that playgoers at the Curtain and Theatre

had come to love and expect. With a move to the Globe now imminent, suppressed differences over these issues resurfaced.

The Chamberlain's Men depended upon the thousands of Londoners willing to pay a penny or more, day in, day out, to see them
perform. For that reason, every play they staged was written with a
popular audience in mind and premièred in the public theatres.
But the company's long-term political security depended on
patronage at court. Fortunately for London's actors and playwrights, the Queen and her court enjoyed seeing plays; but Elizabeth didn't want to pay to keep a retinue of actors for half a dozen
or so command performances a year. She found it easier and much
less expensive to reward the players with a gift of £10 each time
they played at court (though her courtiers patronized the playhouses, Elizabeth herself never set foot in the public theatres). The
fiction – which also happened to be the official position of the
Privy Council – was that public performances were essentially
dress rehearsals whereby the leading companies 'might be the better enabled and prepared to show such plays before her Majesty as
they shall be required at times meet and accustomed, to which end
they have been chiefly licensed and tolerated'.

Shakespeare had had unparalleled success in pleasing both
courtly and popular audiences over the past few years – but these
admirers weren't necessarily drawn to the same things in his plays.
Ordinary Londoners flocked to *The First Part of Henry the Fourth*
for its 'humorous conceits'. The play continued to pack the theatre:
'Let but Falstaff come, Hal, Poins, the rest,' wrote Leonard Digges,
and 'you scarce shall have a room, / All is so pestered.' Courtly
audiences, in contrast, were more caught up in the same play's flirtation with topical political concerns (which explains why the
Lord Chamberlain asked Shakespeare and his fellow players to
perform it when he had to entertain the Flemish ambassador).

Of late, Shakespeare and his fellow players had been invited to
play at court far more than all other companies combined – fifteen

times in the past three years (and his company also gave private performances for aristocrats, both in London or on tour at their great houses in the country). They were keenly aware of how important the support of the Queen, the Privy Council, and the Lord Chamberlain was – all the more so, given the uncertainty about how much longer Elizabeth would reign. They had to prepare against the possibility that only a single company might be protected under a future monarch or singled out for special status as the next 'Queen's' or more likely 'King's Men'.

Just because Shakespeare was able to write plays that appealed to audiences across a wide social spectrum didn't mean that he wasn't frustrated by the limits this imposed on what he could write. As his understanding of drama continued to deepen, his desire to experiment – to push the bounds of comedy and tragedy, to wrestle with increasingly complicated social, historical and political issues, to render how inner states of experience could be conveyed, even to coin new words when English fell short of what his imagination conjured – jarred with the demands of writing plays that had to please all. Those intricate, brilliant sonnets he kept writing provided an outlet, certainly, but that wasn't enough. Here, too, the move to the Globe, whose identity was as yet unfixed, offered a way forward.

The different responses of citizens and courtiers to his work were part of a larger problem Shakespeare faced, having to do with how he was seen as an artist. Though he had written an early Roman tragedy, eight path-breaking English histories, and some of the best comedies that the English stage had ever seen, it was only in the past year or so that contemporary critics had finally begun to acknowledge his talent, and even more frustrating that when they had done so it had invariably been his more sexually charged work – the two long poems *Venus and Adonis* and *Lucrece*, his love tragedy *Romeo and Juliet* and those sonnets that only a privileged few had read or heard – that had won their praise. In

1598, for example, the poet Richard Barnfield celebrated Shake-speare's 'honey-flowing vein' in *Lucrece* and *Venus and Adonis*. John Weever likewise calls him 'honey-tongued Shakespeare' in a poet-ic tribute that year, where 'fire-hot Venus' and 'rose-cheeked Ado-nis' once again come in for special praise. Weever wanted to compliment the plays but was stumped when it came to their names: '*Romeo, Richard*; more whose names I know not.' Shake-speare would not have been flattered.

The most striking praise for Shakespeare at this time appears in Francis Meres's *Palladis Tamia: Wit's Treasury*, also published in 1598. No contemporary writer comes off more favourably in Meres's book than Shakespeare, though once again it's Shake-speare the honey-tongued love poet that commands attention: 'The sweet witty soul of Ovid lives in mellifluous and honey-tongued Shakespeare,' Meres writes, 'witness his *Venus and Adonis*, his *Lucrece*, his sugared *Sonnets* among his private friends, etc.' Meres predictably includes Shakespeare among 'the most passion-ate among us to bewail and bemoan the perplexities of love'. Shakespeare must have been relieved to see this caricature bal-anced by attention to his plays, for Meres also writes: 'As Plautus and Seneca are accounted the best for comedy and tragedy among the Latins, so Shakespeare among the English is the most excel-lent in both kinds for the stage. For comedy, witness his *Gentlemen of Verona*, his [*Comedy of*] *Errors*, his *Love Labour's Lost*, his *Love Labour's Won*, his *Midsummer's Night Dream* and his *Merchant of Venice*. For tragedy, his *Richard the Second, Richard the Third, Henry the Fourth, King John, Titus Andronicus*, and his *Romeo and Juliet*.' But only seven of Shakespeare's plays had been published before 1598 and it wasn't until that year that his name even appeared on a title page of a play.

The 'English Ovid' – the poet of the 'heart-robbing line', as an anonymous contemporary put it a couple of years later – was a hard reputation to shake off. The same anonymous writer even took Shakespeare to task for steering clear of more serious subject matter: 'Could but a graver subject him content / Without love's foolish lazy languishment.' We know too little about the reading and book-buying habits of Elizabethans, but what evidence we have confirms that, especially for younger readers, it was Shakespeare's amorous writing that held the greatest appeal. When, for example, the twenty-one-year-old Scottish poet William Drummond arrived in London in 1606, he kept a list of the titles of books he read. Drummond passed over Shakespeare's histories and major tragedies in his first year in London in favour of *Romeo and Juliet*, *A Midsummer Night's Dream*, *Lucrece*, and *The Passionate Pilgrim*. He may already have read *Venus and Adonis*, for it appears in a separate list of books he owned.

Shakespeare knew that his plays were valued differently at court, where he was recognized as a dramatist alert to the factional world of contemporary politics. Along with *Richard the Second* (whose deposition scene was never printed during Elizabeth's lifetime), *The First Part of Henry the Fourth* had probably done the most to earn him this reputation and had even provoked an angry response from the new Lord Chamberlain, William Brooke, Lord Cobham, who briefly succeeded Shakespeare's company's patron, Henry Carey, Lord Hunsdon, in that office. Shakespeare had portrayed Cobham's namesake, an earlier Lord Cobham named Sir John Oldcastle, as a riotous glutton – a portrait sharply at odds with Oldcastle's reputation as one of England's great proto-Protestant martyrs. It's hard from this distance to determine whether the initial slight was intentional on Shakespeare's part, an attempt to poke fun at a Puritan hero like Oldcastle or a sly dig that aligned Shakespeare with court factions opposed to Cobham and his son. It may simply have been that the prickly new Lord Chamberlain was chagrined that Shakespeare's play about Oldcastle was performed at court under his direct supervision, and the offence was only taken at that time. The long and the short of it is that Shakespeare was ordered to change the name – and he did, turning 'Oldcastle' to 'Falstaff'.

The antagonism did not stop there, however, suggesting that the slight wasn't accidental. If Shakespeare had unknowingly stumbled and insulted the Cobhams the first time around, he probably did so deliberately in his next play, *The Merry Wives of Windsor*, which he interrupted *The Second Part of Henry the Fourth* to write. This time, while careful to call the hero Falstaff and not Oldcastle, Shakespeare gave the name Brook to the disguised, jealous and much mocked husband in the play. The family name of the Lord Cobhams was Brooke, and there could be no mistaking the insult – which the Master of the Revels, Edmund Tilney, who gave his stamp of approval to the play, must have winked at. And Shakespeare also included a gently mocking allusion in the *Merry Wives* to an actual German duke (named Mompelgard) who had been hovering around the English court waiting to be admitted to England's Order of the Garter.

By 1598 Shakespeare's relationship with the court had become increasingly reciprocal. He was not only a regular presence at court but also shaped how England's leading families in turn gave voice to their political experiences and his words entered the court vocabulary as a shorthand for the complicated manoeuvring and gossip that defined court life. Tobie Matthew, for example, can write to Dudley Carleton: 'Sir Francis Vere is coming towards the Low Countries, and Sir Alexander Ratcliffe and Sir Robert Drury with him. "Honour pricks them on, and the world thinks that honour will quickly prick them off again"' – here paraphrasing Falstaff's unvarnished truth about the dangers of pursuing honour in *The First Part of Henry the Fourth*: 'Honour pricks me on. Yea, but how if honour prick me off when I come on? . . . What is that "honour"? Air' (V, i, 129–35). The gist of Matthew's multi-layered observation seems to be that while these ambitious men are spurred ('pricked') on by honour, the consensus at court is that this pursuit will prove disastrous ('to be pricked off' means 'to be marked to die').

It's not the only such example committed to writing to survive (and who knows how many similar allusions in conversation went unrecorded?). At the end of February 1598 the Earl of Essex wrote to Secretary of State Cecil in France: 'I pray you commend me also to Alexander Ratcliff and tell him for news his sister is married to Sir John Falstaff.' This time, the allusion to Shakespeare's character is part of an in-joke about Lord Cobham (now nicknamed 'Falstaff' for his family's opposition to Shakespeare's use of the name Oldcastle) playing the marital field, pursuing Ratcliff's beautiful sister Margaret. Rumour had it that Cobham was also in pursuit of the merchant Sir John Spenser's rich daughter. Essex was at court on 26 February 1598 – a day or so, perhaps, before he wrote this letter – where he might have seen the Chamberlain's Men perform *The Merry Wives of Windsor*, in which a sexually rapacious Falstaff gets his comeuppance. Essex loathed Cobham and alluding to Shakespeare's character was a way of tweaking him (by linking him with Falstaff's multiple wooing in the play) while not alienating Cobham's powerful brother-in-law, Cecil. A year later the Earl of Southampton's wife could write to her husband concerning the latest gossip about Cobham's sexual escapades in similarly veiled Shakespearean terms: 'All the news I can send you that I think will make you merry is that I read in a letter from London that Sir John Falstaff is by his Mrs Dame Pintpot made father of a goodly miller's thumb, a boy that is all head and very little body.'

No other Elizabethan playwright's words or characters served as a similar kind of code for courtiers at this time because no other writer spoke to their preoccupations so directly as Shakespeare. It's no surprise that the few references at this time to popular plays performed in aristocrats' homes are limited to Shakespeare's work, typically his histories. But there was no getting around the danger of alienating one powerful faction while pleasing another. Shakespeare walked a careful line, but as the *Isle of Dogs* episode made clear, the punishment for overstepping the bounds of the acceptable was severe. Trying to satisfy those at court introduced a different set of risks and constraints.

Shakespeare's way out of the dilemma of writing plays as pleasing at court as they were at the public theatre was counterintuitive. Rather than searching for the lowest common denominator, he decided instead to write increasingly complicated plays that dispensed with easy pleasures and made both sets of playgoers work harder than they had ever worked before. It's not something that he could have imagined doing five years earlier (when he lacked the authority and London audiences the sophistication to manage this). And this challenge to the status quo is probably not something that would have gone down well at the Curtain in 1599. But Shakespeare had a clear sense of what veteran playgoers were capable of and saw past their cries for old favourites and the stereotypes that branded them as shallow 'groundlings'. He committed himself not only to writing great plays for the Globe but also to nurturing an audience comfortable with their increased complexity. Even before the Theatre was dismantled he must have been excitedly thinking ahead, realizing how crucial his first few plays at the Globe would be. It was a gamble, and there was the possibility that he might overreach and lose both popular and courtly audiences.

Until recently Shakespeare had been living in north London in rented quarters in St Helen's Bishopsgate. It was a popular area for actors, just a short walk to Shoreditch and the Theatre and Curtain. It was also a comfortable and upmarket neighbourhood, home to musicians and merchants. However, by the time that construction on the Globe had begun, Shakespeare had moved to the Liberty of the Clink in Southwark, a rougher, raunchier neighbourhood outside the City limits, but very close to where the new theatre would stand. The rented quarters on Bankside – he had always rented in London, restlessly moving around, to the frustration of tax collectors – could only have added to the sense of a fresh start, his new surroundings contributing in unpredictable ways to the great surge of creative energies that followed.

As all this was going on, Shakespeare was trying to finish *Henry the Fifth*, which he had been thinking about for several years – as far back as 1596, when he had decided to stretch the plot of his main dramatic source, the anonymous *Famous Victories of Henry the Fifth*, to cover the two parts of *Henry the Fourth* as well as *Henry the Fifth*. And events, professional and political, kept overtaking the play. The scars of revision that *Henry the Fifth* bears – inconsistencies, locales that are specified then altered, characters that are introduced then mysteriously disappear, repetitions that seem to be ghostly remnants of earlier drafts – testify to the extent to which Shakespeare's conception of the play kept changing. It seems to have taken him a lot longer than usual to complete and it's unlikely that it was ready to be performed before late March 1599. Shakespeare knew by then that it would be the last play he would write for the loyal playgoers of the northern suburbs as well as one of the first that would enter the repertory of the Globe. As Shakespeare's melancholy epilogue to *Henry the Fifth* acknowledges – with its backward glance at a decade's worth of history plays with which he had entertained Shoreditch audiences – *Henry the Fifth* marked the end of one stage of his career and the uncharted beginning of another.

WINTER

When carefull man hath carked all the yeare
And sees how god hath prospered his encrease
He killes his swyne And mindsto make good cheare
To passe the tyme while winters Rage doth ceasse

December
Capricornus

the vitiling house

I
A Battle of Wills

Late in the afternoon of Tuesday, 26 December 1598, two days before their fateful rendezvous at the Theatre, the Chamberlain's Men made their way through London's dark and chilly streets to Whitehall Palace to perform for the Queen. Elizabeth had returned to Whitehall in mid-November in time for her Accession Day celebrations. Whitehall, her only London residence, was also her favourite palace and she spent a quarter of her reign there, especially around Christmas. Elizabeth's entrance followed traditional protocol: a mile out of town she was received by Lord Mayor Stephen Soame and his brethren, who were dressed in 'velvet coats and chains of gold'. Elizabeth had come from Richmond Palace, where she had stayed but a month, having been at her palace at Nonsuch before that. Sanitation issues, the difficulties of feeding so many courtiers with limited local supplies, and perhaps restlessness too, made the Elizabethan court resemble a large-scale touring company that annually wound its way

Will Kemp

through the royal palaces of Whitehall, Greenwich, Richmond, St James, Hampton Court, Windsor, Oatlands and Nonsuch. But in contrast with the single cart that transported an itinerant playing troupe with its props and costumes, a train of several hundred wagons would set off for the next royal residence, transporting all that was needed for the Queen and seven hundred or so of her retainers to manage administrative and ceremonial affairs at a new locale.

A century later Whitehall would burn to the ground, leaving 'nothing but walls and ruins'. Archaeological reconstruction would be pointless, for Whitehall was more than just a jumble of Gothic buildings already out of fashion by Shakespeare's day. It was the epicentre of English power, beginning with the Queen and radiating out through her Privy Councillors and lesser courtiers. A cross between ancient Rome's Senate and Coliseum, Whitehall was where ambassadors were entertained, bears baited, domestic and foreign policy determined, lucrative monopolies dispensed, Accession Day tilts run, and Shrovetide sermons preached. Above all, it was a rumour mill, where each royal gesture was endlessly dissected. When the Chamberlain's Men performed at court, they added one more layer of spectacle.

Whitehall figured strongly enough in Shakespeare's imagination to make a cameo appearance in his late play *Henry the Eighth*. When a minor courtier describes how after her coronation at Westminster Anne Bullen returned to 'York Place', he is sharply corrected: 'You must no more call it York Place; that's past, / For since the Cardinal fell, that title's lost.' Henry VIII coveted the fine building, evicted Cardinal Wolsey, and rechristened it: ''Tis now the King's, and called Whitehall.' The courtier who so carelessly spoke of 'York Place' apologetically explains:

> I know it,
> But 'tis so lately altered that the old name
> Is fresh about me.
>   (IV, i, 95–9)

Whitehall's identity was subject to royal whim, its history easily rewritten. That this exchange follows a hushed discussion of 'falling stars' at court makes its political edge that much sharper.

For a writer like Shakespeare, whose plays exhibit a greater fascination with courts than those of any other Elizabethan playwright, visits to Whitehall were inspiring. The palace was a far cry from anything he had ever experienced in his native Stratford-upon-Avon, which extant wills and town records portray as a drab backwater, devoid of high culture. There was little touring theatre, few books, hardly any musical instruments, no paintings to speak of, the aesthetic monotony broken only by painted cloths that adorned interiors (like the eight that had hung in Shakespeare's mother's home in Wilmcote). It had not always been this way. Vivid medieval paintings of the Passion and the Last Judgement had once decorated the walls of Stratford's church, but they had been whitewashed by Protestant reformers shortly before Shakespeare was born.

Whitehall had everything Stratford lacked. It housed the greatest collection of international art in the realm, its 'spacious rooms' hung 'with Persian looms', its treasures 'fetched from the richest cities of proud Spain' and beyond. For an Englishman who (like his Queen) had never left England's shores, it offered a rare opportunity to see work produced by foreign artisans. A short detour, up a staircase into the privy gallery overlooking the tiltyard, led Shakespeare into a breathtaking space. Its ceiling was covered in gold and its walls were lined with extraordinary paintings, including a portrait of Moses said to be 'a striking likeness'. Near it hung a 'most beautifully painted picture on glass showing thirty-six incidents of Christ's Passion'. But the most eye-catching painting in the passageway was the portrait of young Edward VI. Those approaching it for the first time found that 'the head, face and nose appear so long and misformed that they do not seem to represent a human being'. Installed on the right side of the painting was an iron bar with a plate attached to it. Visitors were encouraged to extend the bar and view the portrait through a small hole or 'O' cut in the plate: to their surprise, 'the ugly face changed into a well-formed one'.

A few years earlier this famous picture had inspired Shakespeare's lines about point-of-view in *Richard the Second*:

> Like perspectives, which rightly gazed upon
> Show nothing but confusion, eyed awry
> Distinguish form.
>   (II, ii, 18–20)

It may also have inspired a similar reflection in *Henry the Fifth* about seeing 'perspectively' (V, ii, 321). What the Chorus in this play calls the 'wooden O', the theatre itself, operates much like this Whitehall portrait: its lens is capable of giving shape and meaning to the world, but only if playgoers make the necessary imaginative effort.

Leaving this picture gallery, Shakespeare would next have entered the long privy gallery range that led past the Privy Council chamber, where Elizabeth's will was translated into government policy. The Christmas holiday had not disrupted the councillors' labours; seven of them had met there that day, ordering, among other things, that warm clothing be secured for miserably equipped English troops facing a bitter Irish winter. The councillors adjourned in time for that evening's entertainment and resumed their deliberations the following morning.

The winding corridor next led past Elizabeth's private quarters, including her bedchamber, library and the rooms in which she dressed and dined. When Elizabeth was not residing at Whitehall these rooms were open for viewing. Contemporary reports of their splendours give some inkling of power on display. The ceiling of her bedchamber was gilded, though the room itself was dark, with only a single window. Elizabeth's exotic bath attracted considerable notice, especially for how 'the water pours from oyster shells and different kinds of rock'. The apartments also held organs and virginals that the Queen herself played, as well as 'numerous cunningly wrought clocks in all sizes'; and, of course, the palace held the Queen's fabulously expensive and ornate wardrobe, of extraordinary interest to a player like Shakespeare whose company invested so much of its capital on lavish costumes.

The Queen's library also interested Shakespeare, stocked as it was with books in Greek, Latin, Italian, French and English, along with some of Elizabeth's own manuscripts. This wasn't just show: William Camden records that Elizabeth 'either read or wrote something every day' and that in 1598 she 'turned into the English tongue the greatest part of Horace's *De Arte Poetica* and a little book of Plutarch's *De Curiositate*, and wrote them with her own hand, though the rebellion in Ireland now flamed forth dangerously'. A monarch who wrote every day must have been an especially discriminating critic and perhaps better disposed than most to a playwright who did the same.

As he neared the room in which he would perform that evening, Shakespeare first had to pass the privy chamber (which housed Hans Holbein's famous mural of Henry VII, Henry VIII, and their wives Elizabeth of York and Jane Seymour) and then the large and lofty presence chamber. This was the inner sanctum: only Elizabeth's most intimate circle, her most favoured courtiers, were permitted into the privy chamber, and the distinction between those in and those out was clear-cut. It was decorated with 'a gilded ceiling' and 'pictures of the wars [Elizabeth] ha[d] waged'.

The overall impression, as one foreign visitor wrote in 1600, was that Whitehall was 'a place which fills one with wonder'. In this respect, it resembled those other great wonder-producing sites of Elizabethan England, the public theatres. Like the theatres, it contained space for display as well as a backstage, with secret areas off-limits to spectators that added to its mystery. There was as little concern for the mixing of artistic genres at court as there was in the playhouses. Visitors to Whitehall recorded their impressions of some of its more memorable artefacts, including a bust of Attila the Hun, a picture of 'a cripple being carried on a blind man's shoulders', a Dutch still life, a group of portraits of the leading divines of the Protestant Reformation, a wind-up clock of 'an Ethiop riding upon a rhinoceros', a 'genealogical table of the kings of England', a 'large looking-glass with a silk cover', a portrait of Julius Caesar (which surely caught Shakespeare's attention), a painting of Lucrece (which no doubt did as well), a sundial 'in the form of a monkey', a needlework map of Britain, a 'description of the New World on two boards with maps of the same parts of the New World alongside', and a mother-of-pearl organ bearing an inscription calling England's virgin Queen 'another Mary' (an association sure to annoy Elizabeth's Puritan critics). Other objects also bore mottos or inscriptions, including one that read: 'There are three things which destroyed the sovereignty of Rome: Hidden Hatred, Youthful Council, Self-Interest.' A good deal of the art was intended to flatter Elizabeth, such as the picture of 'Juno, Pallas Athena, and Venus together with Queen Elizabeth'.

Shakespeare would have appreciated the extent to which Whitehall was ultimately about competing, contested histories. Allusions to the Virgin Mary kept company with portraits of Reformation worthies. Fantasies of distant worlds – like the Ethiop astride a rhinoceros – fought for attention with state-of-the-art maps and globes for extending the reach of English trade and colonization. Sundials shared space with the latest in Continental clock technology. The riches contained in the palace were distantly related to those found in that sixteenth-century phenomenon called the *Wunderkammer*, or wonder-cabinet. Ancestor of the modern museum, the wonder-cabinet was usually a room set aside to display exotic objects. The finest of these in London probably belonged to Walter Cope, a merchant-adventurer and a member of Elizabeth's Society of Antiquaries. During his London visit in 1599 Thomas Platter visited Cope's wonder-cabinet, 'stuffed with queer foreign objects in every corner': an African charm made of teeth, the bauble and bell of Henry VIII's fool, an Indian stone axe and canoe, a chain made of monkey teeth, a Madonna constructed of Indian feather, a unicorn's tail, and shoes from around the globe. In another, unnamed house of curios on London Bridge, Platter even saw 'a large live camel'.

What distinguishes Whitehall from the jumble of the wonder-cabinet is that the objects in the latter were connected only by their strangeness and capacity to produce amazement. Whitehall's contents, in contrast, comprised a protean work-in-progress, its objects, rightly interpreted, conveying a complex narrative of dynastic power and political intrigue. No room in the palace better exemplified this than the shield gallery, a long hall overlooking the Thames, through which visitors arriving by boat passed on their way into the court. This gallery was crammed with hundreds of *imprese* – paste-board shields on which were painted pictures and enigmatic Latin mottos.

This strange practice originated under Elizabeth, who required every knight participating in the celebratory royal birthday and Accession Day tilts to present her with a paste-board shield. The pressure to produce just the right *impresa* was a burden for the knights, some of whom sought out the help of poets and artists. Unlike an emblem, which also combined word and image, the *impresa* was highly personal, its message, like that of a sonnet, bound up in the inscrutable relationship of speaker and object of veneration. In this case, the venerated object was Elizabeth herself, and the message of the *impresa* a courtier's attempt to flatter or cajole the Queen. The shield gallery might be said to contain the political history of Elizabeth's reign, the cumulative ups and downs of political aspirants. In its reliance on the enigmatic combination of word and image, and on wonder and interpretive skill, it embodied more than any other room at Whitehall the extent to which the physical world of the court resembled the imaginative world of the stage.

No doubt when Shakespeare entered the shield gallery his eye was drawn to his own anonymous contributions. He was obviously skilled in the genre and would later advertise his talents in *Pericles*, which contains a wonderful scene in which six knights display their *imprese*; Pericles' own shield depicts 'A withered branch, that's only green at top; / The motto, *In hac spe vivo*' – 'In this hope I live' (II, ii, 43–44). For obvious reasons, few records survive of who ghost-wrote *imprese*, though there's a bookkeeper's entry which records that Shakespeare was paid forty-four shillings for providing the *impresa* that the Earl of Rutland displayed at King James's Accession Day tournament in March 1613. That was a lot of money for so few words. And Shakespeare was responsible for just the motto; his fellow actor Richard Burbage, an accomplished artist, was paid handsomely 'for painting and making it'. It's highly unlikely that this commission at the very end of his career was Shakespeare's first freelance job. Who better, after all, to give voice to a courtier's unrequited desires?

Shakespeare's destination at Whitehall was the great chamber, also known as the guard or watching chamber, where the Chamberlain's Men were to perform that evening. It had fallen to them, as the pre-eminent company in the land, to play the first night of the Christmas holidays, as they had now done for five years running. But they couldn't afford to rest on their laurels: they had played three out of five times the previous Christmas season, yet had been responsible for all four court performances the Christmas before that. This season they were sharing the stage with the Admiral's Men, with two performances each. It was not a reassuring trend.

The great chamber was the most intimate playing space at Whitehall. Sixty feet long by thirty feet wide, with a twenty-foot ceiling, it had a wooden floor and a fireplace, and was decorated with woven tapestries. The acoustics were probably much better than those at the next most attractive playing space, the great hall, just beyond it and facing the chapel, which was considerably larger and had a high ceiling and a stone floor. A year earlier, a French ambassador had recorded in his diary that at the Whitehall Christmas celebrations, 'they began to dance in the presence of the Queen and to act comedies, which was done in the great chamber, and the Queen's throne was set up there and attended by a hundred gentlemen, very well ordered, the ladies also, and the whole court'. The French ambassador does not mention it, but there were probably a few children there too. Lady Anne Clifford, who was a girl of nine or so at this time, recalled in later years how, during Elizabeth's reign, at 'Christmas I used to go much to the court and sometimes did I lie at my Aunt Warwick's chamber on a pallet'. It's probable that her Aunt Warwick maintained a company of players earlier in the decade and it would be fitting if she secured a place for her young niece at performances by the leading players of the day.

If the great chamber was to be readied for dancing after the play – including energetic galliards that would have required a good deal of space – the audience, excepting Elizabeth on her throne, would have been seated on easily cleared upholstered benches or stools (or alternatively, as on other occasions, arranged in a shallow bank of temporary seating built against the wall). Many hands pitched in to make the performance a success. The Office of the Revels supervised the lighting and scenery, while the Sergeant Painter and his staff took care of any painting or decoration the performance required. The Chamberlain's staff of ushers, porters, and grooms oversaw cleaning and heating the chamber, as well as seating and decorating. It would have been a tight squeeze to accommodate all those gathered to see the play in the great chamber. John Chamberlain writes at Christmas time 1601: '[There] has been such a small court this Christmas that the guard were not troubled to keep doors at the plays and pastimes.' If this Christmas were more typical, the Queen's guards would have had their hands full.

There was a pecking order about who sat where during performances in the great chamber. This was not the public playhouse, where money could secure a better seat. An excruciating example of how social hierarchy was maintained survives in a letter from a secretary to the Earl of Essex named Edward Jones. Jones, who had married a woman of higher social station, was spotted at Christmas 1596 by the Lord Chamberlain, Cobham, alongside his pregnant wife, in a place reserved for those of higher rank. Shakespeare, whose company was the only one to perform at court that Christmas, may have witnessed the humiliation that followed: Cobham pointed his white staff of office at Jones, publicly berated him and told him to get back to where he belonged. Jones wrote to Cobham a few days later, complaining: 'That which grieveth me most is the public disgrace which your Lordship gave at the play on Sunday night, not only before many of my friends that thought your Lordship did me wrong, but in the hearing of my wife, who being with child did take it so ill as she wept.' Jones protested that he was just checking on his pregnant wife, not presuming to sit where he didn't belong, and didn't deserve to be called 'saucy fellow' and 'other words of disgrace'.

If, as is likely, the Chamberlain's Men presented their resident playwright's most recent work at court during the Christmas season of 1598, they would be staging *The Second Part of Henry the Fourth* and *Much Ado about Nothing*. Against this possible line-up the Admiral's Men were offering relatively lighter fare: two Robin Hood plays co-authored by Anthony Munday and Henry Chettle (Chettle was paid in late November, 1598, 'for mending of *Robin Hood* for the court' – probably inserting changes in the text requested by the Master of the Revels, Edmund Tilney). Tilney, whose responsibilities also included 'calling together of sundry players and perusing, fitting and reforming their matters otherwise not convenient to be shown before her Majesty', would have carefully reviewed every play to be performed at Christmas no later than November, this time not simply vetting the script but scrutinizing a dress performance at the Revels Office to ensure that nothing visual or verbal would give offence.

If the Chamberlain's Men performed *The Second Part of Henry the Fourth* this Christmas, their timing couldn't have been better. Its opening Prologue is spoken by a character named 'Rumour', a familiar presence at court: 'Open your ears, for which of you will stop / The vent of hearing when loud Rumour speaks?':

> Upon my tongues continual slanders ride,
> The which in every language I pronounce,
> Stuffing the ears of men with false reports.
> I speak of peace while covert enmity,
> Under the smile of safety, wounds the world.
>   (I, i, 1–10)

Rumour continues with an image that Shakespeare liked well enough to rework and improve in Hamlet's rebuke to Rosencrantz and Guildenstern: 'Will you play upon this pipe? . . . You would play upon me, you would seem to know my stops' (III, ii, 350–65):

>   Rumour is a pipe,
> Blown by surmises, jealousies, conjectures,
> And of so easy and so plain a stop
> That the blunt monster with uncounted heads,
> The still-discordant wav'ring multitude,
> Can play upon it.
>   (I, i, 15–20)

These words would have struck home at Whitehall that late December day, as rumours of great import swirled around the anxious court: would there be peace or war with Spain? and would the wavering Earl of Essex finally agree to lead an English army to suppress an Irish rebellion?

*

37

When the Chamberlain's Men had staged *The Second Part of Henry the Fourth* at the Curtain, the play had ended with an epilogue spoken by Will Kemp. Characters who deliver Shakespeare's epilogues tend to straddle fictional and real worlds and this play's ending is no exception. As the fifth act comes to a close, Sir John Falstaff – played by Kemp – is hauled off to the Fleet Prison and it looks for once as if Falstaff, that great escape artist, will not be able to wriggle out of trouble. But Kemp suddenly dashes back onstage. A moment or two passes before playgoers realize that the play really is over and that Kemp is delivering an epilogue not as Falstaff but more or less as himself (a slippery distinction, since Kemp always played Kemp whatever role he was assigned):

If my tongue cannot entreat you to acquit me, will you command me to use my legs? And yet that were but light payment, to dance out of your debt. But a good conscience will make any possible satisfaction, and so would I. All the gentlewomen here have forgiven me. If the gentlemen will not, then the gentlemen do not agree with the gentlewomen, which was never seen before in such an assembly.

One word more, I beseech you. If you be not too much cloyed with fat meat, our humble author will continue the story, with Sir John in it, and make you merry with fair Katharine of France. Where, for anything I know, Falstaff shall die of a sweat, unless already 'a be killed with your hard opinions; for Oldcastle died a martyr, and this is not the man. My tongue is weary; when my legs are too, I will bid you good night.

The witty epilogue manages to do several things at once. Kemp's repeated mention of his legs and dancing signals that a jig – a bawdy skit with dancing that concluded every publicly staged play, and at which Kemp excelled – is about to begin. Kemp also conveys the news that Shakespeare, 'our humble author', promises to 'continue the story', so his admirers can rest assured they'll be seeing him again soon. This is the only time Shakespeare ever shared with his audience what he planned to write next – a play that will feature Sir John Falstaff as well as Henry's bride-to-be,

Katharine of France. The work-in-progress is clearly *Henry the Fifth*, capstone to the historical sequence that had begun four years earlier with *Richard the Second* and continued in the two parts of *Henry the Fourth*. Tagged on to the end of the epilogue is a forced apology for using Oldcastle's name in *The First Part of Henry the Fourth* (hence the disclaimer that 'Oldcastle died a martyr, and this is not the man').

This epilogue wouldn't do at court, where plays did not end with ribald jigs. So, like Hamlet scribbling 'some dozen or sixteen lines' to be inserted into 'The Mousetrap', Shakespeare appended roughly the same number of lines to the special Whitehall performance. Once past the opening apology, Shakespeare breaks new ground in this revised epilogue. The speech is brassy and confident and may even have caught his fellow players off guard. Taking centre stage, Shakespeare delivers his own lines ('what I have to say is of my own making'). It's the only time in his plays we hear him speak for and as himself:

First, my fear; then, my curtsy; last my speech. My fear is your displeasure; my curtsy, my duty; and my speech, to beg your pardons. If you look for a good speech now, you undo me, for what I have to say is of my own making, and what indeed I should say will, I doubt, prove my own marring. But to the purpose, and so to the venture. Be it known to you, as it is very well, I was lately here in the end of a displeasing play, to pray your patience for it, and to promise a better. I meant indeed to pay you with this, which if like an ill venture it come unluckily home, I break, and you, my gentle creditors, lose. Here I promised you I would be, and here I commit my body to your mercies. Bate me some and I will pay you some and, as most debtors do, promise you infinitely. And so I kneel down before you; but indeed, to pray for the Queen.

It's a deft piece of work. This time around there's no mention of what the next play will be about and no promise that Kemp will return as Falstaff. The apology for Oldcastle in *The First Part of Henry the Fourth* (perhaps that or the *Merry Wives* was 'the displeasing play' he never quite gets around to naming) is nicely finessed, as Shakespeare offers in compensation the Falstaff play they have just applauded as a way of making amends. Beyond this point, the epilogue's initial acceptance of social deference – all that begging and curtsying – gives way to Shakespeare's novel suggestion that playwright and playgoers are bound in a partnership, sharers in a venture. Those in the audience alert to the echoes of Shakespeare's recent drama may have picked up on key words here – 'venture' and 'credit', 'bating' and 'paying', 'promising' and 'breaking' – central to his play about the new world of venture capital, *The Merchant of Venice*. If Shakespeare offers himself as merchant-adventurer, his plays as treasure, and his audience as investors, then it follows that an 'ill venture' which breaks or bankrupts him will prove as costly to his creditors.

The analogy between a theatrical joint-stock company like the Chamberlain's Men and joint-stock mercantile companies is not far-fetched. Both kinds of joint-stock operations were great levellers, the wealth that they produced transforming long-standing social boundaries. Shakespeare, who had recently translated his theatrical earnings into a coat of arms and joined the ranks of the 'gentle creditors', understood that money helped secure not just property but gentility too. For Shakespeare and the Chamberlain's Men, the rewards of venturing were as palpable as the perils of breaking. Veteran courtiers knew how many talented theatrical companies had come and gone: in the past decade the Queen's Men, Sussex's Men, Pembroke's Men, and Strange's Men had all been applauded at court and had all subsequently broken up. The threat of financial ruin through the loss of a permanent playing space in the city was an actor-sharer's worst nightmare.

When Shakespeare describes his audience as 'gentle creditors', he means not only that they provide the credit or licence to let him write what he wants, but also that they credit or believe in him.

Pursuing the implications of this metaphor, he redefines the terms of their understanding: if they bate him some – that is, if they cut him some slack – he will make it up to them in instalments; and, playing upon how debtors promise infinitely (that is, promise the world), Shakespeare says he will do the same. Like most debtors, when he says 'infinitely' he also means it in the sense of 'indefinitely'. Accept his terms, then, and they'll be repaid with immortal plays for a long time to come. The version of the epilogue spoken by Kemp described 'our humble author' sticking to a successful if by now familiar formula for success; the substitute one that Shakespeare himself delivered on the eve of 1599 couldn't be more different. It's the closest we get in his work to Shakespeare revealing his determination to move in a new direction, one in which he will demand more of his audience, his fellow players, and himself.

What had begun with Shakespeare modestly curtsying to his audience ends with what looks like a second act of deference as the epilogue comes to a close. Kneeling in prayer to conclude a play (itself an outworn Elizabethan convention) would seem to restore the world of deference and hierarchy rather than collaboration and mutuality. But Shakespeare – player and gentleman – catches himself and explains to his audience that while it may look as if he's kneeling 'before them', he's not; he's kneeling in prayer for Elizabeth, in deference to whom, now, one expects, every other subject in the room scrambles to follow suit. Relative to the monarch, debtors and creditors, servants and lords, players and patrons – who are all falling to their knees to join in this prayer for the Queen – are on the same level after all.

This unusual epilogue survives by accident – or rather, due to carelessness. *The Second Part of Henry the Fourth* was published less than two years after this. When the manuscript was passed along to the printing house, both versions of the epilogue were bundled with it. The compositor setting type, unsure of what to do, printed both but left an extra bit of space between the Whitehall and Curtain versions. Had he thought about it more, he might have realized that it made no sense for the speaker to kneel to the Queen midway through the epilogue and then spring up again. When the compositor of the 1623 Folio came upon this crux he too decided not to choose between the two but also melded them into a single epilogue, though he at least tried to mend things by moving the prayer to the Queen to the end of the epilogue. Bizarrely, modern-day editors, who ought to know better, have followed suit, leaving the confusion intact and obscuring why and how Shakespeare redirects his art at this time.

The rupture with Will Kemp hinted at in the revised epilogue became total by the early months of 1599, when Kemp walked (or was shoved) away from his partnership in the Globe and almost surely in the company as well, enabling Shakespeare and the other principals to enrich themselves by carving up his share. The full story of why Kemp changed his mind about the Globe and the Chamberlain's Men will never be known. Given the money he was sacrificing by leaving the partnership, the gulf between how he and others saw his role in the playing company and at the Globe must have been unbridgeable. That Shakespeare chose to cut his comic star out of *Henry the Fifth* defied expectations, for audiences familiar with stage versions of this story took it for granted that they'd be seeing a clown. Whether it precipitated Kemp's decision or was made in response to it is hard to tell, though I suspect the former. Kemp's great predecessor Dick Tarlton had starred as the lead clown, Derick (and perhaps as Oldcastle too), in Shakespeare's main dramatic source, *The Famous Victories of Henry the Fifth*. It would have been a milestone in Kemp's career, at the height of his popularity, to have surpassed Tarlton with his own comic turn in *Henry the Fifth*.

Since at least the eighteenth century critics have struggled to make sense of Shakespeare's change of heart about Falstaff. Why would he abandon one of his great creations – especially after promising that we'd see Falstaff again? Justifying this on artistic grounds wasn't easy, though Samuel Johnson did his best to exonerate Shakespeare: perhaps he 'could contrive no train of adventures suitable to his character, or could match him with no companions likely to quicken his humour, or could open no new vein of pleasantry'. The excuse – that Shakespeare lacked invention – is desperate, and you get the sense that Johnson himself doesn't believe it. What Johnson found especially unforgivable was that Shakespeare went back on his word: 'Let meaner authors learn from this example, that it is dangerous to sell the bear which is not yet hunted, to promise to the public what they have not written.' Johnson apparently hadn't considered reasons for Shakespeare's decision that had nothing to do with character or plot but rather with Kemp and clowning. The parting of ways between Shakespeare and Kemp – ironically if unintentionally mirrored in Hal's icy repudiation of Falstaff – was a rejection not only of a certain kind of comedy but also a declaration that from here on in it was going to be a playwright's and not an actor's theatre, no matter how popular the actor.

Kemp and Shakespeare made an odd pair. Older by a decade or so, Kemp was also the tougher and more physically imposing of the two. He was a powerfully built man, possessed of extraordinary stamina, yet exceptionally graceful. (To play the fat Falstaff he had to wear specially made 'giant hose'). A woodcut executed in 1600 – the only contemporary portrait we have of Kemp – depicts from the neck up a man well into middle age, with a grizzled beard and longish hair. But the rest of his body is that of a much younger man – of average height but muscular, sturdy, erect, light on his feet, dressed in the traditional garb of the morris dancer. Kemp would respond to the break-up with the Chamberlain's Men by dancing his way 'out of the world' (punningly, out of the Globe), out of London, towards Norwich in early 1600, in a morris dance lasting a few weeks, reconnecting with his roots in a solo performance. His demeanour underscored another fundamental difference with Shakespeare, having to do with class. He usually played lower-class country fellows like Bottom, Costard, Peter and Launcelot. Even in the role of the aristocratic Falstaff, Kemp played a man of the people and wore a workingman's cap. For Kemp, this was more than a role, it was a conviction, one that only increased his popular appeal. He loathed social climbers and went out of his way to praise those who didn't stand upon rank. No doubt Shakespeare's pursuit of gentility rubbed Kemp the wrong way.

Kemp was a veteran performer, his career going back at least to the mid-1580s, when he had been a member of the leading company of the time, Leicester's Men. They had been an itinerant company, playing at court, in the English countryside, and on the Continent, including Denmark (Kemp could have regaled Shakespeare with stories of playing before the Danish court at Elsinore). Shakespeare and Kemp may have first crossed paths in 1587, when Leicester's Men passed through Stratford-upon-Avon. If Shakespeare, then in his early twenties, was contemplating a life in the theatre, watching Leicester's Men perform in his home town might have been a deciding factor. Though they may both have belonged to Strange's Men by 1594, the first time their names are officially linked is a year later, 1595, when the two, along with Richard Burbage, are recorded as receiving payments for court performances by the newly formed Chamberlain's Men. The up-and-coming Burbage was by now a promising actor and Shakespeare emerging as an important playwright and poet; but at that time their reputations were easily overshadowed by Kemp's. There could have been no doubt in Kemp's mind in 1594 when he and Shakespeare became fellow sharers, or even in 1599 when his fame was at its height, who would be remembered as the greatest name in Elizabethan theatre.

Gentle as Shakespeare was reputed to be, he was not pliant, especially if that meant subordinating his artistic vision and will to the desires of the extraordinary actors for whom he wrote. It's tempting to read one of the very few contemporary anecdotes about Shakespeare as a gloss on this aspect of his relationship with his charismatic fellow players. This time, however, it's Richard Burbage that Shakespeare displaces in another act of substitution, a curious reversal of the bed-trick that figures so largely in his comedies. The story appears in the journal of John Manningham, a law student who jotted it down in March 1602 (though the apocryphal story may have already been in circulation for a few years):

Upon a time when Burbage played Richard III, there was a citizen grown so far in liking with him, that before she went from the play she appointed him to come that night unto her by the name of Richard III. Shakespeare, overhearing their conclusion, went before, was entertained, and at his game ere Burbage came. Then message being brought that Richard III was at the door, Shakespeare caused return to be made that William the Conqueror was before Richard III.

In the age old struggle for primacy between writer and actor, this round goes to the dramatist, who rewrites the scene, leaving his leading man out in the cold while enjoying his fan's embrace. The protean Shakespeare also gets in the last word.

The parting of ways between Kemp and Shakespeare was less than friendly (a year later, having left the company, Kemp was still muttering about 'Shakerags'). Even if personal differences could be overcome, philosophical ones over the role of the clown and the nature of comedy could not. Performers like Kemp were more than jokesters and at stake was more than simply entertaining audiences. Clowns – closer to what we would call comedians – traced their lineage to older, popular forms of festive entertainment, to the Lord of Misrule, to the Vice figure of morality drama, to traditions of minstrelsy, rusticity, song and dance. Their origins also encouraged leading clowns to think of themselves as the true stars of their companies. It was their job to banter with members of the audience, especially at the ends of scenes, and to stray from the script when occasion presented itself. They weren't intended to be believable characters – that is to say, like real people – not even when playing fully fleshed-out roles like Falstaff. This was because leading clowns were also always playing themselves – or, rather, the stage identity they so carefully crafted.

Playgoers were not the only ones who never forgot that Kemp was Kemp. Even Shakespeare occasionally forgot to distinguish actor and role. When he imagined the clown Peter's entrance in *Romeo and Juliet*, he writes 'Enter Will Kemp'. The same holds true in Act 4 of *Much Ado about Nothing*, where instead of the character 'Dogberry' he writes 'Kemp'. What's so striking is that he rarely does this for other actors in the company. The speech prefixes to the quarto of *The Second Part of Henry the Fourth* similarly reveal traces of what Shakespeare was imagining as he wrote. There's an otherwise inexplicable stage entrance for someone named 'Will' in Act 2, scene 4, which makes no sense other than as an early entry for Will Kemp as Falstaff. Editors who don't accept this are forced to invent a new character, 'Will' or 'William', who is never named onstage, is then given lines assigned to others, and for whom a speedy exit is invented as well. Far more likely is that Shakespeare, as elsewhere in these drafts, couldn't help but think of Will Kemp as Will Kemp, whatever his role. As Shakespeare found himself moving steadily at this time towards a more naturalistic drama in which characters like Rosalind and Hamlet feel real, the traditional clown had become an obstacle.

No less gnawing a problem for Shakespeare was the clown's afterpiece, the jig. It may be hard for us to conceive of the conclusion of *Romeo and Juliet* – with the image of the dead lovers fresh in our minds – immediately followed by a bawdy song and dance, but Elizabethan audiences demanded it. Jigs were basically semi-improvisational one-act plays, running to a few hundred lines, usually performed by four actors. They were rich in clowning, repartee and high-spirited dancing and song, and written in traditional ballad form. Though nominally independent of the plays that preceded them, they were an extension of the clown's part. If comedies were about love, jigs were about what happened after marriage – adultery, deception and irrepressible sexual desire. Jigs – anarchic and libidinal – were wildly popular because they tapped into parts of everyday experience usually left untouched in the world of the play. As such, they provided a counterpoint to the fragile closure of romantic comedy and to the high seriousness and finality of tragedy.

Frustratingly little evidence survives about the Elizabethan jig. There must have been some tacit agreement between the authorities and the publishers not to print them. After several jigs – including a few making much of Kemp's role – appeared in print in the early 1590s, not another was published for thirty years. But even these scripts fail to capture the extraordinary vitality of these performances – the explosive energy, the star clown's side-splitting gestures, the high-spirited singing, the spectacular leaping, the titillating groping. The undisputed master of the jig was, unsurprisingly, Will Kemp – who looked back on his career as one 'spent ... in mad jigs and merry jests'. His stage presence, his comic timing, and more than anything else his dancing skill and stamina made his jigs famous. Dick Tarlton may have been a greater all-round entertainer, but Kemp figured out how to suit his comic gifts to the public stage. By 1598 the popularity of Kemp's jigs was so great that everywhere you turned in London you could hear 'whores, beadles, bawds, and sergeants filthily chant Kemp's jig'. There were spectators so enthralled with jigs that they would only arrive at the theatre after the play was over, pushing their way in to see the jig for free.

Dramatists understandably grumbled about the jigs (which were written not by playwrights but by hack ballad-makers). It could not have been easy surrendering the last word to the clown. Christopher Marlowe had hated jigs, and says so in the prologue to *Tamburlaine the Great*, where he announces that his play rejects 'jigging veins of riming mother wits / And such conceits as clownage keeps in pay'. Even as popular a dramatist as Thomas Dekker had sharp words for what he calls the 'nasty bawdy jig'. Given this friction, it's easy to see how disagreements over the purpose of playing between the Chamberlain's Men's leading clown and its star playwright had reached the breaking point. After Kemp's departure, when a revival of a Falstaff play was called for, fellow sharer Thomas Pope, adept in comic roles, could step in. But Kemp's jigs were a thing of the past; Shakespeare now got in the last word at the Globe.

Shakespeare's victory over Kemp (even if Kemp had left by choice) was so complete that it's hard in retrospect to see what all the fuss was about. In 1638 the dramatist Richard Brome included a scene in *The Antipodes* in which a clown is taken to task for improvising and for bantering with the audience. When the clown defends himself by appealing to the precedent established by the great comedians of the past, he is told that the days of Tarlton and Kemp are over, it's a playwrights' theatre now, and the stage 'purged from barbarism, / And brought to the perfection it now shines'. The battle won, English drama would never be the same.

Kemp bounced around for a while. He drifted back to the Curtain, where he could count on old fans, performed a bit with a company called Worcester's Men, and tried to get a touring company going on the Continent, but nothing really took hold and he had to borrow money. Within a few years he died penniless, his burial entry reading simply 'Kemp, a man'. If not for Shakespeare, Kemp's legacy and verbal style would be long forgotten. After Kemp left the company we no longer find Shakespeare carelessly alluding to particular actors in his drafts, only to characters. It's as if he began to believe more fully in the reality of his own creations.

As Shakespeare's characters became more real and as Shakespeare's name figured more and more prominently on printed editions of his plays, his fellow players, with the exception of Burbage, became increasingly anonymous. Shakespeare had won the battle of Wills, though he would spend much of the following year trying to exorcize Kemp's ghost.

2

A Great Blow in Ireland

Long before returning to Whitehall in late December, Shakespeare knew not to expect much holiday cheer at court. The domestic and international challenges England now faced reverberated through the play he was trying to finish, *Henry the Fifth*, as they would through all the plays he worked on in 1599. Since summer, the news both at home and abroad had been unrelentingly grim. The mood had turned dark in August, with word of the death of the most powerful man in England, Lord Treasurer Burghley, followed by reports of a catastrophic military defeat in Ireland. As Burghley lay dying, Elizabeth visited him and in an extraordinary gesture, hoping to spur his recovery, spoon-fed the minister who had served her faithfully for forty years. On 29 August 1598 Londoners lined the streets between Burghley's residence in the Strand and Westminster Abbey to witness the extraordinary state funeral 'performed . . . with all the rites that

The English army in Ireland

belong to so great a personage'. Watching the five hundred official mourners accompanying the hearse, many of whom were already vying for the spoils of Burghley's lucrative offices, Londoners who remembered the other famous courtiers who had grown old with Elizabeth – Leicester, Walsingham, Warwick and Hatton – may well have sensed that they were witnessing the end of an era.

The ageing Queen knew it and feared it. She had recently confided to a foreign ambassador that she had now 'lost twenty or two and twenty of her councillors', and put little faith in the current crop of aspirants, who 'were young and had no experience in affairs of state'. Burghley's tireless service, his skill at managing conflict, and his occasional ruthlessness had proven indispensable to the Queen. He had helped avert the corrosive effects of the factionalism she herself had encouraged as part of a time-tested strategy of playing her powerful and ambitious courtiers against each other. The most conspicuous mourner that day was Robert Devereux, Earl of Essex, who had been Burghley's ward and who had looked up to him as a father figure. Tall and handsome, with his distinctive square-cut beard and charismatic air, he stood in striking contrast to the man who should have been the centre of attention, Burghley's son, Secretary of State Sir Robert Cecil, a canny, hunchbacked bureaucrat that Elizabeth affectionately called her 'pygmy'. With Burghley's death, the court irrevocably fractured into factions aligned with these two men – the '*Militia*' and the '*Togati*,' court observer Sir Robert Naunton called them: the swordsmen and the bureaucrats.

In the spring of 1598 English policy-makers heatedly debated whether to make peace with Spain. Burghley was the chief advocate of peace and his death was a blow to the hopes of those seeking to reorient English foreign policy. The English had learned in April that their war-weary French allies were ready to make a separate peace. Elizabeth dispatched Robert Cecil to the French court to discover Henri IV's intentions and if possible break off the proposed treaty with Spain; but the French King had already made up his mind. Henri IV's decision left England virtually alone in confronting the Spanish – on the Continent, in Ireland, on the seas, and potentially on its own shores as well. As Lord Treasurer, Burghley knew that the cost of fighting on all these fronts had become nearly intolerable. Even as Burghley lay dying he oversaw a revised agreement with the Low Countries that ensured their covering the expense of auxiliary English troops. If war was unavoidable, Burghley wanted others to pay for it. Only after his death did his fellow countrymen discover how expensive it was to maintain a war footing, one reporting that the Lord Treasurer 'had left the Queen's coffers so bare that there is but £20,000 to be found'.

The arguments favouring peace were compelling. The end of hostilities would go far toward repairing England's international reputation. The English, noted the contemporary historian William Camden, were increasingly seen as 'as disturbers of the whole world, as if they were happy in other men's miseries'. A lasting peace with Spain would also, it was hoped, end Spanish support for Irish rebels and enrich the nation by providing English merchants with access to ports now closed to them; and peace, Camden adds, would let England 'take breath and gather wealth against future events'.

The acknowledged need for England to catch its breath gives some sense of how spent the nation had become in its unending skirmishes with Spain. England's dispatch of troops to the Low Countries and a fleet to the West Indies in 1585 had helped provoke the Great Armada of 1588. This, in turn, had led to English naval expeditions against Spain and Portugal and the conscription of thousands of English soldiers to fight against the Spanish and their surrogates. Spain, for its part, had retaliated with successive (and again unlucky) armadas in 1596 and 1597, plots against Elizabeth's life and support for Irish resistance to English rule. There was little that England could do to forestall future armadas other than send out fleets to loot Spanish shipping, ports and colonial outposts. Like exhausted heavyweights slugging it out, England and Spain exchanged blows, but neither had the luck or strength to land a knock-out punch.

Despite the strong arguments in favour of peace, decades of anti-Catholic propaganda and deep distrust of Spanish motives proved powerful counterweights. From the perspective of those in the war camp, the notion that Spain would change its ways and embrace peace on terms acceptable to England was naïve. Even if this were imaginable, the risks to England were too great to take such a chance. Without the threat of English ships harassing their American treasure fleets and raiding their ports, the Spaniard, they argued, would soon 'heap up such a mass of treasure that if he brake forth into war again, he will be far stronger than all his neighbours'. And if English troops pulled out of the Low Countries, it opened the way for Spain to outflank and invade England.

Court observers were at a loss to tell which faction would prevail. 'It is still in deliberation,' John Chamberlain wrote to his friend Dudley Carleton in early May, 'whether we shall join with France in a peace and leave the Low Countries ... and the balance sways not yet on either side'. The jockeying for influence at court tends to obscure how differently the two camps saw England's national, religious and economic interests best served. With so much hanging in the balance, the debate became heated. At one exchange in the council chamber, after Essex yet again insisted that 'no peace could be made with the Spaniards but such as would be dishonourable and treacherous', the imperturbable Burghley famously reached for his psalter and opened it up to Psalm 55 before conspicuously passing the book to Essex with his finger on verse 23: 'Men of blood shall not live out half their days.'

Burghley's rebuke hit close to home. Essex's father had died in the Queen's service in Ireland in 1576, of chronic dysentery. His funeral sermon was published a year later along with a letter to his eleven-year-old son and heir, reminding the boy that Essex men didn't live long (neither Essex's father nor grandfather had lived past his mid-30s). The letter went on to urge the young Essex to be daring in pursuit of fame: 'Rather throw the helve [handle] after the hatchet, and leave your ruins to be repaired by your prince than any thing to degenerate from honourable liberality.' Essex took that advice to heart.

Once principled disagreements over national policy turned personal, it was inevitable that opponents began accusing each other of acting in self-interest. Essex, stung by such charges, wrote an *Apology* defending himself from allegations of war-mongering. While it had ostensibly been written as a letter to a friend, Essex's supporters made sure that the *Apology* circulated widely, first in manuscript and then in print. There's a good chance that a copy passed through Shakespeare's hands, and not simply because he was a voracious reader who knew how to get his hands on this sort of thing. Through his former patron, the Earl of Southampton, a close friend of Essex, he was well placed to see it; or he might have had access to it through one of the many writers who congregated around Essex House.

Shakespeare would have found Essex's *Apology* fascinating both as a character study and as a daring political tract. Essex saw the current crisis in grand terms, 'as holy a war' as those fought against God's enemies in the Old Testament; but, knowing his Queen, he understood that such enterprises were also judged by their price tags: for £100,000, the war with Spain could be successfully maintained. And, for a serious investment of £250,000, Essex guaranteed that 'the enemy shall bring no fleet into the seas for England, Ireland, and the Low Countries, but it shall be beaten'. In his effort to inspire Englishmen to rally to this call for war, Essex indirectly invoked the example of Henry V, the most celebrated of heroic English conqueror-kings: 'Could our nation in those former gallant ages, when our country was far poorer than it is now, levy arms, make war, achieve great conquests in France, and make our powerful arms known as far as the Holy Land? And is this such a degenerate age, as we shall not be able to defend England? No, no, there is some seed yet left of the ancient virtue.'

Essex had done his best to embody this chivalric code. He had taken his place in the charge at Zutphen in the Netherlands campaign of 1586, where Sir Philip Sidney fell; and, having taken up Sidney's sword (and his widow), he had led the English attack three years later at Lisbon, where he had 'thrust in his pike' into the city gates, challenging any 'Spaniard mewed therein . . . to break a lance'. In 1591, this time in the fields of France, Essex challenged the governor of Rouen. In his subsequent campaign in the Azores, to gain the glory of being the first to land on an island, Essex, though under fire, leapt unprotected into a boat, disdaining 'to take any advantage of the watermen that rowed him'. His daring earned Essex the praise of poets like George Chapman, who describes him in the dedication to his translation of the *Iliad* as 'most true Achilles, whom by sacred prophecy Homer did but prefigure'. But Essex's martial aggressiveness was also dangerously destabilizing: he had personally challenged Sir Walter Ralegh, fought a duel with Charles Blount, and most recently had even challenged the Lord Admiral.

Essex's nostalgia in his *Apology* for the great age of English chivalry echoes Thomas Nashe's similar praise of those times as reenacted in English history plays, 'wherein our forefathers' valiant acts . . . are revived and they themselves raised from the grave of oblivion and brought to plead their aged honours in open presence'. For Nashe, too, Henry V is the exemplar of English greatness: 'What a glorious thing it is to have Henry V represented on stage, leading the French King prisoner, and forcing both him and the Dolphin to swear fealty.' Having promised to write a new version of *Henry the Fifth*, Shakespeare knew exactly how much political baggage the story carried, all the more so after Essex's *Apology* began to circulate.

For an alternative to this martial, masculine stage image, the English only had to look at how their own Queen was depicted on Continental stages. In June 1598 an English merchant described a 'dumb show' or silent play staged lately in Brussels on the hotly debated question of peace between France and Spain. In the midst of Henri IV's onstage negotiations, a fawning, flattering woman enters and attempts to eavesdrop on his conversations before finally 'plucking the French King by the sleeve'. The woman is none other than Queen Elizabeth of England – and, the English merchant angrily reports, the audience members in Brussels 'whisper and laugh at the conceit'. It wasn't just the English who used the stage to satirize contemporary politics; theatre was counted on for its political and topical edge on both sides of the Channel.

News reaching England in September 1598 that King Philip II of Spain had died a slow and agonizing death failed to resolve the debate over the proposed peace treaty. Advocates of war were even more distrustful of his successor, Philip III. As far as Essex was concerned, the young prince's 'blood [was] hotter'. And even as the dying Philip II had extended tentative feelers towards peace, he was also sending assassins to kill Elizabeth.

During this anxious time, when England badly needed his leadership, Essex withdrew from the court in a sulk. While he briefly returned to town for Burghley's funeral, observers wondered whether his heavy countenance that day was best explained by genuine grief or self-pity. In either case, Essex retired once more to his estate at Wanstead, where rumour had it, 'he means to settle, seeing he cannot be received in court'. Essex had relied on this strategy of Achilles-like withdrawal before. It had worked well enough following his disappointing reception after the amateurish Islands Voyage in October 1597. At that time Essex felt that the Queen had unjustly rewarded his rivals with important offices while he was fighting abroad. Essex was only reconciled after being appointed Earl Marshal. But even outsiders could see that this was a dangerous game to play.

The intimate relationship between Elizabeth and her most popular courtier was fast unravelling. Essex refused to conform to the mould of Elizabeth's previous favourites, Hatton and Leicester. Leicester, who nearly became Elizabeth's husband, had also been her age-mate, and there was an understanding and respect between them. Hatton, also of her generation, had ultimately deferred to Elizabeth. Not Essex. He was thirty years younger than Elizabeth, and her relationship with him veered wildly between the maternal and the erotic. For his part, Essex offered protestations of devotion to Elizabeth while waxing indignant when she refused to pursue the policies he advocated. While Essex chafed when he couldn't get his way, Elizabeth grew frustrated at his petulance and his refusal to be subject to her fading mystique. By 1598 the Queen let it be known that Essex 'hath played long enough upon her, and that she means to play awhile upon him'.

By June of that year their quarrel turned violent. The escalation occurred, William Camden reports, in the context of 'this business of the peace' with Spain, and was triggered by a disagreement over a seemingly minor and long-delayed appointment in Ireland. Since Lord Burgh had died the previous autumn, Elizabeth's administration in Dublin had been clamouring for a replacement; but the English court failed to take the Irish problem very seriously. Potential candidates saw the Irish posting as a disastrous career move; the word around court was that Sir Walter Ralegh, Robert Sidney and Christopher Blount had all refused the assignment.

When Elizabeth finally proposed sending Essex's uncle, Sir William Knollys, Essex, wary of losing a trusted ally at court, urged instead that she pack off his enemy Sir George Carew to the Irish bogs. When the Queen baulked at the suggestion, Essex then stepped over the line of what was allowable in her presence. Only a handful of witnesses – including Sir Robert Cecil (who probably leaked the story to William Camden) – witnessed what happened next. Essex, 'forgetting himself and neglecting his duty, uncivilly turneth his back, as it were in contempt, with a scornful look'. Elizabeth had put up with a lot from her headstrong Earl, but this insolence was intolerable. Astounded that Essex would sneeringly turn his back on her, Elizabeth boxed him on the ear 'and bade him be gone with a vengeance'.

Smarting from the royal blow and insult, Essex reached for his sword. He was fortunate that the Lord Admiral restrained him before he treasonously drew on the Queen. As far as Essex was concerned, it was the Queen who, in publicly striking him, had transgressed and he swore 'a great oath that he neither could nor would swallow so great an indignity'. Before stalking out of the royal presence he added one more choice insult, letting Elizabeth know that he wouldn't have submitted to such mortifying treatment at the hands of her father, King Henry VIII. Henry would have beheaded him for such impudence.

Both in the wrong, neither Elizabeth nor Essex would budge. She needed Essex but wasn't about to humble herself to a subject. Essex badly needed to return to court, not only to steer the Queen and Council towards a more confrontational stance towards Spain, but also to ensure that he and his followers reaped the benefits of royal patronage. So Essex boldly wrote to Elizabeth, offering his version of who was at fault, castigating 'the intolerable wrong you have done both me and yourself, not only broken all laws of affection, but done so against the honour of your sex'. Such arrogance led nowhere. Friends tried to intercede, desperate to heal the rift. Sir Thomas Egerton, Lord Keeper of the Seal, urged Essex to back down, reassuring him: 'You are not so far gone, but you may well return.' And then, in words that must have stung: 'You forsake your country when it hath most need of your help and counsel . . . Policy, duty, and religion enforce you to sue, yield, and submit to your sovereign.'

The accusation that he was unpatriotic could not go unanswered. Essex wrote back in words that bordered on sedition: 'Say you, I must yield and submit ... Doth religion enforce me to sue? Or doth God require it? Is it impiety not to do it? What, cannot princes err? Cannot subjects receive wrong? Is an earthly power or authority infinite?' More was going on here than raging egotism. When the principles of honour collided with those of an unconditional submission to a political authority, which prevailed? Essex's challenge to a monarch's absolute power derived from radical Continental political philosophers like the anonymous author of *Vindiciae Contra Tyrannos* – 'A Defence of Liberty against Tyrants' – whose attacks on the unlimited authority of God's anointed were so politically volatile that they could not be printed in England until the revolutionary 1640s. At the same time, Essex invokes an ancient prerogative, a knight's code of honour. From a monarch's perspective, it's hard to imagine a more dangerous combination.

News of a military disaster in Ireland finally forced both Elizabeth and Essex to retreat from their hardened positions without, however, fully reconciling. The report of the annihilation of English troops at Blackwater in Ulster spread quickly. On 30 August, John Chamberlain wrote sombrely to Dudley Cartleton: 'We have lately received a great blow in Ireland ... This is the greatest loss and dishonour the Queen hath had in her time.' Chamberlain was amazed that the enormity of the defeat hadn't sunk in: 'It seems we are not moved with it, which whether it proceed more of courage than of wit I know not, but I fear it is rather a careless and insensible dullness.' Out of overconfidence or perhaps disrespect for the military skill of the Irish rebels, the English had not as yet woken up to what was in store for them. The crushing loss dashed hopes of peace with Spain, put a severe strain on England's financial resources and made the office of Lord Deputy of Ireland a far more vital post than it had been just a month earlier.

The root causes of the disaster can be traced back as far as the twelfth-century Anglo-Norman invasion of Ireland, after which the Kings of England declared themselves Lords of Ireland. The English presence in Ireland over the following centuries had never really displaced the power of local Gaelic lords. Irish politics remained decentralized: clans and their feuding chieftains – who ruled over people, not territory – remained the dominant political force. The influence of the Old English, as the Anglo-Norman settlers were called, didn't extend much further than the major ports, towns, and the area around Dublin, known as the Pale, where the English administration was concentrated. The English made few inroads in the north and west. Successive English kings were content to let surrogate feudal lords, to whom lesser lords paid tribute in exchange for protection, manage things in their absence. This often anarchic state of affairs took a turn for the worse under the Tudors, when Henry VIII decided to declare himself King of Ireland, and also, for good measure, supreme head of its Church. Hereafter the Irish would speak English and abandon their Catholic faith. The Tudor fantasy of imposing English religion, law, language, primogeniture, dress and civility failed to have the desired effect. To the bewilderment of English observers, the rude Irish clung to their strange and barbarous customs. And, to their consternation, many of the Old English settlers had, over the course of several centuries, gone native, adopting Irish customs and marrying into local families, vastly complicating loyalties and alliances between Gaelic, Old English and New English inhabitants – and unnerving those committed to preserving a pure and unsullied Englishness.

Elizabeth's Irish policies were characterized by incoherence and neglect. The Queen was too miserly to pay the huge price to subdue Ireland and too distracted by other concerns to acknowledge the weaknesses of her colonial policies. The impression left on the visiting French diplomat André Hurault, Sieur de Maisse, was that the 'English and the Queen herself would wish Ireland drowned in the sea, for she cannot get any profit from it; and meanwhile the expense and trouble is very great, and she cannot put any trust in that people'. The Elizabethan policy of expropriating huge swathes of Irish land and inviting Englishmen over to settle on these 'plantations' provoked local resentment. Irish rebels looked to Spain for support and rallied followers around their threatened Catholic identity. Meanwhile, each short-lived English viceroy – suspected back at the English court, lacking support for ambitious reforms, bewildered by Ireland's complex political landscape, and often corrupt and brutal – failed in turn to establish either peace or stability. Elizabeth's muddled and half-hearted strategies were penny wise and pound foolish: in the last two decades of her reign she would spend £2,000,000 and the lives of many English conscripts in ongoing efforts to pacify Ireland.

By the mid-1590s chieftains opposed to English rule managed to put their differences aside long enough to unite under the leadership of a small group of Irish lords, most prominent among them the Ulsterman Hugh O'Neill, known to the English as the Earl of Tyrone. Tyrone, now around fifty, had spent some of his formative years among the English of the Pale, was fully versed in English military strategy, and was a brilliant if overcautious commander. William Camden's thumbnail sketch conveys the grudging admiration the English had for this adversary: Tyrone 'had a strong body, able to endure labour, watching, and hunger. His industry was great, his soul large and fit for the weightiest business. Much knowledge he had in military affairs, and a profound dissembling heart.' Tyrone's fellow Irishman, Peter Lombard, rounds out this portrait, describing him as a leader who knew how to keep his 'feelings under control', yet one who also knew how to exercise his charisma: 'He quite captivates the feelings of men by the nobility of his looks and countenance, and wins the affection of his soldiers or strikes terror into them.' By 1598, Tyrone and his allies

O'Donnell and Maguire were ready to strike hard at the English when the opportunity – at Blackwater – presented itself.

The immediate cause of the defeat at Blackwater – also known as the Battle of Yellow Ford – can be traced back a year to the summer of 1597, when Lord Burgh led 3,000 foot soldiers and 500 cavalry from Dublin to the Blackwater River, a strategic junction near Armagh leading to Ulster. The English military in Ireland were convinced that the only way to cut off the head of the Irish rebellion was to go after Tyrone in his home base of Ulster; and the sure way to do that was to land forces by sea at Lough Foyle in the far north – tying up Tyrone's defences and laying waste to his native grounds – while at the same time controlling the entry into Ulster from the south by establishing key garrisons along the way from Dublin through Dundalk, Newry and Armagh.

To this end, on 14 July 1597 Burgh's forces dislodged a contingent of Tyrone's men guarding the Blackwater ford and established a small garrison there. But until it formed part of a longer chain of garrisons leading into Ulster, the Blackwater fort remained vulnerable, its three hundred troops too isolated to resupply. Shortly after, Burgh, like so many of the English commanders in Ireland before and after, took sick and was dead by October. The establishment of another garrison at Lough Foyle and the pincer movement against Tyrone's forces in the north would have to wait.

Tyrone then let one of his periodic truces with the English lapse and he and his allies went on the offensive, catching the English off guard at Cavan, Leinster and Blackwater. Tyrone decided it was easier to starve the English troops than assault them directly and the Blackwater garrison was soon reduced to eating horses and then scrounging for roots and grass. The best military minds the English had in Ireland urged that the fort at Blackwater be abandoned. Their advice was ignored. Sir Henry Bagenal, an old campaigner, volunteered to lead an English army out of Dublin to resupply Blackwater. Bagenal was a bitter enemy of Tyrone, who had eloped with his sister Mabel seven years earlier. The departure of Bagenal's well-equipped army of close to 4,000 foot soldiers and 320 cavalry in early August must have been a comforting sight to English settlers in Ireland, an indication of Elizabeth's commitment to their safety.

Bagenal's army passed through Armagh, and on 14 August marched the final stage toward Blackwater fort, with Bagenal dividing his large army into six regiments. Two regiments marched in front, two in the rear, and two in the main body. The idea was that, if attacked, the three groups would link up. The tactic proved disastrous. After marching a mile through sniper fire, the English vanguard pressed on to a point across the Callan Brook known as the Yellow Ford, where it had to pass through a long trench with bogs on either side. The fort was now in sight, and the starving English garrison at Blackwater could see the lead column coming to their relief. But at this point the English advance fell into disarray. A heavy artillery piece got 'stuck fast in a ford' and the gap between the lead regiment and the main body began to widen. The vanguard received orders to close the gap, but as it turned back it was set upon by the Irish and 'put to the sword without resistance'. The English troops, especially the many fresh conscripts, panicked. Bagenal, leading the second regiment, rushed forward only to be 'shot through his forehead'. His regiment soon suffered the same fate as those in the vanguard.

Retreat was now urgent and commands were given to that effect; but following a huge explosion (probably set off by a spark from the lighted match of an English soldier replenishing his supply of gunpowder), chaos ensued and black smoke enveloped the English troops. Raw recruits ran for their lives and 'were for the most part put to the sword'. Hundreds of hired Irish in Bagenal's army dashed over to their countrymen's side. The detached rearguard went forward in relief but were themselves charged by 2,000 Irish foot soldiers and 400 cavalry. The surviving English captains were barely able to secure a retreat. Only 1,500 English troops, many of them badly injured, made it safely to nearby Armagh, where they took shelter in the local church. Intending to relieve a starving and surrounded force, the English were now themselves surrounded and had enough food to last just eight or nine days. The Irish forces stripped the dead and beheaded those Englishmen too badly wounded to flee.

With Bagenal dead, several thousand troops killed or wounded and the survivors about to starve or be killed, nothing now stood between Tyrone and Dublin, the heart of English rule in Ireland. Were the Spanish to capitalize on the defeat and send Tyrone long-promised reinforcements, the situation would be even more dire. Seeing no alternative, the Lords Justices in Dublin sent Tyrone a grovelling letter begging him not to inflict 'any further hurt' and warning him of Elizabeth's wrath if he should act in 'cold blood'. Elizabeth, upon receiving a copy of this letter, was incensed at their cowardice.

Unbeknownst to the Lords Justices, Tyrone, against the advice of his supporters, decided to extend generous terms not only to the surrounded force in Armagh but also to the famished troops at Blackwater, who were likewise allowed to leave unharmed. Tyrone passed on his chance to drive unimpeded into Dublin because his spies had told him that the English were planning to land forces to his rear, at Lough Foyle. Under such circumstances it was no time for a siege of the force in Armagh. What Tyrone hadn't figured on was that as soon as the news of Blackwater had reached England, the Lough Foyle plans had been scuttled and the 2,000 English troops who had planned to land there hastily diverted to reinforce Dublin. News of Tyrone's 'merciless bounty' in sparing the lives of the survivors in Armagh was greeted back in London with a mixture of relief and cynicism.

While Dublin and its environs were spared, Irish forces elsewhere in the country set to work the rest of the summer and autumn of 1598, determined to uproot the plantations of the New English who had appropriated their land. It was a brutal campaign. Throughout the autumn, fresh reports of English losses reached London. Tobie Matthew wrote to Dudley Carleton in September that since 'the great overthrow' at Blackwater, there were 'four hundred more throats cut in Ireland'. By mid-November, Chamberlain reported that 'messengers come daily' out 'of Ireland ... like Job's servants, laden with ill tidings of new troubles and revolts'. The desire for revenge and the satisfaction that will be derived from Irish blood-letting is conveyed in some lines of verse by the usually level-headed poet, John Donne:

> Sick Ireland is with a strange war possessed
> Like to an ague, now raging, now at rest,
> Which time will cure, yet it must do her good
> If she were purged, and her head-vein let blood.
>   (Elegy 20)

Essex, having returned to the court, weighed in on who should lead a retaliatory force; but when his friend Lord Mountjoy's name was put forward, Essex opposed the idea, arguing that Mountjoy lacked military experience and was, frankly, too bookish. As each candidate was proposed, Essex found grounds for objecting: only 'some prime man of the nobility' would do, he insisted, someone 'strong in power, honour, and wealth, in favour with the military men and which had been before general of an army'. It soon became obvious, as Camden notes, that 'he seemed to point with the finger to himself'. His enemies enthusiastically endorsed sending Essex. At the least, he'd be overseas and unable to interfere with their designs at court. Essex knew well enough that once out of the Queen's orbit his enemies would try to poison her against him. But he was trapped: he could not stand watching a lesser man lead so great an army. To his closest friends, Essex admitted: 'I am tied by my own reputation.' Perhaps the Irish campaign could win him back into the Queen's good graces, 'to be valued by her above them that are of no value'. If not, he might as well 'forget the world and be forgotten by it'.

By December 1598 confirmation that Essex had agreed to go to Ireland was followed by rumours that he had changed his mind. Essex knew that if he were to have any chance of success he would need a very large army, well outfitted and equipped, with promise of replacements. He knew, too, that, despite Elizabeth's reservations, this was the moment to hold out for such an expensive expedition, with soldiers of fortune and second sons of noblemen throughout England clamouring to fight by his side, each one, Chamberlain reports, hoping 'to be colonel at least'. As 1598 came to a close, Essex remained uncommitted. Chamberlain writes: 'The matters of Ireland stand at a stay or rather go backward, for the Earl of Essex's journey thither that was in suspense, is now they say quite dashed.' The reversals were maddening and the nation waited for a sign that its most charismatic military figure would agree to lead the greatest English army into battle since the days of Henry VIII.

3

Burial at Westminster

Shakespeare was not the only major writer at court on the eve of the new year. In late December another arrived bearing letters to the Privy Council from Sir Thomas Norris, President of Munster. He had embarked from Ireland on 9 December 1598, arrived in London within two weeks, and taken up residence on King Street in Westminster, a few minutes' walk from Whitehall. His name was Edmund Spenser, author of the great national epic *The Faerie Queene* and widely acknowledged as the greatest living English poet. For Spenser, the dithering and divisions at court had led to personal ruin and potential disaster for the entire colonial enterprise in Ireland.

Spenser was a prominent member of the Munster Plantation, which extended over nearly 600,000 acres of Irish land appropriated by New English settlers. Spenser himself lived on a 3,000 acre estate on confiscated land at Kilcolman, County Cork (for an annual rent

Detail of map of Whitehall and Westminster, 1593

of about £20), where since 1589 he had done much of his greatest writing and exchanged ideas with his literary neighbour Sir Walter Ralegh (who had commandeered 40,000 prime Irish acres for himself). Spenser imagined himself and Ralegh as a pair of poetic shepherds: 'He pip'd, I sung; and when he sung, I piped.' It was expected that 8,000 Englishmen would emigrate to Munster. One reason that never happened, according to one English settler, was that the new landowners 'ha[d] enticed many honest men over, promising them much but performing nothing'. In 1598, two decades after the plantation was established, only about 3,000 Englishmen had settled in Munster, too few to defend themselves when Tyrone's allies in the south arrived in the aftermath of Blackwater to 'burn and spoil, to murder and kill and to break down the castles of the Englishmen'. The colonists had been dealt with brutally: 'some with their throats cut, but not killed, some with their tongues cut out of their heads, others with their noses cut off; by view whereof the English might the more bitterly lament the misery of their country-men, and fear the like to befall to themselves'. In the face of this onslaught, most of the English settlers had panicked, abandoning rather than defending their estates, and sought refuge within the walls of Cork. Spenser and his wife (who reportedly lost a 'little child new born' in the assault on Kilcolman) had been among them.

Spenser appears to have spent Christmas week near Whitehall, for at the end of the month he was paid £8 for his services to the state, the warrant personally signed by Cecil. Three months earlier Cecil and his fellow Privy Councillors had urged the authorities in Ireland to appoint Spenser – 'a man endowed with good knowledge in learning and not unskillful as without experience in the service of the wars' – sheriff of Cork. In addition to conveying Norris's report on the military situation and the arrival of reinforcements from England, Spenser was able to provide the Privy Council with a first-hand account of the situation that had been unfolding in Munster since early October.

Spenser had lived in Ireland for twenty years, having arrived there in his late twenties in 1580, when he had been appointed private secretary to the new Lord Deputy, Lord Grey, a hard-line Protestant. Shortly after Spenser's arrival, Lord Grey had ordered the massacre of six hundred Spanish and Italian soldiers in a garrison on the south-west coast of Ireland, at Smerwick in County Kerry, after these Catholic troops had already surrendered. Spenser, who along with Ralegh had witnessed the slaughter, vigorously defended Grey's action. Spenser prospered in Ireland, dividing his time between his writing and various administrative posts. He also steeped himself in historical writings on Ireland and found time to compose *A View of the Present State of Ireland*. Though ostensibly written in the form of a dialogue, its two points of view are not all that far apart. Spenser's Irish tract addressed head-on the cause and cure of England's Irish troubles. However complex the roots of the current crisis, Spenser's solution was simple if cold-blooded: the Irish were best brought to heel by starvation. The Privy Council was almost surely aware of this tract, which Spenser had probably completed when he was last in England in early 1596 when he had returned to oversee publication of *The Faerie Queene*. Spenser probably intended his *View* to circulate in manuscript among policy-makers, a likelihood reinforced by the survival of over twenty handwritten copies.

When Spenser passed along Norris's letter to the Privy Council in late December 1598, he is likely to have shared with these government officials an updated position paper 'A Brief Note of Ireland'. It wasn't the only such tract making the rounds. The New English settlers were desperate to influence England's Irish policies. Among those in circulation at this time was *The Supplication of the Blood of the English Most Lamentably Murdered in Ireland, Crying Out of the Earth for Revenge*, whose title captures the desperate state of the dispossessed English settlers. Spenser's 'Brief Note' recapitulates the main point of his *View*: 'Great force must be the instrument, but famine must be the mean[s], for till Ireland be famished it cannot be subdued.'

Spenser knew the consequences of the starvation he advocated. The most powerful paragraph in his *View* renders in graphic detail the effects of a starved and cannibalistic Irish population who 'consume themselves and devour one another':

Out of every corner of the woods and glens they came creeping forth upon their hands, for their legs could not bear them, they looked like anatomies of death, they spake like ghosts crying out of their graves, they did eat the dead carrions, happy where they could find them. Yea, and one another soon after, insomuch as the very carcasses they spared not to scrape out of their graves.

Having seen its effects first-hand, Spenser vigorously advocated mass starvation as a proven policy. A copy of part of Spenser's tract now in the British Library ends with sneering and un-Spenserian verse that punctuates these recommendations with a prophecy of what the Irish and Tyrone had in store:

Mark, Irish, when this doth fall,
Tyrone and tire all,
A peer out of England shall come,
The Irish shall tire all and some,
St Patrick to St George a horse-boy shall be seen,
And all this shall happen in 'ninety-nine.

Spenser's visit to Whitehall coincided with the court's Christmas festivities, a good occasion to meet with old friends and admirers. It was also an ideal time to circulate copies of his new tract and to urge upon those gathered at court the importance of a strong hand in Ireland. His company would have been much sought after by courtiers planning to accompany Essex's on-again, off-again expedition. His depressed and dispossessed fellow planters, holed up with their families in Cork, must have been counting on him to report back on what the government was prepared to do. It could not have been an easy time for Spenser, whose health may have already suffered from the winter crossing of the Irish Sea.

Culture-starved, Spenser was probably eager to see the best plays of the previous year staged at Whitehall, including the two performed by the Chamberlain's Men. We know from his correspondence that Spenser had himself written 'nine English comedies', closet dramas that were never intended for the public stage. They are now lost, perhaps burned at Kilcolman. Critics from John Dryden on have also argued that Spenser admired Shakespeare and acknowledged that high regard in his allusion to 'Our pleasant Willy' in his poem 'The Tears of the Muses', as well as in his reference in 'Colin Clout's Come Home Again' to 'A gentler shepherd . . . Whose muse full of high thoughts invention, / Doth like himself heroically sound'. Whether Spenser was referring to Shakespeare in these poems and not to some other writer (and whether Shakespeare responded in kind in *A Midsummer Night's Dream*), the two were familiar with each other's work. It's unknown if words were exchanged at Whitehall between England's most celebrated poet and its leading dramatist; but it's at least worth speculating about what Spenser would have made of Shakespeare's *The Second Part of Henry the Fourth*, had he attended a performance of it that week – particularly the play's handling of military conscription, an issue vital to a successful resolution of the Irish problem, as Spenser himself had argued in his *View*.

'Rumour', who introduces the play, broaches the issue of military enlistment by asking: 'Who but Rumour, who but only I, / Make fearful musters and prepared defence?' 'Prepared defence' refers to the well-organized local militia; 'musters' was the far more corrupt practice whereby poor men were randomly hauled off to fight, sicken and often die in foreign wars. Musters were 'fearful' not because, as some editors of the play imagine, the enrolment of troops was inspired by fear of invasion but because the musters themselves were a frightening prospect for able-bodied Elizabethan men between the ages of sixteen and sixty, all of whom were potential conscripts. The number of Englishmen rounded up from villages or urban streets to fight abroad kept growing in the late 1590s. Government figures at the time indicate that 2,800 were forced to serve in 1594 and 1,806 in 1595. That figure rose sharply in 1596 to 8,840, dropped to 4,835 in 1597 and then nearly doubled to 9,164 in 1598. The number drafted in the first six months of 1599 alone was 7,300. Apprentices and unmarried men in London of lower social stations had special cause to be fearful. The authorities had no scruples about using required church attendance as a means for rounding up recruits: John Stow reports that on Easter Sunday 1596, after an order came for 1,000 men, 'the aldermen, their deputies, constables, and other officers, were fain to close up the church doors, till they had pressed so many men'. Local authorities didn't hesitate during Elizabeth's reign to raid fairs, alehouses, inns and other popular meeting places. The authorities could count on a good haul at the playhouses too. The only account of recruiting from the theatres survives from 1602, when Philip Gawdy writes: '[There] hath been great pressing of late, and strange, as ever was known in England. All the playhouses were beset in one day and very many pressed from thence, so that in all there are pressed 4,000.'

Something along these lines may have taken place in late December 1598, when the Privy Council directed London's Lord Mayor to send his chief officers to the city's 'privileged places' – that is, the suburban Liberties, where London's theatres were located – to gather forced loans and recruit men who mistakenly believed that they were safe there. Shakespeare and other players, because they performed for the Queen, were exempt from military service. As one of the actors jokingly puts it in John Marston's *Histriomastix*, an old play likely to have been updated around 1599:

> we players are privileged,
> 'Tis our audience must fight in the field for us,
> And we upon the stage for them.

Only onstage were players soldiers, and the audience for *Histrio-mastix* would have enjoyed the scene in which mustered players, their protests ignored, are ordered to march to the wars and encouraged to act as valiantly there as they had onstage.

Opinion was divided over what kind of men to impress. Local authorities were more than pleased to fulfil Privy Council quotas by ridding their neighbourhoods of 'the scum of their country', as Robert Barret writes in a 1598 military treatise. Such men were prone to desertion, if not mutiny. Yet local authorities were loath to round up established citizens; and, given the likelihood that captains would take bribes to free upstanding citizens from conscription, the end result would be that poor men would be sent in their stead anyway. The system was a product of Elizabeth's decision not to have a standing army, unlike her foreign rivals, or to rely on mercenaries. Elizabeth herself apparently thought little of those conscripted to fight her wars. She told the French ambassador de Maisse in 1597 that the English troops stationed in France 'were but thieves and ought to hang'. De Maisse dropped the subject after Elizabeth 'had put herself in a choler about it', uttering imprecations 'between her teeth which [he] did not well understand'.

News in early October 1598 of the desertion of 300 Londoners conscripted for the Irish wars would have circulated widely in the metropolis. When these troops arrived at Towcester, two-thirds of them refused to go further and mutinied, threatening to kill their captain and wounding some of his officers. There may well have been widespread sympathy for such action – by men yanked out of churches, inns or playhouses to die in Ireland, ill fed, poorly armed, poorly trained, even more so after the news trickled back about the disaster at Blackwater a few months earlier. John Baxter, who knew the situation on the ground in Ireland well, spoke of 'the poor English' who 'are half dead before they come there, for the very name of Ireland do break their hearts, it is now so grown to misery'. Richard Bagwell records a Cheshire proverb at the time: 'Better be hanged at home than die like dogs in Ireland.'

Popular broadsides spelled out the fate of those who chose this unpatriotic course, including a ballad whose lengthy title tells the whole story: 'A warning for all soldiers that will not venture their lives in her Majesty's cause and the country's right: wherein is declared the lamentation of William Wrench, who, for running away from his captain, with two other more, were executed'. The execution of Wrench and his mates as an example to potential deserters, like the ballad itself, can be seen as part of a campaign to combat the rising number of deserters – doubly dangerous, once armed and on the loose in England.

To Londoners, the Crown's demand for fresh troops must have seemed insatiable. In November 1598 the Queen once again ordered the lieutenants of London to 'levy, muster, and view, within our city of London, six hundred able men, and furnish them with armor, weapons, and apparel, in such sort as our Privy Council shall direct'. By now the government understood the cost of the shoddy recruiting practices it had long encouraged. The order went out warning lieutenants that they were 'especially to have regard that the men be better chosen, both for ability of body and aptitude for war service, than heretofore, and that they be well appareled'.

One can well imagine, in such a context, what Spenser and others in attendance at Whitehall, like the audiences at the Curtain throughout the autumn of 1598, would have made of the conscription scene in *The Second Part of Henry the Fourth*, in which Justice Shallow arranges for Falstaff to choose from available recruits who are paraded before him. Part of the dark humour is the numbers game being played by those in charge. When 'Captain' Falstaff is assured that Shallow has provided him with 'half a dozen sufficient men' from whom he will select four, only five are trotted out before him: Ralph Mouldy, Simon Shadow, Thomas Wart, Francis Feeble, and Peter Bullcalf. They're a pathetic-looking bunch, sure to get a laugh. Mouldy is old, Shadow slight, Wart tattered, Feeble doddering, and only Bullcalf a sturdy enough fellow, despite his protests that he is 'a diseased man'.

All are initially drafted, save Wart, whom even Falstaff admits is unfit for service. Shadow is no less unsuitable, but as Falstaff jokes, 'we have a number of shadows fill up the muster book' (III, ii, 135–6) – that is, more men will be entered in the books (whose pay he will pocket) than will accompany him. After Falstaff and Shallow depart, Mouldy and Bullcalf bribe Bardolph, each offering the considerable sum of £2 for his freedom. This too is part of the game. Only Feeble doesn't understand that a bribe is obligatory and his last chance to avoid impressment. The irony of watching this frail old man explaining why he wants to fight for his country, offering up bits and pieces of the patriotic propaganda he has swallowed whole, would not have been lost on contemporary audiences: 'A man can die but once. We owe God a death. I'll ne'er bear a base mind. An't be my destiny, so; an't be not, so. No man's too good to serve's prince' (III, ii, 235–8). Falstaff's sidekick Bardolph, having collected £4 in bribes from the men, lies to Falstaff that he has been given 'three pound to free Mouldy and Bullcalf', which he then passes over to Falstaff, keeping the other pound for himself. In the end only Feeble and Shadow, who are too foolish or deluded to play the game, are taken (though Shallow enters four recruits in the muster rolls). Perhaps the funniest, if cruellest, line in the scene is Falstaff's final order to Bardolph to 'give the soldiers coats' (III, ii, 290–91). Here, too, there was money to be made, and we can only imagine what kind of dark laughter the threadbare garments would have provoked in a London playhouse familiar with such corrupt practices. Spenser, for one, who had seen firsthand the effect in Ireland of poorly equipped Feebles and Shadows, would not have been amused. He had warned readers of his *View* of the 'corruption' of English captains who, he said, 'deceive the soldier, abuse the Queen, and greatly hinder the service'.

Shakespeare had not only witnessed such scenes for the past few years on the streets of London, but could also recall from his childhood the time when his father had packed off the Feebles and Shadows of Stratford-upon-Avon to help put down the Northern Rebellion in 1569. As Chief Alderman for Stratford as well as the local Justice of the Peace, John Shakespeare, like Shallow, had been responsible for local musters and militia. The corrupt recruiting for Ireland had a few more wrinkles. Captains like Falstaff would accept bribes from all recruits and arrive at their port of embarkation for Ireland with a troop of invisibles – further lining their pockets with conduct money. Since the Privy Council also had copies of the muster rolls, captains had to produce the right number of men when they arrived at the port of embarkation. To get around this, they worked hand-in-glove with local conspirators, and men, horses and arms would magically appear on the appropriate day when the lists were checked. Once the muster roll was certified correct, these impersonators were paid off and the horses returned. The charade was repeated upon the captain's arrival in Ireland. Any soldier who dared to complain could be hung by his captain as a mutineer. No wonder the Queen was angry at the cost of her wars and her generals perplexed that the number of troops on the ground never squared with those on the books. It was a cheat's game.

One of the most notorious abusers was Sir Thomas North, best known to posterity as the translator of Plutarch's *Lives*, a book that Shakespeare was now reading as a source for both *Henry the Fifth* and *Julius Caesar*. A memorandum of 'the State of Ireland' from December 1596 provides a glimpse of this English captain's corrupt doings. Perhaps North served as Shakespeare's source in more ways than one: 'Of all the captains in Ireland, Sir Thomas North hath from the beginning kept a most miserable, unfurnished, naked, and hunger-starven band. Many of his soldiers died wretchedly and woefully at Dublin; some whose feet and legs rotted off for want of shoes.' Outdoing even Falstaff, 'Sir Thomas North, before his going hence, sold (as is said) the piteous, forlorn band.' Elizabeth later rewarded North with a pension of £40 a year 'in consideration of the good and faithful service done unto us'.

The war was equally unpopular with London's merchants, who would have to foot the bill for it through forced loans they feared would later be declared outright gifts and never repaid. Sure enough, in early December the Privy Councillors informed Lord Mayor Stephen Soame that a six-month loan was required of the City, which the Queen promised to repay with ten per cent interest. Anticipating backsliding, the Privy Councillors forwarded a list with the names of wealthy citizens and the amount they expected from each; and, reaching out for yet another source of funds, they told the Lord Mayor that the Queen wanted to borrow 'the sum of 200,000 French crowns' from London's wealthy alien residents. No group was free of the heavy burden of the war.

By 17 December a shake-down of recalcitrant merchants began: those who refused to pay the forced loan were called in to explain themselves. Even intimidation didn't work. Five days later, furious that London's moneyed classes had refused both loans and summonses to appear daily before them, the councillors wrote again to the Mayor, demanding £20,000 in loans 'before the holidays', and expressing their anger at the 'contempt' of those who had ignored their requests. Yet even this threat wasn't enough to coerce all of London's wealthier citizens to do their part in the war effort. Simon Forman, a prosperous astrologer and physician, also describes regular collections of small sums 'for the soldiers' that were made door-to-door ('I supposed I ought not to pay it,' he wrote in his casebook in early 1599, and wrestled over whether 'it was best to pay it or no' – but in the end he did, paying 'for soldiers' in early January and then again in late February). If Forman's experience was typical, Londoners were already of two minds about supporting the expensive military adventure.

In addition to these financial strains, Londoners had to deal with a refugee problem, as destitute New English settlers in Ireland, men like Spenser who were lucky to have escaped alive, started making their way back to London. The Privy Council directed the Mayor and Lord Bishop of London to take up a 'charitable collection' to assist the 'poor distressed persons of sundry counties of this realm that dwelt in the county of Kerry in Ireland, lately coming hither from thence, that have sustained great losses and spoils by the rebels there'. The sight of these English refugees would have been demoralizing, as would their stories of the rebels' atrocities.

By mid-December, some of those who had adamantly opposed peace with Spain were having second thoughts. John Chamberlain put it bluntly to his friend Dudley Carleton: 'I marvel that they which knew these wants did hearken no more after the peace [with Spain] when they might have had it with good conditions.' Well aware of how unpatriotic these thoughts were, Chamberlain nervously added, 'You see how confidently I write to you of all things, but I hope you keep it to yourself and then there is no danger, and I am so used to a liberty and freedom of speech when I converse or write to my friends that I cannot easily leave it.' Fear of punishment for seditious words was already in the air. Three days before Christmas the Privy Council delivered more unhappy holiday cheer to Londoners: another 600 men were to be rounded up and shipped off to fight in Ireland. Even before the troops had sailed or Essex agreed to lead them, the Irish war was proving to be an unpopular one across a broad social spectrum.

As the Christmas festivities at Whitehall came to an end, all eyes were on the Queen and Essex. Elizabeth decided to send what was for her an unambiguous signal: 'On Twelfth Day,' a court observer notes, 'the Queen danced with the Earl of Essex, very richly and freshly attired.' Another reporter on the scene offered more vivid details of their reconciliation: Elizabeth 'was to be seen in her old age dancing three or four gaillards', the high-spirited dance she so loved (and Essex, always awkward on the dance floor, no doubt loathed). But one didn't say no to the Queen. In early January, Essex wrote to his cousin Fulke Greville that on the eve of the new year Elizabeth had 'destined me to the hardest task that ever any gentleman was sent about'. But Essex was more self-pitying than resigned: in a letter he must have expected would be leaked at court, he went on to complain of how Elizabeth was 'breaking my heart' and how, only after 'my soul shall be freed from this [prison] of my body', shall she 'see her wrong to me and her wound given to herself'. He put on a better face to those preparing to join him, including his naïve supporter (and godson to the Queen), John Harington: 'I have beaten Knollys and Mountjoy in the Council, and by God I will beat Tyrone in the field.'

On Saturday, 13 January 1599, church bells tolled in Westminster. The news was shocking and depressing: Edmund Spenser was dead at the age of forty-six. Three days later Spenser was interred near Chaucer in the south transept of Westminster Abbey, in what would come to be known as 'Poets' Corner'. Essex covered the cost of the funeral, repaying the debt he owed the poet who had praised him as 'England's glory and the world's wide wonder'. William Camden, who eulogized Spenser as one who 'surpassed all the English poets of former times, not excepting even Chaucer himself', recorded the unusual funeral arrangements. As master at the school attached to Westminster Abbey, Camden was well placed to observe the day's events. Spenser's hearse was 'attended by poets, and mournful elegies and poems, with the pens that wrote them, thrown into the tomb'. Camden later added that poets even carried Spenser's hearse. The poems and pens were a nice touch, a change of pace from handkerchiefs wet with tears or the sprigs of evergreen usually tossed into graves at Elizabethan funerals. The verses, which the poets had but three days to compose, would have first been read aloud before being ceremoniously tossed into the grave. Not just a great poet was celebrated this day, but English poetry itself. It's unlikely that many of London's writers would have missed the occasion.

We don't know who the pall-bearers were and few copies of the poems tossed into Spenser's grave survive. Most of these are by second-raters: Nicholas Breton, Francis Thynne, Charles Fitzgeoffrey, William Alabaster, the ubiquitous John Weever, Richard Harvey and Hugh Holland. Holland's couplet got the tone about right: 'He was and is, see then where lies the odds, / Once god of poets, now poet of the gods.' But some, like Breton's ditty, were bad enough to set teeth on edge: 'Sing a dirge on Spenser's death, / 'Til your souls be out of breath.' Three centuries later, hoping to unearth other long-buried tributes, especially one by Shakespeare, Spenser's grave was opened. The grave-diggers failed to find what they were looking for, which was not surprising, since they dug in the wrong place, exhuming the remains of the eighteenth-century poet (and admirer of Spenser) Matthew Prior before sealing things up again.

Unlike most of his fellow writers, Shakespeare had a strong aversion to heaping praise on the work of the living or the dead. Rather than be seen carrying the hearse or ostentatiously tossing a poem into the grave, it's more likely that Shakespeare went home after the funeral and paid a quieter tribute, paging through a well-worn copy of Spenser's poetry. Yet as he heard Spenser publicly eulogized as England's greatest poet, Shakespeare could not have remained disinterested. Spenser, after all, had chosen paths Shakespeare had rejected. He had pursued his poetic fortune exclusively through aristocratic – even royal – patronage, and had done so in

> descriptions of the fairest wights,
> And beauty making beautiful old rhyme
> In praise of ladies dead and lovely knights.

So Shakespeare puts it in Sonnet 106, deliberately echoing Spenser's archaisms.

There were other differences too. Where Shakespeare had purchased a house in his native Stratford, Spenser had moved into a
castle on stolen Irish land. And what had it got him? It's hard not
to conclude that, for Shakespeare, Spenser had built on sand. Premature interment at Chaucer's feet was poor compensation for so
badly misreading history. Spenser had rewritten the course of
English epic and pastoral. Shakespeare would soon enough take a
turn at rewriting each in *Henry the Fifth* and *As You Like It* – and
would have appreciated the vote of confidence expressed in an
anonymous university play staged later this year in which a character announces: 'Let this duncified world esteem of Spenser and
Chaucer, I'll worship sweet Mr Shakespeare.'

Shakespeare knew that Spenser was not alone in following a
career path that led through the wilds of Ireland. The list of
Elizabethan writers who had done so was long and still growing.
It included Thomas Churchyard, Barnaby Googe, Sir Thomas
North, Sir Henry Wotton, Barnaby Rich, Lodowick Bryskett,
Geoffrey Fenton, Sir Walter Ralegh, John Derricke, Sir John
Davies and probably Sir Philip Sidney. This year, their ranks
were swollen by gentlemen-poet adventurers eager to improve
their fortunes, including William Cornwallis and John Haring-
ton.

It's tempting to imagine a Shakespeare who 'was not a company keeper' drifting away from the mournful proceedings that day
at Westminster, distracted by the Chantry Chapel and tomb of
Henry V and the remains of his wife, Queen Katharine, located
close to where Spenser was being interred. Spenser's interment,
and with him, the chivalric world celebrated in his *Faerie Queene*,
may have even led him there. Like Spenser, Henry V, who had
died at thirty-five – Shakespeare's current age – had not lived to
fulfil his great promise. Shakespeare also knew that not even the
most celebrated of English kings, let alone a great poet, could be
assured that posterity would be kind. Shakespeare was interested

in how Henry V was commemorated; he had even staged his funeral in one of his earliest (and probably collaborative) plays, *The First Part of Henry the Sixth*, where mourners compare England's fallen soldier-king to Julius Caesar:

> Henry the Fifth, thy ghost I invocate:
> Prosper this realm; keep it from civil broils;
> Combat with adverse planets in the heavens!
> A far more glorious star thy soul will make
> Than Julius Caesar . . .
>   (I, i, 52–6)

Shakespeare also has Henry imagine his own burial in *Henry the Fifth*, where he tells his followers to 'lay these bones in an unworthy urn, / Tombless, with no remembrance over them', if he fails to return from France a conqueror (I, ii, 228–30). As Shakespeare knew, while there would be a glorious tomb, history would subsequently treat Henry's remains in quite unexpected ways. Yes, Henry was buried with a spectacular effigy covered in silver and gold; but two gold teeth had been pulled from that effigy during the reign of Edward IV, and worse desecration would follow. By 1599 all that remained of Henry's effigy was a headless torso. Shakespeare would have found the fate of Queen Katharine's remains even more poignant. Though buried at Westminster in 1438, her embalmed corpse was 'taken up again in the reign of Henry VII'. Since that time, John Stow writes, 'she was never since buried, but remaineth above ground'. Had he so desired, Shakespeare could have laid hold of the Queen he was bringing back to life onstage. Samuel Pepys did exactly that seventy years later, recording in his diary how, during a visit to Westminster, he took 'the upper part of her body in [his] hands and . . . did kiss her mouth, reflecting upon it that [he] did kiss a Queen'. This was not what Shakespeare had in mind when he spoke of 'making merry with Katharine of France'. For all we know, the fate of this royal pair may have spurred Shakespeare to compose the lines later engraved on his own grave slab:

> Blest be the man that spares these stones,
> And cursed be he that moves my bones.

Shakespeare, who would be buried in Stratford, had no interest in being transplanted to Westminster and the company of Chaucer and Spenser.

All that remained untouched at Westminster, hanging from a thick chestnut crossbeam, was Henry V's saddle, shield (the silk embroidery on the reverse side still intact), and dented helmet. Nearby was his sword, traces of gold still visible on its blade and pommel. These objects were familiar to Londoners and surely the inspiration for Shakespeare's allusion to Henry's 'bruised helmet and his bended sword' that his lords desire to carry 'before him through the city' upon his triumphant return to London (V, Prologue, 18–19). *Henry the Fifth*, like Spenser's death, was turning into a drama that marked the end of an era for Shakespeare. Like the relics of Henry's military campaigns hanging in Westminster, the chivalric world celebrated in Spenser's epic and his own early histories had become increasingly tarnished.

4
A Sermon at Richmond

On 20 February, the last day of playing before the theatres officially closed for Lent, the Chamberlain's Men set off on a short journey from London to the royal palace at Richmond. It had been 'hard weather' of late, making it likely that they travelled overland rather than by boat up the Thames. It was Shrove Tuesday, a day of licence, an unofficial holiday on which London's apprentices often ran wild, vandalizing brothels and occasionally theatres. Shakespeare and his fellow players were no doubt relieved to be far from any mayhem. Elizabeth had just moved her court to Richmond from Whitehall. Though imprisoned at Richmond in 1554 by her half-sister Mary, in later years she had grown increasingly fond of the palace and came to think of it as 'the warm box to which she could best entrust her sickly old age'.

Visitors approaching Richmond from the Thames would have first caught sight of the palace's onion-capped towers, their

Richmond Palace, 1616

weather-vanes painted in gold and azure 'right marvellous' to hear on windy days, for they produced a strange music. Entering the main gate from the direction of Richmond Green, visitors passed through a large outer courtyard leading to a paved inner one, beyond which was the entrance to the royal quarters overlooking 'fair and pleasant gardens'. The inner courtyard was straddled by a pair of impressive and semi-detached buildings, roughly the same in size (each about a hundred by forty feet). To the left was the royal chapel, where religious services were conducted and sermons read; to the right, the great hall, where plays were staged. The hall was impressively decorated, lined with the martial images of England's great kings in 'robes of gold'. Shakespeare and his fellow players were familiar with the venue, having performed there five times in 1595–6.

For this Shrovetide performance Shakespeare dashed off a special eighteen-line epilogue in praise of Elizabeth. Except for the special epilogue to *The Second Part of Henry the Fourth*, it's the only one of his occasional epilogues to survive. Whether Shakespeare himself stepped forward to deliver these lines or whether he passed them along to a fellow actor to memorize and recite is unknown:

> As the dial hand tells o'er
> The same hours it had before,
> Still beginning in the ending,
> Circular account lending,
> So, most mighty Queen, we pray,
> Like the dial, day by day,
> You may lead the seasons on,
> Making new when old are gone.
> That the babe which now is young,
> And hath yet no use of tongue,
> Many a Shrovetide here may bow,
> To that empress I do now;
> That the children of these lords,

Sitting at your council boards,
May be grave and aged seen,
Of her that was their father[s'] Queen.
Once I wish this wish again,
Heaven subscribe it with 'Amen'.

At this moment of seasonal change, Shakespeare imagines Elizabeth as a timeless and rejuvenating force, likening her to a clock
hand perpetually circling, resistant to the ravages of time, outliving
generations. There's a slight undertow to the conceit, the claustro-
phobic sense of being trapped in time, the uncomfortable thought
that Elizabeth will still be around in a half-century. Shakespeare
knew better, his flattering words to the Queen ignoring what he
declares in his sonnets: only 'in my verse', he wrote, would the
object of his devotion 'ever live young' (Sonnet 19).

The epilogue's style and diction are unmistakably Shakespearean,
as are the trochaic rhythm and rhymed couplets that appear a score
of times in songs and poems in his work. The only time that
Shakespeare had ended a play in this metre had been in *A Midsummer Night's Dream*, whose conclusion, with its call to bless the
chambers of 'this palace' and its 'owner', would have had special
resonance at Richmond that day:

With this field dew consecrate,
Every fairy take his gait,
And each several chamber bless,
Through this palace, with sweet peace;
And the owner of it blest
Ever shall in safety rest.
  (V, i, 410–15)

Rhythmically, the transition between Oberon's final lines in that play
and the special epilogue (which would have replaced Puck's final
speech in the public playhouse) would have been seamless. If one had
to venture a guess, it seems likely that Shakespeare wrote this special

epilogue for a revival of *A Midsummer Night's Dream*. That comedy's mild anarchy dovetails especially well with the festive release of Shrove Tuesday and Oberon's words – 'We the globe can compass soon, / Swifter than the wand'ring moon' (IV, i, 96–7) – nicely double as an allusion to their planned playhouse in Southwark.

It was brave of Shakespeare to broach the touchy subject of Elizabeth's age. As Elizabeth's godson John Harington put it, 'There is almost none that waited in Queen Elizabeth's court and observed any thing, but can tell, that it pleased her much to seem, and to be thought, and to be told, that she looked young.' Her age and looks mattered a great deal to Elizabeth. The French diplomat de Maisse describes the care she took in presenting herself: 'She had a petticoat of white damask, girdled and open in the front, as was also her chemise, in such a manner that she often opened this dress and one could see all her belly, and even to her navel ... When she raises her head she has a trick of putting both hands on her gown and opening it insomuch as all her belly can be seen.' De Maisse adds, when 'anyone speaks of her beauty she says that she was never beautiful, although she had that reputation thirty years ago. Nevertheless she speaks of her beauty as often as she can.' But he is quick to add that as 'for her natural form and proportion, she is very beautiful'. Elizabeth was very much the fading Cleopatra: she knew that her age was working against her and recognized the need to silence those who drew attention to her years – and by extension her failing powers. But she also enjoyed and saw through flattery, and, as her flirtation with de Maisse makes clear, she remained a skilled enough performer to summon her charms when she wanted to, when politics demanded it.

Given her sensitivity to the matter of ageing, mishandling the subject of Elizabeth's mortality in her presence could be dangerous. Shakespeare may have heard the story of how, on Good Friday 1596, Anthony Rudd, Bishop of St David's, had incautiously raised the same topic in his sermon to Elizabeth. Harington, who was present that day, writes: 'This good bishop being appointed to preach before her . . . and wishing in a godly zeal, as well became him, that she would think some time of mortality, being then full sixty-three years of age, he took this text, for that purpose . . . "O teach us to number our days."' Like everyone else in the chapel, Elizabeth knew that this psalm was part of the Burial Service. After impatiently sitting through Rudd's citation of many 'passages of Scripture that touch the infirmity of age', Elizabeth cut him off, saying 'he should have kept his arithmetic for himself'. The good bishop wasn't invited back again until Lent 1602, and he seemed not to have learned his lesson, this time preaching on the verse from the 82nd Psalm: 'Ye are all the children of the most Highest, but ye shall die like men, and fall like one of the princes.' Once again Elizabeth couldn't restrain her sarcasm, dismissing him with the words, 'You have made me a good funeral sermon; I may die when I will.'

When the Chamberlain's Men performed at Richmond on the evening on 20 February, they would have been unable to return to London until the following day. At some point on 21 February, the six shareholders in the company – Burbage, Kemp, Shakespeare, Heminges, Phillips and Pope – would meet with Cuthbert Burbage and Nicholas Brend to sign the lease on the Globe site. They may have delayed signing it until the first day they knew they would neither rehearse nor perform: Ash Wednesday, the beginning of Lent. Or perhaps they wanted to wait until they were sure that Giles Allen had failed in his initial legal efforts to prevent them from using the timber of the Theatre to build the Globe.

There was a powerful incentive to linger at Richmond: Lancelot Andrewes was at court to deliver a sermon ushering in Lent and he liked to preach his Lenten sermons in the morning, before the service of Communion. Andrewes was arguably England's greatest preacher in an age notable for its oratory. For Shakespeare, that morning in court would offer a chance to hear and study a remarkable performer. Post-Reformation England had dispensed with the Catholic practice of daubing foreheads with ashes to signify repentance. Public sermons were now the primary means of conveying the spiritual meaning of the day that marked the end of Shrovetide frivolity (one need only look at Bruegel's famous painting *The Battle of Shrovetide and Lent* to get a sense of the sharp clash of values implicit in the turning of the clock from Shrove Tuesday to Ash Wednesday, physically reinforced at Richmond by the change of venue from the great hall to the chapel). This symbolic shift from pleasure to serious reflection well suited a nation on the verge of war.

It wasn't simply Andrewes's distinctive prose style and powerful delivery that would have captured Shakespeare's attention that day. Andrewes didn't flinch from taking on topical issues in his sermons. True to form, he had chosen as his text for this Lenten sermon Deuteronomy 23:9, where Moses goes off to war. His sermon's title makes its contemporary political relevance unambiguous: 'Preached before Queen Elizabeth at Richmond, On the 21st of February, A.D., 1599, being Ash Wednesday, at What Time the Earl of Essex was Going Forth, upon the Expedition for Ireland'. The chapel walls, decorated with carvings of ancient British monarchs 'whose life and virtue was so abundant that it hath pleased almighty God to . . . recount as saints', formed a perfect backdrop for his sermon aligning Church and State. It is probable that Elizabeth, during this volatile period before Essex's departure for Ireland, had advance notice of what Lancelot Andrewes intended to preach. Peter Heylyn recalled after her death that when Elizabeth 'had any business to bring about amongst the people, she used to tune the pulpits, as her saying was; that is to say, to have some preachers in and about London, and other great auditories in the kingdom, ready at command to cry up her design'. Andrewes would not disappoint her.

The past two months had seen their share of turmoil over the Irish campaign. Infighting at court had intensified, including 'high words' between Essex and the Lord Admiral. Chamberlain ominously observed: 'Many things pass which may not be written'; and he added: '[The] Earl of Essex is crazed, but whether more in body or mind is doubtful.' Essex only secured at the last moment permission 'to return to her Majesty's presence at such time as he shall find cause'. Essex's 'whole forces [were] said to be 16,000 foot and 1,400 horse,' but, Chamberlain adds, 'when they shall come to the poll I fear they will fall short'.

All that remained was for the government to justify the campaign and for the Church to bestow its blessings. Christopher Barker, printer to the Queen, would publish 'The Queen's Majesty's proclamation declaring her princely resolution in sending over her army into the realm of Ireland'. In it Elizabeth declares that the Irish have 'forgotten their allegiance, and (rebelliously taking arms) have committed many bloody and violent outrages upon our loyal subjects'; but she is careful to admit that the rebellion had many causes, including the abuses of some of her deputies there. The most striking lines in the proclamation have to do with Elizabeth's defensiveness about accusations that she 'intended an utter extirpation and rooting out of that nation and conquest of the country'. The charge is utterly rejected. Ireland, after all, is her own: 'The very name of conquest in this case seemeth so absurd to us, as we cannot imagine upon what ground it could enter into any man's conceit.' Barker would also print the official 'Prayer for the good success of her Majesty's forces in Ireland', asking God 'to strengthen and protect the forces of thine anointed, our Queen and Sovereign, sent to suppress these wicked and unnatural rebels'.

Andrewes's sermon – no less than Shakespeare's *Henry the Fifth* – needs to be understood within the context of the huge obstacles such official pronouncements ignored. Essex feared that the Irish climate would consume 'our armies, and if they live, yet famine and nakedness makes them lose both heart and strength'. Logistics, too, were nightmarish: 'If victuals be sent over, yet there will be no means to carry it.' Essex had enough military experience and knowledge of the court to see that he was walking into a trap: 'All those things, which I am like to see, I do now foresee . . . Too ill success will be dangerous . . . Too good will be envious.'

If Essex was doomed, those loyal to him might suffer the same fate. John Harington's kinsman, Mr Robert Markham, at considerable danger to himself, warned Harington of just this outcome. His extraordinary letter provides further evidence of how wary some contemporaries were of this military adventure even before the expeditionary force had set sail:

I hear you are to go to Ireland with the Lieutenant, Essex. If so, mark my counsel in this matter: I doubt not your valor nor your labour, but that damnable uncovered honesty will mar your fortunes. Observe the man who commandeth, and yet is commanded himself. He goeth not forth to serve the Queen's realm, but to humour his own revenge. Be heedful of your bearings. Speak not your mind to all you meet. I tell you I have ground for my caution. Essex hath enemies; he hath friends, too.

Markham offers his inexperienced kinsman a quick sketch of the political landscape. This was advice that might save Harington's life: write down everything, say little, and don't play the fool. In a world of surveillance, be a spy yourself, for 'there are overlookers set on you all':

You are to take account of all that passes in your expedition, and keep journal thereof, unknown to any in the company. This will be expected of you . . . I say, do not meddle in any sort, not give your jesting too freely among those you know not. Obey the Lord Deputy in all things, but give not your opinion; it may be heard in England. Though you obey, yet seem not to advise, in any one point. Your obeisance may be, and must be, construed well; but your counsel may be thought ill of, if any bad business follow.

Markham well knew that if his letter were intercepted he would be in grave trouble, so gave the letter to his sister to deliver, first ensuring that she was unaware of its contents – 'danger goeth abroad', and 'Silence is the safest armour.'

Fear and scepticism extended well beyond the court. The popular astrologer Simon Forman was kept busy in the early months of 1599 by clients hoping to learn through the signs of the heavens the fate of loved ones going off to the war. Forman even privately cast a horoscope 'to know how . . . Essex shall speed in his voyage into Ireland, and whether he shall prevail or no'. Here's what he learned:

There seems to be in the end of his voyage negligence, treason, hunger, sickness and death, and he shall not do much good to bring it to effect. But at his return much treachery shall be wrought against him and in the end will be evil to himself, for he shall be imprisoned or have great trouble. For he shall find many enemies in his return and have great loss of goods and honour and much villainy and treason shall be wrought against him to the hazard of his life . . . He shall escape it with much ado after long time and much infamy and trouble.

That this horoscope could double as the plot summary of a romantic tragedy owes something to Forman's love of theatre (in fact, he repeatedly visited the Curtain this spring, though his mind seems to have been more on a young woman he was pursuing than on the Chamberlain's Men's plays). Horoscopes, like plays, though more clumsily, give voice to hopes and fears that might otherwise remain unspoken. Unlike Forman, Shakespeare didn't consult astrological signs to register the deep anxieties the Irish campaign was raising. The play he was completing, its timely subject matter Henry V's military exploits overseas, would resonate deeply with the conflicting feelings of a nation committed to war – a nation hoping for the best, but knowing that 'treason, hunger, sickness and death' were just as likely the fate that awaited Essex and his followers.

*

When scholars talk about the sources of Shakespeare's plays, they almost always mean printed books like Holinshed's *Chronicles* that they themselves can read; but Shakespeare's was an aural culture, the music of which has long faded. Lost to us are the unrecorded sounds reverberating around him – street cries of vendors, church bells, regional and foreign accents, scraps of overheard conversation, and countless bits of speech and noise that filled the densely packed capital. Some of these made their way into Shakespeare's writing, others impeded it, and still others were a kind of precondition for it. In a culture where so little was written down, memories had to be strong. Only a tiny percentage of Elizabethan sermons were committed to print, so it's a stroke of luck that Andrewes's war sermon was one of them, for the evidence suggests that elements of it inspired (or uncannily parallelled) the play that Shakespeare was now completing.

Andrewes began his sermon in the usual fashion by quoting the Scripture upon which he would elaborate – 'When thou goest out, with the host against thine enemies, keep thee then from all wickedness' – before launching into a dramatic start that underscored just how directly the Bible spoke to the current military crisis in Ireland. 'To entitle this time to this text, or to show it pertinent to the present occasion, will ask no long preface. "When thou goest forth, etc." This when is now. There be enemies; and we have an host: It is going forth.' It's worth quoting at length (like Shakespeare's prose, it's best read aloud) to catch Andrewes's distinctive voice – abrupt, jagged, full of emphases, crammed with witty conceits and word-play – a style beloved of the Elizabethans: 'This our host so going forth, our hearts desire and prayer unto God is, that they may happily go, and thrice happily come again; with joy and triumph, to her sacred Majesty; honour to themselves; and general contentment to the whole land.' Note the thumping reiteration of 'this time' and 'this day':

These former years, this time of the fast, and this day, the first day of it (both) ministered an occasion to call from an abstinence from sin. This day, and this time being set out by the Church's appointment to that end. Now, besides that ordinary, of other years, God, this year, hath sent us another, this time of war, and that, a very seasonable time too, wherein to repent and retire from sins . . . This is the sum . . . that our giving over sin might procure the good speed to our going forth; even an honourable and happy return.

Just five weeks later London audiences would hear far more rousing sentiments in a similar celebration of troops going into battle 'this day' in *Henry the Fifth*:

This day is called the Feast of Crispian.
He that outlives this day and comes safe home
Will stand a-tiptoe when this day is named
And rouse him at the name of Crispian.
He that shall see this day and live old age
Will yearly on the vigil feast his neighbours
And say, 'Tomorrow is Saint Crispian.'
Then will he strip his sleeve and show his scars,
And say, 'These wounds I had on Crispin's Day.'
(IV, iii, 40–48)

The thrust of Andrewes's speech is to sanction, if not bless, the plan to crush Tyrone, who has broken faith: 'Here, here have been diverse princely favours vouchsafed, and most unkindly rejected; means of clemency many times most graciously offered, and most ungraciously refused; yea, faith falsified, and expectation deluded; contempt upon contempt heaped up, that the measure is full. These then are the enemies against, and this the time when.' Though offering unconditional support for the campaign, Andrewes doesn't shy away from chiding the government for its past habit of sending over ill-equipped soldiers. This time must be different: 'Victuals must be supplied . . . Pay must be thought of . . . We must "go forth with our host" . . . "with our host", not a heap of naked or starved men.' And perhaps turning directly to Essex (who had recently boasted that he 'would have thought danger a sport and death a feast'), Andrewes warns: 'War is no matter of sport.' It 'may be "sport" in the beginning; it will be "bitterness in the end", if it hold long.' It was a sermon sure to meet with his monarch's approval.

There are a number of moments in *Henry the Fifth* that owe nothing to either the chronicles or to Shakespeare's dramatic sources. They are related to the two strands of Andrewes's argument in this sermon: the theological justification for an aggressive offensive war and the need for those who go off to war to purge themselves of sin. *Henry the Fifth* opens with English clergymen debating an imminent military campaign, followed not long after by one of the longest speeches in any of Shakespeare's plays, a virtual sermon by the Archbishop of Canterbury insisting on the legitimacy of Henry's offensive war against his neighbouring country. Even as Andrewes assures Elizabeth, Essex and the rest of the court that war is 'no sin, but lawful' and that 'not only defensive war, but offensive war too hath his "when"', Canterbury argues in Shakespeare's play that Henry's cause is lawful, just, and has the clergy's blessing.

The connection between Andrewes's sermon and Shakespeare's play extends to the scene in which the disguised Henry V argues with his troops on the eve of the battle of Agincourt. At the climax of this scene the King refuses to accept his soldiers' argument that if the war is unjust, their guilt is upon his head. When Henry insists rather that 'every subject's soul is his own' and that every soldier should 'wash every mote out of his conscience', he might as well be paraphrasing Andrewes's contention that the act of going to war demands a collective renunciation of sin: 'What a thing this is, how great, gross and foul and incongruity it is, to pour ourselves into sin at the very time when we go forth to correct sin: To set forth to punish rebels when we ourselves are in rebellion against God?' Finally, Andrewes's belief that the victory belongs to God

not man – 'that the safe and speedy coming again of them that
"now go forth" . . . dependeth upon God's "going forth with them"'
– is echoed in the play by Henry's assertion that the victory is
God's alone:

> O God, thy arm was here!
> And not to us, but to thy arm alone,
> Ascribe we all.
>   (IV, viii, 106–8)

With Andrewes's cadences ringing in his ears, Shakespeare
returned to London that day to sign off on the Globe contract.
The break for Lent left him a few precious weeks to finish the play
before he had to turn it over, first to the Master of the Revels for
approval and then to the actors to learn their lines in time for the
reopening of the theatres in late March.

5
Band of Brothers

A month later, crowds of playgoers streamed north through Bishopsgate to the Curtain in Shoreditch, while others walked south across London Bridge to Henslowe's Rose in Southwark. Boatmen ferried playgoers across the Thames in both directions. Flags flying from the tops of the playhouses confirmed that playing had resumed following a month-long break for Lent. The titles of the plays to be performed that afternoon by the Chamberlain's and Admiral's Men – 'Painted in play-bills, upon every post' – had already been widely advertised throughout the city. Musicians were dispatched to literally drum up business, while trumpets called out to the tardy from the playhouse rooftops. The rival playing companies were blessed with exceptional weather this week, the kind likely to draw audiences to the outdoor playhouses in large numbers. Between 22 and 27 March the days were 'bright and clear and very hot', Simon Forman recorded, 'like summer'. Days

The Earl of Essex, *c.*1599

were also getting longer; with the play and jig lasting roughly three hours, from two to five in the afternoon, there would still be an hour or so of daylight after the performance for spectators to find their way home before dark.

While no records survive for what the Chamberlain's Men earned at the Curtain, we know that the Admiral's Men did poorly at the Rose both this week and the next: Henslowe records receipts of £3 18s followed by just over £2, a fraction of the weekly average of £9. Coming on the heels of their excellent gate receipts right before the theatres closed for Lent, this poor attendance can best be explained by the competition. It looks as if far more Londoners went to see the Chamberlain's Men, including Shakespeare's much awaited *Henry the Fifth*; but playgoers at the Curtain were not rewarded with the kind of play they had expected or that Shakespeare had promised. Their comic favourite, Will Kemp, wasn't even in the cast, nor was there much merrymaking with Katharine of France.

Plays about Henry V had been a staple of the Elizabethan stage since the mid-1580s. The most popular of them, *The Famous Victories of Henry the Fifth*, had been in the repertory of the Queen's Men, and after they disbanded it continued to be performed by other companies. Henslowe's records give some sense of its popularity: in one eight-month stretch in the mid-1590s it was staged an extraordinary thirteen times. Shakespeare knew it intimately. When looking for incidents to develop in both parts of *Henry the Fourth* and again in *Henry the Fifth*, it was the first place he turned, and he went back to it repeatedly, ransacking it for episodes, lifting everything from the highway robbery scene that opens *The First Part of Henry the Fourth* to the wooing of Kate that ends *Henry the Fifth*. And he had done so from memory, for the anonymous play was only belatedly published in 1598. Shakespeare's easy familiarity with *The Famous Victories* strongly suggests that on more than one occasion, as both he and the play moved from company to company in the early 1590s, he had regularly acted in it and perhaps reflected on how he might rework it. Shakespeare knew that audiences didn't love *The Famous Victories* for its complexity. Its prose was workaday and its characters two-dimensional – more a series of skits than a coherent play, it was a perfect vehicle for a great clown like Richard Tarlton. And playgoers enjoyed its untroubled patriotism: the French are silly and the war is a romp, even when the English are badly outnumbered. *The Famous Victories* had no ambition to leave audiences wrestling with any great moral issues and it certainly didn't make any intellectual demands on them. If you were paying to see a play about Henry V you could expect to have a few laughs and cheer on your nation and its heroic past.

Playgoers at the Curtain in late March 1599 were in for a surprise the moment that Shakespeare's *Henry the Fifth* began. Unlike *The Famous Victories*, it opened not with a famous clown bantering with his prince, but with a very serious Chorus dressed in a long black velvet cloak, who announces new ground rules. The Chorus, which scholars have argued was played by Shakespeare himself, picks up where the revised epilogue to *The Second Part of Henry the Fourth* had left off. This was going to be work; and work not just for the playwright straining for inspiration, or for the actors who have 'dared / On this unworthy scaffold to bring forth / So great an object', but for the audience too. The playwright and players cannot manage alone: 'Let us, ciphers to this great account, / On your imaginary forces work.' The burden, the Chorus repeats, falls squarely on the playgoers: 'Think, when we talk of horses, that you see them.' The play will fail without their imaginative effort: they are urged to 'Piece out' the play's 'imperfections', and 'make imaginary puissance' – another dense phrase, meaning 'Picture an army in your mind's eye' (Prologue, 9–26).

This was the first of several times in 1599 that Shakespeare, in breaking with the past and underscoring how much had changed, rewrote an old familiar story. In so doing, one of the most challenging tasks he set for his audience was insisting that they keep the two plays, old and new, simultaneously in mind. *Henry the Fifth* becomes a much more original and complicated work when you realise that playgoers couldn't help but see it unfold in juxtaposition to what they were expecting: a play like *The Famous Victories*, in which the gritty realities of war had never intruded.

An uncritical sense of England's heroic past (forgivable when *The Famous Victories* was first staged for a nation that dreaded and then miraculously escaped a punishing Spanish Armada) was no longer credible. And in 1599 it was impossible to recall Henry V's celebrated invasion of France without reflecting on the fate of Essex's much anticipated campaign in Ireland. Ireland, which never intruded in *The Famous Victories*, haunts Shakespeare's play and as much as anything else defines what is new in Shakespeare's version, while also suggesting what his own preoccupations were at this time.

Ireland seeps into the play at the most unexpected and even unintended moments, such as when the Queen of France, who has never met her future son-in-law Henry V, greets him with the words, 'So happy be the issue, brother Ireland, / Of this good day and of this gracious meeting' (V, ii, 12–13). The mistake is not the nervous Queen's but Shakespeare's, who slipped when intending to write 'brother England' (and whose error modern editors silently correct). That this confusion of identity occurs in the context of the 'issue' or union of English King and French Princess makes the error all the more revealing, for anxiety over pure and hybrid national identity runs through the play even as it preoccupied those who wrote about England's Irish problem.

For much of the play, allusions to the current crisis in Ireland are fleeting, such as the offhand remarks about Irish kerns and bogs. When Gower, an English captain, speaks of a soldier who wears 'a beard of the General's cut', his reference to the Earl of Essex's distinctive square-cut beard, which collapses the distance between

Henry V's world and their own, would not have been lost upon London playgoers. There are also glancing allusions to the kind of bitter conditions their conscripted fellow countrymen were facing at that moment in Ireland, with 'winter coming on and sickness growing / Upon our soldiers' (III, iii, 55–6). And the stage direction in Act III, scene vi – 'Enter the King and his poor soldiers' – would also have evoked with surprising realism England's poorly outfitted forces in Ireland.

Only in the play's final act does Essex's imminent Irish campaign, long submerged, break the surface of the play. Temporarily abandoning the make-believe world of theatre, Shakespeare invites his fellow Londoners to think not about Henry V but about the near future, the day when they will pour into the streets of London to welcome home Essex, 'General of our gracious Empress' Elizabeth. It's an extraordinary moment and the only time in his plays that Shakespeare breaks theatrical allusion and directs playgoers' attention away from the make-believe world of his play to the real world outside the theatre:

> But now behold,
> In the quick forge and working-house of thought,
> How London doth pour out her citizens!
> The mayor and all his brethren, in best sort,
> Like to the senators of th'antique Rome
> With the plebeians swarming at their heels,
> Go forth and fetch their conquering Caesar in;
> As by a lower but loving likelihood,
> Were now the General of our gracious Empress,
> As in good time he may, from Ireland coming,
> Bringing rebellion broached on his sword,
> How many would the peaceful city quit
> To welcome him! Much more, and much more cause,
> Did they this Harry.
>   (V, Prologue, 22–35)

As we shift perspective from Henry's triumphant return to Julius Caesar's to Essex's then back to Henry's, much gets blurred. The passage speaks to the audience's understandable desire to leap over time, for the imminent Irish campaign to be over.

When examined more closely, however, the Chorus's comparisons prove disquieting. Caesar had entered Rome harbouring thoughts of returning the Republic to one-man rule and his short-lived triumph and tragic end were already on Shakespeare's mind as he looked forward to his next play, *Julius Caesar*. Scratch the surface and the analogy to Essex's forecast return 'with rebellion broached on his sword' is no less troubling. Henry was a king. In contrast, Essex, like Caesar, was a military hero feared by rivals, who sought his overthrow because they believed he would be king. Essex's enemies, William Camden noted, seeing how the Earl wished 'nothing more than to have an army under his command', feared that Essex 'entertained some monstrous design, especially seeing he showed his contumacy more and more against the Queen that had been most bountiful to him'. His enemies may have felt their concern justified when Essex's own followers claimed that he was descended from 'the blood royal of England' by Cecily Bourchier, his great grandmother, who was descended both from Thomas of Woodstock, the youngest son of King Edward III, and also from Richard Earl of Cambridge, and that 'hereupon he had better title to the sceptre of England than any of the competitors' hoping to succeed Elizabeth.

If Shakespeare was aware of this lineage it throws into a new light his handling of Essex's ancestor, the same Richard Earl of Cambridge, who has a cameo part in *Henry the Fifth* as a traitor who betrays his monarch for foreign gold and is sent to his death. What Shakespeare knew from his sources, but buries too deeply in his play for audiences to readily see, is that the Earl of Cambridge really did have a strong claim to the throne, a better one than Henry V. It's a point that is made much of in *Sir John Oldcastle*, staged the following November, in which Cambridge argues that Henry IV and Henry V are 'false intruders and usurp the crown'. Heir of the third son of Edward III's eldest son, Cambridge was unfairly passed over by these Lancastrians, who can only trace their descent from the fourth son of Edward III's eldest son.

While it is unlikely that Shakespeare would deliberately link Essex with the traitorous Cambridge, the politics of *Henry the Fifth* are so inscrutable that it's difficult to know for sure. Nowhere is the play more slippery than in its description of Essex returning from Ireland 'with rebellion broached on his sword'. The line allows for the possibility that the unpredictable Essex, in command of a conquering army, could, like Henry V's father Bolingbroke, enter England at the head of such an army, rebelliously returning to London and counting on the commoners to come to his side. Had she heard these lines, Elizabeth might have shuddered.

In all likelihood she never did hear them. There's no evidence that the play was ever performed before her. By the end of the year political events would have made that impossible. Despite its initial popularity, its focus on sensitive contemporary events assured *Henry the Fifth* – at least in its original form – one of the shortest first runs of any of Shakespeare's plays. After it was 'sundry times played' by the Chamberlain's Men in 1599, a copy of it was first 'stayed', or delayed, and then, having undergone extensive cuts, rushed into print in 1600 in a stripped down version that eliminates the Choruses, all mention of Essex, Ireland, Scotland, collusion between the Crown and the Church, and anything else that might remotely cause political offence. It certainly looks as if the company, in the light of unfolding events, was trying to cover its tracks. This sanitized version was twice reprinted before the fuller, original version finally appeared in the 1623 Folio; but by then the play had dropped out of the repertory. Before the Restoration, Pistol is quoted or mentioned a couple of times, dramatists recalled enough to poke fun at one or two bits in it, and a version of the play was once performed for King James (surely trimmed of its slurs against the 'weasel Scot' [I, ii, 170]). Otherwise, silence.

Those seeking to pinpoint Shakespeare's political views in *Henry the Fifth* will always be disappointed. The play is not a political manifesto. Shakespeare resists revelling either in reflexive patriotism or in a critique of nationalistic wars, though the play contains elements of both. *Henry the Fifth* succeeds and frustrates because it consistently refuses to adopt a single voice or point of view about military adventurism – past and present. Shakespeare was aware that on some deep level, as their brothers, husbands and sons were being shipped off to fight in Ireland, Elizabethans craved a play that reassuringly reminded them of their heroic, martial past. What better subject than the famous victories of Henry V? The siege at Harfleur would be a triumph (compensating for the humiliating defeat of besieged Blackwater). But Shakespeare also knew that this same audience – already weary of military callups and fresh demands to arm and victual troops, and unnerved by frightful reports from settlers and soldiers returning from Ireland – were, by the eve of Essex's departure, of two minds about the campaign. *Henry the Fifth* thus takes its place among the many stories circulating in London at this anxious time – from the gossip at court and in the taverns to the official sermons and royal pronouncements justifying the imminent military expedition – and yet somehow manages to encompass them all. It wasn't a prowar play or an anti-war play but a going-to-war play.

In responding to his audience's mixed feelings – their sense that the war was both unavoidable and awful – Shakespeare fills the play with competing, critical voices: the backroom whispers of self-interested churchmen, the grumblings of low-life conscripts, the blunt criticism of worthy soldiers who know that leaders make promises they have no intention of keeping, the confessions of so-called traitors, the growing cynicism of a young boy off to the wars, the infighting among officers, the bitter curses of a returning soldier. Much of the play, from beginning to end, is composed of scenes in which opposing voices collide over the conduct of the war. In truth, there's not much else to the plot. Critics who complain that 'a siege and a battle, with one bit of light love-making cannot form a drama' are not wrong as far as that goes. What they overlook is that all the debate about the war is the real story.

King Henry is himself responsible for a lot of this arguing and exhorting and speaks in many voices, each perfectly tuned to the demands of the moment. He is, when he needs to be, the inspiring battlefield leader, the cold-blooded commander ordering his men to execute their prisoners, the pious general giving thanks to God alone, the self-effacing wooer, and (while disguised amongst his troops on the eve of battle) the defensive, isolated leader. We see here signs of Shakespeare's increasing interest in biography and character, spurred, perhaps, by his recent reading of North's translation of Plutarch's *Lives* of the great Greek and Roman leaders. Shakespeare also knew enough from observing Elizabeth that the successful monarch was one with an intuitive sense of theatre, one who not only knew how to perform many roles but who also knew (like Henry V) how to steer others into playing less attractive parts. Henry turns out to be a lot like Shakespeare himself: a man who mingles easily with princes and paupers but who deep down is fundamentally private and inscrutable.

With the innovative (and for Shakespeare unique) experiment of introducing each act with an extended prologue spoken by the Chorus, a sense of counterpoint sharply defines the structure and rhythm of the play, as the Chorus and the ensuing stage action offer competing versions of what is taking place. The idea of using a Chorus in this way probably came to Shakespeare late in his conception of the play – for the speeches were sufficiently detachable to be eliminated when the play was first printed. The Chorus keeps giving the story away in advance; but what Shakespeare loses in dramatic surprise he makes up for in the tension between what audiences are told and what they see for themselves – which becomes, far more than the antagonism between the French and English, the main conflict in the play. Adjudicating between the competing claims of the Chorus and the action is demanding, though perhaps it would have been less so to Elizabethan audiences, who saw the widening gulf between official propaganda and the harsh reality around them (and knew what could, and what could not, be said aloud about the war effort). Take, for example, the Chorus to Act II, which offers a stirring vision of a nation responding to a call to arms:

> Now all the youth of England are on fire,
> And silken dalliance in the wardrobe lies.
> Now thrive the armourers, and honour's thought
> Reigns solely in the breast of every man.
> They sell the pasture now to buy the horse,
> Following the mirror of all Christian kings,
> With winged heels, as English Mercurys.
> For now sits Expectation in the air
> And hides a sword from hilts unto the point
> With crowns imperial, crowns and coronets,
> Promised to Harry and his followers.
>   (II, Prologue, 1–11)

By March 1599 this inflated rhetoric would have produced a wince or two among muster-weary Londoners, few of whom, except for a handful of hopeful gentlemen volunteers, were planning to 'sell the pasture now to buy the horse' and follow Essex into battle for greater rewards. The cheery, official view of this Chorus is belied by the action that immediately follows onstage. It's not the 'winged heels' of young men eager to fight that we next see, but rather a group of foot-dragging, thieving conscripts, Nym, Bardolph and Pistol, who grudgingly 'must to France together' (II, i, 91) and who fall to fighting amongst themselves. Their quarrel is set aside only when Pistol announces that he will sell provisions to the army (another deeply corrupt business) 'and profits will accrue' that will ensure their 'friendship' and 'brotherhood' (109–12). The sole motivation these soldiers have to fight is that there's money to be made by cheating the army that is cheating its troops. The alternation of Chorus and action re-enacts the pattern of expectation and disenchantment that characterized the campaign to subdue Ireland. The competing views of the Chorus and these underworld characters do not so much qualify as disqualify each other.

This Chorus's breathless patriotism would have been familiar enough to audiences from works like the just published poem by Thomas Churchyard, 'The Fortunate Farewell to the Most Forward and Noble Earl of Essex'. These thumpingly alliterative lines from Churchyard's poem are typical:

Now when green trees begin to bud and bloom,
On Irish seas Eliza's ships shall ride.
A warlike band of worthy knights, I hope,
Are armed for fight, a bloody brunt to bide,
With rebels shall both might and manhood cope,
Our country's right and quarrel to be tried.
Right makes wrong blush, and truth bids falsehood fly,
The sword is drawn, Tyrone's dispatch drawn nigh.

But even Churchyard, who had been writing this kind of propaganda since the reign of Edward VI and was the author of a now lost book *The Scourge of Rebels in Ireland*, recognized that this effusive support for the campaign was a necessary counterweight to the misgivings contemporaries had about the military adventure. He defends his proselytizing poem on the grounds that it was important 'to stir up a threefold manly courage to the mercenary multitude of soldiers, that follow this marshal-like General'. Of course, the need to encourage backsliding troops suggests something less than total enthusiasm on the part of these citizen-soldiers. After a long life as a poorly requited poet-soldier, now almost eighty years old and probably forced to churn out this kind of stuff to make ends meet, Churchyard knew better, but also knew that somebody was going to make money from this kind of publication, so why not him? Propaganda was necessary as a country went off to war; but few could have been naïve enough to swallow it whole – whether they came across it in Churchyard's poem or Shakespeare's Chorus. Shakespeare's audience knew this, and he expected them to.

Shakespeare also introduces in *Henry the Fifth* what later became a staple of English comedy: the stage Irishman. Captain Macmorris appears in Act III, entering in the company of a Scottish captain, Jamy. Tellingly, both disappear from the play before the decisive battle at Agincourt, unlike their fellow captains – the Welsh Fluellen and the English Gower. A scene that shows Irish, Welsh, Scottish and English captains united against a common enemy prophetically anticipates the notion of a united kingdom. But these kingdoms were far from united in 1599 and some were downright hostile during the reign of Henry V. That Shakespeare portrays these nations as allied is all the more strange, given the warning earlier in the play that if Henry is not careful, as soon as he goes off to the wars in France, the Scots will attack England's 'unguarded nest'. With the King of Scots the leading contender to succeed Queen Elizabeth, Henry's warning that 'the Scot . . . hath been still a giddy neighbour to us' (I, ii, 144–5) seems uncharacteristically impolitic on Shakespeare's part. Many in the audience no doubt knew that Scottish mercenaries, fighting alongside the Irish, were awaiting Essex's forces in Ireland (even as anyone familiar with the chronicles upon which Shakespeare drew would have known that Scottish and Welsh forces fought alongside the French against Henry V while, confusingly, the Irish fought alongside Henry).

The collision of past and present alliances becomes even more complicated when we turn to the fantasy of English and Irish fighting side by side in the play. Even before the desertion of hired Irish troops at Blackwater when the battle started going badly, the English had been ambivalent about paying Irishmen to fill out their ranks. After that defeat a serious effort was made to purge the army of Irish soldiers. Irish captains were held especially suspect. It's no surprise, then, that when the Welshman Fluellen starts telling the Irish captain Macmorris that 'there is not many of your nation–', he is angrily cut off by the Irishman before he can complete the thought: 'Of my nation? What ish my nation? Ish a villain, and a bastard, and a knave, and a rascal? What ish my nation? Who talks of my nation?' (III, ii, 120–23). The stereotypical hot-blooded Irishman even threatens to cut off Fluellen's head.

Macmorris's name may provide a clue to his defensiveness. The so-called Old English or Anglo-Norman, who had settled in Ireland centuries earlier, had adjusted to local custom by changing their names' original prefix 'Fitz' to the Gaelic 'Mac'. No wonder, then, the part-English, part-Irish, and part-Norman Macmorris is so touchy about his unfixed national identity: what is his nation? English? Irish? An Anglo-Irish mix? If so, what of his loyalties? As a frustrated Irish captain in the English army named Christopher St Lawrence put it: 'I am sorry that when I am in England, I should be esteemed an Irishman, and in Ireland, an Englishman.'

Even as Shakespeare was exposing contemporary prejudices towards England's Gaelic neighbours, he was revealing traces of his own. If we look at the Folio text of this scene (which can be traced back to Shakespeare's own manuscript), the speech prefixes permit a glimpse of how Shakespeare himself imagined his own characters. Throughout the scene, stage headings for Macmorris and Jamy substitute for their names their national types, for Shakespeare thought of them less as individuals than as 'Irish' and 'Scot'. The Welsh occupy a middle ground: Fluellen is first called Fluellen before he too is reduced to national type, 'Welsh'. In contrast, the Englishman Gower is always called 'Gower'. There were some deep cracks in the edifice of cheerful British allies standing shoulder to shoulder.

Shakespeare's interest in national stereotypes is closely related to his obsessive interest in the play in dialects and in the connection between nationality and language. In addition to the distinctive and often comic English dialects spoken by Macmorris, Jamy and Fluellen, there's the broken English spoken by Katharine of France, the schoolboy French that Henry falls back on when wooing Katharine, and the slightly muddled French spoken by the prisoner Monsieur le Fer. We are even treated to an extended and obscene English lesson in which the sexual surrender of Katharine is prefigured.

One result of all this mangled English is that characters have a great deal of trouble understanding what others say or mean. English lessons notwithstanding, language stands as an insurmountable barrier to erasing national difference because identity is so intertwined with how one speaks. Henry embodies Englishness precisely because he can't – or won't – speak French. As he tells his future wife, 'It is as easy for me, Kate, to conquer the kingdom as to speak so much more French' (V, ii, 185–6). Katharine speaks for many in the play when she admits: 'I cannot tell wat is dat' (V, ii, 178). The audience comes to know just how she feels, for Shakespeare invents over a score of new words or phrases in the course of *Henry the Fifth*, including 'impawn', 'womby vaultages', 'portage', 'nook-smitten', 'sur-reined', 'congreeted', 'enscheduled', and 'curselarie'. These, and rare words like 'leno', 'cresive' and the recent Dutch import 'sutler', keep spectators struggling to get a firm grasp on what is said and what is meant. There's a further irony here, one that Shakespeare is keenly aware of: in the act of expanding its linguistic boundaries, the English language must appropriate (or from another perspective, be contaminated by) other languages.

There's a telling example of this cross-cultural confusion, with an Irish twist, in the scene in which the braggart Pistol can't believe his good fortune that a wealthy Frenchman has surrendered to him. Pistol's second-hand language tends to be stitched together from old discarded scraps, including Marlovian rant. When he hears French and sees treasure in this scene, his mind immediately runs to a popular Irish ditty, 'Calen O costure me', which he characteristically mangles:

PISTOL Yield, cur!
FRENCH SOLDIER Je pense que vous êtes le gentilhomme de bonne qualite.
PISTOL Qualtitie calmie o custure me. Art thou a gentleman? What is thy name? Discuss.
    (IV, iv, 1–5)

'Calen o costure me' is itself a corrupt rendering of the original Irish for 'Young maiden, my treasure': *Cailin og a' stor* (further debased by Pistol to 'calmie o custure me'). The Irish language, like its land and people, is inexorably anglicized, corrupted and appropriated. The brief exchange also offers insight into the ways in which Shakespeare was perfecting the art of creating characters who feel real: though he's no Hamlet, we grasp who Pistol is by following his idiosyncratic train of associations.

Such commixtures were proving to be much less humorous when played out in Ireland itself. The underlying threat to English identity produced by conquering and intermarrying is given rich expression in the anonymous New English tract *A Discourse of Ireland*, written in 1599, which notes: 'It is a thing observed in Ireland and grown into a proverb, that English [settlers] in the second generation become Irish but never English,' adding that the cause is that 'the evil overcometh and corrupteth the good'. To preclude any more of this mix of 'English with the Irish', the author urges that the English simply relocate, rather than annihilate, the Irish: 'The removing of the Irish may happily alter their dispositions when they shall be planted in another soil.'

Ideally, they'll be shipped off to provide a servant class 'throughout England' (though the author of this tract never considers the possibility that they would mate there with the English). Spenser himself in his *View* discusses how the English living in Ireland are 'grown almost mere Irish' and asks rhetorically in lines that anticipate Macmorris's defensiveness about his national identity: 'Is it possible that an Englishman brought up naturally in such a sweet civility as England affords can find such barbarous rudeness that he should forget his own nature and forgo his own nation? How may this be?'

Conquest, national identity, and mixed origins – the obsessive concerns of Elizabethan Irish policy – run deep through *Henry the Fifth* and sharply distinguish it from previous English accounts of Henry's reign. Earlier in Shakespeare's play, it is the French who complain about the mongrel English. The Dauphin asks:

> Shall a few sprays of us,
> The emptying of our fathers' luxury,
> Our scions, put in wild and savage stock,
> Spurt up so suddenly into the clouds
> And overlook their grafters?
> (III, v, 5–9)

The impossibly dense metaphors of breeding and grafting almost obscure the Dauphin's point: in 1066 the Normans who conquered England went about impregnating English women – the 'wild and savage stock'. Centuries later, how dare Henry and his army of upstart half-breeds challenge us, 'their grafters'? A fuming Bourbon can only concur in one of the funnier lines in the play: 'Normans, but bastard Normans, Norman bastards!' (III, v, 10). Yes, the English are Normans – after the Norman Conquest – but bastard ones. From the Dauphin and Bourbon's point of view, the French are the only pure-breds, but they worry that 'Our madams mock at us and plainly say'

Our mettle is bred out, and they will give
Their bodies to the lust of English youth
To new-store France with bastard warriors.
(III, v, 28–31)

The danger of polluted national purity runs through the play
and locates *Henry the Fifth* midway between Shakespeare's
extended exploration of inter-racial marriage in *The Merchant of
Venice* a few years earlier and his return to this preoccupation in
Othello a few years later. Henry's threat of turning his soldiers
loose to rape the French maidens of Harfleur raises the stakes
considerably:

What is't to me, when you yourselves are cause,
If your pure maidens fall into the hand
Of hot and forcing violation?
(III, iii, 19–21)

This time the Frenchwomen are the root-stock and the English
soldiers the potential scion grafted on. The result is much the same
and part of the collateral damage of wars of conquest. The over-
riding irony of *Henry the Fifth* is that its happy ending leads to just
such a union, romanticized of course, with the English Henry
wedded to the French princess. The language of breeding persists
to the very end, as Henry tells Katharine:

thou must therefore needs prove a good soldier-breeder. Shall not thou
and I, between Saint Denis and Saint George, compound a boy, half
French, half English, that shall go to Constantinople and take the Turk
by the beard? Shall we not?
(V, ii, 206–10)

The spectre of Islam will help the French and English temporarily forget their differences. A final Chorus, which doubles as an
epilogue, reminds us that their 'half French, half English' son,
Henry VI, will never make it to Constantinople; in fact, he'll lose

France and then his own crown. Having inflated expectations, the Chorus now punctures them.

There's the added irony that Pistol learns that his wife, a bawd, 'is dead / I'th'spital of a malady of France' (V, i, 80–81). Through the sexual transmission (often by returning soldiers) of the so-called French disease, syphilis, the French are ultimately revenged and the English fatally contaminated. The news of his wife's death confirms Pistol's decision to return to a criminal life in England:

> Well, bawd I'll turn
> And something lean to cutpurse of quick hand.
> To England will I steal, and there I'll steal.
>   (V, i, 84–6)

Overlooked in the spectacle of Henry's (and Essex's) imagined homecoming is the largely suppressed and unhappy story of the return of war veterans like Pistol. Though England was taking the war to Ireland, it was clear that, in the aftermath of the campaign, English soldiers would be bringing their Irish experience home. This was a different but no less disturbing kind of contamination. The reach of the war extended into every corner of England, including Shakespeare's native Stratford-upon-Avon, which in June 1601 petitioned to 'be eased of the charge of one Lewis Gilbert, a maimed solder in Ireland'. Gilbert was a butcher (a member of a trade that Shakespeare's father, a glover who dealt in animal skins, knew well, and perhaps the young man or his family was known to the Shakespeares). We don't know what Gilbert was like before he came back maimed from Ireland; but in the years after his return he was a public burden and a danger to his community – he was accused of forcible entry into a local shop, he failed to pay his debts and, finally, he stabbed a neighbour to death with 'a long knife' in a quarrel. Through bitter war veterans like Pistol, Shakespeare also hints at the corrosive and unavoidable national cost of the Irish war.

Interwoven with the recurrent fantasy in *Henry the Fifth* of national purity is the fond hope that war will do away with the social barriers that divide the men who fight as one on the battlefield. The great speech on this subject is delivered by Henry himself as he prepares his soldiers for battle:

> We few, we happy few, we band of brothers.
> For he today that sheds his blood with me
> Shall be my brother; be he ne'er so vile,
> This day shall gentle his condition.
>   (IV, iii, 60–63)

No speech better expresses the loyalties forged in combat; but, like much in the play, its sentiments are belied by what follows. The battle won, Henry immediately reverts to the familiar divisions between aristocratic brethren and everyone else. When, for example, he scans the list of the Englishmen who died at Agincourt, he tells his army of the deaths of

> Edward the Duke of York, the Earl of Suffolk,
> Sir Richard Keighley, Davy Gam, esquire;
> None else of name, and of all other men
> But five-and-twenty.
>   (IV, viii, 103–6)

'None else of name'. Battlefield deaths have not gentled the condition of the anonymous soldiers who fought alongside Henry. It's painful witnessing the soldiers' frustrated expectations. If any one of them deserved to be knighted, it is the worthy captain Gower. When he and the foot soldier Williams (who exchanged blunt words with the disguised King the night before) enter in mid-conversation after the battle, they are discussing the news that Gower has been invited to attend the King at his tent. That can only mean one thing: Williams expects, mistakenly, 'I warrant it is to knight you, Captain' (IV, viii, 1). It was the aspiration of every gentleman volunteer who would follow Essex to Ireland knowing that the Earl had generously knighted dozens of men in his previous military campaigns. But Williams is wrong: there will be no knighting. Gower is simply called in to act as peace-maker between Fluellen and Williams, as Henry tries to extricate himself from an uncomfortable quarrel with Williams.

The defeated French aristocrats, like their English counterparts, are also eager to restore the division between nobility and commoners, even among the dead on the battlefield, and ask for permission

> To sort our nobles from our common men.
> For many of our princes – woe the while! –
> Lie drowned and soaked in mercenary blood;
> So do our vulgar drench their peasant limbs
> In blood of princes.
> (IV, vii, 73–7)

While brotherhood figures repeatedly in the final act of the play, it refers not to the battle-forged fraternity but to pre-existing ties of family and rank. Henry and the French King pointedly call each other 'brother', and Henry refers to his aristocratic kin, Gloucester and Bedford, as brothers too. Even Alexander Court calls his fellow foot soldier 'Brother John Bates' (IV, i, 86). But in the end this fraternal good will doesn't cut across social lines: Henry, for example, refers to Court's and Bates's friend, Michael Williams, as 'this fellow'. The battle over, traditional divisions are restored; and as the final Chorus reminds us, all that Henry V won was soon lost. For audiences at the Curtain, and later that year at the Globe, it was a quietly deflating ending to an exhilarating theatrical experience, though one that cannot erase the pleasures of the victory at Agincourt or the patriotic feelings stirred up by Henry's speeches on the eve of battle.

A week or so later, in the early afternoon of 27 March, the Earl of Essex and his followers finally assembled at Tower Hill, an open field just north of the Tower of London. Their departure for the wars was theatrical, down to the timing, for the procession got under way at just the hour that plays began. It was a scene that called to mind the lines from the opening Chorus to *Henry the Fifth*, which exhorts spectators to picture just such a martial scene: 'Think, when we talk of horses, that you see them / Printing their proud hoofs i'th' receiving earth.' John Stow writes:

[At] about two o'clock in the afternoon, [Essex] took horse in Seething Lane, and from thence being accompanied with diverse noblemen and many others, himself very plainly attired, rode through Grace Street, Cornhill, Cheapside, and other high streets, in all which places and in the fields, the people pressed exceedingly to behold him, especially in the highways for more than four miles' space, crying and saying, 'God bless your Lordship, God preserve your Honour,' and some followed him until the evening, only to behold him.

But this dramatic sight of a powerful English army heading off to crush the Irish rebellion was undermined – at least for the superstitious – by the weather, which the army could no more control than the players could. Out of nowhere, historian John Speed writes, there struck 'a strange thunderclap in a clear sunshine day'. Simon Forman, another eyewitness, offers a more detailed account. After an hour or so, he writes, 'it began to rain and at three 'till four there fell such a hail shower that was very great'. The weather then turned even darker: 'It thundered withal and the wind turned to the north and after the shower was past it turned to the south-east again, and there were many mighty clouds up, but all the day before one of the clock was a very fair day and clear.' Anxious Londoners read it as an ominous sign. It made so powerful an impression upon the translator John Florio that, over a decade later, he included it in a dictionary as the definition of the word 'Ecnéphia': 'a kind of prodigious storm coming in summer, with furious flashings, the firmament seeming to open and burn, as happened when the Earl of Essex parted from London to go for Ireland'. Shakespeare also took notice, and would soon work the disturbing image of this 'civil strife in heaven' into his next play, *Julius Caesar*:

> When these prodigies
> Do so conjointly meet, let not men say,
> 'These are their reasons, they are natural,'
> For I believe they are portentous things
> Unto the climate that they point upon.
> (I, iii, 28–32)

SPRING

Sol in Aries
Marche

Now windy marche doth wittnesse winter worne
And blooming budds doth courage men to toyle
some graffe ther trees some sowe ther barly corne
some eke prepare by warrs ther foes to spoyle

6
The Globe Rises

From Shakespeare's new lodgings near the Clink prison in the
parish of St Saviour's in Southwark it was just a few minutes' stroll
to the construction site of the Globe. It is likely that through late
winter and early spring he kept a close eye on progress there.
Whether it was the relief of working in a playhouse free of the
ghosts of the past or the sense of potential that the new theatre
offered, the Globe clearly had a lot to do with the great surge of
energy and creativity at this moment in Shakespeare's career. His
surroundings could only have contributed to this vitality. Located
outside the jurisdiction of the London authorities, Bankside had a
reputation for free-wheeling independence. It was notorious for its
criminality, prostitution, inns, theatres and blood-sports – both
bull- and bear-baiting. Puritan preachers called it a 'licensed stew'.
Some of this local colour began finding its way into Shakespeare's
plays. Everyone in the audience at *Troilus and Cressida* knew what

Interior of the Swan Theatre in 1596, giving an idea of how
the Globe might have looked

Shakespeare meant when he mentioned 'some galled goose of Winchester' (V, x, 54): a syphilitic Bankside prostitute. And Antonio's advice to Sebastian in *Twelfth Night* that it was 'best to lodge' in 'the south suburbs, at the Elephant' (III, iii, 39) – a local brothel converted to an inn – would also have produced a knowing smile.

In his new neighbourhood, Shakespeare would have found himself rubbing elbows with watermen (who made up a quarter of all workers in St Saviour's) rather than with the merchants and musicians of St Helen's in upmarket Bishopsgate. Southwark was a community in transition. Its population was swelling, tenements were going up all around, and the streets lining the Thames and leading from London Bridge were crammed. But a hundred yards from the Thames, Southwark took on a more bucolic appearance, and to the south and west were fields, farms, ponds and scattered marshland.

Because of his proximity to the Globe site and because decisions about stage design constrained the kinds of scenes he could write, Shakespeare was probably consulted at various points during the theatre's construction. Though its external dimensions were necessarily identical to the Theatre's, much else about it – the direction that its stage faced in relation to the afternoon sun, trapdoors, the balcony, special machinery for descents, the backstage, and stage doors for entrances and exits – could be customized to suit the actors' and their resident playwright's needs. The only document to survive about the property during the spring of 1599 (dated 16 May and in Latin), speaks of a newly built house with a garden 'in the occupation of William Shakespeare and others'. Whether this 'house' refers to the Globe, still under construction, or more likely to another dwelling on the two-parcel site, remains unclear; but this slender piece of evidence suggests that Shakespeare played a visible role in the new venture.

By spring, with the arrival of longer thaws, it was obvious that the soggy property off Maiden Lane that had been leased so hurriedly back in December was far from ideal for a playhouse. No wonder, then, that a year later the Lord Admiral would justify relocating his playing company from the adjacent Rose to the northern suburbs on the grounds that the site of the Rose was 'very noisome' – that is, unpleasant, even noxious – 'for resort of people in the winter time'. As Ben Jonson later observed, the low-lying Bankside land, on which the Globe also sat, better suited the defensive terrain of a 'fort'. The Globe, Jonson adds, was 'flanked with a ditch and forced out of a marsh'. Fortunately for the Chamberlain's Men, Elizabethan playgoers don't seem to have been particularly fussy about muck and smells.

Had Shakespeare visited the construction site in late spring, he would have stepped over the newly dug foundation trenches and found himself within a large-scale version of the shape Prospero would later draw onstage in *The Tempest*, where the stage direction reads: 'They all enter the circle which Prospero had made, and there stand charmed' (V, i, 57). The master carpenter Peter Street had carefully measured the exact dimensions of the Theatre's foundations after the timber structure had been dismantled. Once the location and centre-point of the Globe had been decided upon, Street took his surveyor's line and, probably sprinkling lime to indicate where the exterior wall would stand, marked off a ring with a diameter of seventy-two feet. The charmed circle stopped there. It was agreed upon that, unlike the Rose, the stage at the Globe would be entirely in afternoon shadow. Playgoers rather than actors would have the sun in their eyes; they'd have to squint at times, but they'd feel warmer.

The Chamberlain's Men probably hoped to be able to move to the Globe by June, since Peter Street wouldn't have to build the frame from scratch. They were still paying rent at the Curtain through late April (Simon Forman writes of going to the Curtain three times that month). Because its foundations could not have been dug much before April, it was increasingly clear that the

Globe couldn't open before late July. The reason for the delay was an extended cold spell. March, April, and May had been dry – which ordinarily would have accelerated the construction schedule – but, John Stow records, they had also been unseasonably cold, mocking the almanac's forecast of the arrival of 'goodly pleasant weather' by the first new moon in April.

Raising the Globe's frame could only take place after the foundation work was completed. The late cold spell brought frost, and frost was the bane of labourers who had to break through the foot or so of frozen ground to excavate the foundation and prevent frost heave before sinking elm piles and filling the shallow trenches with limestone and pebbles for drainage. It was also the enemy of the bricklayers who then took over, constructing out of bricks and mortar the foundation plinth, a short, squat wall rising a foot above the ground level of each of the two roughly concentric rings of the multi-sided structure. The plinth was needed to keep the groundsills or bottom-most layer of timber from rotting. Because frost compromised the bond holding bricks and mortar together, it would have been foolhardy – and unsound Tudor building practice – to begin laying the brick foundation until the risk of freezing weather was safely past. Twenty-first-century builders faced with such conditions might pour antifreeze into the mix to prevent the bond holding the bricks together from disintegrating. Elizabethan builders simply had to wait for warmer temperatures if they wanted to ensure, in the words of a contemporary theatre contract, that there be a 'good sure and strong foundation of piles, brick, lime, and sand'.

Londoners learned first-hand of the dangers of shoddy construction in overcrowded playing spaces in August 1599. Thirty to forty people were injured and five killed – including, John Chamberlain reports, 'two . . . good handsome whores' – when a crammed house on St John Street in London's north-west suburbs collapsed while a 'puppet play' was being performed. There had been an earlier disaster in 1583 at the Paris Garden bear-baiting ring in Southwark, when too many spectators packed the amphitheatre: the gallery that 'compassed the yard round about was so shaken at the foundation that it fell as it were in a moment flat to the ground'. Eight people were crushed to death and many others injured. As far as those involved in raising the Globe were concerned, it was better to wait until the risk of frost was past, and the foundations of their future playhouse and prosperity could be secure.

William Shepherd, who was probably brought in by Street to lay the foundations of the Globe, couldn't have waited too long to finish the work. While the weather so far had remained unseasonably dry, spring would bring rains and flooding – as it did in late May, when, John Stow reports, on Whitsunday, London was inundated with 'great rain, and high waters, the like of long time had not been seen'. When the Thames overflowed its banks it ran downhill towards the building site. Even thirty years later, when the Globe site was drained by ditches along its northern and southern boundaries, the land was still subject to flooding at spring tides. The window between frost and flood in which the Globe foundations could be built that spring was a narrow one.

Shakespeare and his fellow sharers faced other problems this spring, including the ongoing legal battle with Giles Allen over the dismantling of the Theatre. One can only imagine how furious Allen must have been when he returned to where the Theatre had stood and found it gone, the grass trampled, his field littered with mounds of plaster and shattered tile. The first legal action had taken place at Westminster on 20 January, when Allen, pursuing his case with 'rigour and extremity', sued Peter Street in the King's Bench for trespassing and damages. Street didn't need this kind of trouble and it would have fallen to the Burbages and their partners to pay for the builder's defence. And so began what both sides

understood was a complicated game. Allen may have guessed that
the Burbages would counter with a lawsuit in the Court of
Requests, even as they may have anticipated that Allen would then
respond with another lawsuit at the King's Bench. Both sides
knew that, if all else failed, Allen could always cry foul and take
things to the Star Chamber (which in fact he would). The last
thing that the Chamberlain's Men needed was for Allen to delay
or halt Street's progress; and even if they were to triumph sooner
or later, legal costs were mounting.

The growing number of rival playing companies was another
worry. The Admiral's Men continued to play at the Rose; and
there was no guarantee that the Swan would remain off-limits to a
permanent playing company. It wouldn't be easy selling out the
Globe with three active theatres (plus bear-baiting) on Bankside.
Meanwhile, the owners of the Boar's Head Inn, just outside London's western boundary, had invested heavily in transforming their
playing space into a full-scale theatrical venue by summer; and as
soon as the Chamberlain's Men vacated the Curtain, some hungry
itinerant company was sure to move in.

More troubling still was word that, after a decade's hiatus, the
boys of St Paul's would shortly resume playing for public audiences
at the Cathedral. And if he had not done so already, Henry Evans
would soon approach the Burbage brothers to see if he could rent
their indoors Blackfriars theatre for another boys' company. It had
sat unused since adult playing had been banned there in 1596.
Within a year the deal was done: the benefits of the steady rent for
the heavily indebted Burbages outweighed the risk of losing customers to this second children's company. Shakespeare's subsequent complaint – in lines later added to *Hamlet*, that 'children . . .
are now the fashion' and that boy players so 'carry it away' that they
threaten the Globe, 'Hercules and his load too' – suggests that
Shakespeare himself was considerably less enthusiastic about this
arrangement (II, ii, 341–62). As theatres popped up like mush-

rooms, new entrepreneurs tried to cash in on what must have been seen as a lucrative business. Shakespeare may have heard around this time that the printer John Wolfe had plans – as Middlesex court records for the following April indicate – 'to erect and build a playhouse in Nightingale Lane near East Smithfield' not far from the Tower of London.

In the face of all this unexpected competition, Shakespeare and his fellow investors must have wondered what had happened to the Privy Council's year-old decree that only they and the Admiral's Men would be allowed to perform in London. Like the Council's earlier threat to tear down London's theatres, it looked to be more honoured in the breach than the observance. The decision to invest in the Globe must have depended, in some measure, on this promise of a duopoly, and, as a result, the explosion in the number of competing playhouses must have been especially demoralizing. There simply weren't enough spectators to go round. Now competition for new plays to supplement Shakespeare's offerings would be even stiffer. Expansion also meant the potential dilution of quality in the fare offered. Innovation – from all-boy companies to aristocrats dabbling at play-writing – was a dangerous thing for a veteran, protected company like the Chamberlain's Men. The sooner the Globe was up, the sooner Shakespeare could offer plays there that set a new standard and attracted a regular, charmed clientele.

There was greater pressure than ever, then, to distinguish the Chamberlain's Men from their rivals. No other company could match their experience – so it's not surprising that Shakespeare committed himself to writing plays that showcased his company's depth. *Julius Caesar* is exemplary in this regard, requiring strong performances by four adult actors playing the parts of Brutus, Caesar, Cassius and Antony. Throughout 1599 Shakespeare also seems to have gone out of his way to showcase a pair of leading boy actors in his company (whose names are unfortunately unknown). One of

them seems to have specialized in playing romantic leads, the other
both younger and older women. Consider the extraordinary pairs
of roles Shakespeare wrote for them in a little over a year, beginning
with Beatrice and Hero in *Much Ado* and Katharine of France and
Alice in *Henry the Fifth*. In *Julius Caesar* Shakespeare created for
them another pair of sterling roles, Portia and Calphurnia. Most
audiences remember Portia's famous lines about showing proof of
her constancy to Brutus, when she reveals how she gave herself 'a
voluntary wound / Here, in the thigh' (II, i, 301–2); but it is her first
and longer speech that reveals how much confidence Shakespeare
must have had in one young actor in particular, and how this
speech, whose difficult rhythms, wit, gestures and shifts in tone,
captures both Portia's character and the story of her marriage:

> You've ungently, Brutus,
> Stole from my bed. And yesternight, at supper,
> You suddenly arose, and walked about,
> Musing and sighing, with your arms across,
> And when I asked you what the matter was,
> You stared upon me with ungentle looks.
> I urged you further; then you scratched your head
> And too impatiently stamped with your foot.
> Yet I insisted, yet you answered not,
> But with an angry wafture of your hand
> Gave sign for me to leave you. So I did,
> Fearing to strengthen that impatience
> Which seemed too much enkindled, and withal
> Hoping it was but an effect of humour,
> Which sometime hath his hour with every man.
> It will not let you eat, nor talk, nor sleep,
> And could it work so much upon your shape
> As it hath much prevailed on your condition,
> I should not know you, Brutus. Dear my lord,
> Make me acquainted with your cause of grief.
>   (II, i, 238–57)

Shakespeare may have realized, watching the pair of boys handle such challenging roles, that they were capable of handling even more taxing ones, for he would next reward them with the extraordinary parts of Rosalind and Celia in *As You Like It* followed by those of Ophelia and Gertrude in *Hamlet*.

By early May the Globe was finally rising. Once the foundation work was finished, Street's carpenters and sawyers took over the construction site for ten weeks or so. Shakespeare and his fellow investors had to reach deeper into their pockets, for these expensive labourers had to be paid weekly and fresh supplies were constantly required. Even as unused sand, bricks and lime were hauled away, horse-drawn carts manoeuvred down Maiden Lane or along paths leading down from docks along the nearby Thames, loaded with seasoned lumber for the rafters, joists, rakes and floorboards as well as with fir poles for scaffolding. Sawyers would have already picked a convenient spot to set up a sawpit to cut these pieces to the carpenters' specifications; and if any of the main oak pieces of the Theatre frame had been damaged when being dismantled and moved, now was the time for teams of sawyers to cut their replacements and finish them off with side axe and adze.

What followed would be by far the most challenging stage of construction. The pressure now was on the master carpenter, Peter Street, who, in determining how the parts of the reassembled frame would fit together, somehow had to keep in mind the relationship of the floor sills (which rested on the foundations) to the wall plates (the topmost part of the frame on which the roofing sat) thirty feet above. Measurements were especially tricky because no two pieces of hand-cut timber were alike, and yet each one had to dovetail perfectly with all those connected to it. Each one of the towering back posts, for example, was fitted to twenty-six other timbers on three of its four sides. Getting the sequence right – and all the workers in place to execute it – required the skill of a chess master who could play out in his mind dozens of moves ahead.

It helped that Street had been responsible for dismantling the Theatre; and it's likely that the dozen or so carpenters who had worked under his direction at that time were now employed at the Globe. Street may also have brought down from Windsor the same crew of carpenters that he employed a year later at this stage at the Fortune. 'Erecting', as this stage of construction was called in the trade, was not to be left to inexperienced hands. Even illiterate carpenters could easily identify the familiar set of long and ornate slashes that were gouged in the wood, still to be found on Tudor frame buildings (and even on timber-frame buildings raised in North America by their descendants), marks that all of them had learned early on in their apprenticeship indicating where sections were to be joined.

Sections of the extremely heavy pre-assembled outer wall frames were hoisted into place first, and then, as they were held in place, cross frames and curved braces added for stability. Once the inner wall frames and floor frames were slotted into position, joined just as they had been at the Theatre, the carpenters were able to move the scaffolding and repeat the procedure at each of the twenty or so bays. If the timber had arrived in good enough condition, and not too many new pieces had to be hewn from scratch in the sawpits, this stage of construction would have gone very quickly. The rising skeletal frame of the Globe was a new addition to the silhouette of Bankside and let Londoners know that playing there would begin in the summer. Henslowe, who had to pass the Globe every day on his walk to the ageing Rose, knew that his theatre's days were numbered.

Time lost to frost would also have to be made up in the next and most laborious stage of construction: 'setting up'. New joists, floorboards, rafters, partitions and seating all had to be measured, cut and fitted. The staircases, the tiring house and the five-foot-high stage itself had to be knocked together as well. Fresh loads of seasoned lumber continually arrived as Street pressed his regular suppliers. The torrential rains and flooding at the end of May were a setback, but the work must have gone on after that at a torrid pace.

The Globe was the first London theatre built by actors for actors, and Shakespeare and his fellow player-sharers would have worked with Street closely during the setting up, especially on last-minute decisions about the tiring house and stage. Heminges was probably responsible for handling the finances, while the Burbage brothers, who had watched their father, a joiner by profession, supervise the building of the Theatre (and more recently the indoor stage at Blackfriars), no doubt drew on their experience to ensure that Street built exactly the kind of stage they and their fellow investors wanted. They brought a good deal of practical experience to the task – and they knew the strengths and weaknesses of each of London's playhouses, having performed in all of them. Only a playwright who knew something about construction problems and cost overruns could have recently (in *The Second Part of Henry the Fourth*) written:

> When we mean to build,
> We first survey the plot, then draw the model;
> And when we see the figure of the house,
> Then must we rate the cost of the erection,
> Which if we find outweighs ability,
> What do we then but draw anew the model
> In fewer offices, or at least desist
> To build at all?
>   (I, iii, 41–8)

Once the setting up was completed, new teams of skilled workers began to appear on the site: glaziers (for the tiring-house windows), plumbers (for a lead gutter), smiths (for doors and windows), thatchers and plasterers (for the roof and exterior), and painters (for interior details). Specialists also had to be brought in to handle the marbling of the pair of wooden columns onstage, a skill that took years to master. The exterior had to be plastered with 'lathe, lime and hair' – completely covering the timber frame, so that from a distance the building looked as if it was made of stone, perhaps calling to mind a Roman theatre – a fitting touch for a play about Julius Caesar; and, unhappy as the idea might seem to us, the Chamberlain's Men may also have asked Street to fence the lower gallery (as he would at the Fortune) with 'strong iron pikes' in order to prevent those who only paid to stand from slipping over the railing into the more expensive seating in the galleries.

As Street's workmen struggled to make up for lost time, London's fickle weather finally cooperated: June and July were for the most part hot and dry – perfect for painting and plastering. If the Chamberlain's Men's luck held, it now looked as though playing could begin, even if all the detail work wasn't completed, sometime in late July. As it happens, when Street contracted with Henslowe the following January to build the Fortune, he promised to finish the job by 25 July; there's a strong chance that they agreed on this date based on Street's recent experience at the Globe. Shakespeare, eager to have a new play in hand to inaugurate the theatre, had probably begun writing *Julius Caesar* around March and may have been ready to hand the play over to the Master of the Revels for official approval by May. *Julius Caesar* would certainly be among the earliest of the offerings at the Globe, if not the first.

7
Book Burning

While Shakespeare could count on his fellow investors to share the headaches of construction delays and Allen's lawsuits, the burden of opening the Globe with a brilliant play was his alone. His decision about what kind of play to write after *Henry the Fifth* was shaped by countless factors, prominent among them an unfolding political drama in the publishing world.

An Elizabethan curious about the ruler who had deposed Richard II would have found two titles on the subject in London's bookstalls this spring: *The First Part of the Life and Reign of King Henry IV* and *The History of Henry the Fourth*. One was Shakespeare's, the other written by a thirty-five-year-old lawyer named John Hayward, though it wasn't immediately clear to book-buyers who had written which. Adding to the confusion, it was Hayward's and not Shakespeare's book that was called 'The First Part' – though only Shakespeare had written a sequel. Shakespeare's

Henry the Fourth was selling well. The print run of the two editions of the 1598 first quarto had sold out rapidly and in 1599 a third edition was printed (of all his plays only *Richard the Second* had sold this well). But it was Hayward's book, not Shakespeare's, that everyone was talking about. Its publisher, John Wolfe (the same man who tried to build a theatre in East Smithfield), bragged that 'no book ever sold better'.

Before Hayward turned his manuscript over to his publisher he had had to secure a licence to have it printed. Concerned about how censors might respond, he had omitted a dedication and preface. Authors could apparently choose which official examined their books and Hayward may have heard that Samuel Harsnett was more lax than most. The custom, according to Harsnett, was for 'the author himself to present the book unto the examiner and to acquaint him with his scope and purpose'. But Hayward had evaded this direct questioning, persuading a friend to present the book to Harsnett on his behalf. Harsnett later admitted that he hadn't examined the book very carefully, looking no further than the first page before giving it his approval. Hoping to drive up sales and capitalize on contemporary events, John Wolfe persuaded Hayward to add a preface and dedicate the book to Essex, 'he being a martial man and going into Ireland, and the book treating of Irish causes'. There were many dedications to the popular and generous Earl around this time, but none quite so daring: 'You are great indeed, both in present judgment and in expectation of future time.' These were not reassuring words to those who feared Essex's ambitions.

Hayward's history went on sale in early February 1599. By the end of the month, with sales brisk and the book already much talked of, Essex wrote to Archbishop Whitgift, suggesting that Hayward's dedication be looked into. It's not clear why Essex did so. Perhaps, in the midst of tense negotiations with the Queen over his demands for Ireland, the last thing he wanted was to antagonize her. Or perhaps he had waited before contacting Whitgift in order to have it both ways – allowing Hayward's dedication to attract notice while seeming to distance himself from it. Sceptics like Francis Bacon believed that Essex knew full well 'that forbidden things are most sought after'. A year or so later, Essex's enemies insisted that he had enjoyed Hayward's book and accused him of being 'often present at the playing thereof, and with great applause giving countenance to it'. It's impossible to know just what is meant here by the frequent 'playing' of Hayward's history, which had to have taken place in February or early March, before Essex left for Ireland. Were there staged readings at Essex House of dramatic speeches from Hayward's history? Was Hayward's work confused with a play on the same subject, privately performed for Essex's circle? Or was the accusation imaginary and fantastic, just the kind of thing that fed Essex's paranoia?

Whatever the case, by late March, after half of the thousand-copy print run had sold, Archbishop Whitgift instructed the Stationers' Company to tear out the dedication to Essex from all unsold copies. Predictably, the Archbishop's order only heightened interest in the book and the rest of the print run quickly sold out. In early March, John Chamberlain wrote to Dudley Carleton that there 'hath been much descanting about' Hayward's book, especially 'why such a story should come out at this time, and many exceptions taken, especially to the epistle which was a short thing in Latin dedicated to the Earl of Essex'. He went on to tell Carleton that 'there was a commandment that it should be cut out of the book', but did his best to get his friend a copy of the offending dedication: 'I have got you a transcript of it that you may pick out the offence if you can. For my part, I can find no such bugswords, but that everything is as it is taken.'

As Chamberlain's letter makes clear, the big question on everyone's mind was: 'Why should such a story come out at this time?' The 'descanting' or political analysis he mentions eventually led the authorities to ask a host of related questions. Did Hayward 'pretend to write a history past but intend to point at this very time'? 'Who made the preface to the reader?' 'What was the true cause of setting forth this single story?' 'What moved him to maintain . . . that it might be lawful for the subject to depose the king?' And why did his book presuppose 'that there should be ill success in Ireland'?

By Easter, Wolfe reports, with 'people calling for' the book 'exceedingly', Hayward submitted to his publisher a revised and expanded text, including a new preface that aggressively challenged 'the many imputations and secret senses' attributed to his work by those Hayward dismissively calls the 'deep searchers of our time'; but one didn't have to search very deeply to find obvious similarities between the reigns of Richard II and Elizabeth I, especially when it came to 'benevolences' (a punishing form of taxation) and the dangers to the state of a childless ruler. The similarities to Elizabeth's disastrous Irish policies were especially hard to miss. Then as now, 'The naked and fugitive Irish have shaken off our shackles and glutted themselves upon us, with massacres and spoils.' Queen Elizabeth saw the parallels all too clearly, and famously said, 'I am Richard the Second, know ye not that?' The authorities were concerned that Londoners might draw the same conclusions as their rebellious ancestors had two centuries earlier, when they had supported a charismatic aristocrat's overthrow of a childless monarch who had taxed them ruthlessly and mismanaged Ireland.

Just as few playgoers at a performance of *Richard the Second* or *The First Part of Henry the Fourth* would have been as knowledgeable as Hayward about how Shakespeare transformed his sources, few readers in the early months of 1599 would have grasped as readily as Shakespeare what Hayward had accomplished in his account of how Henry overthrew King Richard. Shakespeare knew all the chronicles that Hayward drew on and would have immediately seen what Hayward invented or exaggerated. Along with Plutarch's *Lives* (his main source for *Julius Caesar*), Hayward's best-seller was undoubtedly one of the books that Shakespeare was reading closely this winter.

Shakespeare didn't need to read far into Hayward's history to see that he was an avid theatregoer, for the set speeches in the work had great dramatic intensity. Hayward was one of the first English historians since Sir Thomas More to understand how invented speeches made the past come alive and there are a number of points where his work reads more like a prose play than a chronicle history. As the words of his title – 'The Life and Reign' – made clear, Hayward was interested in character and he broke new ground in showing the extent to which history was shaped by personality. Here's Henry exhorting his followers after agreeing to depose King Richard (lineated as rough verse, it's easy to see what an actor could do with it):

If we prevail, we shall recover again our liberty.
If we lose, our state shall be no worse than now it is.
And since we must need perish,
Either deservingly or without cause,
It is more honourable to put ourselves
Upon the adventure either to win our lives or die for desert.
And although our lives were safe, which indeed are not,
Yet to abandon the state and sleep still in this slavery
Were a point of negligence and sloth.

Hayward had missed his calling. It's easy to imagine dramatic speeches like this 'played' by professional actors for Essex's appreciative followers, stymied as they were by rival factions at court and frustrated by the parsimonious and ageing Queen.

If Shakespeare had any doubt about how indebted Hayward was to his own work, he needed to look no further than Hayward's insistence on Henry's pursuit of popularity with the common folk:

[Henry] for his part was not negligent to uncover the head, to bow the body, to stretch forth the hand to every mean person, and to use all other complements of popular behaviour, where with the minds of the common multitude are much delighted and drawn ... The standings in all the streets where he passed were taken up to behold him, and the unable multitude, who otherwise could not, yet by their good words, wishes, and wills did testify unto him their loving affection.

Hayward knew his Shakespeare, for Henry's pursuit of popularity had been Shakespeare's invention, not to be found in any source other than his play's innovative depiction of a crowd-pleasing Henry, encapsulated in the passage in *Richard the Second* where York describes Henry's entry into London:

> You would have thought the very windows spake,
> So many greedy looks of young and old
> Through casements darted their desiring eyes
> Upon his visage, and that all the walls
> With painted imagery had said at once,
> 'Jesu preserve thee! Welcome, Bolingbroke!'
> Whilst he, from the one side to the other turning,
> Bareheaded, lower than his proud steed's neck,
> Bespake them thus: 'I thank you, countrymen.'
> And thus still doing, thus he passed along.
>   (V, ii, 12–21)

As he read Hayward's best-seller, what made Shakespeare really sit up and take notice wasn't the provocative dedication, the implied comparison between Richard II and Elizabeth, the allusions to Ireland, or even what was lifted from his own version of the story, so much as Hayward's sense of how history worked, an approach closely identified at this time with the dark world-view of the Roman writer Tacitus. By comparison, it made his own histories feel old-fashioned and a bit tame. Until now, it was Shakespeare who had consistently made other writers' work feel dated, not the other way around. Even when Shakespeare's plays had staged the deposition and murder of God's anointed, they still couldn't be seen as advocating regicide (except when it came to the king deposed by the Tudors, Richard III). Whatever his own beliefs, Shakespeare did not – and, if he wanted to see his plays staged and printed, could not – write history that broke quite so radically with a Providential world-view. In the spring of 1599 he had to wonder whether these unspoken rules were changing.

What little we know about what ordinary Elizabethans thought about their leaders survives from trials in which those who criticized the government were punished. So we can only guess about the extent to which the ideas in Hayward's *History* resonated with what people were thinking or beginning to say aloud. On 23 February 1599, for example, Joan Bottinge of Chiddingstone told Elizabeth Harris that things wouldn't improve until 'the rich men's throats were cut and then poor men should be rich'. She added that she 'did pray up rising and down lying to God to take away the Queen's Majesty, and that she would be one that should help to cut the rich men's throats . . . and help the Queen's enemies'. Harris reported this to the authorities and Bottinge was found guilty and sentenced to hang. A couple of months later, Mary Bunton of Hucking was equally blunt, declaring: 'I care not a turd for the Queen nor her precepts.' She was sentenced to be put in the stocks with a paper above her head (probably detailing her crime) and then whipped. When ordinary Englishwomen could question the Elizabethan regime so brazenly, the kind of history found in Hayward was seen, in Queen Elizabeth's own verdict of the *History*, as 'a seditious prelude to put into the people's heads boldness and faction'.

In the late sixteenth century Tacitus had become a byword for an unflinching view of history. Tacitus, who wrote of the dark days of Nero's rule, knew how treacherous politics could be. His republican and radical leanings also set his work apart from more moralizing Roman historians such as Plutarch. Tacitus' writings were eventually rediscovered and newly appreciated in the decades following the Reformation in a strife-torn Europe that for many observers resembled the ruthless ancient world he depicted. It took a few years for the cult of Tacitus to reach England after the great Continental scholar Justus Lipsius first edited his works in 1574, having found in Tacitus 'a theatre of everyday life'. Sir Philip Sidney (who corresponded with Lipsius) played an important role in importing Tacitus, though Sidney was also aware of the dangers of this kind of history, warning his younger brother Robert to beware of the 'venom of wickedness' he would encounter reading Tacitus. Sir Philip steered his brother to Henry Savile, the Oxford classicist (and Latin Secretary to the Queen) who in 1591 published the first English version of Tacitus' writings, dedicating it to Elizabeth, and making available to a far wider readership this history of the dark days of Rome. When Savile's translation was first published it may have seemed more relevant to France, torn by civil war, than to England; but by the time it was reprinted in 1598, things at home looked a lot different.

Savile attracted an eager following that included the Greek scholar Henry Cuffe (a radical type whom Essex pulled out of the ivory tower and appointed as his personal secretary). Among other young thinkers and writers drawn into this Tacitean orbit were Francis Bacon, William Camden, Henry Wotton, William Cornwallis and Richard Grenewey (who rendered most of what Savile had left untranslated into English in 1598, in a text that included both his own and Savile's translations and a dedication flatteringly comparing Essex to the Roman commander Vespasian).

According to Ben Jonson, Essex himself had ghostwritten the preface to Savile's translation. For the ambitious men in Essex's circle whose advancement was thwarted in the late 1590s, Tacitus must have sounded like the great diagnostician of the age. If Essex were indeed the author of that preface, he would have been responsible for arguing that in this 'story thou shalt see all the miseries of a torn and declining state'. Tacitus' account of Rome under Nero is a portrait of a weak monarchy in which principle has given way to political scheming, the state crumbling from within. Essex also found attractive – because it suited his sense of injured merit – Tacitus' juxtaposition of political wranglers with men of action and honour. While Tacitus provided Essex with political and military guidelines, he also offered a powerful alternative to writers and readers who found moralizing history increasingly discredited.

If Shakespeare was drawn to Tacitus it was the briefest of flirtations. He may well have glanced at the 1591 edition of Savile's translation when depicting the disastrous reign of Henry VI, especially the painful scene in which a son kills his father in battle. There's also a chance that he picked up the 1598 English edition of Tacitus while writing *Henry the Fifth*. The debt occurs in the scene in which Henry walks incognito among his troops on the eve of battle, a scene that may in part be inspired by one that Grenewey had just translated from Tacitus. There, a Roman leader named Germanicus, eager to 'sound the soldiers' mind', went out disguised at night 'in secret and unknown places' to observe the 'watch'. He went 'from one place to another, stood listening at the tents' and (far more than Shakespeare's Henry) was reassured by his experience.

Leafing through Hayward's *History*, Shakespeare, with just a passing familiarity with the translations, could not have missed Hayward's explicit borrowings from recent English renderings of Tacitus. Even a summary of what Hayward lifted from Tacitus would run to a dozen pages. Years later Francis Bacon recorded how an infuriated Queen Elizabeth refused to believe that Hayward had written the *History* himself and was convinced 'that it had some more mischievous author, and said, with great indignation, that she would have him racked to produce his author'. She then asked Bacon if he could 'find any places in it that might be drawn within case of treason'. Bacon wittily responded, "'For treason surely I found none, but for felony very many." And when her Majesty hastily asked me "Wherein?" I told her, "the author had committed very apparent theft; for he had taken most of the sentences of Cornelius Tacitus, and translated them into English, and put them into his text.'"

Hayward's Tacitean history arrived on the heels of a revival of another popular classical genre, satire, which similarly courted censorship by ridiculing the follies of the age. Shakespeare faced a difficult situation. He had to decide, and fairly quickly, whether the authorities were now loosening restrictions on what could be said, or, alternatively, whether a crackdown that could affect his own livelihood was imminent. He could play it safe, but doing so did not come without risks. By avoiding writing about the things that his fellow Elizabethans were excited by he'd lose his audience to writers whose works spoke more directly to their concerns.

Shakespeare had lived through enough official and seemingly arbitrary acts of suppression to know that another would come soon enough if his fellow writers pursued their current course. Of all the major playwrights of the 1590s he alone had managed to avoid a major confrontation with those in power. He had seen the innocent Thomas Kyd broken by torture on the rack, Christopher Marlowe possibly assassinated, and Ben Jonson imprisoned for his role in *The Isle of Dogs*. His rivals were now either dead or impoverished. Genius also meant knowing what you could get away with writing. In the end, he chose to write about the problem of censorship rather than, like Hayward and the satirists, inviting it.

No play by Shakespeare explores censorship and silencing so deeply as the one he was writing during these months, *Julius Caesar*. In one of the few scenes that is Shakespeare's invention an angry mob fatally mistakes a poet for a conspiring politician. 'Cinna the Poet' is accosted by a crowd of Plebeians who surround and interrogate him. He does his best to humour and distract the mob, but when he tells them his name – Cinna – he is lost. A plebeian yells, 'Tear him to pieces! He's a conspirator!', obviously confusing him with the Cinna who had stabbed Caesar. The poet desperately repeats, 'I am Cinna the Poet, I am Cinna the Poet!' It makes no difference. Another rioter chants, 'Tear him for his bad verses, tear him for his bad verses!' Though Cinna again insists, 'I am not Cinna the conspirator,' his words cannot save him. That same rioter sways the crowd, saying, 'It is no matter, his name's Cinna. Pluck but his name out of his heart, and turn him going' (III, iii, 4–36).

In a grim replay of the scene in which Caesar is hacked to death in the Capitol, an innocent poet is savagely murdered onstage. It's hard not to conclude that the haze of Elizabethan censorship hanging in the air at this time seeps into the play at such moments; but it's also hard not to wonder at how little sympathy Shakespeare shows either for Cinna the Poet or for the other writer who appears in the play and gets caught in the maw of politics, the unnamed poet who tries to insert himself into the political action by attempting to reconcile the feuding Brutus and Cassius. When Cassius tries to excuse the poet's intrusion, explaining that's what poets foolishly do – ''tis his fashion' – Brutus will have none of it:

> I'll know his humour when he knows his time.
> What should the wars do with these jigging fools?
> Companion, hence!
>   (IV, iii, 135–7)

The message seems to be that it's a wise poet who knows his place and time, who doesn't go looking for trouble in a dangerous political world. As Ben Jonson, no stranger to trouble, put it a few months later in *Every Man Out of His Humour*:

>   take heed,
> The days are dangerous, full of exception,
> And men are grown impatient of reproof.
>   (I, i, 123)

Even as censors and sympathizers were combing Hayward for 'bugswords' or coded terms, Shakespeare may have been reflecting on other aspects of Hayward's *History* that had been largely overlooked. One was its emphasis on a political aspirant's pursuit of popularity. The meaning of the word 'popularity', familiar to us today in the sense of 'being admired by many', has undergone a sea-change since Shakespeare's day. In the mid-sixteenth century it was used to describe a radical form of democracy that was the opposite of tyranny. Then, in the late 1590s, a new sense of the word emerged, having to do with courting popular favour. Shakespeare was one of the first to employ it in this sense. It appears only twice in his work, within a very narrow time frame, first in *The First Part of Henry the Fourth* (1596) and then again in *Henry the Fifth*. By now, this highly charged notion of 'popularity' had become loaded, and the word itself best left unspoken by playwrights wary of censors; but the issues underlying this complex term nonetheless suffuse the play he was now writing, for Shakespeare returns to the problem of popularity in *Julius Caesar* relentlessly – from the opening scene of holiday and triumph to Casca's eagerness to enlist the support of a Brutus who 'sits high in all the people's hearts' (I, iii, 157), to the posthumous reading of Caesar's will and his extraordinary generosity to the commoners. Shakespeare was well aware, as Hayward was learning to his peril, that popularity was dangerous, made all the more so by Elizabeth's and Cecil's deep anxiety about Essex's cultivation of the people.

It was Francis Bacon who had recently begged Essex to banish popularity from his thoughts, 'to take all occasions to speak against popularity and popular causes vehemently'. It was Bacon who criticized Essex for embracing public displays of piety, 'knowing there were no such strong and drawing cords of popularity, as religion'; and it was Bacon again, a few years later, who wrote a biographical sketch (in Latin and never intended for publication) that acknowledged that 'greatness of mind he undoubtedly had in a very high degree; yet such as aspired more after personal aggrandizement than merit towards the public. For he referred everything to himself, and was himself the true and perfect centre of all his own actions.' His great flaw, Bacon concludes, was his 'desire of popularity'. But the subject of Bacon's biographical sketch wasn't Essex, as one might expect, but Julius Caesar. From the Chorus to *Henry the Fifth* that compares Essex to a conquering Caesar to Bacon's unpublished character study – which surely had Essex in mind – the similarity between these aspiring, charismatic, martial men was obvious to many. In *Julius Caesar*, Shakespeare is not so much interested in drawing a one-to-one comparison – that was never his style – but in steeping classical history in contemporary political concerns.

While writing *Julius Caesar*, Shakespeare also paid close attention to those passages in Hayward's *History* that reproduced the language of Continental theorists who sought to justify the overthrow of bad rulers. It was dangerous, for example, for Hayward to have Henry tell his followers that he could not decide 'whether they be termed rebels or subjects' until they made clear that their 'allegiance was bound rather to the state of the realm than the person of the prince'. From a monarchist's perspective, for Hayward to suggest that one could be loyal to the state yet not to its ruler was treasonous; but, like the precise civil lawyer that he was, Hayward had carefully juxtaposed these passages with others that refuted these arguments, point for point. If anything, his work came down on the side of the monarchy. It wasn't Hayward's fault that censors and other 'deep searchers' ignored these royalist counter-arguments. Shakespeare didn't. One of the lessons Shakespeare had confirmed by reading Hayward was the dramatic advantage of juxtaposing competing political arguments, balancing them so neatly that it was impossible to tell in favour of which the scales tipped. He would put the insight to good use as he explored the tragic collision of Brutus and Caesar, individuals who embodied irreconcilable political positions. *Julius Caesar*, then, would repeat the arguments for deposing tyrants, even as it offered powerful arguments for those bitterly opposed to regicide. Shakespeare also understood that, given the nature of Elizabethan censorship, which was far more concerned with the printed word than with what was spoken onstage, there were things that he could get away with that Hayward couldn't.

When the Plebeians gather to hear Brutus' justification for the killing of Caesar, we overhear two of them gossiping: 'This Caesar was a tyrant.' 'That's certain,' the other affirms. 'We are blest that Rome is rid of him' (III, ii, 70–71). The word 'tyrant' and its cognates, so central to republicanism, sound a steady drum beat in the play, reinforcing the view that Caesar was justifiably slain. As early as the first act, Cassius asks: 'And why should Caesar be a tyrant then?' (I, iii, 103). Brutus similarly invokes the language of tyrannicide, leading the fight against 'high-sighted tyranny', while Cinna leads the cry 'Liberty! Freedom! Tyranny is dead' over Caesar's fallen body (II, i, 118; III, i, 78).

Rulers revealed their tyrannical tendencies by how they came to power or by how they exercised it; and one of the most keenly debated issues in Shakespeare's play is whether Caesar is tyrannical in one, the other, or both of these respects. Cassius argues that Caesar is tyrannical in his pursuit of power, wondering aloud that 'this man / Is now become a god', and demanding of Brutus: 'Upon what meat doth this our Caesar feed / That he is grown so great?' (I, ii, 115–16; 149–150). Caesar's suppression of opponents, the frequent comparisons of Brutus to his ancestor Junius Brutus who first banished kings from Rome, and most of all Brutus' conclusion that Caesar is like 'a serpent's egg / Which, hatched, would, as his kind, grow mischievous', and who therefore must be killed 'in the shell' (II, i, 31–4), tilt the play heavily towards the Plebeians' conclusion. A Caesar who speaks of himself in the third person, who considers the Senate his own, and who in his next-to-last words compares himself first to the northern star, which has 'no fellow in the firmament', and then to an immovable Mount Olympus (III, i, 61, 75), was indeed a tyrant, or would have been so if given the chance.

Yet even as Shakespeare carefully constructs this pro-republican case, he just as skilfully undermines it, altering his source material to achieve a neater balance, omitting, for example, Caesar's unlawful appropriation of royal powers and prerogatives. Indeed, Caesar's refusal to place himself first and foremost proves his undoing, for when he is approached by a petitioner intent on warning him about the assassination plot, he insists: 'What touches us ourself shall be last served' (III, i, 8). Even Brutus, for all his moral certitude, admits that he knows 'no personal cause to spurn at him' (II, i, 11). The case against republicanism and legitimate deposition is also reinforced by Shakespeare's portrayal of the conspirators, who, with the exception of Brutus, are more driven by jealousy than principle. Despite Brutus' exhortation that they kill Caesar 'boldly, but not wrathfully', and that they 'carve him as a dish fit for the gods' rather than 'hew him as a carcass fit for hounds' (II, i, 173–5), what we actually see onstage is a savage murder, the conspirators' arms bathed in blood 'Up to the elbows' (III, i, 108). By the end of Antony's funeral oration, the same Plebeians who minutes earlier had called Caesar a tyrant, now remember him as 'royal Caesar' and rush off to set alight the houses of the 'traitors' who assassinated him (III, ii, 245, 255).

One measure of Shakespeare's success in employing this balanced dramatic structure is that four centuries later critics continue to debate whether he sides with or against Brutus and his fellow conspirators. Shakespeare didn't conceive of his tragedy in Aristotelian terms – that is, as a tragedy of the fall of a flawed great man – but rather as a collision of deeply held and irreconcilable principles, embodied in characters who are destroyed when these principles collide. It would take another couple of centuries before Friedrich Hegel in his *Philosophy of Fine Art* described the kind of tragedy Shakespeare was writing, one that hadn't been attempted since works like *Antigone* in the great age of Sophoclean Athens.

What Shakespeare brought to the play was not just cerebral. There's a visceral quality to the play that keeps it from turning into an intellectual exercise – a defect of many other contemporary plays about ancient Rome. It is most palpable in those bloody scenes where the conspirators hack Caesar to death and the Plebeians dismember Cinna the Poet before our eyes. Shakespeare was no stranger to butchery. It's likely that as a youngster he accompanied his father to local butchers to purchase skins for making gloves. One seventeenth-century Stratford tradition even held that Shakespeare had been 'bound apprentice to a butcher' before running off to the London stage; and John Aubrey was told that when Shakespeare 'was a boy he exercised his father's trade, but whenever he killed a calf he would do it in high style and make a speech'. As an adult, when he had to write speeches that conjured the brutality of assassination, his childhood recollections served him well. Perhaps only a talented whittawer's son might liken Caesar's death to that of a slaughtered animal: when Polonius brags in *Hamlet* that in his university days he 'did enact Julius Caesar. I was killed i' th' Capitol; Brutus killed me,' Hamlet replies: 'It was a brute part of him to kill so capital a calf there' (III, ii, 103–6).

Though the unrivalled master of the English history play, Shakespeare nonetheless decided at this time to abandon this comfortable genre and return to the political landscape of classical Rome, which he had previously explored in *Titus Andronicus* and *Lucrece*, two of his most popular works. No doubt the Hayward affair merely nudged Shakespeare in a direction he was already moving. He put away his well-worn copy of Holinshed's *Chronicles*. Hayward's best-seller, its lessons learned, was shelved as well; and Shakespeare buried himself more deeply in North's translation of Plutarch's *Lives*. If others were following Tacitus in writing about the decline and fall of the Roman Empire, he would begin by returning to the starting point of this decline, the moment when the republic was replaced by imperial rule.

Shakespeare's decision to do so reminds us of how intensely politics preoccupied him at this moment. What's too often forgotten, though, is that there's a difference between being fully engaged with politics and history and espousing a particular political view. When it came to the assassination of Julius Caesar, it was especially difficult for writers to disguise their political sympathies, as Shakespeare managed to do: Dante, after all, had sent Brutus to the bowels of Hell, while Milton would praise him as a republican hero – which is another way of saying that Shakespeare's nuanced handling of the assassination at this tense moment was, paradoxically, both daring and cautious. Daring, because, to depict the killing of Julius Caesar at a time of official hypersensitivity about seditious writing, had to be risky. At the same time, his choice of working through Plutarch – who had been largely overlooked as a source by London's professional playwrights – was a careful and canny one. He knew, as did everyone else who was within earshot of the court, that Queen Elizabeth herself had been absorbed in translating Plutarch ('On Curiosity') just a few months earlier. Even as Tacitus leaned towards republicanism, Plutarch was at heart a monarchist. And, it's worth noting, Shakespeare named his play after Caesar (who only appears in a few scenes, and except for his ghost is gone midway through the play), rather than Brutus, hero to republicans, who occupies centre-stage throughout. It was, again, one thing to stage such a play, another to publish it. There would be no quarto editions of this popular play in Shakespeare's lifetime: twenty-four years would pass before English men and women could buy and read *Julius Caesar*.

Shakespeare's main source, Thomas North's translation of Plutarch's *Lives*, had first been published in 1579 by a French immigrant, Thomas Vautrollier. Vautrollier apprenticed Richard Field, who, after his master died, took over the business, and, among other things, published a revised and expanded edition of Plutarch's *Lives* in 1595. Field and Shakespeare had been school-mates in Stratford's grammar school. Their fathers knew each other professionally: Field's was a tanner and Shakespeare's at one point appraised his inventory. The young Field had arrived in London a decade before Shakespeare and may have helped him find his way there. When Shakespeare decided to publish *Venus and Adonis* and *Lucrece* he turned to Field. They were close enough friends for Shakespeare to casually insert Field's name into *Cymbeline*, when the disguised Imogen is asked the name of her master and says that it's 'Richard du Champ' (IV, ii, 380) – that is, Richard Field (Field used to call himself 'Ricardo del Campo' in his Spanish publications). Shakespeare probably worked from a copy of Plutarch given or lent to him by Field, an expensive and beautiful folio that cost a couple of pounds.

Shakespeare had thumbed through a copy of Plutarch's *Lives* as early as 1595: searching for characters' names for *A Midsummer Night's Dream*, he had lifted a handful from its pages. By late 1598 he had begun to read the *Lives* in earnest. *Henry the Fifth* is the first play to bear the marks of that engagement, not just in the obvious ways, such as in Fluellen's digressive comparison of Henry V to Alexander the Great (imitating Plutarch's pairing of Greek and Roman leaders). In *Henry the Fifth* Shakespeare turns towards biography more directly than he had ever done before; and to this end, Plutarch's brief lives made available to him a model for conveying interiority, something he had until now failed to do in a sustained way in his plays. A chasm divides an avenger like Titus Andronicus from Hamlet, or even the self-revelations of Richard III from those of Brutus. Plutarch enabled Shakespeare to bridge that divide.

Reading Plutarch closely also seems to have shaken Shakespeare's preconceptions of Brutus and Caesar – both of whom are mentioned now and again in his earlier plays. These earlier allusions suggest that Shakespeare had not really thought very much about the famous assassination and accepted the commonplace that it was a heinous act. When a decade earlier Queen Margaret in *The Third Part of Henry the Sixth* cast about for an example of something as terrible as the murder of her son (and England's heir), the analogy she drew was to Caesar's death at the conspirators' hands. Shakespeare even seems to have subscribed early in his career to the belief that Brutus was Caesar's illegitimate son and that the assassination had also been an act of patricide: 'Brutus' bastard hand / Stabbed Julius Caesar' (*Second Part of Henry the Sixth*, IV, i, 137–8). But Shakespeare's engagement with Plutarch seems to have shifted his interest in this chapter of Roman history from the familial to the political and made him impatient with his earlier take on the story.

Something extraordinary was beginning to happen as Shakespeare wrote *Julius Caesar* in the spring of 1599. The various strands of politics, character, inwardness, contemporary events, even Shakespeare's own reflections on the act of writing, began to infuse each other. Brutus' and Antony's long funeral orations notwithstanding, Shakespeare was writing in an exceptionally spare and compressed style. The play's 2,500 lines, for a change, were almost all in verse and it was 800 lines shorter than *Henry the Fifth*. It's as if all his energies were self-consciously focused on a new and different kind of invention. Though Shakespeare couldn't resist introducing new words, he does so less frequently here than in any other play (though we have *Julius Caesar* to thank for the first recorded appearances of 'gusty', 'chidden', 'unscorched', 'insuppressive', 'misgiving' and 'honeyless'). In contrast to all the inconsistencies and second thoughts that characterized the writing of *Henry the Fifth*, the streamlined *Julius Caesar* feels as if it was written without interruption in a few short weeks.

The result was a significant breakthrough. Take for example the extraordinary lines of Brutus, deep in thought, as he sets in motion one of the most consequential events in Western history. It is one of Shakespeare's first great soliloquies and conveys a sense of inwardness new to the stage:

Between the acting of a dreadful thing
And the first motion, all the interim is
Like a phantasma or a hideous dream.
The genius and the mortal instruments
Are then in council; and the state of man,
Like to a little kingdom, suffers then
The nature of an insurrection.
  (II, i, 63–9)

Read one way, it's a portrait of a brooding intelligence struggling to understand itself. Read another, it's a justification of tyrannicide even as it recognizes that a mind desperate to commit itself to action resembles nothing so much as insurrection itself. From this point on, even when he is most Stoic and cheerful in his resolve, we can never forget the ghosts that haunt Brutus. Read a third way, it's about Shakespeare's craft, what happens between conception and execution, the transformation of the workings of his mind into the staging or 'acting of a dreadful thing'. It's not too much of a stretch to claim that *Macbeth* was born at this moment, its plot stored away for a few years in the recesses of Shakespeare's imagination:

My thought, whose murder yet is but fantastical,
Shakes so my single state of man,
That function is smothered in surmise,
And nothing is but what is not.
  (I, iii, 140–43)

And, for many at the Globe that spring and summer, the final lines of Brutus' speech also brought to mind a different interim as they anxiously waited for a resolution to the insurrection their state was experiencing in that 'little kingdom' Ireland.

Shakespeare was also discovering that what characters didn't say mattered too. He had curbed the tendency to excess of display in *Henry the Fifth*, whose long speeches are more stirring than revealing. In *Julius Caesar* the most memorable speeches are also the shortest: Caesar's 'Et tu, Brute,' and Brutus' 'Portia is dead,' each sum up a character and a world.

Around mid-May, fifteen hundred copies of the new edition of Hayward's *History* were printed and readied for sale at Wolfe's bookshop in Pope's Head Alley near the Royal Exchange. The Bishop of London, Richard Bancroft, responsible along with the Archbishop of Canterbury for censoring printed works, had had enough. After Whitsunday, on 27 May, Bancroft ordered the second print run seized by the wardens of the Stationers and delivered to his house in Fulham, where he burned the lot of them. Though it was done quietly, everyone, including those clamouring for a copy of the sold-out book, soon learned what had happened. Wolfe could curse the loss of his investment, but he had no recourse. From now on, there would only be one book for sale about Henry IV in London's bookstalls: Shakespeare's.

Hayward's *History* turned out to be kindling for a much larger conflagration. A week later, on the first of June, John Whitgift and Bancroft ordered that more than a dozen other titles be confiscated and burned. The list included, first and foremost, the works of satirists: Joseph Hall's *Biting Satires* and *Virgidemiarum*, John Marston's *The Metamorphosis of Pygmalion's Image* and *The Scourge of Villainy*, Everard Giulpin's *Skialetheia*, Thomas Middleton's *Micro-cynicon: Six Snarling Satires*, Thomas Cutwode's *Caltha Poetarum*, and John Davies's *Epigrams*, which was bound with the *Elegies* of Christopher Marlowe, were all destroyed. Thomas Nashe's and Gabriel Harvey's works were singled out for special attention: 'none of their books be ever printed hereafter'. Even two anti-feminist works that could be read as critical of the unmarried Elizabeth – *The Book Against Women* and *The Fifteen Joys of Marriage* – were tossed into the flames.

The Bishops' Ban made clear that the vogue for topical satire was officially over: 'No satires or epigrams' were to 'be printed hereafter'. Hayward had also poisoned the well for those writing national history: 'no English histories' are to 'be printed except they be allowed by some of her Majesty's Privy Council'. For the time being, then, only political and not ecclesiastical authorities could approve the publication of histories; an author of an even mildly critical history would have to be unusually bold to approach the councillors for permission to publish. Not even London's dramatists escaped the ban, which also decreed that 'no plays [were to] be printed except they be allowed by such as have authority'. Left unexplained was exactly why some works were called in and others spared. The ambiguity, perhaps deliberate, had a chilling effect. Looking over the seemingly arbitrary list of prescribed books, English writers, some of whom were forced to abandon work-in-progress, must have been left wondering whether it was topical satire itself or rather the drift by some satirists toward the obscene or the explicitly political that had provoked the bishops.

Shakespeare hadn't had any of his works banned, but even he was singed by the flames. Neither the popular *Richard the Second* nor *The First Part of Henry the Fourth* were published again during Elizabeth's lifetime. The Chamberlain's Men took extra precautions with his two other works on the hypersensitive Lancastrian reign: both *The Second Part of Henry the Fourth* and *Henry the Fifth* were sanitized and seen into print far more quickly than any other plays Shakespeare wrote before or after. Both plays had unfortunately painted an Archbishop of Canterbury in a particularly unfavourable light, especially *The Second Part of Henry the Fourth*, which when published eliminated such potentially offensive lines as 'the Bishop / Turns insurrection to religion' (I, i, 200–1). With the opening of the Globe, this was not a time to take unnecessary risks. The publishing history of Shakespeare's plays at this time suggests that it was wiser for the Chamberlain's Men to publish lightly sanitized versions and pull offending plays from the repertory, rather than let linger the memory of what might otherwise be regarded as seditious history.

8

'Is this a holiday?'

Since the end of the seventeenth century critics and editors of *Julius Caesar* have focused almost exclusively on the play's unforgettable characters and gripping political drama. From their perspective, the religious bits that surface throughout the play were 'palpable blunders' and for a long time they did their best to ignore or repair them. When, in 1693, Thomas Rymer condemned the play's anachronisms as 'a sacrilege', his language ironically registers the extent to which a fixed notion of what Shakespeare's Roman play ought to be – classical, political and pagan – had displaced the mix of religion and politics that Shakespeare's audience would have taken for granted. Issues Elizabethans confronted in their world and in the theatre – assassination, succession, tyrannicide, holidays – were not only steeped in but produced by religious division. Part of Shakespeare's genius was discovering in Plutarch's old story the fault lines of his own milieu.

'Squires's Practice to Poison the Queen', George Carleton

From the time of Henry VIII's break from Rome, changes in state religion had invited new, sometimes radical, political thought. With every twist and turn in the Tudor dynasty – with its various Acts of Supremacy, Submission and Uniformity and its official shifts from Catholic to Protestant to Catholic to Protestant once again in little more than a quarter-century – the effort to reconcile political and religious authority grew increasingly strained. Pope Pius V's bull of 1570, excommunicating Elizabeth and absolving her subjects from allegiance to her, only made things worse for English Catholics torn between loyalty to their Church and to their country. If you accepted Rome's verdict – though only the most radical Catholic fringe in England went this far – you could, in good conscience, support the assassination of Elizabeth as a tyrant.

Once it was clear that Elizabeth was not going to marry or bear children, her advisers were worried enough about the possibility of Catholic succession to fall back upon quasi-republican positions to ensure Protestant rule. Elizabeth had to be offended by what their argument implied: that the people and not just their monarch had a say in such matters. You can see the effects of such arguments in works like Thomas Wilson's unpublished manuscript on 'The State of England', written in 1600, where Wilson writes that an English monarch has 'no authority to make laws nor to dispose of the crown; that must be done by general consent of all in Parliament. Yea, the king's eldest son, though the kingdom be hereditary, shall not be crowned without the consent of the Parliament after the death of his father.' Though his manuscript was never intended for print, Wilson could not bring himself to come out and say that it was her subjects, not Elizabeth herself, who would confirm her successor. Peter Wentworth recently had, in his *Pithy Exhortation to Her Majesty for Establishing Her Successor to the Crown*. For his bluntness, Wentworth, a Member of Parliament, died imprisoned in the Tower of London, and his tract, posthumously published in Scotland in 1598, was ordered by the Elizabethan authorities to be burnt by the hangman.

The authorities did their best to suppress talk of succession. Even a tourist like Thomas Platter quickly learned not to ask twice after being told that it was 'forbidden on pain of death to make enquiries as to who is to succeed her on her decease, for fear that if it were known, this person in his lust for government might plot against the Queen's life'. But because Elizabeth refused to name a successor, speculation was rife. Political tracts advocating rival contenders were published overseas and in Scotland. In England, their publication or sale was illegal.

In the waning years of the reign, loyal Englishmen like Thomas Wilson were quietly handicapping the prospects of each of the dozen or so leading contenders for Elizabeth's crown. Moreover, Elizabeth must have suspected that some of her Privy Councillors – including Essex and Cecil – were in secret correspondence with the King of Scots if not others as well, each doing his best to ingratiate himself with her likeliest successor. Gossip was rampant. Those eager for a Catholic monarch to ascend the English throne still lived in hope, abetted by the prophecy circulating in Spain that Elizabeth would not outlive the year.

Thomas Fitzherbert, an English Catholic living in Spain, wrote to a friend in early March 1599 that while many believed 'the King of Scots will win the game if the Earl of Essex be not in his way', he himself remained sceptical: 'I think they are deceived, and that the other takes him for his competitor – which will be well for the Infanta' – that is, the leading Catholic claimant. He added that, with Essex and James both itching to succeed Elizabeth, the Spanish Infanta at least had an outside chance: 'When two dogs fight for a bone, you know what follows?'

It's risky, then, to read history backwards and assume that contemporaries viewed the King of Scots' path to the throne as unobstructed. And his position was further undermined by rumour-mongers who questioned the depth of his commitment to Protestantism. Word spread in late April 1599 to the effect that the King of Scots 'intends to gather grapes before they are ripe' and that 'for a kingdom he will become a counterfeit Catholic'. William Camden writes of 'certain lewd fellows there were, I know not out of what shop, to whom it was good as a reward to disturb the quiet peace. These men, to the end to break off by secret and wicked practices the amity betwixt the Queen and the King of Scots, spread rumours abroad that he inclined to the Papist's faction, and was of a most averse mind to the Queen.'

If this were not enough, Camden adds, a man named Valentine Thomas appeared on the scene, 'accusing the King of Scots of ill affection towards the Queen'. This claim was taken more seriously. On 4 August 1598 Sir William Knollys wrote to the absent Essex that he had missed out on a 'great debate' among the Privy Councillors 'whether Valentine Thomas should be arraigned or no. It was concluded he should; but I think it is at a stand, the King of Scotland having desired that some for him might be at his arraignment.' In the end, Elizabeth overruled her councillors: 'The matter she commanded to be concealed in silence, and thought not good to have the man put to death, lest any aspersion should be laid upon the King's reputation.' You couldn't kill Thomas or people would mutter that he knew too much; but you had to put him to silence, lest he do more damage. So he was left to rot in the Tower of London.

A much more dangerous threat came from Catholic assassins. For the likeliest way to assure Catholic succession was to kill Elizabeth, triggering an uprising of English Catholics supported by a Spanish invasion that would restore Catholic rule to England. If anything, the defeat of the Armada in 1588 had intensified Spanish efforts to effect regime change by other means, and the closing years of the century saw some of the most notorious of such attempts on Elizabeth's life. The King of Scots, as a likely Protestant successor, was also a target. John Chamberlain wrote to Dudley Carleton in mid-January 1599 that there 'was a plot laid by certain Jesuits and priests to murder or poison the Scottish king, as it is confessed by some that are taken'. In such a climate, it wasn't easy, nor could it have made much sense, to distinguish political from religious motivation.

For Shakespeare in particular, political assassination wasn't some costume drama that took place long ago and far away (and it is to his *Macbeth* that we owe the introduction of the word 'assassination' into English literature). When he was nineteen years old, still living in Stratford a few months after the birth of his first child, Shakespeare learned that his relative, John Somerville, a Catholic, had been implicated in a failed attempt to assassinate Queen Elizabeth. The Oxford-educated Somerville, just a few years older than Shakespeare, was married to Margaret, the daughter of Edward and Mary Arden of Park Hall (how closely they were related to the Ardens from whom Shakespeare's mother descended is unclear – and may even have been unclear to the Shakespeares themselves). On 25 October 1583 Somerville left his home a few miles from Stratford and headed to London intending to shoot the Queen. But he was intercepted the next day on the London road, near Aynho, and conveyed to the Tower. His interrogators quickly learned that his orders came from 'his allies and kin' and a warrant was issued to apprehend all 'such as shall be in any way akin to all touched and to search their houses'.

The leaders of the plot were put to death and Somerville himself was found strangled on the eve of his execution – perhaps to prevent him from revealing too much about the conspiracy from the scaffold. His head, along with Edward Arden's, was mounted on stakes atop London Bridge. What Shakespeare knew about the plot, whether any of his Arden relations were investigated or suspected, even what his own sympathies were, is lost to us; but apparently he didn't forget Somerville. There's an otherwise inexplicable moment in *The Third Part of Henry the Sixth* where the Earl of Warwick looks for his enemy, Clarence, in the wrong direction, and is corrected by a Warwickshireman who speaks briefly, then disappears. This bit character's name, efficiently immortalized, is Somerville.

In the months preceding the composition of *Julius Caesar* there was a rash of attempts upon Elizabeth's life. The government eagerly publicized them, striking a propaganda blow against a much hated domestic enemy, the tireless and hounded English Jesuits. Word of the most notorious of these plots – by a hapless Englishman named Edward Squires – circulated widely. During his travels in England in the autumn of 1599, Thomas Platter recorded in his journal that 'but a short time before, an attempt had been made to poison the queen by smearing powder on the chair she was accustomed to sit and hold her hands on'. Platter got the facts slightly wrong, though perhaps he was only recording a version of the story in currency at the time.

Edward Squires was a down-on-his-luck scrivener from Greenwich who had found employment in the Queen's stables and then sought to improve his fortunes by joining Sir Francis Drake's privateering voyage of 1595. Squires sailed in the *Francis*, which was captured by the Spanish and its crew taken prisoner of war and imprisoned in Seville. English Jesuits in Spain, from where they plotted the restoration of Catholicism in England, were given access to these prisoners and singled out those who could potentially be converted and persuaded to infiltrate England and act against the Queen. This process of recruiting prisoners – which included years of threats, isolation, confrontation and confusion – depended on a kind of brainwashing. Of course, the Jesuits could never be sure if they had succeeded or whether those they were releasing were merely good actors who had won parole.

Squires and his friend Richard Rolles were released in the summer of 1597 and headed home. Upon reaching London, Squires immediately signed on with Essex's fleet, bound for the Azores, during which voyage, he later confessed, he poisoned 'the Earl's chair where he used to sit and lay his hand'. Before setting sail he visited his old workplace, the Queen's stables, and, by his account

understanding that her Majesty's horses were preparing for her to ride abroad, as the horse stood ready saddled in the stable yard, I went to the horse and in the hearing of divers thereabouts, said 'God save the Queen,' and therewith laid my hand on the pommel of the saddle, and out of a bladder, which I had made full of holes with a big pin, poisoned the pommel, it being covered with velvet and soon after, her Majesty rode abroad.

Both assassination attempts failed and, after returning from the Azores, Squires went back to work in the stables. His actions were only exposed a year later when John Stanley and William Monday, another pair of Englishmen similarly released from Spain by Jesuit handlers with plans to take the Queen's life, arrived in London. Stanley's insistence upon a private audience with Elizabeth quickly attracted attention, and under interrogation he implicated not only himself but Squires and Rolles as well.

The conspiracies were taken seriously at the highest levels of government, and Essex, Cecil, Francis Bacon and Edward Coke all personally participated in interrogating the suspects. Some of the conspirators were tortured and all were executed, Squires being hung, disembowelled, then quartered at Tyburn on 13 November 1598. Francis Bacon anonymously authored the semi-official version of the story, published in 1599: *A Letter Written out of England . . . Containing a True Report of a Strange Conspiracy*. The English Jesuits, whose cause was damaged by the case, opted for denial, and had Martin Array publish in Rome a counter-blast, *The Discovery and Confutation of a Tragical Fiction*.

For Shakespeare's audiences, then, the re-enactment of the greatest of political assassinations in *Julius Caesar* followed a series of religiously motivated assassination attempts at home. They were not ignorant of the turmoil into which an assassination could throw a nation; but they may also have accepted its utility. Sir Walter Ralegh, for example, wrote to Robert Cecil in October 1598 suggesting that the Irish problem be resolved by assassinating Tyrone. Ralegh goes so far as to say, '[It] can be no disgrace if it were known that the killing of a rebel were practised, for you see that the lives of anointed princes are daily sought and we have always in Ireland given head money for the killing of rebels.' Ralegh is at pains to make clear that Cecil wouldn't be implicated in the scheme ('But for yourself, you are not to be touched in the matter'), apparently unaware that just a few months earlier Cecil had himself written to Sir Geoffrey Fenton, the Irish Secretary of State, with instructions to assassinate Tyrone.

Moral qualms aside, the real problem with political assassination for Elizabethans – and Shakespeare's play makes this abundantly clear – was that it unleashed forces that could not be predicted or controlled. Assassination was linked with chaos, blood-letting and potential civil war because this was what it invariably led to. However noble Brutus' motives, however morally and politically justified his actions, it would have been clear to many in Shakespeare's audience that he hadn't thought things through. Critics who fault *Julius Caesar* for being a broken-backed play, who are disappointed by the final two acts and who feel that the assassination takes place too early in the action, fail to understand that the two parts of the play – the events leading up to the assassination and the bloody civil strife that follow – go hand in hand. Even as Shakespeare offers compelling arguments for tyrannicide in the opening acts of the play, he shows in the closing ones the savage blood-letting and political breakdown that, if the English history he had so compellingly chronicled was any example, were sure to follow. Recent French history – borne out in the Admiral's Men's collaborative four-part drama of the civil wars in France onstage the previous autumn and winter at the Rose – only confirmed this.

If succession and assassination were long-standing problems with special contemporary relevance, there were other conflicts, no less inflected by religious divisions, that were more deep-seated in the culture and preoccupied Shakespeare as he wrote *Julius Caesar*. Foremost among these were those concerning the official calendar. To grasp the resonance of these issues – both for the culture and for Shakespeare himself – requires a brief digression, going back in time to the early 1570s, when the theological shards that barely protrude in this play but are embedded deeply within it cut deeply into Shakespeare and his society.

On Midsummer's Day 1571, when Shakespeare was seven years old, the townsfolk of Stratford-upon-Avon gathered opposite the Guild Chapel on Church Street. The 'right goodly Chapel' had stood at the heart of Stratford's religious and civic life since the thirteenth century. It had last been refurbished during the reign of Henry VII with the help of Hugh Clopton, who had also built a home for himself, New Place (which Shakespeare would later own), and whose gardens faced its beautiful stained-glass windows. Adjoining the chapel was a schoolhouse as well as almshouses for old folk, who could remember a time during the reign of Henry VIII when four priests had been employed to say masses in the chapel.

The crowd had gathered to witness an historic event: a glazier was knocking out the chapel's stained-glass windows, replacing the coloured glass with pieces of 'white' or clear glass. It was a considerable undertaking. The children in the crowd may have been more excited by the sound of shattering glass than by the knowledge that the glazier, paid 23 shillings 8 pence for his labour, was furthering the work of the English Reformation. For advocates of Protestant reform, who feared that, in William Prynne's words, 'Popery may creep in at a glass window as well as at a door,' the light of clear day would at last shine in the chapel, no longer reflected through the images of Catholic saints. For others, who had grown up and grown old worshipping in the shadows cast by those figures and who in troubled times had prayed to these saints for intercession, it was a sad day. Some may have stooped to retrieve as souvenir or relic a jagged fragment of the Virgin Mary or St George.

There's no way of knowing whether the decision to destroy the stained glass on Midsummer's Day was deliberate. It could have been that the long days of late June were best suited for the job; it may simply have been when the unnamed glazier, who must have come from a neighbouring town, was available (glass windows were a rarity in Stratford). But the timing may have struck some as intentional. When England had been Catholic, Midsummer had been a day of festive release, a time to light bonfires and 'for youths and girls [to] dance all day with flowers in their hands'. For proponents of reform, however, what Shakespeare would speak of playfully in *Twelfth Night* as 'midsummer madness' (III, iv, 61) smacked of the worst of papistry and paganism, and they had already succeeded in squelching most of this merrymaking. In London, John Stow lamented, the great Midsummer celebrations of his youth had all but died out by mid-century. A young Shakespeare may have asked his elders about what they did at Midsummer, but by the time he was old enough to hear their stories, those rites (some of which would be re-imagined in his *Midsummer Night's Dream*) were fading memories.

When, decades later, Shakespeare searched for a metaphor that captured a sense of melancholy loss, and compared the silhouette of trees' naked branches to the bare window tracery in a ruined Gothic choir or chancel, he may have drawn on this childhood memory of 'Bare ruined choirs where late the sweet birds sang' (Sonnet 73). The chapel's stained glass had been its last vestige of Catholic imagery. A few months before Shakespeare was born there had been an earlier and massive 'defacing [of] images' in the chapel's interior. At that time Stratford's governing council (which included Shakespeare's father) had ordered workmen to white-wash the extraordinary paintings that covered the interior of the chapel. Some of the more zealous workers had got carried away, gouging overtly Catholic images, but, for the most part, it seems that the workmen had been instructed to follow a less reckless course, painting over the interior but otherwise leaving the art-work intact (and sparing the wall paintings in the chancel, which had been partitioned off). After all, the Protestant reforms insti-tuted under Edward VI in the early 1550s had been reversed when Mary restored Catholicism later in that decade. Though the engine of reform had once again begun to churn under Elizabeth, who knew when it might be reversed, especially since the pre-sumed heir to the throne was the Catholic Mary Queen of Scots? A safer and less expensive policy was to apply a couple of coats of whitewash that could one day be removed (as they were in 1804 when the paintings were temporarily uncovered). Other reversible changes were made as well. The chapel's rood loft was taken down and a communion board replaced the altar; but it wasn't until October 1571 that Catholic vestments, including copes of white damask that had been in storage for over a decade, were finally ordered to be sold off, perhaps as bed-covers or as stage props for touring players.

Retreating from the severity of Edward VI's iconoclasm, Eliza-beth had made clear that stained glass need not suffer the same fate as painted images and that no one should 'break down or deface any image in glass windows in any church' without official permission. However, in the aftermath of the Catholic-led North-ern Rebellion in 1569 and the replacement of Stratford-upon-Avon's Catholic-leaning vicar, schoolmaster and curate with those of more confirmed Protestant credentials, it appears that the bal-ance in town had shifted in favour of the reformers, and the chapel's stained-glass windows, whose bright images had stood out starkly for the past six years against the background of unadorned walls, were doomed.

Once the chapel was sanitized of visual distractions, the power of the word would predominate: the Bible, Foxe's *Acts and Monuments*, and the official *Book of Homilies* and *Book of Common Prayer* – works that would leave a different though no less profound impact on Shakespeare's writing. Reform in Stratford-upon-Avon and throughout England was met with a degree of confusion and ambivalence. Confusion, because the government kept sending mixed signals about the extent of reform, as the Queen sought to avoid sectarian strife by accommodating both Puritans clamouring for radical change and Catholic subjects longing for a return to the old ways. Ambivalence, because every adult in Stratford had either been raised as a Catholic or had lived under Catholic rule. Many, if they had abandoned the faith in which they had been raised, had done so grudgingly. Even if Shakespeare's parents, like most Elizabethans with Catholic roots, were reconciled to the latest change in state religion (and scholars are divided on this point), it's easy to imagine John and Mary Shakespeare pointing out to their curious eldest son in visits to the Guild Chapel precisely where, beneath the whitewash, Doomsday had been visible, where lost souls could once be seen falling into hell-mouth, and where the Virgin Mary had been painted. To argue that the Shakespeares were secretly Catholic or, alternatively, mainstream Protestants, misses the point that except for a small minority at one doctrinal extreme or other, those labels failed to capture the layered nature of what Elizabethans, from the Queen down, actually believed. The white-washed chapel walls, on which perhaps an image or two were still faintly visible, are as good an emblem of Shakespeare's faith as we are likely to find.

Of all the images in Stratford's chapel that young Will Shakespeare must have longed to see, the painting of St George fighting with the dragon, plunging his spear into the monster's neck, is a strong candidate (the pommel even resembles the one on the Shakespeare coat of arms). Shakespeare, who was probably born either on St George's Day, 23 April, or on the day before, may well have had a special affinity for this saint, who, as well as being England's patron saint, was a particular favourite in Stratford. There had been a special altar in his name in Stratford's Holy Trinity Church and among its ceiling paintings yet another depiction of St George defeating the dragon. For much of the sixteenth century one of the town's most popular celebrations was the annual pageant of St George, held on Holy Thursday. Though suppressed after 1547, the pageant was revived during Mary's reign. Stratford's wardens' accounts at that time include payments for 'dressing' and 'bearing' the dragon, gunpowder, scouring St George's harness, and two dozen bells – which suggests a lively show, with St George riding on horseback through Stratford's streets, children running from the dragon shooting gunpowder smoke, and perhaps a clown, adorned with bells, dancing in the rear of the procession. It must have been sorely missed. The town of Norwich was so reluctant to abandon its famous pageant that officials salvaged the production by banning St George but allowing the dragon to march, unopposed, for the rest of Elizabeth's reign.

By the 1570s it was unclear whether St George's Day, along with other days printed in red ink on the calendar, remained a holiday. When, in 1536, Henry VIII overhauled the traditional Catholic calendar, cluttered with saints' days, St George miraculously survived the cut and was still celebrated 'as in time past hath been accustomed'; but he didn't fare as well under his son Edward VI, who seems to have had a personal antipathy to St George. When Edward trimmed the number of official holidays – that is, days on which people didn't have to work – to twenty-seven (plus Sundays), only the Knights of the Garter were granted a special dispensation to observe St George's Day as the feast of their order. The *Book of Common Prayer* issued under Edward in 1552 made clear that St George's Day was no longer a red-letter or holy day. Seven years later, when that Prayer Book was republished under Elizabeth, St George's Day, to the relief and delight of many, was restored to its holiday status and a year later was included in a list of official holidays. Excitement about its restoration was premature, however, for in the following year new guidelines made clear that the only holidays to be observed were those recognized as holidays in the 1552 calendar (which had excluded St George's Day). A young William Shakespeare might have been forgiven for waking up on 23 April and asking: 'Is this a holiday?'

It wasn't just a semantic question for a non-labouring schoolboy. Shakespeare needed to know how to dress. In 1571 Parliament had decreed that on all official holidays every male from age six and up (excluding gentlemen) was required to wear what Shakespeare calls in *Love's Labour's Lost* the 'plain statute-caps' (V, ii, 282). These knitted woollen caps signified that it was a holiday while at the same time supporting the ailing wool trade. The unpopular legislation was strengthened two years later and only repealed in 1591, when Shakespeare was in his mid-twenties. From a very early age, then, Shakespeare understood well enough that the calendar was subject to religious, economic and political pressures.

Shakespeare came of age when time itself was out of joint: the Western calendar, fixed by Julius Caesar in 46 BC (a meddling with nature deemed tyrannical by some of his fellow Romans), had by the late sixteenth century drifted ten days off the celestial cycle. Something had to be done. In 1577 Pope Gregory XIII proposed skipping ten days and in 1582 Catholic Europe acted upon his recommendation: it was agreed that the day after 4 October would be 15 October. Elizabeth was ready to go along with this sensible change, but her bishops baulked, unwilling to follow the lead of the Pope on this issue or any other. Other Protestant countries also opposed the change and, as a result, nations began to keep different time. By 1599 Easter was celebrated a full five weeks apart in Catholic and Protestant lands.

There's an odd moment in *Julius Caesar* when Brutus, on the eve of Caesar's assassination, unsure of the date, asks his servant Lucius: 'Is not tomorrow, boy, the first of March?' (II, i, 40) and tells him to check 'the calendar' and let him know. Virtually all modern editions silently correct Brutus' 'blunder' (how could such an intelligent man be so wrong about the date?), changing his question to: 'Is not tomorrow, boy, the ides of March?' Elizabethans, though, would have smiled knowingly at Brutus' confusion in being off by a couple of weeks – as well as at his blindness to the significance of a day that would resound through history. They also knew, watching the events in the play that culminate in the ides of March, that virtually all the political upheaval their own nation had experienced since the Reformation – from the Pilgrimage of Grace in 1536, to the Cornish Rebellion of 1549, to the Northern Rebellion of 1569, coincided with or had roots in feasts and holidays. As recently as 1596 the planners of the abortive Oxfordshire Rising had agreed that their armed insurrection, in which they would cut down gentlemen and head 'with all speed towards London' to foment a national uprising, would begin shortly after Queen Elizabeth's Accession Day, 17 November. 'Is this a holiday?' was a question that touched a deep cultural nerve.

Shakespeare, then, was born into an England poised between worlds. While the Elizabethans didn't suffer the bloody religious wars that wracked much of the Continent, its reformations meant, among other things, a stripping away of altars, paintings, ceremonies, vestments, sacramental rituals and beloved holidays. At least in theory, for reformers seeking to purify a Church they saw encrusted with idolatry, this made good sense; but in practice it also left a tear in the fabric of daily life. Traditional seasonal rhythms were disrupted, the long-standing equilibrium between holiday and workday unbalanced. The reformist effort to do away

170

with the distracting rituals of Catholic worship resulted in a kind of sensory deprivation, for the rush to reform had overlooked the extent to which people craved the sights and sounds of the old communal celebration. It soon became obvious to Tudor authorities that reform had left a potentially dangerous vacuum. The official and avowedly Protestant *Book of Homilies* acknowledged as much when it incorporated into the homily 'Of the Place and Time of Prayer' an imaginary dialogue between two churchgoing women confused by all these changes: 'Alas, gossip,' one says to her friend, 'what shall we do now at church, since all the saints are taken away, since all the goodly sights we were wont to have are gone, since we cannot hear the like piping, singing, chanting, and playing upon the organs, that we could before?'

In such a climate, new cultural forms – especially those that offered 'goodly sights' – prospered, including the public theatre. In retrospect, it seems natural enough for the stage to fill a need once met by Catholic ritual, for English theatre emerged out of the liturgical plays of the twelfth and thirteenth centuries and, in the three hundred years of mystery, miracle and morality drama that followed, continued to be deeply suffused with religious ritual and subject matter. The extent to which the Elizabethan theatre retained some of the energies that had been the domain of the Church may help explain why Protestant reformers, who at first embraced the stage as a means of promoting their own views, soon turned against it. John Stockwood complained from the outdoor pulpit at London's St Paul's Cross in 1578, 'Will not a filthy play, with the blast of a trumpet, sooner call thither a thousand, than an hour's tolling of a bell, bring to the sermon a hundred?' And five years later the extremist Philip Stubbes decried how drama had reintroduced the 'false idols, gods, and goddesses' that reformers had worked so hard to suppress: 'If you will learn to condemn God and all his laws, to care neither for heaven nor hell, and to commit all kind of sin and mischief, you need go to no other school, for all

these good examples may you see painted before your eyes in inter-
ludes and plays.'

The history in the making that Midsummer's Day in Stratford-
upon-Avon in 1571 and in villages across England in the 1560s and
1570s marked the decline of one form of communal expression and
the renaissance of others, most notably a drama that was no less
rooted in spectacle, magical transformation and wonder. As it
turned out, in the hands of Shakespeare and his fellow playwrights, this theatre not only absorbed social energies that had
become unmoored in a post-Reformation world, but also explored
in the plays it staged the social trauma that had enabled it to
thrive, the repercussions of which the culture had not fully
absorbed.

From the start of his career as dramatist and poet Shakespeare
was compulsively drawn to epochal moments, to what it meant to
live through the transformation of so much that was familiar. His
early Roman tragedy *Titus Andronicus* ends with the empire tot-
tering on its last legs, the Goths already within Rome's gates; and
his great narrative poem *Lucrece* returns to a much earlier moment
of Roman political history, when a rape led to the banishment of
the last of the Roman kings and the birth of republicanism. When,
in 1599, he turned again to Rome in *Julius Caesar*, he addressed a
pivotal moment in that empire's (if not the world's) tumultuous
history. But even as he was writing about Rome, he felt and re-
imagined these stories as a Christian Elizabethan.

Notably, when Shakespeare has Brutus and Antony address the
crowds following Caesar's death, he has them speak from a 'pulpit'
(the only time this word appears in his work). It's an anachronism,
of course, for what he imagines is more characteristic of the architecture of Elizabethan London – with its outdoor pulpit at Paul's
Cross – rather than any detail he might have read about how
Romans addressed crowds. It's a small point but one that reveals a
good deal about the extent to which Shakespeare was always writ-

ing out of his own cultural moment. Put another way, without the destruction of Midsummer's Day 1571, replicated in communities large and small throughout England, there could not have been a *Midsummer Night's Dream* a quarter-century later, nor, more to the point, a play like *Julius Caesar*. A seven-year-old Shakespeare listening to glass shatter outside Stratford's chapel could not have known it, but his future calling was in good measure made possible that day.

All this helps explain why the opening scene of *Julius Caesar* is so fraught and electrifying. Flavius and Marullus, tribunes of the people, burst in upon a crowd of labourers. Flavius sternly rebukes them – 'Hence! Home, you idle creatures, get you home!' – and demands to know:

> Is this a holiday? What, know you not,
> Being mechanical, you ought not walk
> Upon a labouring day without the sign
> Of your profession?
>   (I, i, 1–5)

Why are these labourers dressed in their holiday finest (including, as we later learn, the familiar 'sweaty' woollen caps) instead of bearing the tools of their trade? When Flavius asks whether it's a holiday, he obviously doesn't think it is, or should be; and when the jocular commoners, clearly in a festive mood, bandy words with the two tribunes, Flavius presses his point, and challenges one of their ringleaders, a cobbler:

> But wherefore art not in thy shop today?
> Why dost thou lead these men about the streets?
>   (I, i, 27–8)

The cobbler jokingly deflects the question before getting to the point. It's the last funny line in a play in which Shakespeare had again chosen to omit a clown's part: 'Truly, sir, to wear out their shoes, to get myself into more work. But indeed sir, we make holiday to see Caesar and to rejoice in his triumph' (29–31). The victorious Caesar has returned to Rome in celebratory triumph, cause enough for the commoners to put work aside and 'make holiday'.

Marullus, hearing this answer, cannot restrain himself and explodes in anger and frustration in the first long speech of the play. Caesar's bloody victory over Pompey's sons is no cause for communal celebration. It wasn't so long ago that the people had turned out to witness Pompey's homecoming, described in a passage whose topography, with its walls, towers, windows, chimney tops, crammed streets and great river, would have been familiar to Londoners:

> O you hard hearts, you cruel men of Rome,
> Knew you not Pompey? Many a time and oft
> Have you climbed up to walls and battlements,
> To towers and windows, yea, to chimney tops,
> Your infants in your arms, and there have sat
> The livelong day, with patient expectation,
> To see great Pompey pass the streets of Rome.
> And when you saw his chariot but appear,
> Have you not made an universal shout,
> That Tiber trembled underneath her banks
> To hear the replication of your sounds
> Made in her concave shores?
> And do you now put on your best attire?
> And do you now cull out a holiday?
> And do you now strew flowers in his way
> That comes in triumph over Pompey's blood?
> Begone!
> Run to your houses, fall upon your knees,
> Pray to the gods to intermit the plague
> That needs must light on this ingratitude.
>   (I, i, 36–55)

As the commoners depart in silence, Flavius turns to Marullus and approvingly observes, 'See whe'er their basest mettle be not moved. / They vanish tongue-tied in their guiltiness' (61–2) – though for all we know the labourers have simply headed off to another part of town, where they won't be bothered by these kill-joys.

Flavius, encouraged by their retreat, instructs Marullus to take matters a step further:

> Go you down that way towards the Capitol;
> This way will I. Disrobe the images
> If you do find them decked with ceremonies.
> (I, i, 63–5)

Stripping the images or statues of Caesar raises the stakes considerably. It also tells us something about Flavius, who, rather than confronting danger himself, urges Marullus to head towards a likely clash at the Capitol, where Caesar and his close supporters are gathered. Marullus, fearful of pressing things too far, nervously asks: 'May we do so? / You know it is the Feast of Lupercal' (66–7). This line comes as a bit of a shock: so it is a holiday after all. The Saturnalian Lupercal was a major Roman festival, a mid-February carnival that resembled England's Shrove Tuesday – a semi-official holiday associated with excess and violence. Shakespeare would have discovered in Plutarch's *Life of Romulus* an explanation for why on the Lupercal young men '[ran] through the city, striking and laying on them which they [met] in their way with their goat thongs'. It was to re-enact the violent founding of Rome, when 'Remus and Romulus ran from Alba unto that place with their drawn swords in their hands'. Plutarch further explained that the young men touched 'their forehead with a bloody knife' in 'remembrance of the danger' that these founders of Rome 'stood in at that time'. Shakespeare could not have found a more suggestive image of mayhem passing itself off as a ritual purgation and political commemoration.

Something complicated is happening in the play at this point, though the dialogue rushes by almost too fast to follow its implications. Rome on the Lupercal is a dangerous place, made more dangerous by the triumph of a man deliberately following in Romulus' footsteps. Anything could happen. Elizabethan audiences were likely to grasp more quickly than modern ones what's implied but won't be made explicit until the following scene: the appropriation of a religious holiday for political ends; for it's obvious to the two tribunes that Caesar's triumphant entry into Rome was intended to capitalize upon the anarchic holiday energies released on this festive day. But to oppose these makes the consuls resemble, in Elizabethan terms, puritanical reformers, eager to strip 'images' and do away with 'ceremonies'.

Shakespeare knew exactly what he was doing when he substituted theologically loaded terms for the more neutral ones in his source, where instead of 'ceremonies' Plutarch writes that the statues were decked with 'trophies' and 'scarves'. Where Plutarch places Caesar's triumphant entry into Rome in October 45 BC, the Lupercal a full four months later on 15 February and the assassination itself on the ides of March, Shakespeare radically compresses events so that Caesar's triumph and the Lupercal are simultaneous, and the assassination hard upon that. It's also worth noting that the day of Caesar's entry, with which the play begins, comes near the end of Plutarch's *Life of Caesar*. It's as if Shakespeare read patiently, circling the text, waiting for just the right point of entry into the story, before recognizing and seizing the opening that his contemporaries would find most explosive.

So when Flavius brushes off Marullus' reservations – 'It is no matter' – Elizabethans knew well enough that the issue could not be so easily dismissed, especially when Flavius urges a more aggressive course of action, one that can be read as sacrilegious or politically desperate:

> Let no images
> Be hung with Caesar's trophies. I'll about
> And drive away the vulgar from the streets;
> So do you too, where you perceive them thick.
>   (I, i, 68–71)

One of the nicer ironies here is that Flavius' disrespect for the image of Caesar echoes the contemporary controversy over the biblical injunction to render 'unto Caesar what is Caesar's'. It was defamatory and punishable to deface a ruler's image (the fact that Flavius is doing so in order to prevent Caesar from becoming a ruler is almost beside the point). The Queen's Catholic opponents had taken to abusing her royal image. In 1591, for example, a religious extremist, aptly named Hacket, took a knife to a panel portrait of the Queen and stabbed her through the breast. A few years later, the Irish Catholic rebel O'Rourke had a wooden image of Elizabeth dragged through the street while children pelted it with stones.

Catholic and Anglican polemicists had been battling over the treatment of political images for decades. Few things struck Catholics as more two-faced than the Protestants' worship of political icons and suppression of religious ones. The Catholic writer Nicholas Sanders challenged his hypocritical Protestant adversaries in his 1567 *Treatise of the Images of Christ*: 'Break if you dare the image of the Queen's Majesty.' Sanders was jabbing at an especially sensitive nerve here, given the extent to which Elizabeth's image was treated as near-sacred. Royal apologists were hard-pressed to answer. The Protestant Thomas Bilson, in his treatise on subjection and rebellion, does his best to walk a fine line, condemning outright abuse of political images but ruling idolatrous any overenthusiastic response: 'The images of princes may not well be despised or abused, least it be taken as a sign of a malicious heart against the prince, but bowing of the knee or lifting up the hand to the image of a prince is flat and inevitable idolatry.'

Shakespeare was deeply interested in the issue of how one represented rulers and draws a good deal of attention in this play to the difference between Caesar's infirm body and his idealized image (Calphurnia even dreams of her husband's statue rather than the man himself). We learn that Caesar is hard of hearing, a weak swimmer, endured fever like a 'sick girl' (I, ii, 128), and is subject to epileptic fits. The discrepancy between an admired leader's image and actual physical condition was familiar to Elizabeth's subjects as their Queen entered her sixty-seventh year. One measure of Elizabeth's concern with how she was depicted was the extraordinary control she exercised over her portraits. Every few years she would sit for a court artist whose work would then serve as a model for others to copy. Some time around 1592 Isaac Oliver made the mistake of accurately rendering the Queen as an old lady. Elizabeth let her Privy Council know that portraits based on this model were unacceptable. A few years later the councillors directed officers to seek out and destroy all portraits of the Queen which were to her 'great offence'. Some were immediately burnt; others met that fate more slowly. John Evelyn writes that some of the engravings that were called in were used for years at Essex House for 'peels for the use of their ovens'. From that time on, all royal portraits would show Elizabeth as an eternally young woman, her true complexion hidden by a so-called 'mask of youth'. Years later, Jonson acknowledged what it would have been fatal to say while the Queen was still alive: 'Queen Elizabeth never saw her self after she became old in a true glass.' It's far more likely that she in fact did – which is why, like the physically flawed Caesar, she reacted so aggressively to how the image of that self was treated. Elizabethan audiences would not have been surprised to learn that Flavius and Marullus, for abusing Caesar's image, were 'put to silence' (I, ii, 286).

The opening scenes of the play feel more contemporary than classical. The theologically tinged language, the casual references to Elizabethan dress codes, professions, guilds and shops, chimney tops and windows, and soon enough to pulpits, clocks, books with pages, and nightgowns, all contribute to a sense that either Shakespeare cared little about historical accuracy, or wanted to collapse the difference between classical Rome and Elizabethan London. This is especially true of Marullus' description of a Roman triumph – the one thing that modern audiences might consider foreign to Shakespeare's London: the famous procession of a victorious general from outside Rome's wall through the Forum to Jupiter's Temple, with politicians, spoils and captives in tow.

But it wasn't. Many in the audience at Shakespeare's play would have recalled that great day a decade earlier when, on 24 November 1588, Queen Elizabeth staged a triumph – 'imitating', as John Stow put it, 'the ancient Romans'. Dressed in 'robes of triumph', Elizabeth rode in a specially built 'chariot-throne', drawn by a pair of white horses through the streets of London from Whitehall to St Paul's. For those who missed the event a Latin collection celebrating the triumphs of the victorious Elizabeth soon appeared in print.

Late sixteenth-century Londoners, who regularly witnessed both royal and mayoral triumphs, lived in a golden age of civic pageantry. And many of Shakespeare's fellow dramatists – though tellingly not Shakespeare himself – sought work scripting civic triumphs, including Ben Jonson, George Peele, John Marston, Thomas Heywood, John Webster, Anthony Munday and Thomas Dekker. Jonson carefully annotated his copy of the great Renaissance handbook of triumphs, François Modius' *Pandectae Triumphales*, a thousand pages illustrating triumphs from Romulus' to those of sixteenth-century European rulers. Dekker spelled out the triumph's attractions for both rulers and ruled: 'Princes themselves take pleasure to behold them: they with delight, the common people with admiration.'

Elizabeth sufficiently enjoyed riding in triumph to make it part of her repertory of public display (she didn't appear in the streets all that often, and this was a powerful way of eliciting a 'universal shout' of approval and celebration). One of the most remarkable paintings executed towards the end of her reign – entitled by Sir Roy Strong *Eliza Triumphans* – depicts just such a scene. Elizabeth was not the first English monarch to wrap herself in the trappings and symbolism of a Roman triumph. Her grandfather, Henry VII, had followed up his victory over Richard III by displaying captive spoils in a triumphant procession to St Paul's. And a century before him, Henry V, after his victory at Agincourt, had led French prisoners through London. Shakespeare considered this triumph significant enough to include a description of it in *Henry the Fifth*, even if it meant confusing the audience by transporting Henry home to London for his triumph before whisking him back to France to woo Kate:

> So let him land,
> And solemnly see him set on to London.
> So swift a pace hath thought that even now
> You may imagine him upon Blackheath,
> Where that his lords desire him to have borne
> His bruised helmet and his bended sword
> Before him through the city. He forbids it,
> Being free from vainness and self-glorious pride,
> Giving full trophy, signal, and ostent
> Quite from himself to God.
> (V, Prologue, 13–22)

Shakespeare also underscores the extent to which Henry V's homecoming is a Roman triumph. In case we miss the point, he draws the analogy for us:

> The Mayor and all his brethren, in best sort,
> Like to the senators of th'antique Rome
> With the plebeians swarming at their heels,
> Go forth and fetch their conquering Caesar in.
> (V, Prologue, 25–8)

Shakespeare didn't invent this blurring of Roman past and Elizabethan present – he found it all around him. The Tower of London, it was believed, was built by Caesar himself – at least that's what tourists were told. Shakespeare himself repeats and questions this myth of origins in *Richard the Third*, when one of the doomed young princes asks Richard: 'Did Julius Caesar build that place?' – and is told: 'He did, my gracious lord, begin that place, / Which, since, succeeding ages have re-edified' (III, i, 70–71). It was a myth, of course, though one of value to the state and, as late as 1576, William Lambarde, Keeper of the Records in the Tower, defended this tradition. It was useful to have one's own authority linked in a line of direct descent to that of imperial Rome – ceremonially and architecturally. And it fitted nicely with the concurrent myth that London was Troynovant – 'Troy Revived' – and Britain founded by Brutus, a mythical nephew of Aeneas.

Nowhere was the affinity between ancient Rome and Elizabethan England more pronounced than at court. Visitors to Woodstock Palace were told that it had been built 'in Julius Caesar's time', while those arriving at Nonsuch Palace were struck by its exterior, 'built entirely of great blocks of white stone on which are represented numerous Roman and other ancient stories'. Continuing this architectural theme, 'above the doors of the inner court' stood 'stone statues of three Roman emperors'. Elizabeth's palace at Greenwich housed a bust of Julius Caesar. And when Shakespeare and his fellow players visited Hampton Court, they would have seen displayed in the room next to Elizabeth's quarters 'a gold embroidered tapestry on the walls' which 'told the history of the murder of Julius Caesar, the first emperor'. If that were not enough, by 'the door stood three of the emperor's electors in customary dress painted in life-like fashion'. It seems that the desired effect of the *trompe-l'oeil* was to make viewers feel as if they were momentarily transported back in time. But, as they stood near the large tapestry of Caesar's assassination and faced the three life-like Roman electors painted by the door, did visitors feel like co-conspirators or witnesses to a heinous political crime? Caesar also appears in two spectacular tapestries depicting triumphs at Hampton Court – *The Triumph of Chastity Over Love* and *The Triumph of Fame over Death*, both based on Petrarch's poem 'I Trionfi'. These tapestries had hung at Hampton Court since Cardinal Wolsey had purchased them early in the century, before the building, like Whitehall, was taken from him by Henry VIII. These 'triumphs' quickly caught the eye of poets, including John Skelton, who described how 'all the world stares' at the 'Triumphs of Caesar / And of Pompeius' war'. Ceasar's legacy, his triumphs and his assassination, loomed large in Shakespeare's England.

Fifty lines into *Julius Caesar*, as they grappled with the motives underlying Caesar's triumph, Elizabethan playgoers were confronted with a dizzying overlap of religion and politics, past and present. The start is symphonic: all of the play's major themes are established, the fundamental questions driving the drama set out. Before we even catch a glimpse of the protagonists – Caesar, Brutus, Antony, and Cassius – two disposable minor characters and a crowd make clear what's at stake and what's contested. Is this a holiday – and if so, a political or religious one? Has a high-flying Caesar overreached, or have his overzealous opponents read too much into his actions? Is the tribunes' sense of the commoners as an easily manipulated rabble correct, or have they underestimated their political savvy?

As if to compensate for keeping the protagonists offstage at the play's outset, in the scene that immediately follows Shakespeare brings all the main characters onstage at once, though most of them don't even speak. While Flavius and Marullus exit by one door, Caesar, Antony, Calphurnia, Portia, Decius, Brutus, Cassius, Casca and the Soothsayer sweep in from the other. Shortly thereafter, Marullus and Flavius return, only to see their greatest fears realized. Caesar speaks first, overseeing the rites of the holiday of Lupercal, including the foot race in which young men strike sterile women: 'The barren, touched in this holy chase, / Shake off their sterile curse' (I, ii, 7–8). He also engages in a bit of choreography, directing his wife to stand 'in Antonius' way' and reminding Antonius to 'touch Calphurnia' – a not so subtle hint that he's anxious for a political heir (an inappropriate desire in republican Rome, which had long since banished dynastic succession). Plutarch tells us that Lupercal's murky origins were variously associated with symbolic violence, collective purification, ritual sacrifice, the killing of enemies, even the preservation of Rome. These mysterious origins suited Shakespeare's needs perfectly, even as they enabled him to anchor the play in how the genre of tragedy itself is historically rooted in the nexus of religion, collective communal identity and bloody sacrifice – all this in a play whose central action, the slaughter of Caesar, re-enacts this complex ritual.

The crucial event of the second scene in *Julius Caesar* takes place offstage: Antony's attempt to crown the triumphant Caesar in the midst of the revelry. Brutus and Cassius, who have stayed behind rather than follow the Lupercalian race, are told by Casca that Caesar was offered a crown, 'and, being offered him, he put it by with the back of his hand, thus, and then the people fell a-shouting'. Twice more, it turns out, Antony offered Caesar a crown – or rather, Casca says, ''twas not a crown neither, 'twas one of these coronets'. To Casca's thinking, Caesar was 'loath to lay his fingers off it'. As Antony yet again offered it and Caesar refused it for the third time, 'the rabblement hooted and clapped their chapped hands, and threw up their sweaty nightcaps, and uttered such a deal of stinking breath because Caesar refused the crown that it had almost choked Caesar' (I, ii, 237–48). Once again, the meaning of the scene is left ambiguous: was Caesar earnestly rejecting the crown? Or was Casca right in suggesting that he wanted it – and would, if he could, rule over them all?

In his main source for this scene Shakespeare came across material he chose to suppress, for Plutarch makes clear that the coronation scene was anything but spontaneous. When Antony entered 'the market place' he 'came to Caesar and presented him a diadem wreathed about with laurel':

Whereupon there rose a certain cry of rejoicing, not very great, done only by a few, appointed for that purpose. But when Caesar refused the diadem, then all the people together made an outcry of joy. Then Antonius offering it him again, there was a second shout of joy, but yet of a few. But when Caesar refused it again the second time, then all the whole people shouted. Caesar having made this proof, found that the people did not like of it, and thereupon rose out of his chair, and commanded the crown to be carried unto Jupiter in the Capitol.

The scene had been orchestrated: planted in the crowd were 'a few' supporters, 'appointed for the purpose', who were ready to cry out when Antony offered Caesar the crown; but they failed to carry the rest of the crowd. Making the best of this staged show, Caesar recognized that the people only cheered when he refused the crown; it was pointless to force the issue at this moment.

Shakespeare may well have been startled when he came across this account in Plutarch, for he had himself invented a version of this scene before ever picking up a copy of the *Lives*. *Richard the Third* includes a wonderful moment when Richard, with his crony Buckingham, tries to manipulate the crowd in much the same way. This incident too is described rather than enacted. Buckingham assures Richard that he did everything he could to persuade the citizens to join in his cry for 'Richard, England's royal king' – but they refused to join in and declare Richard king. Buckingham even employs the same strategy as Antony and Caesar had in Shakespeare's source, planting supporters in the crowd to galvanize support:

> Some followers of mine own,
> At lower end of the hall, hurled up their caps,

And some ten voices cried, 'God save King Richard!'
And thus I took the vantage of those few:
'Thanks, gentle citizens and friends,' quoth I,
'This general applause and cheerful shout
Argues your wisdoms and your love to Richard.'
   (III, vii, 34–40)

But the terrified English subjects see through the charade, and, as in Plutarch, the manoeuvre fails. The revelation of this political chicanery further damns Richard in our eyes – which helps explain why Shakespeare chose not to base the scene on what Plutarch wrote, for he goes out of his way in *Julius Caesar* never to tilt the balance so decisively against Caesar.

Even as *Julius Caesar* anticipates *Hamlet*, it also looks back to *Henry the Fifth*, for Caesar's appropriation of a religious holiday for political ends recalls Henry V's similar efforts. The historical Henry V may have said a lot of things to his troops on the eve of the battle of Agincourt. He may have prayed to God, he may have prayed that the English longbow or the hedge of stakes planted to protect his forces from the French cavalry might carry the day. But we can be sure that he didn't say anything about how the longed-for victory on St Crispin's Day ought to be commemorated as a civic holiday. Only in a post-Reformation world would this have been imaginable. When Henry suggests that Crispin's Day henceforth be associated with England's great victory over France, Shakespeare has him speaking as a late sixteenth-century monarch. We are no longer invited to remember the religious figures – the fraternal Saints Crispin and Crispinian – but rather the English military heroes who fought that day:

> Then shall our names,
> Familiar in his mouth as household words –
> Harry the King, Bedford and Exeter,
> Warwick and Talbot, Salisbury and Gloucester –
> Be in their flowing cups freshly remembered.

This story shall the good man teach his son;
And Crispin Crispian shall ne'er go by,
From this day to the ending of the world
But we in it shall be remembered.
      (IV, iii, 51–6)

For all of Henry's insistence that the glory of the victory be
attributed to God, it is not God's saints but rather he and the other
English leaders who will be eternally celebrated. It's hard to imagine a better example of the displacement of the religious by the
nationalist. When these stirring lines were spoken on a London
stage in 1599, the victory at Agincourt was no longer celebrated
(it's only because of Shakespeare's words that its memory has been
kept alive). England had lost even its final toehold in France,
Calais, which had been turned back over to the French a few
months before Elizabeth came to the throne in 1558. So much for
'From this day to the ending of the world'. What distinguishes
Henry the Fifth from *Julius Caesar* is that, in the former, triumph
and holiday are kept apart; in the latter, they form a combustible
mixture.

The Elizabethans had their own 'Crownation Day', as some called
it: 17 November, generally known as Accession Day – commemorating the day in 1558 that Queen Mary died and Elizabeth's rule
began. Whether it was officially a religious or political holiday
depended on whom you asked. For the first couple of decades of
Elizabeth's reign 17 November, if celebrated at all, had been
observed as St Hugh of Lincoln's Day, in memory of a popular
regional saint whose holiday had nonetheless been struck from the
national calendar.

After Elizabeth's forces crushed the Northern Rebellion in 1569,
however, 17 November took on a special status, with 'bonfires,
ringing of bells, discharging of ordinance at the Tower of London
in the honour of the Queen and other signs of joy' including 'tri-

umphs used now yearly before Whitehall'. Elizabeth's Accession Day was probably the first political holiday in modern Europe and it initiated the string of nationalist holidays that are now a staple of the Anglo-American calendar. While holidays like Guy Fawkes' Day or Independence Day seem perfectly normal today, the notion of a non-religious holiday, or even of a holy day celebrating a living figure, was simply unimaginable before this in Europe. Though authorities preferred to speak of these celebrations as the spontaneous effusions of loyal subjects, Elizabeth's government quietly provided guidelines intended to promote the holiday, including a reprinted *Form of Prayer with Thanksgiving to be Used . . . the 17th of November* (1578). Works like Edmund Bunny's *Certain Prayers . . . for the Seventeenth of November* (1585), which included a helpful folding chart of the main points preachers should use in their Accession Day sermons, furthered these governmental aims.

While most Elizabethans, suffering from the dearth of holidays (especially in autumn), were happy enough for any excuse to carouse, those on the religious extremes – both Catholics and Protestants – immediately saw the danger of mixing politics and religion, triumph and holiday, in this way. In 1581, for example, the Puritan malcontent Robert Wright challenged a parson named Barwick over a sermon that the latter had preached. As far as Wright was concerned, Barwick had no business calling 17 November a 'holiday'. Barwick tried to backtrack, claiming that he had merely referred to it as a 'solemn day', but Wright wouldn't let the matter rest. In an attack that anticipates Cassius' bitter words about Julius Caesar – 'And this man / Is now become a god' (I, ii, 115–16) – Wright argued that to 'have a sermon on the Queen's day and to give God thanks for her Majesty was to make her a god'. Reports of Wright's claim that the point of the holiday was to turn the Queen into a god reached Elizabeth and angered her; he was charged with slander and thrown in prison.

Sometimes the conflicts over the celebrations on this day verged on the comical. The students at Lincoln College, Oxford – which had strong Catholic leanings – would annually on 17 November commemorate their patron saint, St Hugh of Lincoln. Some time around 1580, Oxford's mayor caught them in the act of ringing bells at All-Hallows Church, and accused them of doing so in memory of the passing of Queen Mary. The quick-witted students avoided punishment by claiming that they were simply ringing bells in honour of Elizabeth's accession. The chastened mayor, we are told, then ordered the rest of Oxford's churches to ring their bells too. Historians have noted that, in some parts of England where payments were made for bell-ringing on this day, accounts sometimes specify that they are to honour Elizabeth and some-times St Hugh. If the authorities were unsure for whom the bells tolled, how could those toiling in the fields that day know with any certainty who was being honoured: St Hugh? Mary? Elizabeth?

Where Puritan critics saw in Accession Day a reversion to Catholic ritual, Catholic ones condemned the holiday as pagan, having 'no better ground than the idolatrous rites and pastimes exhibited by the heathenish to Jupiter, Mars, Hercules, etc.' Catholic polemicists also derided Accession Day as a naked attempt to supplant the cult of the Virgin Mary with an unholy cult of Elizabeth. Edward Rushton was outraged that on 17 November at St Paul's Cathedral an 'antiphonal or hymn' once sung in praise of the Virgin was now 'converted ... to the ... hon-our of Queen Elizabeth, thereby to sound her praises'. The appro-priation of religious ritual for political ends had gone too far. Defenders of Elizabeth's regime confronted with this charge were left sputtering.

In November 1599 Londoners who had seen *Julius Caesar* in performances over the past few months at the Globe would have been treated to a scene in which life imitated art. On 17 and 18 November, a Saturday and Sunday, Hugh Holland and John

Richardson preached back-to-back sermons at Paul's Cross pulpit. If the public theatres could hold upwards of 3,000 spectators, the crowded outdoor space around the raised pulpit outside St Paul's Cathedral could hold twice that number. When Brutus and Antony take turns speaking at the open-air 'pulpit' in *Julius Caesar*, it is just such a site that Shakespeare and his audience would have had in mind.

Holland, preaching on Accession Day, played what might be described as Brutus' role, for he used the pulpit to defend the actions of the state. His appointed task was to defend 'the honour of this realm [that] hath been uncharitably traduced by some of our adversaries in foreign nations, and at home, for observing the 17th of November yearly in the form of a holy-day'. Richardson, for his part, got to play the role of Antony (though without Antony's rhetorical flair or success), using as his point of departure Matthew 22: 21 – 'Give unto Caesar that which is Caesar's' – subtly challenging the position of those in power. The crowd, alert to 'bugswords' or coded language, got the point and news quickly spread that Richardson, 'in open pulpit, spoke much of the misgovernment in Ireland; and used many words of the duty of subjects to their princes'.

The story of these rival pulpit speeches reveals a good deal about political sensitivities at the time, and about the extent to which the issues Shakespeare explores in *Julius Caesar* reflected contemporary concern with the uses of the classical past, republicanism, tyranny, holiday, popularity, censorship, political spin and the silencing of opposing voices. The analogies in this case are particularly strong: the government was greatly concerned that Elizabeth was portrayed as tyrannical; it was no less sensitive about accusations that the Queen was appropriating a holiday to promote her political cult. The incident offers a sharper sense than we might otherwise have of the power of the public sermon, the risks and dangers (so evident in *Julius Caesar*) of that favourite phrase of the Queen, 'tuning the pulpits'. Secretary of State Cecil himself scribbled worried notes on a copy of Richardson's sermon.

Classical stories could be dangerous – especially one that called to mind the Tacitean narrative of Nero's reign that had caused John Hayward such anguish. Even if Richardson had no knowledge of Tacitus, his sermon was read as if he did, one report claiming that 'he used a Latin phrase borrowed out of Tacitus'; and the same pair of powerful churchmen that had censored Hayward – Whitgift and Bancroft, the Archbishop of Canterbury and Bishop of London – now turned their attention to Richardson and demanded to know 'whether he had conferred with any man or were advised or instructed by any person to enter into that part, point, division, or application of his sermon'.

The authorities who had invited Richardson to speak felt as taken advantage of as Brutus after he turned the pulpit over to Antony. The official immediately responsible, Edward Stanhope, Bishop Bancroft's diocesan chancellor, was clearly caught off guard ('I least listened for novelties at his hands, as he was never of a turbulent spirit') and noted that, in the aftermath of the sermon, Whitgift and Bancroft responded by silencing Richardson: he 'now stands sequestered in a private house to his chamber, with the same restraint of resort to him, and silence, as before'. It was not just on the stage of the Globe that those who challenged the authorities were, to recall Flavius and Marullus' ominous fate, 'put to silence'.

The issues at stake over Accession Day were the same that kept coming back to haunt post-Reformation England, and they haunt Shakespeare's play as well. Ultimately, like the controversy over defacing the royal image, they cut to the heart of the cult of political leadership; and with this came disagreement over how history and time itself could be bent to accommodate a ruler's whim. For Elizabeth's flatterers her Accession Day marked the start of a new age 'wherein our nation received a new light after a fearful and bloody eclipse'. According to Edmund Bunny, the day commemorated England's deliverance from 'the power of darkness'. A Lancashire rector named William Leigh asserted that God himself had ordained 17 November as a holy day and John Prime preached in Oxford: 'Never did the Lord make any such day before it, neither will he make any such day after for the happiness of England.' What Prime failed to grasp was that the day Elizabeth died – and it couldn't be that far off – would be a new holiday: her successor's Accession Day. Inevitably, accession days were moveable feasts; one holiday drives out another, and Elizabeth's, much like St Crispin's and St Hugh's Days, would soon enough join the list of holidays that had become relics.

Yet such was the force of the argument that Elizabeth's accession ushered in a new historical age that it produced a romanticized view of her reign that persists to this day. And one of the great ironies of *Julius Caesar* is that the epoch-making political holiday that Caesar failed to create for himself on the Lupercal nonetheless led to a new calendrical moment – known to this day as the ides of March – that marked the end of the republic and the triumph of Caesarism. By locating within *Julius Caesar* a remarkably similar collision between political holiday and religious triumph, Shakespeare effectively translated a Roman issue into an Elizabethan one. No Elizabethan dramatist had ever done anything quite like this, and audiences must have been struck by how Shakespeare's retelling of this classical story seemed to speak so clearly to their moment.

Reaction to *Julius Caesar* was immediate. Even a tourist with only a smattering of English, like Thomas Platter, who went with a group of friends to see it when it was still in repertory at the Globe on 11 September, thought it was 'very pleasingly performed'. Shakespeare had written a brilliant, torrid play, fast-paced and relentless, with finely drawn and memorable characters and scenes that stuck in people's minds. The rival pulpit orations came in for special praise. The poet John Weever, who just a year earlier hadn't been able to distinguish between *Richard the Second* and *Richard the Third*, captured the tug of emotions as theatregoers, like the Plebeians in the play, found themselves siding first with Brutus, then with Antony:

> The many-headed multitude were drawn
> By Brutus' speech, that Caesar was ambitious.
> When eloquent Mark Antony had shown
> His virtues, who but Brutus then was vicious?

Weever's account dovetails with Leonard Digges's subsequent description of the intensity of this theatrical experience, with Digges paying special tribute to the fraught confrontation between Brutus and Cassius on the eve of the battle of Philippi:

> So have I seen, when Caesar would appear,
> And on the stage at half-sword parley were
> Brutus and Cassius, Oh, how the audience
> Were ravished, with what wonder they went hence.

One looks in vain for another play from this period that is described as leaving its audience 'ravished' and struck with 'wonder'.

SUMMER

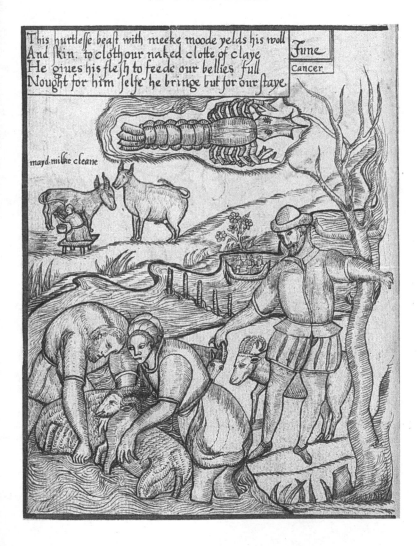

This hurtleſſe beaſt with meeke moode yelds his woll
And ſkin. to clóth our naked clotte of claye
He giues his fleſh to feede our bellies full
Nought for him ſelfe he bringe but for our ſtaye.

June
Cancer

mayd. milke cleane

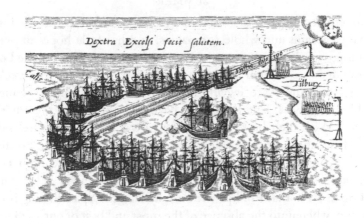

Dextra Excelfi fecit falutem.

9
The Invisible Armada

By late July political events began to overtake *Julius Caesar*. Brutus' castigation of Cassius for denying him 'gold to pay my legions' (IV, iii, 77) may have induced a grimace among playgoers after word got out of 'a mutiny threatened among the soldiers in Ireland, for want of pay and scarcity of victuals'. Hopes for a speedy and decisive victory in Ireland had been dashed: 'The Irish wars go slowly,' Sir Anthony Paulett wrote, as spring gave way to summer, 'and will not so soon be ended as was thought.' Never before under Elizabeth had the authorities cracked down so hard on what could be said or written, or been so willing to silence those who overstepped. George Fenner explained to news-hungry friends abroad that it 'is forbidden, on pain of death, to write or speak of Irish affairs'. Francis Cordale similarly apologized that he could 'send no news of the Irish wars, all advertisements thence being prohibited and such news as comes to Council carefully concealed'.

'The Invincible Armada', George Carleton

Nonetheless, he confided that our 'part has had little success, lost many captains and whole companies, and has little hopes of prevailing'. Fresh recruits were conscripted to replace those killed or wounded: '3,000 men are to go . . . from Westchester this week, and 2,000 more are levying.' 'It is muttered at court', Fenner added, that Essex 'and the Queen have each threatened the other's head'. With their best troops in the Low Countries and Ireland, the English knew how vulnerable they were to invasion. So did their Spanish foes. Current events began to take on the contours of Shakespearean history: 'The furious humour of the . . . Hotspurs of Spain,' Thomas Phillips writes, 'may lead the Spanish king into action, whereunto the absence of the most and best of our soldiers, as they conceive, and the scarceness of sea provisions this year may give encouragement.'

These were more than paranoid musings. Reports were arriving with disturbing frequency from spies, escaped prisoners and merchants that the Spanish were outfitting another armada to sail against England. By mid-July English spies reported home that the Spanish were ready to attack: the 'whole force will be about 22 galleys and 35 galleons and ships out of Andalusia . . . They report greater sea forces and 25,000 landing soldiers, and that he goes for England, hoping with this sudden exploit to take the shipping. They go forward in their old vanity of 1588.' The Spanish were coming, eager to avenge the humiliating defeat of the Great Armada eleven years earlier. A two-pronged assault was feared, with the Spanish attacking at some point along the southern coast while simultaneously sailing up the Thames, their land forces sacking and pillaging London as they had notoriously done to Antwerp. Even as plasterers, thatchers and painters were attending to the final touches on the Globe, Shakespeare had to contemplate the prospect that the gleaming playhouse might soon be reduced to ashes – along with the artistic and financial capital he had poured into it.

The Privy Council began requisitioning some of England's best ships to protect the coast and the Queen postponed her summer progress (no doubt a relief, since she had extended the one she had planned after hearing that her 'giving over of long voyages was noted to be a sign of age'). Hoping to raise morale, and seeing the obvious similarities to the threat of the Great Armada, the Archbishop of Canterbury suggested to Cecil that the special prayers that 'were used in the year 1588 are also fit for this present occasion and cannot be bettered'. By late July (the time when the Spanish had planned to land on the English coast in 1588), anxiety was running high. On the night of 25 July, Lieutenant Edward Dodington, one of the defenders at Plymouth, dispatched a messenger to London with the news of 'a fleet at this instant coming in upon us, the wind at north-west, and in all likelihood it is the enemy'. The letter's endorsement conveys his great sense of urgency, spurring on the messenger's race from one post horse to the next to let the Privy Council know the invasion had begun: 'For Her Majesty's special use; haste, post haste for life; haste, haste, post haste for life.' It was a false alarm, the first of many. John Chamberlain, who had excellent sources at court, wasn't sure of the true nature of the threat: he writes from London to Dudley Carleton on 1 August: 'Upon what ground or good intelligence I know not but we are all here in a hurle as though the enemy were at our doors.'

There was considerable scepticism both at home and abroad that the defensive preparations were intended solely to fend off a Spanish attack. The word on the Continent was that the 'Queen is dead'. The same was suspected in England. Henry Wake informed Cecil that it was 'secretly spread and whispered that her Majesty should be either dead or very dangerously sick'. Rumours were piled on rumours. One correspondent reported that 'the King of Scotland has taken arms against the Queen', 'the Earl of Essex, viceroy, is wounded, and his soldiers leave him', and 'in England there is tumult and fear, and many fly into the southern parts.

Some say the Queen is dead; it is certain that there is great mourning at Court.'

John Billot, an English prisoner in Spain, escaped and returned home with a smuggled Spanish proclamation, written in English, hidden in his boot. It revealed that King Philip III had commanded his forces to reduce England to 'the obedience of the Catholic Church'; and it instructed all Catholics in England to join forces with the Spanish invaders and take up arms against the English 'heretics'. Those who because of the 'tyranny' of English Protestants were too scared to change sides openly were urged to defect during 'some skirmish or battle' or 'fly before . . . the last encounter'. The Spanish threat was now coupled with a fear of disloyal English Catholics rising and joining forces with the invaders. To ensure that the dying embers of religious strife did not get blown into a civil war that would engulf the nation, the English government acted forcefully. On 20 July the Privy Council directed the Archbishop of Canterbury to round up leading recusants – those who remained committed enough to Catholicism to pay fines for refusing to participate in mandatory Protestant worship – and imprison them. In addition, orders were given 'to sequester all the able horses of the recusants'. If Catholic gentry were to join forces with the Spanish, they would have to walk. Some felt that these moves didn't go far enough. Sir Arthur Throckmorton warned that Protestant men with Catholic wives were even more dangerous than professed recusants and should be restrained and disarmed.

William Resould reported to Cecil that the Spanish planned to replace Elizabeth with an English Catholic, and though he wasn't prepared to name names, he wrote that 'there is some great personage' in England prepared to claim the throne. Catholic treachery was feared in the City as well. The Lord Mayor of London warned the Privy Council on 9 August: 'There are lately crept into this city diverse recusants, who in their opinions and secret affections being

1 RICHMOND PALACE This anonymous painting, executed circa 1620, shows Richmond Palace from across the Thames, with Morris dancers performing in the foreground. The Chamberlain's Men played before the Queen here on the evening of Shrove Tuesday, 1599, for which occasion Shakespeare wrote a special epilogue, probably for a revival of *A Midsummer Night's Dream*. The following morning, Ash Wednesday, with Shakespeare most likely in attendance, Lancelot Andrewes, England's leading preacher, delivered a Shrovetide sermon, its subject Essex's imminent campaign to crush the Irish rebellion.

2 THE EARL OF ESSEX Robert Devereux, 2nd Earl of Essex – the charismatic hero referred to by Shakespeare in *Henry the Fifth* as 'the General of our gracious Empress' – held centre-stage thoughout much of 1599. He is portrayed here by Marcus Gheeraerts the Younger, circa 1596, with his distinctive square beard (also alluded to in Shakespeare's play).

3 QUEEN ELIZABETH I This is the celebrated 'Rainbow Portrait' of Elizabeth, executed around 1600 (attributed by some to Marcus Gheeraerts and by others to Isaac Oliver). Though in her late sixties when this was painted, Elizabeth appears much younger, wearing the 'Mask of Youth' characteristic of portraits of her in her declining years. The flattering painting is heavily symbolic: the Queen is depicted here as Astraea and her garment is covered with eyes and ears (suggesting that she sees and hears all).

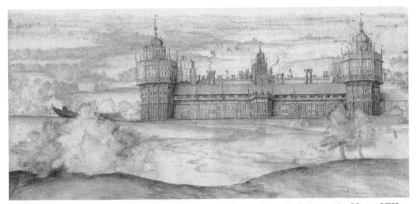

4 NONSUCH PALACE The splendid royal palace at Nonsuch was built in 1538 by Henry VIII, in Cuddington, near Epsom in Surrey. It was here, in late September 1599, that Essex, hastening back to court from Ireland, burst in unannounced upon Elizabeth in her bedchamber, while she was 'newly up, her hair about her face'.

5 ELIZABETH IN TRIUMPH Attributed to Robert Peake and long called *Queen Elizabeth Going in Procession to Blackfriars in 1600*, it has been aptly retitled *Eliza Triumphans*. The painting vividly captures the ceremonial and public nature of an Elizabethan procession. A half-dozen Knights of the Garter precede the Queen, wheeled by her grooms.

6 SHAKESPEARE The celebrated and contested 'Chandos' portrait of Shakespeare that hangs in the National Portrait Gallery, traditionally attributed to John Taylor.

7 RICHARD BURBAGE A portrait of the multi-talented Richard Burbage, star tragedian of the Chamberlain's Men, for whom Shakespeare wrote some of his greatest parts.

8 BEN JONSON Shakespeare's great rival Ben Jonson – poet, playwright and masque-maker – left an extended and generous tribute to Shakespeare in the First Folio of his plays.

9 ROBERT ARMIN The diminutive comic actor and author who joined the Chamberlain's Men after the popular clown Will Kemp broke with the company.

10 SERMON AT ST PAUL'S John Gipkyn's diptych, painted in 1616, captures a familiar sight in early modern London: a sermon at Paul's Cross. A pair of such sermons were delivered back to back on 17 and 18 November, 1599, for and against governmental policy, by Hugh Holland and John Richardson, respectively.

11 IRELAND, 1599 This colourful and in some details fanciful map of Ireland was executed by Baptista Boazio and engraved by Renolde Elstrack in 1599. It was probably commissioned for Essex's Irish expedition, for Boazio had previously produced maps of Calais (1596) and the Azores (1597) in advance of Essex's earlier campaigns.

12 EDMUND SPENSER Author of *The Faerie Queene* and Elizabethan England's most celebrated poet, Spenser died in early January 1599. Essex paid for his funeral at Westminster.

13 THE WILD IRISH WOMAN From the margin of the map of the 'Kingdom of Ireland' in John Speed's *Theatrum Imperii Magnae Britanniae* (1616).

15 SHAKESPEARE'S COAT OF ARMS A rough sketch of Shakespeare's coat of arms, which had been granted in 1596, appears in the so-called 'York Herald's Complaint' of 1602.

14 ST GEORGE AND THE DRAGON An early nineteenth-century copy of a painting of St George and the Dragon from the west wall of the Guild Chapel in Stratford-upon-Avon.

16 A PERSPECTIVE VIEW OF NEW PLACE This view of New Place (on the left) and the Guild Chapel and the Guild Hall and Grammar School (on the right), at the corner of Chapel Street and Chapel Lane in Stratford-upon-Avon, was drawn by John Jordan, a local artist, in 1793. This was years after Shakespeare's house had been pulled down in 1759.

17 LONDON (detail) The earliest printed map of London, it first appeared in 1574 in the second edition of G. Braun and F. Hogenberg's *Civitatis Orbis Terrarum*, an atlas of European cities. London's boundaries were expanding beyond the old Roman walls as the city's population would approach 200,000 by the end of the century. The map, executed two years before London's first permanent playhouses were built in Shoreditch, shows the bear and bull baiting rings in Southwark.

averse from the present state, may prove very dangerous to the state and city, if any opportunity should offer itself.' Everywhere one turned, it seemed, there were signs of Catholic plotting. A pair of illiterate London bricklayers stumbled upon what they thought was a handkerchief but turned out to be a letter. They dutifully took it to a scrivener, who directed them to a constable, who in turn alerted a local justice, who wrote to Cecil. The intercepted letter was from the Catholic Irishman the Earl of Desmond and was intended for the King of Spain. It urged 'the recovery of Christ's Catholic religion' in England, and justified such action on the grounds that Elizabeth was a tyrant ('Nero was far inferior to the Queen's cruelty'). Who dropped or planted this letter on the streets of London is anyone's guess.

The imagined threat didn't stop with the Spanish troops and their recusant supporters. A letter to Cecil about what the English now feared is worth quoting at length:

I thought it my duty to advertise you of the strange rumours and abundance of news spread abroad in the city, and so flying into the country, as there cannot be laid a more dangerous plot to amaze and discourage our people, and to advance the strength and mighty power of the Spaniard, working doubts in the better sort, fear in the poorer sort, and a great distraction in all, in performance of their service, to no small encouragement of our enemies abroad, and of bad subjects at home; as that the Spaniard's fleet is 150 sail of ships and 70 galleys; that they bring 30,000 soldiers with them, and shall have 20,000 from the Cardinal; that the King of Denmark sends to aid them 100 sail of ships; that the King of Scots is in arms with 40,000 men to invade England, and the Spaniard comes to settle the King of Scots in this realm.

London preachers fanned the flames, including one who 'in his prayer before his sermon, prayed to be delivered from the mighty forces of the Spaniard, the Scots and the Danes'. Nobody was sure what to believe: 'Tuesday at night last, it went for certain the Spaniards were landed at Southampton and that the Queen came at ten of the clock at night to St James's all in post; and upon Wednesday, it was said the Spanish army was broken, and no purpose of their coming hither: with a hundred other strange and fearful rumours, as much amazing the people as [if] the invasion were made.' Such anxious and conflicting accounts of the destination and size of the enemy fleet would be echoed a few years later in the opening act of Shakespeare's *Othello*, where Venice's leaders argue over intelligence reports: 'My letters say a hundred and seven galleys,' says one; 'And mine, a hundred and forty,' says another; 'And mine,' adds a third, 'two hundred . . . yet do they all confirm / A Turkish fleet, and bearing up to Cyprus' – a consensus immediately contradicted when news arrives that the 'Turkish preparation makes for Rhodes'. This latest intelligence is quickly dismissed: ''Tis a pageant / To keep us in false gaze' (I, iii, 4–21). As Shakespeare recognized, such crises were rich in drama.

By the first week of August defensive preparations around London, at sea and along the coast had intensified. Rowland Whyte reported to Sir Robert Sidney, who was with English forces in the Low Countries, that in London 'there [was] nothing but alarms and arming for defence'. From every ward in London, he added, ten or a dozen men were conscripted to man Her Majesty's fleet. John Chamberlain provides additional details: London 'is commanded to furnish out sixteen of their best ships to defend the river and 10,000 men, whereof 6,000 [are] to be trained presently and every man else to have his arms ready'. Letters were sent to the bishops and noblemen ordering them to 'prepare horses and all other furniture as if the enemy were expected within fifteen days'. The national mobilization was extraordinary. The objective was to mass upwards of 25,000 men in and around London to repel the invaders. The historian John Stow, who lived through it, believed that 'the like had not been seen in England since Queen Elizabeth came to the crown'. Sir Francis Vere was ordered to send home 2,000 of his best troops from the Low Countries. Messengers were sent to fifteen counties with instructions to send cavalry and rendezvous at prearranged sites around London. Orders also went out to twelve counties to provide thousands of foot soldiers. Earls and barons were told to gather forces, repair to the court and protect the Queen herself. The Earl of Cumberland was put in charge of the defence of the Thames, Lord Thomas the high seas, and the Lord Admiral the southern front.

As forces began to crowd London and its suburbs, great precautions were taken in the jittery capital. On Sunday, 5 August, by royal command, Stow writes, 'chains were drawn athwart the streets and lanes of the city, and lanterns with lights, of candles (eight in the pound) hanged out at every man's door, there to burn all the night, and so from night to night, upon pain of death, and great watches kept in the streets'. The danger of a sneak attack under cover of darkness outweighed even that of fire in a city containing so much combustible timber and thatch. The next day, Chamberlain writes, panic struck upon 'news (yet false) that the Spaniards were landed in the Isle of Wight, which bred such a fear and consternation in this town as I would little have looked for, with such a cry of women, chaining of streets and shutting of the gates as though the enemy had been at Blackwell. Our weakness and nakedness disgrace us, both with friends and foes.' Military leaders like Sir Ferdinand Gorges worried that civilian defenders weren't up to the task, 'for when things are done upon a sudden, and especially amongst people unenured to the business, they are amazed and discouraged'.

The Thames remained a weak link and a major concern. Initially, the Earl of Cumberland intended 'to make a bridge somewhat on this side Gravesend, after an apish imitation to that of Antwerp'. Given the failure of such a defence in Antwerp – it hadn't stopped the Spanish troops who laid waste to that city in 1585 – it was probably not the best plan. Still, Cumberland swore that 'with 1,500 musketeers he would defend that bridge or lose his life upon it'. This plan was soon succeeded by another: a shipwright named Ayde suggested blockading the river by sinking ships at a narrow point in the Thames, near Barking Shelf. The Privy Councillors were so taken with his idea that they instructed the Lord Mayor to put it into effect. It was an indication of just how desperate things were, for if the Spanish didn't destroy London's commerce, Ayde's plan surely would. The Mayor and aldermen begged the councillors to forgo this desperate measure and rely instead on a score of highly manoeuvrable boats to 'annoy the enemy and impeach his passage'. They had done the calculations and it had frightened them: Ayde proposed sinking eighty-three ships, their value roughly £25,000. Once sunk, these ships would flood the adjoining marshland, causing £40,000 worth of damage. Recovering the sunken hulks – and it wasn't at all clear that it would prove possible to do so – would cost £20,000 more. If they failed to, the 'Thames [would] be choked and spoiled, and the trade of the city wholly overthrown'. To the great relief of London's merchants, the Privy Council was prevailed upon and Ayde's plan abandoned.

The call to arms was heeded in the city by both rich and poor. This wasn't Ireland; they were defending their families, their homes, their Queen and country. John Chamberlain declared: 'Though I were never professed soldier, to offer my self in defence of my country . . . is the best service I can do it.' After casting a horoscope to learn whether the Spanish would attack, the enthusiastic astrologer Simon Forman went overboard, purchasing 'much harness and weapons for war, swords, daggers, muskets, corslet, and furniture, staves, halberds, gauntlets, mails, &c.' A contemporary survey of the mustering of the 'Armed and trained companies in London' in 1599 gives a vivid impression of its citizen army. Many of the captains leading their neighbours had served in a similar capacity in 1588. John Megges, draper merchant, led 125 men from Queenhyth Ward, while 250 men of Cripplegate Ward followed merchant tailor John Swynerton, and so on, throughout the various wards. All told, this London muster lists fifteen captains leading 3,375 men from twenty-five wards.

And what about Shakespeare? As a servant of the Lord Chamberlain, did he join up with those who wore the Privy Councillor's livery and attend upon the Queen herself at Nonsuch? If so, did his new status as a gentleman lead him to acquire a horse? Or did he decide instead to ride out of town against the sea of defenders heading south, heading back home to Stratford-upon-Avon, convincing himself that at this time of crisis it was best to be by his family's side and out of immediate harm's way? The answer to this would tell us a great deal about what kind of person Shakespeare was; but we don't have a clue what he did. The best guess is that, like others in the theatre, he stayed in London, followed events closely, and kept performing and writing. There's no indication that the authorities banned playgoing at this time, and there's a likelihood that, with thousands of volunteers in town milling about with nothing to do but drill and wait for the invaders to land, the theatres may have done brisk business – and from the government's perspective proved a helpful distraction, keeping the armed and idle forces preoccupied.

Henslowe's *Diary* certainly shows no sign of interruption in the regular routine of commissioning and writing plays through this crisis. Chapman, Dekker and Jonson were particularly busy. At the end of July, Chapman was at work on a 'pastoral ending in a tragedy', for which he received forty shillings on 27 July. Dekker was caught up in a frenzy of play-writing, taking payment on 1 August for *Bear a Brain* and nine days later sharing an advance with Ben Jonson for *Page of Plymouth*, a tragedy that they finished in three weeks. The two teamed up again at the beginning of September along with Henry Chettle 'and other gentlemen' on another lost tragedy, *Robert the Second, King of Scots* (capitalizing on the current of anti-Scottish sentiment, for Robert II, James's lineal ancestor, was one of the weakest monarchs ever to rule in that kingdom). If any of London's playwrights could be expected to bear arms it would have been Jonson, a native of the City, who had seen military service in the Low Countries (and bragged about killing an enemy soldier there in single combat). Yet even he was devoting this time to writing – not just collaborative work for the Admiral's Men but also a solo-authored sequel to *Every Man In His Humour* that he hoped to sell to the Chamberlain's Men. Henry Chettle and Thomas Haughton were also paid for plays at the height of the armada scare, the former for *The Stepmother's Tragedy*, and the latter for *The Poor Man's Paradise*. And if Michael Drayton, Wilson, Hathaway and Anthony Munday were to complete the *First Part of Sir John Oldcastle* and begin its sequel by mid-October, it's likely that they were already collaborating in August on the first part. Finally, John Chamberlain's allusion to the collapse of a house on St John's Street where a puppet show was being staged in mid-August offers further evidence that, armada or not, London's entertainment industry did not come to a halt.

Two plays in the Chamberlain's Men's repertory were particularly well suited to the moment. One was *Henry the Fifth*, celebrating as it did English military greatness (though, in the light of doubts raised about Essex's Irish campaign and rumours that this mobilization had something to do with him, the play's allusion to our 'General' returning from Ireland 'with rebellion broached on his sword' was probably dropped). Shakespeare's company would probably have dusted off another timely play in their repertory, *A Larum for London: Or, the Siege of Antwerp*, published not long after. The opening of the play graphically recounts how Antwerp was overrun when its citizens ignored the Spanish threat and put self-interest ahead of the common good:

> The citizens (were they but politic,
> Careful and studious to preserve their peace)
> Might at an hour's warning, fill their streets,
> With forty thousand well appointed soldiers.

It wasn't a particularly good play – and it gives a sense of how uneven the offerings of Shakespeare's company could be – but it got its point across: spectators would have looked on in horror as a family of four, including a blind father, was butchered. An Englishman in the wrong place at the wrong time was tortured, literally strappadoed onstage – yanked up and down by a rope by his arms, which were pinioned behind him. Virgins and matrons were attacked and threatened with rape and the libidinous Spaniards even began to strip one of their victims onstage. It was the Elizabethans' worst nightmare, all the more powerful if revived at this time, for playgoers knew that the same treacherous enemy was heading their way. Unlike their negligent fellow Protestants in Antwerp, though, Londoners were armed and ready.

As August dragged on there was still no sign of the Spanish. The more time passed, the wilder the speculation about what was really happening. Chamberlain writes:

> The vulgar sort cannot be persuaded but that there was some great mystery in the assembling of these forces, and because they cannot find the reason of it, make many wild conjectures, and cast beyond the moon, as sometimes that the Queen was dangerously sick, otherwhile that it was to show to some that are absent, that others can be followed as well as they, and that if occasion be, military services can be as well and readily ordered and directed as if they were present with many other as vain and frivolous imaginations as these. The forces in the west country are not yet dismissed, for there, if anywhere, may be some doubt of danger.

His cryptic allusions to those that 'are absent' and to the 'danger' expected by the defensive forces in the 'west country' both point to Essex, suggesting that there were fears that he might abandon Ireland, land with a military force in Wales, and march against his adversaries at court.

By the third week of August the strain, both psychological and financial, was enormous. The Privy Council continued to receive conflicting reports about Spanish plans and didn't know what to believe. Unscrupulous tradesmen were overcharging the gathered troops and the Lord Admiral had to publish a decree outlawing profiteering. The treasury, already drained by the Irish campaign, was nearly dry, yet somehow had to cover the enormous expense of supporting all these soldiers and sailors. By mid-August Elizabeth made a point of asking Thomas Windebank to remind Cecil to keep a closer eye on the rocketing costs of the mobilization: 'Yester evening,' he wrote to the Secretary of State, 'at her Majesty's going to horse, she called me to her' and 'willed me to write unto you these few words: "that there should not be too much taken out of an emptied purse, for therein was no charity".' In addition, the vast numbers of labourers drawn from their fields during harvest could lead to large-scale rioting or rebellion. After a string of crop failures from 1594 to 1597 due to terrible weather, the government couldn't afford to induce yet another bad harvest because of misguided policy. On 17 August, the defenders in the south – the Earl of Bath, Sir Ferdinand Gorges and others – dismissed those gathered to defend the coast, justifying their decision on the ground that they had 'received this day credible intelligence that no part of the enemy's fleet is at Brest or Conquet'. For the troops, it was not a moment too soon: 'Their estate had been most pitiful if they had not been sent home to help in their harvest, for by reason of the foul weather and want of help, their corn was almost utterly lost.'

By 20 August Elizabeth had had enough and told the Lord Admiral to 'dismiss our loving subjects assembled together by virtue of our former commandment'. He thought it a mistake but not an order he could refuse. So the city began to empty again, the danger thought to be past. On the 23rd, a much relieved John Chamberlain wrote cheerfully: 'The storm that seemed to look so black [is] almost quite blown over ... Our land forces are daily discharged little and little, and this day I think will be quite dissolved.'

Yet even as Chamberlain sent off his letter, new and terrifying reports arrived at court. One, from Plymouth, reported that the Spanish were about to 'land in some part of England 15,000 men, and assure themselves of another 15,000 English papists ready to assist them at their landing'. Their likely destination: Milford Haven. By Saturday the 25th there was no longer any doubt, and the Privy Council informed the Lord Mayor and the Earl of Cumberland that the Spanish 'must needs be on the coast of England by this time'. The troops so recently dismissed had to be recalled, 'the armed force of the city' put 'in readiness', and the Thames defended 'to impeach the coming up of the [Spanish] galleys'. It was 'now high time', the councillors added, 'for every subject to show his duty and affection to their sovereign and country'. The following days were tense and spectacular. On 26 August 3,000 citizen soldiers 'were all in armour in the streets, attending on their captains till past seven of the clock, at which time, being thoroughly wet by a great shower of rain', they 'were sent home again for that day'. The following morning 'the other 3,000 citizens, householders and subsidy men, showed on the Mile's End', where they trained all that day.

The drilling and martial display continued unabated until 4 September. Whatever the threat had been, by then the danger really had passed, and an exhausted country did its best to return to normal. Elizabeth quietly removed to Hampton Court where, according to one report, she was seen through the windows of the palace, 'none being with her but my Lady Warwick' – 'dancing "The Spanish Panic"' to pipe and tabor. The tune was aptly named. Elizabeth had a right to high-step it: she had nimbly dodged disaster yet again. The crisis was over. What had caused it remained disputed. The well-placed Francis Bacon refused to accept the official version. The claim that the Spanish were coming, he wrote, was 'a tale . . . given out by which even the wiser sort might well be taken in'. Perhaps if he had had access to all the intelligence reports and intercepts in Cecil's possession he might have thought differently. Perhaps not. Cecil himself, who knew for certain of Spanish preparations (though against whom was the sticking point), admitted in the midst of the crisis that he had overreacted, but defended himself on the grounds that the 'world is ever apt to cry *crucifige* [crucify him] upon me, as they have done on my father before me, whensoever I do dissuade these preparations'.

Bacon later maintained that 'all this was done to the end that Essex, hearing that the kingdom was in arms, might be deterred from any attempt to bring the Irish army over into England'. It was as good a theory as any. Why else had the Queen forbidden Essex from returning to England without her permission? To the English farmers called away from their fields the false alarm was an embittering experience. They had seen the effects of dearth and some had buried kin and neighbours who had died of famine or famine-related disease. A year before the armada threat of 1599 a Kentish labourer had been brought up on charges for saying the real war to be fought was between the rich and the poor, and that 'he hoped to see such a war in this realm to afflict the rich men of this country to requite their hardness of heart against the poor'. Francis Bacon also remembered the people 'muttering that if the Council had celebrated this kind of Maygame in the beginning of May, it might have been thought more suitable, but to call the people away from the harvest for it (for it was now full autumn) was too serious a jest'. Bacon saw that the English people were shrewd enough to see through their government's story, 'insomuch that they forbore not from scoffs, saying that in the year '88 Spain had sent an Invincible Armada against us and now she had sent an Invisible Armada'.

The difference was clear. The two armada threats framed the closing years of Elizabeth's reign and the comparison was not a flattering one. In 1588 the Queen had girded herself for battle and, according to a later report, reassured her subjects as they gathered in defence of the realm at Tilbury that she was 'resolved in the midst and heat of the battle to live and die amongst you all, to lay down for my God and for my kingdom and for my people mine honour and my blood even in the dust'. They were words that rivalled the stirring speeches of Henry V to his outnumbered troops at Agincourt. This time around she did not appear in public; like a queen bee she stayed hidden in her hive, protected by thousands who swarmed to her defence. She must have sensed that propagandistic speeches or even a royal appearance would no longer be effective. Her people were now too suspicious, their scepticism fed by seemingly endless conscription, faction at court and uncertainty about political and religious succession. It was also nurtured by the historical drama of Shakespeare and his fellow playwrights, who over the past decade had taught them, among other things, to be wary of the motives of rulers. Censorship over what could be said about Ireland or royal succession and the control over royal images, satire and history couldn't stop the muttering and certainly couldn't bring back that sense of promise and Providence that had followed the victory over the 'Invincible Armada' of 1588. Politically and artistically, there was no going back.

London's dramatists responded to the armada threat of 1599 in markedly different ways. For some, like John Marston, it offered a chance for a throwaway line and a sardonic laugh – 'The Spanish are coming!' – in his *Histriomastix*, probably performed by Paul's Boys later that autumn. Others worked the threat into the fabric of plays-in-progress, most notably Thomas Heywood, whose two-part *Edward the Fourth*, entered in the Stationers' Register on 28 August and rushed into print before the end of the year, must have been revised with the crisis in mind. Playgoers attending a performance of Heywood's play at the Boar's Head Inn during the armada scare would have had the uncanny experience of watching their ancestors confront a threat nearly identical to their own. The third scene of the play, which opens with the Mayor leading his fellow citizen-defenders – 'whole companies / Of mercers, grocers, drapers, and the rest' – explicitly collapses the distance between past and present. The Mayor asks, 'Have ye commanded that in every street / They hang forth lights as soon as night comes on?' We soon learn that London's 'streets are chained, / The bridge well manned, and every place prepared'. Heywood even has his historical Mayor wonder, anachronistically, 'What if we stop the passage of the Thames / With such provision as we have of ships?' The analogy is far more complicated, though, for in *Edward the Fourth* Londoners defend their city not against foreign invaders but against an English army, led by Falconbridge, intent on freeing the deposed King Henry VI from the Tower. And Heywood quietly suppresses the fact that the Earl of Essex's ancestor had come to the aid of London's citizens. As the political winds kept shifting this year, so too did the meaning of Heywood's play.

Other playwrights made no pretence of masking current events in past histories. In October, for example, an anonymous and now lost play – whether it was staged publicly or privately is unclear – celebrated the recent victory of English troops over Spanish forces at Turnhout in the Low Countries. The actors were deliberately made up to resemble English leaders down to their distinctive beards and doublet and hose: 'This afternoon I saw *The Overthrow of Turnhold* played,' writes Rowland Whyte, 'and saw Sir Robert Sidney and Sir Francis Vere upon the stage, killing, slaying, and overthrowing the Spaniard.'

It took some time for Shakespeare to digest what was happening around him and turn it into art. Before 1599 was over he would hit upon how his next tragedy would begin – with jittery soldiers, at night, standing guard. One of them isn't even sure what he's guarding against and wonders if anyone can tell him the reason for the frenzied military preparation going on around him:

Why this same strict and most observant watch
So nightly toils the subject of the land,
And with such daily cost of brazen cannon
And foreign mart for implements of war,
Why such impress of shipwrights, whose sore task
Does not divide the Sunday from the week?
    (*Hamlet*, I, i, 71–6)

The time is out of joint, the mood dark, the threats multiple and uncertain. For many Londoners, recalling their experience of the past August, the opening scene of *Hamlet* would have brought a shudder of recognition. But this is getting ahead of our story.

THE
PASSIONATE
PILGRIME.
By W. Shakespeare.

AT LONDON
Printed for W. Iaggard, and are
to be fold by W. Leake, at the Greyhound in Paules Churchyard.
1599.

IO

The Passionate Pilgrim

We don't know who first mentioned to Shakespeare, no later than April or May, that a new book of his poems, '*The Passionate Pilgrim* by W. Shakespeare', was for sale at William Leake's bookshop at the sign of the Greyhound in Paul's Churchyard (and perhaps elsewhere as well). At long last some of his prized sonnets, which until now had circulated only among those Francis Meres called Shakespeare's 'private friends', were available in print. The news would have come as a surprise. While Shakespeare couldn't deny that some of the sonnets in *The Passionate Pilgrim* were his, he had had nothing to do with their publication; and though the book advertised his authorship – testimony to his growing popularity – he didn't profit from its sale.

How and under what auspices his poetry was published mattered a great deal to Shakespeare, especially early on in his career. He had carefully seen *Venus and Adonis* into print in 1593; a year

Title page of *The Passionate Pilgrim*, 1599

later he had shown similar care in publishing *Lucrece*, this, too, handsomely produced by his friend Richard Field. But in the ensuing five years he hadn't published a single poem, including any of his sonnets. He had begun writing sonnets around 1590, well before he turned his hand to the two long narrative poems, and he would continue writing and revising them for many years. Other than sharing his sonnets with a select few, Shakespeare guarded them closely – so closely that not a single commonplace book or manuscript collection from the 1590s records even one of them. We can only assume that he made clear to his friends that the poems shouldn't circulate and, except for those that appeared in *The Passionate Pilgrim*, they would remain under wraps until a sequence of 154 of them was published in 1609.

Disconcerting as it must have been to see his poetry surreptitiously published – along with poems that weren't even his – there was little Shakespeare could do about it. In Elizabethan England publishers, not authors, held copyright. The publisher of *The Passionate Pilgrim* was William Jaggard, famous to posterity for helping to produce the 1623 First Folio of Shakespeare's plays; but that was a quarter-century later. In 1599 Jaggard was at the beginning of his career, already keen on, though apparently unknown to, Shakespeare. He had somehow got hold of two of Shakespeare's sonnets that were in circulation: 'When my love swears that she is made of truth' and 'Two loves I have, of comfort and despair'. With this provocative pair of sonnets in hand, Jaggard had then filched three other irregular sonnets (spoken by young gallants, all three of them second-rate poets) from Shakespeare's *Love's Labour's Lost*, which had just appeared in print.

Five of Shakespeare's poems did not stretch far enough to warrant a whole book – nor enough to generate a decent profit, since there were rules about how much he could charge for a book (no more than a penny for every two sheets of text). So Jaggard padded things out by beginning each brief poem on a fresh page, leaving most of the reverse sides of the pages blank and adding fifteen other poems of varying lengths (the Elizabethan definition of a sonnet was fairly elastic). Four of these were about the erotic encounters of Venus and Adonis. Jaggard must have hoped, reasonably enough, that they might pass for Shakespeare's. He also went out of his way to put the real thing at the front of the volume. Four of the first five sonnets are unquestionably Shakespeare's, so that hesitant buyers flipping through the opening pages would be reassured that they were getting what they paid for.

Jaggard put *The Passionate Pilgrim* up for sale at William Leake's bookshop rather than his own shop near the Royal Exchange. While it might cut into his profits, the move offered a veneer of legitimacy for the unauthorized volume. Leake had recently acquired the rights to sell Shakespeare's best-selling *Venus and Adonis*, now in its fifth edition. To the unsuspecting consumer it looked as if Leake had cornered the market in Shakespeare's amorous poetry. The strategy worked. Not only did *The Passionate Pilgrim* sell out and quickly go into a second edition before the end of 1599, but its brisk sales also boosted those of *Venus and Adonis*, which for the first time ever went through two editions in a calendar year. *The Passionate Pilgrim* was so popular that it was nearly read out of existence: just fragments of a single copy of the first edition (rediscovered only in 1920) and a couple of copies of the second 1599 edition survive.

Londoners with a few shillings to spare now had access to what until now only a privileged few had previously enjoyed. They were also as free to gossip about the sonnets' intimate (if fictional) biographical details, for these teasingly allusive poems almost beg for that sort of response. Who were the man and 'ill-coloured' woman – the two loves 'of comfort and despair' – with whom the poet was sexually entangled? If word of the book spread far enough, Shakespeare may have had a bit of explaining to do the next time he went home to his wife in Stratford.

It's likely that Shakespeare went to see for himself what the book was doing at Leake's bookshop, at the least to discover who was behind it. He was no stranger to London's book world and must have been a familiar presence in the bookshops. There's no way that Shakespeare could have bought or borrowed even a fraction of the books that went into the making of his plays. Besides his main sources for his British histories and Roman tragedies, which he probably owned – Holinshed's *Chronicles* and Plutarch's *Lives* – he drew on hundreds of other works. From what we know of Shakespeare's insatiable appetite for books, no patron's collection – assuming that Shakespeare had access to one or more – could have accommodated his curiosity and range. London's bookshops were by necessity Shakespeare's working libraries and he must have spent a good many hours browsing there, moving from one seller's wares to the next (since, unlike today, each bookseller had a distinctive stock), either jotting down ideas in a commonplace book or storing them away in his prodigious actor's memory. Between his responsibilities vetting potential plays for the Chamberlain's Men's repertory and his time spent paging through recently published books, it's hard to imagine anyone in London more alert to the latest literary trends.

The one surviving anecdote that links Shakespeare with London's bookshops dates from 1599. Around this time another widely read Elizabethan, George Buc – government servant, Member of Parliament, writer, and theatregoer – sought out Shakespeare's advice about the authorship of an anonymous play he had recently purchased. Like everyone in the theatre world, Shakespeare knew that Buc was next in line for Edmund Tilney's job as Master of the Revels, so we can assume he would have done his best to help him. Buc was also one of the first serious collectors of Elizabethan drama; and though Buc's play collection has since broken up, scholars have identified his handwriting in copies of sixteen plays now scattered in archives around the world. How many other quartos from Buc's collection survive, unmarked or unexamined, is anybody's guess. We know from his marginalia that Buc purchased at least four old plays belatedly published in 1599: *Alphonsus King of Aragon*, *Edward I*, *Sir Clymon and Clamydes*, and *George a Greene, the Pinner of Wakefield*. While all were published anonymously, Buc was well enough informed to write on their title pages that Robert Greene was the author of *Alphonsus* and George Peele of *Sir Clymon* and *Edward I*. He was stumped, though, by *George a Greene*. The group of plays overlaps with those Shakespeare may have consulted this year – for in the course of writing *As You Like It* he probably looked at the depictions of Robin Hood in *George a Greene* and *Edward I*, and may have lifted the name of the old shepherd Corin from *Clymon and Clamydes*. In the course of 1599 Buc and Shakespeare may have crossed paths at London's bookstalls on more than one occasion.

After purchasing *George a Greene* at Cuthbert Burby's shop near the Royal Exchange, Buc went about finding out who had written it, at which point he either ran into or sought out Shakespeare. Shakespeare recalled that the play had been written by a minister, though at this point his memory failed him: he couldn't remember the minister's name. The oversight was excusable. It had been over a decade since the play was first staged. But Shakespeare did volunteer an unusual bit of information: the minister had acted in it himself, playing the Pinner's part. A grateful Buc scribbled on the play's title page his findings: 'Written by .... a minister, who acted the pinner's part in it himself. *Teste* [i.e., witnessed by] W. Shakespeare.' He'd have to fill in that blank another time. Their conversation probably took place near the Royal Exchange, though it may as well have occurred after a performance at the Curtain or Globe or at a court performance. The story suggests not only that plays were becoming valued as printed texts to be read and collected but also that dramatic authorship was beginning to matter – at just the moment that Shakespeare was coming into his own.

Jaggard's title – *The Passionate Pilgrim* – says a good deal about the target audience for a book by 'W. Shakespeare'. He was exploiting a market as much as he was creating one. The title deliberately echoes the language of Romeo and Juliet's romantic first encounter, where the young lovers speak, touch, then kiss, in the course of sharing a sonnet. While Romeo addresses his beloved in the well-worn language of the Petrarchan lover, the division of the sonnet between the young man and the usually silent object of his love offers a new twist. The lovers' shared sonnet begins with each speaking in a quatrain, Romeo, the passionate pilgrim, going first:

> If I profane with my unworthiest hand
> This holy shrine, the gentle sin is this:
> My lips, two blushing pilgrims, ready stand
> To smooth that rough touch with a tender kiss.

To which Juliet replies:

> Good pilgrim, you do wrong your hand too much,
> Which mannerly devotion show in this;
> For saints have hands that pilgrims' hands do touch,
> And palm to palm is holy palmers' kiss.
>   (I, v, 94–101)

The title appealed to those who could not get enough of the passionate language of *Romeo and Juliet*. Writers at the time joked about young men who slept with a copy of *Venus and Adonis* under their pillows and about others who rifled Shakespeare's work for pick-up lines. Just a year earlier John Marston had mocked young men about town from whose 'lips . . . doth flow / Naught but pure Juliet and Romeo'. It was a stock joke, retailed in a university play performed at Cambridge in late 1599 called *The Return from Parnassus, Part One*, in which one character predicts that another is sure to plagiarize Shakespeare: 'We shall have nothing but pure Shakespeare and shreds of poetry that he hath gathered at the theatres.' He's right. A moment later that character tries to pass off romantic lines from *Romeo and Juliet* as his own. In case anybody missed the point, when Jaggard published a third edition of Shakespeare's *Passionate Pilgrim* in 1612, he advertised on the title page that the volume contained 'Certain Amorous Sonnets'.

Because of Jaggard's clever packaging, most readers of *The Passionate Pilgrim* assumed that the entire volume was by Shakespeare; and admirers of Shakespeare continued to believe this for the next two hundred years. Not until the nineteenth century would sceptical researchers reassign half of the lyrics in *The Passionate Pilgrim* to other poets. Today, ten of its poems still remain unattributed. The case is still occasionally made for Shakespeare's authorship of the four poems about Venus and Adonis. As scholars who have made headlines in recent years for claiming that Shakespeare wrote such poems as 'Shall I die' and the 'Funeral Elegy' would grudgingly admit, it's surprisingly hard to distinguish Shakespeare on an off day from one of his imitators on a very good one. Some of the greatest names in the history of Shakespeare criticism from the eighteenth and nineteenth centuries – Malone, Theobald, Furnivall, Dyce, Collier, Dowden and Halliwell-Phillipps – maintained that most of the poems in *The Passionate Pilgrim* were Shakespeare's. We can only assume that, except for a small coterie of poets and their admirers, few in 1599 would have known better or thought otherwise.

Some writers might have been flattered by Jaggard's gambit. Not Shakespeare, who was offended by what Jaggard had done and let it be known; the publication of *The Passionate Pilgrim* would only make it more difficult to undo his reputation as poet of the 'heart-robbing line'. Our source is his fellow poet and dramatist Thomas Heywood (whose work was later stolen by the unscrupulous Jaggard and passed off as Shakespeare's to flesh out the third edition of *The Passionate Pilgrim*). At that time Heywood complained loudly about this 'manifest injury' – he wanted to make it clear that it was Jaggard, not he, who was guilty of theft. Heywood recalled that Shakespeare himself had suffered similar treatment at Jaggard's hands when *The Passionate Pilgrim* had first been published: Shakespeare, he writes, was 'much offended with M. Jaggard (that altogether unknown to him) presumed to make so bold with his name'.

As Shakespeare thumbed through the volume that bore his name, it's hard to know what would have offended him most. Was it the shock of seeing his sonnets there – and, by implication, possible evidence of betrayal by a friend who had surrendered them to Jaggard? Or would he have been more irritated by the yanking out of context of the three intentionally bad poems from *Love's Labour's Lost*? The weakest of these appears as the fifth poem in the collection, and is served up in limping alexandrines. The first eight lines are enough to give the gist:

> If Love make me forsworn, how shall I swear to love?
> O, never faith could hold, if not to beauty vowed:
> Though to my self forsworn, to thee I'll constant prove,
> Those thoughts to me like oaks, to thee like osiers bowed.
> Study his bias leaves, and makes his book thine eyes,
> Where all those pleasures live, that art can comprehend.
> If knowledge be the mark, to know thee shall suffice:
> Well learned is that tongue that well can thee commend.

As Polonius might have said at this point, 'This is too long' (and had he read the third poem, also lifted from *Love's Labour's Lost*, he might have called 'vapour-vow' an 'odious phrase'). Shakespeare had written 'If love make me forsworn' for the young gallant Berowne, and, to further deflate its effect, had the poem read aloud not by the lover himself but by a curate. It's unlikely that Shakespeare appreciated the irony of life imitating art, for in the play, too, the sonnet ends up in the wrong hands, having 'accidentally . . . miscarried' (IV, ii, 138).

Rather than offering the dazzling linguistic virtuosity of what would come to be known as a 'Shakespearean' sonnet – just the kind of verbal play readers had encountered in the opening two poems of *The Passionate Pilgrim* – Berowne's effort simply rehearses stale Petrarchan conceits. In *Love's Labour's Lost* Shakespeare leaves no doubt about how weak a poem it is and the best thing any of those onstage can find to praise about it is the writer's penmanship. Shakespeare was left to wonder which was worse: readers dismissing it as one of his weaker efforts or, alternatively, thoroughly enjoying its conventional style and hoping he'd write more like it.

It was one thing for Shakespeare to be confused with second-raters; it was another, and a much more uncomfortable experience, to have a poem arguably better than any that he had ever published ascribed to him:

> Live with me and be my love,
> And we will all the pleasures prove
> That hills and valleys, dales and fields,
> And all the craggy mountains yield.
>
> There we will sit upon the rocks,
> And see the shepherds feed their flocks,
> By shallow rivers, by whose falls
> Melodious birds sing madrigals.
>
> There will I make thee a bed of roses,
> With a thousand fragrant posies,
> A cap of flowers and a kirtle
> Embroidered all with leaves of myrtle.

Even in this abbreviated version, 'Live with me and be my love' is one of the finest expressions of pastoral in English poetry, its vision so precarious that it cries out for a response or refutation. And contemporary poets, including Sir Walter Ralegh and John Donne, responded in these ways. Nowadays, we know that

Christopher Marlowe wrote these extraordinary lines and that Ralegh was reputedly the author of the most famous response, a stanza of which is appended to the lyric in *The Passionate Pilgrim*:

> If that the world and love were young,
> And truth in every shepherd's tongue,
> These pretty pleasures might me move,
> To live with thee and be thy love.

In 1599, however, neither poem had been published or attributed. Only a year later, in the rival collection *England's Helicon*, was Marlowe's poem correctly attributed (while Ralegh's was signed '*Ignoto*' – Unknown). But for most readers of *The Passionate Pilgrim* the attribution to Shakespeare the amorous poet made good sense, and support for Shakespeare's authorship of 'Live with me and be my love' lingered into the nineteenth century.

Shakespeare himself was keenly aware of Marlowe's authorship. He was also familiar with Marlowe's own send-up of it in the wildly popular *The Jew of Malta*, where an exaggerated version of this innocent pastoral fantasy is recited by Ithamore, a slave and a villain, while lying in the lap of a prostitute, Bellamira:

> The meads, the orchards, and the primrose lanes,
> Instead of sedge and reed, bear sugar-canes:
> Thou in those groves, by Dis above,
> Shalt live with me and be my love.
> (IV, ii, 101–4)

Marlowe had not only invented the perfect pastoral, he had shown how easily its fragile vision could be parodied.

Shakespeare himself had offered his own tribute to the poem just a year earlier in *The Merry Wives of Windsor*, where lines from 'Live with me' are delivered in a slightly garbled version in the thick Welsh accent of Parson Evans. Evans is nervously waiting to fight a duel and his mind drifts helplessly from Marlowe's love lyric to the despairing lines of Psalm 137:

> To shallow rivers, to whose falls
> Melodious birds sings madrigals;
> There will we make our peds of roses,
> And a thousand fragrant posies.
> To shallow—

Mercy on me! I have a great dispositions to cry.

> Melodious birds sing madrigals –
> Whenas I sat in Pabylon –
> And a thousand vagram posies.
> To shallow, etc.
>   (III, i, 16–25)

This kind of direct quotation of another Elizabethan writer – mis-pronunciations and confusions notwithstanding – is unusual in Shakespeare's work, and until now in his plays virtually unprece-dented. Even before the publication of *The Passionate Pilgrim*, Marlowe, though dead for six years, was still on Shakespeare's mind.

The publication of *The Passionate Pilgrim* would amount to little more than a footnote to his career if not for the impact it had upon Shakespeare's thinking about his stolen sonnets, about Marlowe and the pastoral and, through both, about *As You Like It*. After it appeared as the opening poem in *The Passionate Pilgrim*, Shake-speare went back to 'When my love swears that she is made of truth' and changed it. The copy Jaggard had got hold of may have introduced a few errors, but the difference between the two ver-sions (especially when compared with the versions of the compan-ion sonnet Jaggard published with it) makes clear that the revisions were Shakespeare's. While he could have revised it at any time between 1599 and 1609 (when it reappeared in his collected *Sonnets*), it's likely that Shakespeare was spurred to make the changes soon after it appeared in print. It's impossible to know whether he saw himself reclaiming a poem that had been untimely ripped from his possession or whether seeing it in print had made him see its faults. He didn't change much, but the cumulative effect is astonishing. Like Michelangelo chiselling free a figure trapped in stone, Shakespeare, with a few well-placed strokes, enables a far more complex poem to emerge. The transformation points the way to a new comic vision, one at the heart of *As You Like It*.

Shakespeare may well have tinkered with other sonnets over the ten, fifteen, even twenty years between their conception and publication (no surprise, then, that he speaks in Sonnet 17 of his papers 'yellowed with their age'). Shakespeare kept close at hand a sheaf of forty or more folded sheets, each sheet with four writing sides, covered with sonnets in various stages of completion (it wasn't until the early seventeenth century that writers began using single sheets of paper). A handful of the poems that appear in 1609 don't seem quite finished. Others are so highly polished that a syllable can't be altered without serious damage to the poem's architecture. Unlike rival poets such as Michael Drayton and Samuel Daniel, who also reworked their sonnet sequences over several decades but chose to publish each successive version, Shakespeare kept his poems-in-progress private, which suggests that they had a different kind of value for him, filled different creative needs, which included serving as sounding boards, rough drafts for the larger themes and dynamics of his plays.

We know very little about how Shakespeare went about writing – where he liked to write, how much he revised, what was hard for him and what was easy. What evidence we have is from his plays and poems, and one of the few scenes of writing Shakespeare does describe – in *Lucrece* – includes a healthy share of blotting, a rush of thoughts trying to force their way through at once, and a ruthless insistence on getting it right. It may be the closest we get to Shakespeare's own writing process, a portrait of the artist at work, the autobiographical 'Will' at war with 'wit', trying to control the great press of ideas. Here is Lucrece as she 'prepares to write',

> First hovering o'er the paper with her quill.
> Conceit and grief an eager combat fight;
> What wit sets down is blotted straight with will;
> This is too curious-good, this blunt and ill.
> Much like a press of people at a door
> Throng her inventions, which shall go before.
>   (1297–1302)

What Shakespeare describes in these lines is not so much writing as intense revision. This fits with what we know about how he tended to work, which was by reworking rather than inventing stories. A glance at the plays he had written so far in 1599 confirms this. The play he was currently writing – *As You Like It* – recasts the story of Thomas Lodge's popular *Rosalind*. Shakespeare had a gift for reading or hearing something and unspringing its unrealized potential. It couldn't have been easy for him to resist the impulse to improve things as he read or performed another writer's work. With 'When my love swears' Shakespeare turned that same severe critical eye – 'This is too curious-good, this blunt and ill' – upon his own creation.

First, the version that appeared as the opening poem in *The Passionate Pilgrim*:

> When my love swears that she is made of truth,
> I do believe her (though I know she lies)
> That she might think me some untutored youth,
> Unskilful in the world's false forgeries.
> Thus vainly thinking that she thinks me young,
> Although I know my years be past the best:
> I, smiling, credit her false-speaking tongue,
> Outfacing faults in love with love's ill rest.
> But wherefore says my love that she is young?
> And wherefore say not I that I am old?

224

O, love's best habit is a soothing tongue,
And age (in love) loves not to have years told.
Therefore I'll lie with love, and love with me,
Since that our faults in love thus smothered be.

The premise of the sonnet is straightforward, if a bit cynical: it's a doomed relationship, built on lies. He knows that she lies to him about being faithful, but he doesn't challenge her, hoping thereby that she'll think he's new to this game; and he lies to her about his age (though he knows his 'years be past the best'). She's the bigger liar, though, for she not only lies about fidelity, but also lies about her age ('But wherefore says my love that she is young?').

The speaker of the sonnet is self-protective, isolated and comfortably misogynistic. We see the affair from his perspective and his alone. There's no reciprocity here, only sex and deception. It's but a small step to the disillusionment and dark anger of Sonnet 129 ('Th'expense of spirit in a waste of shame / Is lust in action'). The central lines here are those in which we learn that the speaker plays his cards close, giving nothing away. He's convinced that he's better at this game than she is: 'I, smiling, credit her false-speaking tongue, / Outfacing faults in love with love's ill rest.' The language here anticipates Hamlet's bitter words about Claudius' deception ('smile, and smile, and be a villain' [I, v, 108]), with hints as well of Iago-like bluffing, 'outfacing' those he deceives.

The most remarkable thing about Shakespeare's revision of this poem is how much he alters economically. Here's the revised version as it appeared in the 1609 collected *Sonnets*:

When my love swears that she is made of truth,
I do believe her though I know she lies,
That she might think me some untutored youth,
Unlearned in the world's false subtleties.
Thus vainly thinking that she thinks me young,
Although she knows my days be past the best:
Simply I credit her false-speaking tongue,

On both sides now is simple truth suppressed.
But wherefore says she not she is unjust?
And wherefore say not I that I am old?
O, love's best habit is in seeming trust,
And age in love loves not to have years told.
Therefore I'll lie with her, and she with me,
And in our faults by lies we flattered be.

The first quatrain is largely unchanged, 'Unlearned' substituted for 'Unskilful' and 'subtleties' for 'forgeries', softening the edges a bit, though not much more than that (and replacing words that only occur in the first half of Shakespeare's works with those – 'unlearned' and 'subtleties' – that he preferred later in his career).

The most significant change is also the subtlest. By turning 'I know' to 'she knows', in line 6, a shared understanding and subjectivity is introduced. We are now witnesses to a lovers' game, one in which role-playing leads to mutual understanding. As Edward A. Snow (who has written cogently about these poems) observes, it 'is the difference between "I may be able to deceive her but I can't deceive myself," and "I might be able to deceive myself if I weren't aware of how well she knows me, how obvious the truth of me is to her."' Only in the revised version does the speaker learn to see himself through his lover's eyes. We're no longer listening to someone brag about an affair; instead, we're experiencing the excitement and confusion of what it feels like to be in love.

The crassest pair of lines in the earlier version of the poem (in which the speaker hides behind his mask) is scuttled, replaced by: 'Simply I credit her false-speaking tongue, / On both sides now is simple truth suppressed.' This is the heart of the revised poem: simple truth is mutually suppressed so that a greater and more complex truth that the lovers share can thrive, and it is this truth that defines and sustains their love.

Shakespeare also goes back and recasts the lies (in the revised poem things are symmetrical: each lover now tells just one lie).

Falsehoods once meant to deceive now appear as both playful and purposeful. As Edward A. Snow concludes, the 'earlier version makes us feel the impossibility of the relationship, the later one, its fittingness, its inevitability'. In the version of the poem that appeared in *The Passionate Pilgrim* the speaker is only fooling himself when he 'lies with love'; in the revised version he lies with his beloved in both senses of the word, their playful falsehoods securing their affection. In the new ending, their love is forgiving, not smothering. This sense of mutuality, of merging selves, ring outs in the chiming sounds of the concluding couplet: 'She ... me ... we ... be.'

T was a louer and his laſſe, With a haye ,with a hoe and a haye nonie

no and a haye nonie nonie no , That o're the green come fields did paſſe in ſpring time,ij,ij.

II
Simple Truth Suppressed

At the heart of *As You Like It* is the relationship of Orlando and Rosalind, which moves from a love that is self-centred to one that is complex and mutual. Like the revised version of 'When my love swears', *As You Like It* achieves this through role-playing and the suppression of simple truths. What Shakespeare sketches out in the revised sonnet he transfers onto a larger canvas in the play and the result marks a significant advance in his handling of character and intimacy. Shakespeare manages to create a relationship so emotionally complex that the love feels genuine (even if, paradoxically, he does so by setting up and knocking down literary conventions). We may love Romeo and Juliet and agonize over their fate, but we respond to the intensity, not the complexity, of their feelings. With *As You Like It* that's no longer the case; intensity has become a liability. As Rosalind, though deeply in love herself, observes in her devastating put-down of dying for love, it's just one more lie that lovers tell: 'But these are all lies. Men have died from

'It was a lover and his lass', Thomas Morley, *First Book of Ayres*, 1600

time to time, and worms have eaten them, but not for love' (IV, i, 100–101).

Shakespeare lifts a conventional heroine out of a popular story and transforms her into someone we feel we know or want to know. How he does so, and how he then endows her with the ingenuity to educate the 'untutored youth' she loves about who she is and what intimacy means, is one of the mysteries of literary creation. This jolt of realism may well have surprised Elizabethans schooled in a drama that until now had only rarely been this naturalistic. Unlike the contemporary praise for Shakespeare's recent successes in history and tragedy, there is only silence regarding *As You Like It*. The play, one of the most frequently staged today, was not published until the 1623 Folio and over a century would pass before it was mentioned or staged again. It may well be that Shakespeare made such novel demands upon audiences, introduced so much that was not easily absorbed, that spectators left the Globe unsettled. It was a play not only of its time but also ahead of it.

There's a great deal going on in *As You Like It* and on many levels. Ultimately, though, everything in this relatively plotless drama – its political frame, its clown and satirist, its multiple marriages, its gender-bending, its reflections on poetry and pastoral – is subordinate to the story of the central lovers, Orlando and Rosalind. Their relationship is the engine that drives *As You Like It* and the success or failure of the play turns on how convincingly Shakespeare tells their story.

With the exception of Romeo, Orlando is the most passionate hero Shakespeare had yet created. In the first 300 lines of the play we see him at the throat of his cruel older brother Oliver (who has withheld his patrimony and formal education) and then, though overmatched, manhandling a champion wrestler. In these opening scenes Orlando speaks as forcefully as he fights; but his eloquence deserts him after he and Rosalind fall in love at first sight. When

Rosalind offers him a present, Orlando is so tongue-tied he can't even thank her. Despite her efforts to keep their flagging conversation alive he still 'cannot speak to her'. Orlando may be in love, but at this point he doesn't have a clue what this love means. If he is to win as extraordinary a heroine as Rosalind – and if audiences are to give the match their blessing – he must be more than in love. He needs to learn what love is as much as what it's not; and he needs to learn who Rosalind is.

But he goes about it disastrously, seizing on the medium of poetry to express his love. He roams through the Forest of Arden, defacing trees – pinning poems on them and carving Rosalind's name into their bark. We overhear him as he enters in Act III, scene ii, part-way through a poem, and what we catch is the last ten lines (two quatrains and a couplet) of a Shakespearean sonnet (with its distinctive rhyme scheme – *abab cdcd efef gg*):

> Hang there, my verse, in witness of my love;
> And thou, thrice-crowned queen of night, survey
> With thy chaste eye, from thy pale sphere above,
> Thy huntress' name that my full life doth sway.
> O Rosalind! These trees shall be my books,
> And in their barks my thoughts I'll character,
> That every eye which in this forest looks
> Shall see thy virtue witnessed everywhere.
> Run, run, Orlando, carve on every tree
> The fair, the chaste, and unexpressive she.
> (III, ii, 1–10)

It's wretched stuff. Orlando is a second-rate poet and as yet an inadequate lover. He has no idea that Rosalind is also in the forest, nor does it seem to matter. Only obsessively declaring his love does. Shakespeare's challenge (and soon Rosalind's) is to move Orlando beyond this stilted view of love. Shakespeare had included sonnets in *Love's Labour's Lost* and *Romeo and Juliet* and had done so as recently as the epilogue to *Henry the Fifth*; but in the wake of *The*

Passionate Pilgrim he rarely introduced one into a play again. They only appear in *All's Well* (III, iv, 4–17) and *Cymbeline* (V, iv, 93–110); the one in *As You Like It* is incomplete, missing its first quatrain, discouraging the kind of theft that Jaggard had engaged in.

Orlando cannot help himself and we are subjected to one bad poem after another, the play, like a parody of *The Passionate Pilgrim* itself, offering an anthology of earnest but terrible love poetry. The worst is a tedious eight-line poem with a thumping four-stress line made worse by its monotonous rhyming. Rosalind finds it in the woods and enters reading it aloud:

> From the east to western Ind,
> No jewel is like Rosalind.
> Her worth, being mounted on the wind,
> Through all the world bears Rosalind.
> All the pictures fairest lined
> Are but black to Rosalind.
> Let no face be kept in mind
> But the fair of Rosalind.
> (III, ii, 86–93)

It doesn't take much to churn out this sort of jog-trot verse, and the fool, Touchstone, who overhears Rosalind reading, cannot resist offering an obscene version of his own, that ends:

> Sweetest nut hath sourest rind;
> Such a nut is Rosalind.
> He that sweetest rose will find
> Must find love's prick and Rosalind.
> (III, ii, 107–10)

Shakespeare goes out of his way to make Orlando a hopeless case, desperately in need of a cure for his bad versifying, if not his adolescent love-sickness (mirrored in and fostered by his stale Petrarchism). This passionate pilgrim's longest and last poem in praise of Rosalind unravels metrically as it reaches its final couplet:

Thus Rosalind of many parts
By heavenly synod was devised
Of many faces, eyes, and hearts
To have the touches dearest prized.
Heaven would that she these gifts should have,
And I to live and die her slave.
   (III, ii, 147–52)

Rosalind can stand no more of it: 'Oh, most gentle Jupiter, what tedious homily of love have you wearied your parishioners withal' (153–4). She also can't resist pointing out the lines' metrical flaws, 'for some of them had in them more feet than the verses would bear' (163–4). By mid-play Shakespeare stacks the deck against his lovers, the distance between this artificial poetry and genuine intimacy seemingly unbridgeable. In a comedy otherwise lacking much conflict – there are no rival suitors or angry fathers here to divide the lovers – this is the obstacle that must be overcome.

Shakespeare took the plot of *As You Like It* from Thomas Lodge's prose romance *Rosalind*. In the late 1580s Lodge had signed on for a profiteering voyage to the Canary Islands, taking along for idle hours a copy of a fourteenth-century poem called 'The Tale of Gamylon', thought at the time to be by Chaucer. In 1590 Lodge published a greatly revised version, transforming an all-male outlaw story into a pastoral romance laced with Petrarchan lyrics. *Rosalind* was so popular that it went through three more editions by the time that Shakespeare gave it his full attention, in 1599. We don't know which edition he used, but given the extent of his indebtedness he must have owned or borrowed a copy. Part of *Rosalind*'s appeal a decade after its publication was nostalgic: it was a product of a golden moment in Elizabethan history, the period following England's great triumph over the Spanish Armada in 1588.

The nostalgia exercised its hold on Shakespeare as well. Like many of the other sources Shakespeare turned to this year, *Ros-*

alind dates from around the time that he moved to London and began writing. A decade into his career, as his work began to turn in new directions, Shakespeare needed to take his bearings. He found himself reflecting back to that time when he had first fully immersed himself in the literary culture, measuring how much had changed, what kind of writing was no longer possible.

For the past decade Elizabethan playwrights in search of stories to turn into plays had passed *Rosalind* by; it didn't seem to have enough plot to sustain a comedy. Not even Lodge, who was a competent playwright, tried his hand at dramatizing it. Though flimsy, *Rosalind*'s narrative stretched just far enough for Shakespeare's needs. He borrows wholesale the story of how the lovers end up in the woods as well as the sub-plot of political usurpation and restoration that frames Lodge's work; and he retains all of the main characters, though he changes a few names (including that of Lodge's hero – Rosader – to Orlando).

Shakespeare intuitively saw what Lodge failed to develop. Part of the problem was that *Rosalind* was sorely lacking in irony and humour; and while the material was all there, opportunity after opportunity had been squandered. Lodge had had the wonderful idea of Rosalind cross-dressing as a young man named Ganymede (with all the suggestive homoerotic associations that went with the name of Jove's beloved cup-bearer) and, in this guise, flirtatiously role-play with the man she loves: 'I will represent Rosalind and thou shalt be as thou art, Rosader.' But in Lodge this mostly serves as an excuse for the two to launch into poetic duets like 'The Wooing Eclogue Betwixt Rosalind and Rosader'. Lodge also invents the lovers' mock marriage, with Rosalind still disguised as a man. But from Shakespeare's perspective, Lodge failed to see how much more could have been done with this and other extraordinarily rich scenarios. Why other dramatists didn't recognize this potential says a good deal about Shakespeare's particular gifts as reviser as well as about his deep understanding of how comedy worked. It also suggests that there was some truth to Robert Greene's jealous attack on Shakespeare, in 1592, when he warned his fellow playwrights to beware of this young rival, an 'upstart crow, beautified with our feathers'. He saw how easily Shakespeare could ransack others' styles, making those he imitated feel passed by.

As Shakespeare cast his eye over Lodge's story, he saw to what good use he could put bad poetry. The kind of unquestioned adoration of Petrarchism that defines *Rosalind* – so fashionable when it was written in the 1580s – was overripe. There's a particularly excruciating poem in Lodge called 'Rosalind's Description', a Petrarchan anatomy from head to foot, including tone-deaf lines about her breasts, or 'paps':

> Her paps are centres of delight,
> Her paps are orbs of heavenly frame,
> Where nature moulds the dew of light,
> To perfection with the same,
> Heigh ho, would she were mine.

The word seems to have lodged in Shakespeare's memory and had already inspired Bottom's part – as the lover Pyramus – in a send-up of romantic fluff in the play-within-a-play in *A Midsummer Night's Dream*:

> Come, tears, confound,
> Out, sword, and wound
> The pap of Pyramus;
> Ay, that left pap,
> Where heart doth hop.
> (V, i, 291–5)

Lodge's story – with its cross-dressed heroine, its mix of high and low, and its movement from city to country and back again – already contained many of the basic ingredients of Shakespearean comedy. And its minimal plot was elastic enough to allow Shakespeare to complicate the play's movement without damaging its basic choreography. To that end, Shakespeare crowds it with a larger cast of characters, including the melancholy Jaques, the clownish fool Touchstone and the rustics William and Audrey. The storyline follows a series of seemingly random encounters in the woods: Rosalind and Orlando run into Jaques, who in turn confronts Touchstone, who challenges William and woos Audrey, and so on. Their brief encounters turn into sparring matches in which everything from the philosophical to the mundane is debated, as characters from court and country find themselves drawn to and mystified by each other. There's a lot more talk than action. By the end, the lovers are coupled up and political threats removed. Lodge's story ends in three weddings; Shakespeare can't resist adding a fourth.

About the only words Shakespeare takes virtually unchanged from *Rosalind* come from its Preface, where Lodge tells his readers, 'If you like it, so; and yet I will be yours in duty, if you be mine in favour.' Shortened and thoroughly transformed in its implications, it worked nicely as a title: *As You Like It*. The words encapsulate what Shakespeare is up to here, seemingly offering the audience just the kind of conventional story they went to the playhouse to see, yet at the same time expanding the horizons of what they thought they were looking for in a comedy.

That Shakespeare was able to create a play with so commanding and complicated a female lead is a tribute to the qualities of the nameless young actor for whom he wrote Rosalind's part. Shakespeare had so much confidence in this young man's ability that he gave him over a quarter of the play's lines. Not even Cleopatra would speak as much. This was unprecedented and may not have pleased his experienced fellow sharers, used to playing the leading roles themselves. *As You Like It* turns on what happens when the high-spirited Rosalind, disguised as 'Ganymede', decides to speak to Orlando 'like a saucy lackey and under that habit play the knave with him' (III, ii, 291–3). Shakespeare's other cross-dressed heroines all change back into women's clothing at the first opportunity. We would expect Rosalind to shed her doublet and hose once secure in the knowledge of Orlando's love for her; but she won't until Orlando's education and transformation are complete. To that end, the first thing that she does as Ganymede is offer Orlando advice about love:

There is a man haunts the forest that abuses our young plants with carving 'Rosalind' on their barks, hangs odes upon hawthorns and elegies on brambles, all, forsooth, defying the name of Rosalind. If I could meet that fancy-monger, I would give him some good counsel.
    (III, ii, 351–6)

The tone is both teasing and critical. 'Defying' – that is, demeaning – 'the name of Rosalind' is a bit harsh and unexpected (so much so that the troubled editor of the 1632 Second Folio changed it to 'deifying'), but it also sets the tone for Rosalind's attack on Orlando's conventional view of love. Breaking from Lodge's model here, Shakespeare has Rosalind propose to cure Orlando of what ails him. The two, she suggests, should role-play the parts of lovers, and she invents a precedent in which she has successfully done so with another man so deeply in love:

He was to imagine me his love, his mistress; and I set him every day to woo me. At which time would I, being but a moonish youth, grieve, be effeminate, changeable, longing and liking, proud, fantastical, apish, shallow, inconstant, full of tears, full of smiles; for every passion something and for no passion truly anything, as boys and women are for the most part cattle of this colour; would now like him, now loathe him; then entertain him, then foreswear him; now weep for him, then spit at him; that I drave my suitor from his mad humour of love . . .
    (III, ii, 396–407)

Orlando agrees to the game and it's the last we hear of his poems. To succeed, Rosalind must lie to Orlando about who she is and what she's up to. As a woman playing a man playing a woman (played by a young male actor), Rosalind steadily chips away at Orlando's conventional responses. By Act IV, scene i, the once-silent Orlando is bantering with 'Ganymede' in a punning exchange that underscores how much has changed. They now speak a shared language, their witty dialogue barely concealing a subtext that explores how they imagine what life would be like with each other. She insists that she won't be a silenced wife and Orlando makes clear that he'll value her on her terms: Close 'the doors upon a woman's wit', Rosalind suggests, 'and it will out at the casement; shut that, and 'twill out at the keyhole'. To which Orlando replies, at once playful and earnest, 'A man that had a wife with such a wit, he might say, "Wit, whither wilt?"' (IV, i, 153–8). It's a start.

If their game is to succeed it must be reciprocal. It's not just Rosalind who must disguise what she knows; Orlando must also suppress simple truths. Paradoxically, the only way Shakespeare can show that Orlando has matured in his understanding of love is to show him masking what he's learned, having him playing and lying in love, learning to appreciate Rosalind's deception. Much depends, then, on when it dawns on Orlando that 'Ganymede' is actually Rosalind. Modern productions often miss Shakespeare's signals and as a result don't allow Orlando to discover the truth until it's far too late. In doing so they turn Orlando into a cloddish figure, unworthy of Rosalind's affections (in George Bernard Shaw's words, a 'safely stupid and totally unobservant young man'). Other productions have him conspiratorially wink and nod at playgoers too early on, to let them know that he hasn't been taken in by Rosalind's deception, thereby reverting to the cynicism of the unrevised 'When my love swears'. But when it works right, it works beautifully: 'I know she knows': Orlando comes to know that 'Ganymede' is Rosalind pretending to be a man playing a woman; and we know he knows she knows he knows it.

But when, exactly, do we know it? Much of the pleasure of tragedy depends upon our ignorance, our failure to see what's coming. The greater the shock, the more intense the tragic experience. When Shakespeare had King Lear enter with Cordelia dead in his arms, he caught his audience by surprise, all the more so because those familiar with his sources expected Cordelia to live. Comedy is pleasurable because we're told what's coming, know better than the characters themselves about who is disguised, about lost and separated twins, and about who is really in love with whom. When we are armed with this knowledge, there are few things more satisfying than watching a well-orchestrated comedy unfold, anticipating the moment at the end when the characters discover what we already know. But in *As You Like It* Shakespeare bends the rules, creating situations where we can no longer be as confident as we'd like to be about what characters know – even who they really are. We're forced to question our judgement and go back, as the play progresses, and replay a good deal of the action – especially about when it is that we are sure that Orlando knows that 'Ganymede' is his Rosalind.

My own guess – and Shakespeare sets things up so that it can only be a guess – is that the first inkling we have that Orlando sees through her disguise comes when Rosalind playfully asks for his hand and tells Celia to 'be the priest and marry us' (IV, i, 116–17). It's a lot more obvious in performance, where, once Orlando takes her hand in his own, the physical reality of who she is becomes palpable to him, clear enough for him to turn to Celia and agree to what Rosalind (as 'Ganymede') has said: 'Pray thee marry us.' Their game has gone too far for Celia's comfort. Playgoers at the Globe knew that Celia was being asked to participate in a 'handfast', or legally binding betrothal, and at first she adamantly refuses: 'I cannot say the words.' She won't be implicated in this contract and, if truth be told, she's more than a little in love with Rosalind herself. But Rosalind insists: 'You must begin, "Will you, Orlando" –' Celia at last gives in, reciting the familiar words: 'Will you, Orlando, have to wife this Rosalind?' Orlando's reply, in the future tense – 'I will' – fails to satisfy Rosalind, who immediately asks: 'But when?' Once more, Orlando hedges on his commitment, responding: 'Why now, as fast as she can marry us.' This won't do for Rosalind. Shakespeare's contemporaries knew the difference between saying 'I do' and 'I will' (Elizabethan lawyers called the first *sponsalia per verba de praesenti*, the latter – less binding, because it only commits to a marriage at some unspecified future time – *sponsalia per verba de futuro*). Rosalind persists – she wants to know where he stands: 'Then you must say, "I take thee, Rosalind, for wife."' Orlando knows what he is doing, understands the difference between the playful and the real and, hand in hand, repeats the words that bind him to her: 'I take thee, Rosalind, for wife' (IV, i, 120–29). This is the closest Shakespeare would ever come to staging an espousal. Though a Friar had appeared at the end of *Much Ado*, like Friar Lawrence in *Romeo and Juliet*, he must urge the lovers to join him offstage – 'to the chapel let us presently' (V, iv, 70) – to perform the rite. In so far as holy sacraments, including that of matrimony, could not be performed in the theatre, Elizabethan audiences would have found the espousal scene in *As You Like It*, where contractual words are spoken, especially powerful. For Rosalind and Orlando, there could be no turning back.

Though legally joined, their play-acting and deception aren't over. It's not yet time for Rosalind to shed her disguise or for Orlando to admit what he knows. Orlando is not perfect, though, and he lets his guard slip once or twice. The first time occurs in Act V, scene ii, when 'Ganymede' enters and Orlando tells his brother Oliver, 'here comes my Rosalind', rather than, 'here comes Ganymede'. Oliver, who saw Rosalind faint when he brought her news of Orlando's fight with a lion, also sees through her disguise, for when 'Ganymede' says to him, 'God save you, brother,' he replies, 'And you, fair sister' (18). A few lines later, the game is up, pushed as far as it can be when Rosalind, as 'Ganymede', asks Orlando whether tomorrow she can 'serve your turn for Rosalind', and Orlando firmly responds to the double-edged line (since 'serve your turn' means to satisfy sexually as well as to act as substitute): 'I can live no longer by thinking' (49). She's ready to lie with him and he with her. When Rosalind formally reveals herself at the end of the play, we're denied the pleasure of a traditional recognition scene: there's no shock on Orlando's part, no mention that she had been 'Ganymede', just the conditional, 'If there be truth in sight, you are my Rosalind' (V, iv, 117). Touchstone is there to remind us that the truest lovers, like the best poets, are liars, 'for the truest poetry is the most feigning, and lovers are given to poetry, and what they swear in poetry may be said as lovers they do feign' (III, iii, 17–20). It's as good a paraphrase of the paradoxical truth of Sonnet 138 – 'When my love swears that she is made of truth / I do believe her though I know she lies' – and of *As You Like It*, as one could ask for.

In retelling this story, Shakespeare not only overhauls Lodge, but also revisits two of his earlier amorous works, *Romeo and Juliet* and *Love's Labour's Lost*, both of which feature heroines named Rosalind or Rosaline (as Rosalind's name is also sometimes spelled in the Folio text of *As You Like It*). Again, Shakespeare glances back as he goes forward. In both of those plays Rosalind figures as a heart-breaker, the unattainable object of a Petrarchan lover. In *Romeo and Juliet* she's much talked of but never actually appears. Romeo's commitment to a young woman we never see him with and who for all we know isn't aware of his existence is fair game for the cheerfully obscene Mercutio, who has no patience for this passionate but meaningless Petrarchan stuff:

> I conjure thee by Rosaline's bright eyes,
> By her high forehead and her scarlet lip,
> By her fine foot, straight leg, and quivering thigh,
> And the demesnes that there adjacent lie.
> (II, i, 18–21)

To be in love with Rosaline is to 'lie with love', and it's a fantasy Romeo abandons when he meets Juliet and discovers a love that is genuine and reciprocal.

Rosalind – or at least her namesake – had also appeared in *Love's Labour's Lost*, where she is also the object of a young man in love, the same Berowne whose uninspired sonnet appears in *The Passionate Pilgrim*. In a play where both male and female lovers are so conventional that they border on the indistinguishable, Rosalind stands somewhat apart. Though she speaks in the same formal couplets as the other characters, her wit and spirit shine through, especially at the end when she playfully mocks her wooer: 'That same Berowne I'll torture ere I go . . . How I would make him fawn, and beg, and seek' (V, ii, 60–62). The return of Rosalind in *As You Like It* (Shakespeare obviously is working from Lodge, but he could have changed her name as easily as he did Rosader's) is all the more striking in a play that has so many characters who share names – inexplicably, and confusingly, Shakespeare writes parts for two Olivers and two Jaques. It's hard to avoid the impression that this is something of a private joke on Shakespeare's part. In a play so intimately aware of literary antecedents, there's probably yet one more in-joke, for Rosalind had also been the name of the heartless lover (and despiser of bad poetry) in Edmund Spenser's poetry. Spenser's autobiographical double, Colin Clout, complains in *The Shepherd's Calendar* (1579) about how his beloved Rosalind 'laughs [at] the songs, that Colin Clout doth make' ('January', 66) and is still nursing his wounds over a decade later in *Colin Clout's Come Home Again*. Given a voice and a will, the Rosalind of *As You Like It* makes her earlier incarnations seem two-dimensional.

She's the most beloved of Shakespeare's heroines and for good reason. It's not just her intelligence and wit that account for this. Rosalind's emotions are close to the surface, and we see – and are able to experience through her – an extraordinary range of feelings, from the exhilaration and pain of love to terror and embarrassment. Like Shakespeare's other great creations – Falstaff, Hamlet, Iago and Cleopatra – Rosalind loves to plot, to banter, to direct and play out scenes; and, like these other unforgettable characters, she begins to take on a life of her own, and in doing so comes close to wresting the play away from her creator.

In *Shakespeare's Language*, Frank Kermode rightly calls *As You Like It* 'the most topical of the comedies'. It's not topical, though, in the transparent way that *Henry the Fifth* (and its allusion to Essex and Ireland) or *Julius Caesar* (and its concern with holiday and republicanism) had been. From its casual allusions to Ireland to its mention of the celebrated new fountain of Diana in West Cheap (IV, i, 145) – the one that was 'for the most part naked', John Stow writes, 'with Thames-water pilling from her breasts' – there's no mistaking that *As You Like It* is rooted in its place and time; but its real topicality resides elsewhere, in its attentiveness to evolving notions of Elizabethan comedy and pastoral. Comedy tends to have a briefer shelf life than other genres even as it's more popular (there were, for example, as many comedies as histories and tragedies combined in 1599). What's funny or delightful to one generation often feels pointless and strained to the next. When conventions and social expectations change, comedy must too. Shakespeare didn't need Marston or Jonson to remind him that it was no longer possible to write the kind of comedy that he had been writing for most of the past decade. In *As You Like It* we can feel that a cultural page had turned, even if that page is no longer fully legible to us, and that Shakespeare knows it and moves to act on this knowledge.

Frank Kermode is also on the mark when he concludes that the play 'has too much to say about what was once intimately interesting and now is not', for there 'is no play by Shakespeare, apart perhaps from *Love's Labour's Lost*, that requires of the reader or spectator more knowledge of Elizabethan culture and especially of its styles of literature'. Even the play's most devoted admirers must admit that Shakespeare's often opaque reflections on literary matters are distracting. Few today read or see *As You Like It* for the pleasure of immersing themselves in literary issues that only matter now because they once mattered to Shakespeare; but this liability turns out to be a godsend for the literary biographer, for whom Shakespeare has left all too few clues about how and why he wrote what he did. That having been said, what clues there are often feel like riddles. When he does allude to another writer in *As You Like It*, it is to one that was no longer alive:

> Dead Shepherd, now I find thy saw of might,
> 'Who ever loved that loved not at first sight?'
>   (III, v, 80–81)

The lines are spoken by Phoebe, a young shepherdess desperately in love with 'Ganymede', who quotes from Christopher Marlowe's masterpiece *Hero and Leander*, posthumously published in 1598. It's the word 'now' in the first line that carries particular emphasis for Phoebe, dumbstruck in love, and for Shakespeare as well. The line recalls the time back in the early 1590s when he was working on *Venus and Adonis* and Marlowe on *Hero and Leander*. Poetry would never be quite so simple or pure as that again. Shakespeare also goes out of his way to recall Marlowe as 'Dead Shepherd', the celebrated author of the pastoral lyric 'The Passionate Shepherd to His Love'. That the misattribution of this poem in *The Passionate Pilgrim* is still on his mind appears likely from another passage in the play, though this one is so obscure that it's unclear who would have caught the allusion. Shakespeare seems to be speaking to himself when he has Touchstone say: 'When a man's verses cannot be understood, nor a man's good wit seconded with the forward child, understanding, it strikes a man more dead than a great reckoning in a little room' (III, iii, 10–13). This oblique allusion to Marlowe's violent death (stabbed over the 'reckoning', or bill) and the echo of his famous line in *The Jew of Malta* about 'infinite riches in a little room' seem to be linked here to how deadly it is to a writer's reputation – Marlowe's, but undoubtedly Shakespeare's as well – to be misunderstood. It's hard not to feel that these recollections are but the tip of the iceberg. Lurking beneath the surface of the play is a decade-long struggle on Shakespeare's part to absorb and move beyond his greatest rival's work, an engagement that is at its most intense in 1598–9 in *The Merry Wives of Windsor*, *Henry the Fifth*, *As You Like It* and, finally, *Hamlet*. After that, the battle won, and Marlowe's innovations and 'mighty line' thoroughly absorbed, Shakespeare was troubled no longer.

But Marlowe's ghost still visited Shakespeare as he turned to pastoral in *As You Like It* – for Marlowe had been there before him, both in refashioning and debunking the genre. One of the lessons Shakespeare learned from Marlowe, which he puts to good use in *As You Like It*, is that the most effective way to talk about love without sounding clichéd is to turn what others have written into cliché. Rosalind does this in dismissing Marlowe's tale of tragic lovers as a fiction. Leander didn't die for love, as Marlowe had it, in a desperate attempt to swim the Hellespont to reach his beloved Hero, but drowned while bathing, victim of a cramp:

Leander, he would have lived many a fair year though Hero had turned nun, if it had not been for a hot midsummer night; for, good youth, he went but forth to wash him in the Hellespont and being taken with the cramp was drowned; and the foolish chroniclers of that age found it was – Hero of Sestos.

(IV, i, 94–9)

What Marlowe's characters experienced was invented; what Rosalind feels in this most artificial of plays is real.

As Shakespeare was caught up in writing *As You Like It*, pretty clearly by late summer 1599 he was more concerned with living rivals than dead ones, including those with a strongly satiric bent, like Jonson. Jonson was collaborating on plays at the Rose and working by himself on his best play yet, a comical satire called *Every Man Out of His Humour*. Espousing a coolly critical form of comedy devoted to exposing human foibles, Jonson offered Londoners a dazzling alternative to Shakespearean romantic comedy. Shakespeare would have had advance notice, having heard the gist of it when Jonson read or pitched the play to him and his fellow sharers, for the Chamberlain's Men purchased it and staged it that autumn. Jonson took some clever swipes at Shakespeare in his play (at everything from his coat of arms to his recent *Julius Caesar*), but for the Chamberlain's Men profits mattered more than personal slights. This was Jonson's breakthrough play and they were glad to have it.

Jonson's timing couldn't have been better. The banning and burning of verse satire in early June had done nothing to sate the public's hunger for this caustic stuff. Satire quickly found an outlet on the stage. Shakespeare, alert to the shift, offers a rare piece of editorializing about the ban and its aftermath in *As You Like It*: 'for since the little wit that fools have was silenced, the little foolery that wise men have makes a great show' (I, ii, 85–7). Whatever misgiving he may have had about the genre, Shakespeare, who would soon write the trenchantly satiric *Troilus and Cressida*, was motivated to try his hand at satire for the first time in *As You Like It*, in the person of Jaques.

Jaques is something of an enigma. He has a significant presence in the play (speaking almost a tenth of its lines), but no effect on it. He changes nothing, fails to persuade or reform anyone. Mostly, he likes to watch. He's melancholy, brooding and sentimental, and some have seen in him a rough sketch for Hamlet; others find him little more than a self-deluding, jaundiced one-time libertine. Shakespeare himself is careful to suspend judgement. For audiences at the Globe, whether or not they found Jaques sympathetic, his insistence that his aim was to 'Cleanse the foul body of th'infected world, / If they will patiently receive my medicine' (II, vii, 60–61) signalled unambiguously that he was cut from the same cloth as the satiric types popularized by Jonson. Shakespeare even does his best to turn the type into a cliché, and other characters refer to Jaques generically as 'Monsieur Melancholy' and 'Monsieur Traveller' (III, ii, 290; IV, i, 30).

Jaques's obsession with purging society helps explain the name Shakespeare gives him – pronounced like 'jakes', the Elizabethan word for privy or water-closet, with a nod here at John Harington's *The Metamorphosis of Ajax* (pronounced 'a-jakes'). In case we miss Shakespeare's joke, Touchstone is there to remind us, calling Jaques not by his distasteful name, but rather, out of a dignified politeness, 'Master What-ye-call't' (III, iii, 68). In portraying Jaques, Shakespeare manages to have it both ways, which wasn't easy to do. He creates a memorable satirist who nonetheless finds himself trumped at every turn. Touchstone gets the better of him, as does Rosalind. Even Orlando vanquishes him in their verbal sparring. These encounters also make Rosalind and Orlando feel more human and believable.

Jaques's finest moment is his famous speech on the seven ages of man, the one that begins: 'All the world's a stage, / And all the men and women merely players' (II, vii, 138–9). It ends with a grim portrait of old age:

> Last scene of all,
> That ends this strange, eventful history,
> Is second childishness and mere oblivion,
> Sans teeth, sans eyes, sans taste, sans everything.
> (II, vii, 162–5)

Just as we find ourselves nodding in agreement, Shakespeare reverses course, repudiating Jaques's cynicism with the dramatic entrance of 'Orlando with Adam'. What we witness at this moment – Orlando bearing his ancient servant Adam on his back – is no portrait of a toothless second childhood, or of the inevitability of isolation as we age, but an emblem of devotion between old and young.

For Shakespeare, this undermining of the grim vision of Jonsonian comical satire was personal, and there's a good chance that he wrote himself into this scene. An anecdote set down in the late eighteenth century records how a 'very old man' of Stratford-upon-Avon, 'of weak intellects, but yet related to Shakespeare – being asked by some of his neighbours what he remembered about him, answered – that he saw him once brought on the stage upon another man's back'. Another independent and fuller version of this tradition from around this time provides more corroborating details, recalling how Shakespeare played the part of 'a decrepit old man', in which 'he appeared so weak and drooping and unable to walk, that he was forced to be supported and carried by another person to a table, at which he was seated among some company, who were eating, and one of them sung a song'. The descriptions bear a close resemblance to Adam's role. Scholars have long surmised that Shakespeare, not the finest actor in his company, may have taken 'old man' parts for himself. There aren't any other anecdotes quite like this that describe which roles Shakespeare created for himself and, while there's no way of authenticating it, this tradition sounds plausible.

Jaques's most poignant moment comes at the very end of the play. Though the Duke begs him to 'Stay, Jaques, stay' for the imminent wedding festivities, Jaques cannot find it in himself to join in the dance, that timeless symbol of communal harmony: 'I am for other than for dancing measures' (V, iv, 192–3). Unable to change society, Jaques turns his back on it. While the others leave Arden and return to court, Jaques remains behind. Like Shylock before him and Malvolio not long after, he is an outsider whose isolation reminds us that Shakespearean comedy, too, can be harsh, and draws a sharp line between those it includes and those who remain outside its charmed circle.

*

Shakespeare faced other challenges in this comedy, not the least of which was satisfying his audience's desire for a clown. *As You Like It* accommodates both clown and satirist, though their roles – exposing the foolishness of others – overlap considerably. As disappointed playgoers at the Globe had already discovered, Kemp was no longer with the company. However personally relieved Shakespeare may have been, he and his fellow sharers still needed to find a suitable replacement. By the time Shakespeare wrote *As You Like It*, Kemp's successor, Robert Armin, had at last been found.

The Chamberlain's Men would have known Armin by reputation as a goldsmith turned ballad-writer and pamphleteer who had then turned playwright and comedian. They may have seen him perform as a member of Chandos' Men or attended one of his performances for private, aristocratic audiences (Armin seemed to do a good bit of freelancing). Had they seen an early version of *Two Maids of More-Clack*, they would have been impressed by his intellect and versatility, for Armin not only wrote it, he also starred in two comic roles. Armin may even have allowed the Chamberlain's Men a look at his works-in-progress, a pair of books about the art of the clown, *Fool upon Fool* and *Quips upon Questions*, both about to be published. If he read the latter, Shakespeare would have seen that Armin was gifted at riddling and engaging others in witty, catechizing dialogue. It wasn't long before Shakespeare was drawing on this particular skill, creating for him the memorable role of the riddling Gravedigger in *Hamlet*.

Armin was everything Kemp was not. He couldn't dance but he was a fine singer and mimic. Though a veteran performer, he was still young, having just turned thirty. He didn't do jigs. He didn't insist on being the centre of attention. And he was physically unintimidating: a contemporary woodcut portrait suggests that he was almost dwarfish. He was someone Shakespeare could work with and learn from. Armin was more of a witty fool than a clown, though when called upon he had no problem stepping into a role like *Much Ado*'s Dogberry that Shakespeare had written specifically for Kemp. All told, Armin's talents fitted neatly with the trajectory of Shakespeare's art and had a liberating effect on it, culminating in Armin's role as the Fool in *King Lear*. It proved to be a good match. In the short term, however, it remained to be seen if audiences would embrace him, as they had Kemp. It had taken several years for Shakespeare to write parts that fully capitalized on Kemp's strengths; he would not have the same luxury in Armin's case and must have felt considerable pressure to make Armin's debut a success.

The first role he would create for Armin would be Touchstone. Touchstones are literally objects that take the measure of things, tell us if they are real or fraudulent, which is very much Armin's role in the play (there's also a bit of a private joke here, given Armin's training as a goldsmith, for London's goldsmiths had a touchstone as their emblem). Breaking with the tradition of Kemp's country fellows, Armin is cast as a court or professional fool, dressed in motley. He loyally accompanies Celia and Rosalind into the woods, though he misses life at court. Once in Arden, he's a fish out of water, a situation that provides ample opportunity to show off Armin's dry wit. He has an unusually large part for a fool; excepting Feste in *Twelfth Night*, his 300 lines in *As You Like It* are the longest part Shakespeare wrote for any fool. Surprisingly, Shakespeare didn't take advantage of his singing ability (unless, that is, Armin also doubled the part of the play's professional adult singer, Amiens). Like any professional clown, Armin also had his set routines, and, when the play needs to stall for time near the end, he launches into one of them about the 'Seven Degrees of the Lie' in Act V. Written specifically for Armin, it now feels dead on the page as well as in performance. Without his touch, its magic has evaporated.

In contrast to Jaques, his opposite number and self-appointed commentator, Touchstone finds himself becoming more of a participant in Arden than an observer. The fool who holds his nose and announces upon entering the pastoral world ('Ay, now am I in Arden; the more fool I' [II, iv, 14]), eventually surrenders to the impulses he has ridiculed and at the end of the play marries a country wench, Audrey. How long this marriage will last is anyone's guess (Jaques gives it two months, and he may be right). This, too, marked a signal change from Kemp, who consistently steered clear of romantic entanglements in his stage roles. Spectators still missed the charismatic Kemp, but from the perspective of the Chamberlain's Men, and surely from Shakespeare's, Armin was a welcome addition.

Shakespeare had more to worry about than clowns and fools. He knew that children's companies were about to start attracting more privileged audiences in London. In early May a new choirmaster, Edward Pearce, had taken over at St Paul's, and it was under his tenure that the boys resumed playing for the first time in nearly a decade. Paul's Boys had a great advantage, for they performed on the grounds of the centrally located Cathedral, in the City itself, an area off-limits to adult players; and their advertised 'private' performances, limited to 200 or so spectators, allowed them to operate independently of the licensing control of the Master of the Revels. They were therefore free to put on plays that were more daringly satiric and topical. They also had some powerful backers: Rowland Whyte would report in November that William Stanley, the sixth Earl of Derby, had 'put up the plays of the children in Paul's to his great pains and charge'. The success of Paul's Boys soon led to the creation of the Children of the Chapel, who began playing at the indoor Second Blackfriars by 1600.

The boys' pint-size appearance was perfect for parodying their rivals; and their uncracked voices were a strong selling point in so musically attuned a culture (Elizabethan England only produced a few painters of note, such as Isaac Oliver and Nicholas Hilliard, but the talent in musical composition was deep). Adult players could sword-fight, dance and carry a tune, but only a handful, including Armin, could compete musically with the children, who were after all trained choristers. The Chamberlain's Men would find themselves caught between the popular fare of rival adult companies and the intimate offerings of the boys.

If the children's companies highlighted boys and song, the Chamberlain's Men could too. *As You Like It* includes an unprecedented six boy actors (as opposed to the usual pair). A lesser dramatist might have simply responded to the vogue for boys and their singing by adding a tune or two. Shakespeare chose to write more songs – five in all, three sung by adults, two by boys – than he would in any other play. Thinking of *As You Like It* as an embryonic musical may help explain why critics have had such a hard time with its meagre, episodic plot, its rich vein of contemporary satire, its over-the-top climax where the god Hymen enters, and all its song and dance. The same ingredients, viewed from the perspective of musical comedy, make perfect sense. It's as if Shakespeare was feeling his way towards something not yet imaginable, for over a century would pass before the first English musical, John Gay's *The Beggar's Opera*, was staged in 1728. It's not entirely clear whether Shakespeare was fully aware of where his art was leading him and, in retrospect, this turns out to be one of the paths not taken, its tracks almost fully covered over.

That wasn't the case in the years after the English musical became a sensation. Producers immediately recognized how little reworking it took to turn *As You Like It* into a fully fledged musical. When it was revived in 1740, for example, it was padded out with a song lifted from *Love's Labour's Lost*; and by the time it was put on at the Theatre Royal in York in 1789, Celia, Phoebe and Amiens all had singing parts, and more music – including a hornpipe solo at the end of Act I – was added as well. By 1824, at Drury Lane, you couldn't call it anything else but a musical, with a liberal helping of songs added from *A Midsummer Night's Dream*, *Twelfth Night*, *The Passionate Pilgrim*, and *Venus and Adonis*, and a new finale – 'An Allegorical Dance and Chorus of Aeriel Spirits' – brought in to replace the older and tired one starring Hymen.

Some of the songs Shakespeare wrote for *As You Like It* have a thematic function; others seem to be included simply to satisfy the audience's desire to hear good singing. The most accomplished of these songs is 'It was a lover and his lass', which appears in Act V, scene iii – a scene with no other purpose than to introduce it. It's sung by two boys, introduced as the 'Duke's pages', who go out of their way to remind us that they're professionals who sing without making excuses, 'without hawking or spitting or saying we are hoarse, which are the only prologues to a bad voice':

> It was a lover and his lass,
> With a hey, and a ho, and a hey-nonny-no,
> That o'er the green cornfield did pass
> In springtime, the only pretty ring-time.
> When birds do sing, hey ding a ding, ding.
> Sweet lovers love the spring,
> And therefore take the present time,
> With a hey, and a ho, and a hey-nonny-no.
> For love is crowned with the prime.
> In springtime, etc.
> (V, iii, 16ff.)

Original music for 'It was a lover and his lass' survives, set for voice, lute and bass-viol, and was published shortly after it was first staged in Thomas Morley's *The First Book of Ayres* in 1600. Morley was one of the leading musicians and composers of the day and until recently had been Shakespeare's neighbour in Bishopsgate Ward. The best explanation for why the same song appears in both Shakespeare's and Morley's published work is that Shakespeare had sought out Morley as a collaborator. Lyrics in musical theatre don't count for much unless they are accompanied by first-rate tunes. It looks as if the two artists worked on this song together, Shakespeare providing the words, Morley the music, leaving both free to publish the joint venture independently. If so, audiences at the Globe would have been treated to an inspired collaboration between England's leading lyricist and one of its finest composers. If there are any lost Shakespearean lyrics still to be discovered, it's likely that they will be found in the anonymous songs in collections like Morley's *Book of Ayres*.

In the final scene of the play, Shakespeare pulls out all the stops. There is nothing in his earlier works – or indeed in earlier scenes of *As You Like It* – to prepare audiences for this grand finale. He had taken naturalism unusually far in this artificial pastoral, but, as he subsequently showed in his late romances, naturalism too had its limits and was not an end in itself. Rosalind (as 'Ganymede') slips offstage, promising to return and magically produce the actual Rosalind. She returns, along with Hymen, god of marriage. This divine intervention is unnecessary, for Shakespeare has already resolved all outstanding conflicts. Shakespeare again offers his audience more than they expected, for the scene is the first masque in his work, anticipating by roughly a decade those in *The Winter's Tale*, *Cymbeline* and *The Tempest*. Bridging the divide between courtly and popular theatre, Shakespeare makes available to ordinary playgoers a taste of the expensive and spectacular symbolic drama of the court.

Modern directors, drawn to the play's naturalism, are mystified by the Masque of Hymen and most go to any length to work around it, playing it as a joke rather than the transcendent scene Shakespeare has written. Nowadays, as often as not, the actor playing Corin, or another minor rustic character, recites Hymen's lines and the scene becomes a little playlet stage-managed with a wink and a nod by Rosalind. From the perspective of these directors, the play has already worked its magic, and they're at a loss to deal with Shakespeare cutting back across the grain, introducing a god in his search for a more profound comic pattern.

While we don't know what audiences made of it four hundred years ago at the Globe, we do know that the Masque of Hymen marshals all the special effects that Shakespeare had at his command. The stage directions don't make clear how Hymen enters, but there's a possibility that, like the divine entrances in Shakespeare's late plays, Hymen appears from above, descending in a throne from the cover of the Globe's stage. If so, it shows off for the first time at the Globe the stage technology previously unavailable to Shakespeare's company at the Theatre or Curtain. Hymen enters to the sound of 'still music' and intones:

> Peace, ho! I bar confusion.
> 'Tis I must make conclusion
> Of these most strange events.
> Here's eight that must take hands
> To join in Hymen's bands,
> If truth holds true contents.
>   (V, iv, 124–9)

The four pairs of lovers – Rosalind and Orlando, Celia and Oliver, Phoebe and Silvius, and Audrey and Touchstone – come forward and are confirmed in their vows, and a final song follows, celebrating the act of marriage that is at the heart of comedy:

> Wedding is great Juno's crown,
> O blessed bond of board and bed!
> 'Tis Hymen peoples every town;
> High wedlock then be honoured.
> Honour, high honour and renown,
> To Hymen, god of every town!
>   (V, iv, 140–45)

Duke Senior, following up on Hymen's order that the eight lovers 'must take hands', calls for the formal dance that symbolically ends both masque and play, specifying 'measures' or a stately court dance like a pavan: 'Play, music! And you, brides and bridegrooms all, / With measure heaped in joy, to th' measures fall' (177–8). Shakespeare seems to have gone a step further here than he had recently done with the ending of *Julius Caesar*. After seeing *Julius Caesar* at the Globe, Thomas Platter recorded in his notebook: 'At the end of the play they danced together admirably and exceedingly gracefully, according to their custom, two in each group dressed in men's and two in women's apparel.' Alan Brissenden persuasively argues that the extremely elegant ('*überausz zierlich*') dance Platter describes was most likely a court dance, such as a 'pavan, almain, or even the faster coranto'. The formal dance tagged on to the end of *Julius Caesar* in lieu of a jig had become with *As You Like It* part of the fabric of the play itself.

If this were not enough to absorb, one last innovation follows, for the play ends but doesn't stop here. Once the dance is over and the other characters exit, the young actor who played Rosalind steps forward to interact with the audience directly, in an epilogue. The audience would have been shocked by this and the actor must begin by defending why 'Rosalind' defies convention in this way: 'It is not the fashion to see the lady the epilogue; but it is no more unhandsome than to see the lord the prologue' (Epilogue, 1–3). Now that the play is over, does this young actor recite these lines in his own voice or is he still playing a woman's part? If he hasn't dropped his voice a register (speaking, say, as 'Ganymede') or taken off his wig, how are we to know if we are supposed to be hearing a man or a woman? Halfway through the epilogue the actor himself takes up this delicate question, making unambiguous that, though still dressed as a woman, he's really a young man: 'If I were a woman I would kiss as many of you as had beards that pleased me, complexions that liked me, and breaths that I defied not' (Epilogue, 16–19). Though he assures us that he's not a woman, seconds later he curtsies rather than bows to us. This is more realism that we bargained for. But, Shakespeare is quick to remind us, human as we feel Rosalind is, there's a young actor who really is human and deserves our applause; Rosalind is a fiction and realism a convention, an illusion. To the very end, Shakespeare insists that we share the play's scepticism about conventionality. One last time he confounds our expectations, forcing us to abandon the self-satisfaction that comes from watching the characters discover in the end what we knew all along. Rosalind's last conditional 'If' (a word repeated about once a minute in the play) reminds us that unlike comic closure, real life is open-ended and provisional.

Nowhere else in his works does Shakespeare break the frame in quite so disconcerting a way, confronting us with the fact that we are watching cross-dressed actors and that we are complicit in the lie upon which Elizabethan theatre depends. Even as we believe that Shakespeare's plays are made of truth, he reminds us that we know he lies. We are left, in the end, in Orlando's shoes: educated and delighted by Rosalind, forgetful at times that we are listening to a boy playing the part of a woman, and in danger of being a bit too comfortable with conventions – with how we like it.

The suppression of simple truth – cousin to what Coleridge called 'the willing suspension of disbelief' – turns out to be at the core of the theatrical experience. In exchange for forgetting that Rosalind is really a boy playing a woman's part, we, like Orlando, are rewarded with more complex truths. In the end, play is what's real, and in the epilogue, Rosalind – or whoever it is that is speaking to us – won't let us forget it:

I charge you, O women, for the love you bear to me, to like as much of this play as please you; and I charge you, O men, for the love you bear to women – as I perceive by your simpering, none of you hates them – that between you and the women the play may please.

(Epilogue, 11–16)

Jaques had it right: all the world's a stage, and all the men and women merely players. The epilogue is an assertive ending to a daring play. Shakespeare had offered more and demanded more in return. If playgoers missed the point, it would have been underscored for them a final time as they filed out of the new theatre. On the sign the Chamberlain's Men displayed outside the Globe was a reminder: '*Totus mundus agit histrionem*' – 'We are all players.'

12
The Forest of Arden

It was time for Shakespeare to head home. Neighbours told the seventeenth-century biographer John Aubrey that Shakespeare 'was wont to go into Warwickshire once a year', though he probably made the trip more often than that, even if in 1599 he may have had to postpone visiting during the hectic months in which the Globe was under construction. By late summer, though, a great deal was going on in Stratford that demanded his presence.

His family needed him. Joan Hathaway, his wife's mother (or possibly stepmother), was dying. Shakespeare was close enough to the Hathaway family to have recently looked into buying 'some odd yardland' – an open-field holding of thirty or so acres – near their farmhouse in Shottery, on the verge of the Forest of Arden. Joan, who had been widowed since Richard Hathaway's death in 1581, lived with Anne's brothers (or stepbrothers), John, Thomas and William, and her sister Margaret. They were helped by the family's long-time shepherd, Thomas Whittington. If Shake-

Warwickshire, Michael Drayton, 1612

speare needed a model for the generous and devoted servant Adam in *As You Like It*, he didn't have to look further than Whittington, who left in his will £50 for 'the poor people of Stratford', including the 'forty shillings that is in the hand of Anne Shakespeare, wife unto Master William Shakespeare'. Ties still bound Anne, and by extension her husband, to her old household. Anne had been nineteen when her stepbrother John was born and lived under the same roof for nine more years until she married Shakespeare. She probably helped Joan raise the younger children and must have been concerned when John was mustered in November 1596 and then again this summer, when he joined other trained men ordered to drill with muskets at nearby Alcester on 19 July. There's no record of whether he was subsequently called up to defend against the Spanish threat or shipped off to fight in Ireland. Shakespeare may have found in his young brother-in-law a good source of information on mustering and the military.

If Shakespeare missed Joan Hathaway's funeral on 5 September, he may have arrived home in time for a wedding. No later than this summer, though perhaps sometime earlier, there was cause to celebrate: his sister Joan, age thirty, got married. We don't know the exact date Joan wedded William Hart, a hatter; but we know that by November she was pregnant with their first child, a son who would be given his godfather's name: William. It was not a wedding that Shakespeare would have missed. She was his only surviving sister, a first Joan having died in infancy in 1558, followed by Margaret, a baby, in 1563, and Anne, age eight, in 1579. Joan was also Shakespeare's only sibling to marry (his brothers – Gilbert, who was two years younger, Richard, born when he was about to turn ten, and Edmund, born in 1580 when Shakespeare was sixteen – all died bachelors). For Shakespeare's mother and father, who were around seventy, an advanced age at the time, Joan's marriage must have been a mixed blessing, for she had lived with them in their house on Henley Street and would now have to attend to her husband's and soon her child's needs as well as theirs (the newly-weds moved into the western part of the house). Joan must have been attached to the place, which Shakespeare inherited, and he allowed her to stay there for life for the nominal fee of twelve pence a year. Shakespeare appears to have remained on warm terms with his sister and eventually bequeathed her 'twenty pounds and all my wearing apparel'.

Family demands aside, there were practical reasons for Shakespeare to travel home during the summer months. The season was sunnier and drier, which meant that the roads would be in better shape. The most direct route from London to Stratford, by way of High Wycombe and Oxford, was ninety-four miles, a three-days' journey by horse when the weather was fair and the roads decent. Had Shakespeare set forth by early September, when the sun rose and set around six, he would have had a comfortable twelve hours of daylight in which to ride, four fewer than in mid-July, but four more than in the dark days of December.

Shakespeare's trip home probably began at the Bell Inn on Carter Lane near St Paul's Cathedral, where he would likely have hired a gelding for the journey from William Greenaway. Greenaway was Stratford's main carrier. He had been plying the route between his home town and London since at least 1581, and for the next twenty years played an indispensable role carrying letters, messages, food, goods and gossip back and forth. The Greenaways were near neighbours of the Shakespeares, living a few houses down on Henley Street. Greenaway probably conveyed the terrible news to Shakespeare of his son Hamnet's death as well as of the devastating fires in Stratford in 1594 and 1595 (the house where Shakespeare's family lived narrowly escaped the flames; the Greenaways were not so fortunate). Leading citizens in Stratford who needed to contact Shakespeare had Greenaway serve as a go-between: 'Your letter of 25 of October came to my hands the last of the same at night per Greenaway,' Abraham Sturley wrote to Adrian Quyney on 4 November 1598, 'which imported that our countryman, William Shakespeare, would procure us money.'

Greenaway carried goods along with messages – he was a draper as well as a carrier and leased a couple of small shops in Middle Row in Stratford. His trade told a story of the complementary desires of country and city. He left home with his saddlebags laden with the traditional offerings of pastoral England: lamb skins, rabbit skins, woollen shirts and cheeses; and he carried back for Stratford's wealthier consumers imported riches from London's markets. So, for example, when Richard Quyney was in London for an extended stay in autumn 1598, his wife employed Greenaway to bring him tobacco, silver and twenty pounds of cheeses, and Greenaway brought her back oranges. Taking advantage of her husband's stay in London, she also asked that he send home 'raisins, currants, pepper, sugar and some other grocery, if the prices be reasonable'. Anne Shakespeare may have requested much the same luxury items from her husband.

Greenaway charged five shillings for a horse for the trip between London and Stratford. For some travellers he also provided company. When Shakespeare's neighbour John Sadler had to travel to London, he hired a horse in Stratford and 'joined himself to the carrier', who knew the best routes and inns. More than once, surely, Shakespeare and Greenaway's trips home or back must have overlapped, and they would have ridden together and perhaps shared lodging and conversation. Greenaway probably had as good a sense of how Shakespeare juggled his roles as London playwright and well-to-do Stratford citizen as anyone, but what passed between the men perished with them.

The age of Chaucer's pilgrims, a time when Catholic English men and women of all ranks criss-crossed England to visit shrines at Canterbury, Norwich and elsewhere, was long over. Royal statutes against vagabonds now outlawed unrestricted travel. Itinerants were likely to be whipped and sent packing. The problem was particularly acute in Arden. Vagrants, some of whom had lost their homes owing to harvest failures and the pace of enclosure, had become so severe a problem in Stratford-upon-Avon that an act was passed in 1597 to prevent overcrowding, allowing no more than one family to a household; and in 1599 the authorities began to track down those who had entered town in the past three years.

By the end of Elizabeth's reign only a small number of people travelled far and wide across the English countryside, a list that included judges on circuit, carriers, soldiers, clandestine priests, those migrating to London to look for work and, of course, strolling players. As a Chamberlain's Man, Shakespeare had toured in south-east England and had probably toured more extensively earlier in his acting career. What Shakespeare saw on the road during the stretch of terrible harvests in the mid-1590s must have been an especially sobering experience. Only someone who had seen the effects of crop failure could write so poignantly in *A Midsummer Night's Dream* of how 'the green corn'

> Hath rotted ere his youth attained a beard;
> The fold stands empty in the drowned field,
> And crows are fatted with the murrain flock.
>   (II, i, 94–7)

Shakespeare had also seen first-hand, as few others could have, the widespread effects of enclosure and deforestation upon the English landscape.

A trip home to Stratford in late summer 1599, with days spent bouncing on a small, hard, English saddle along rutted roads, and nights enduring strange and flea-infested beds, was no holiday. A 1555 statute put it bluntly: 'Highways are now both very noisome and tedious to travel in, and dangerous to all passengers and carriages.' Even during the relatively dry months of late summer and early autumn the roads could be impassable. That October, for example, Thomas Platter failed to make it from Oxford to Cambridge by private coach. His coachman, who had leased his vehicle from a wealthy lord in London, begged off, explaining that the route was 'uninhabited and rather deserted, [and] further that it had recently been raining, so that he did not wish to take the risk'. Newfangled four-wheeled coaches might do in London's immediate environs, but horse or foot was the only sure way of overland travel through rural England, and sometimes even that wasn't good enough. When Will Kemp made his famous morris dance from London to Norwich in the spring of 1600, he found himself having to detour around muddy roads 'full of deep holes'.

Shakespeare added his name to a list of seventy or so people who in 1611 contributed to supporting a Parliamentary bill 'for the better repair of the highways and amending diverse defects in the statutes already made'. He was acting out of self-interest, knew that travel on the poorly maintained roads was travail, labour – and said as much in Sonnet 27:

> Weary with toil, I haste me to my bed,
> The dear repose for limbs with travel tired;
> But then begins a journey in my head,
> To work my mind when body's work's expired.

His obligations to his parents, his wife and her family, his daughters and his business affairs drew Shakespeare to Stratford. But if Sonnet 50 can be said to offer any insight into his private life, the journey home must at times have produced mixed feelings, separating him as it did from other, more intimate relationships in London:

> How heavy do I journey on the way,
> When what I seek, my weary travel's end,
> Doth teach that ease and that repose to say,
> 'Thus far the miles are measured from thy friend!'
> The beast that bears me, tired with my woe,

Plods dully on, to bear that weight in me,
As if by some instinct the wretch did know
His rider loved not speed being made from thee.
The bloody spur cannot provoke him on
That sometimes anger thrusts into his hide,
Which heavily he answers with a groan
More sharp to me than spurring to his side;
For that same groan doth put this in my mind:
My grief lies onward and my joy behind.

Riding out of London, however ambivalent, Shakespeare passed through Holborn, St Giles in the Field, past Tyburn's gallows, over Hanwell Common to Northcote. His path led him to Hillingdon Heath, through Uxbridge towards Buckinghamshire; and, after crossing the Colne and riding through Beaconsfield, he arrived at High Wycombe, twenty-five miles from London, a good place to stop for the night. If he were travelling in late summer, he would have seen roads still clogged with mustered men hurrying back to their unharvested fields, now that the threat of the 'Invisible Armada' had passed. There would also have been those back from Ireland – walking wounded or deserters. Shakespeare's decision to disguise Rosalind as a soldier on her way to Arden must have struck some playgoers as an apt one.

The dominant sight would have been of farmers harvesting their fields. Perhaps like the German traveler Paul Hentzner, who toured England at this time of year in 1598, Shakespeare witnessed the popular and pagan celebration of 'harvest-home', when farmers crowned 'their last load of corn ... with flowers, having besides an image richly dressed, by which perhaps, they would signify Ceres; this they keep moving about, while men and women, men and maid servants, riding through the streets in the cart, shout as loud as they can till they arrive at the barn.' There would have been few idle hands in the rich agricultural country through which Shakespeare was riding.

The next stage of his journey took him the twenty miles through Stokenchurch, Aston Rowant, Tetsworth and Wheatley, into Oxford. Because of his father's economic problems, Shakespeare, unlike schoolmates of his social standing in Stratford, had been denied a chance to study at the university; Oxford was the career path not taken. Tradition has it that Shakespeare lodged in Oxford at the Crown Inn. The proprietor was the father of William Davenant, who would later become a leading English playwright. Over time, the story was embellished and it was alleged that Shakespeare lodged there to carry on an affair with Davenant's beautiful mother – and Davenant himself wasn't ashamed to declare that he 'seemed contented enough to be thought' Shakespeare's illegitimate son.

The final leg of the journey – and the longest, at forty miles – would have taken Shakespeare from Oxford through Wolvercote and Begbroke to Woodstock, where he could have stopped and visited the rooms in which Elizabeth, before she was queen, under close guard, had awaited her doom, and scrawled in charcoal upon a window shutter a poem that was still legible when Paul Hentzner transcribed it in 1598:

> O Fortune! how thy restless wavering state
> Hath fraught with cares my troubled wit!
> Witness this present prison whither fate
> Hath borne me, and the joys I quit . . .
>   ELIZABETH prisoner.

Hers was a dramatic story and it was a pity that the life of the reigning queen remained off-limits to a playwright who could have made so much of it.

From Woodstock he followed the route past Kiddington, through Neat Enstone into Chipping Norton. He was now twenty miles from home. This stage of the journey led through a rich stratum of English history: on his way to Long Compton he would pass by the Rollright Stones – a local Stonehenge rich in legend. The story went that, in the days of the Danish King Rollo, an army of men had been turned to stone on the spot. After passing through this relatively isolated area, he neared Shipston-on-Stour. Shakespeare was approaching familiar ground, passing through Tredington and Newbold. He knew he was but eight miles out when he crested a hill, crossing the Roman road to Leicester, the great Fosse Way. Another five miles, through Ettington and Alderminster, would lead him to Atherstone. He was now squarely in the feldon – the rich and cleared agricultural expanse planted with wheat and other crops. In the distance, the River Avon marked the boundary separating feldon from woodland, chalk from cheese, not simply an agricultural boundary but a social, architectural and economic one as well. His native town straddled it.

Shakespeare rode into Stratford over Clopton Bridge, perhaps stopping long enough to notice where the stone he had recently sold the town (left over from renovations on his home) had been used in patching the bridge. His trip nearly over, he rode past Middle Row, turned left on High Street, past Sheep Street, and ended his journey on Chapel Street. Along this final stretch he saw how much the Stratford of his childhood and adolescence had changed. The terrible fires of 1594 and 1595 had claimed 200 houses and caused as much as £12,000 worth of damage. The first fire had struck the town centre, the one a year later its northern edge. The disasters were a national story: Thomas Beard bent the facts to suit his providential view of history when he wrote in *The Theatre of God's Judgment* (1597) that the 'whole town hath been twice burnt for the breach of the Sabbath by the inhabitants'. More likely, the conflagrations were caused and spread by small businesses in town, especially those turning barley to malt, which required stockpiles of fuel. The town went begging for relief – to neighbouring counties for hand-outs and to London in order to be spared the steep taxes and subsidies demanded by the crown in 1598 – and succeeded in both efforts.

During the summer of 1599 the town was still rebuilding. In late April Stratford's leaders appointed a commission to see how reconstruction was progressing and their report provides a snapshot of how the town looked at this moment. Shakespeare would have seen Stratford in the slow process of recovery. There had been a flurry of activity in Wood Street Ward, where John Locke, Thomas Lempster and Widow Cooper had finished rebuilding. Abraham Sturley still had some tiling to finish. Closer to his home, Shakespeare would have seen that, in defiance of new regulations, Hamnet Sadler had used flammable thatch in re-covering his roof. The area around Sadler's house and north, along Ely Street, had seen some of the worst destruction. Throughout Stratford, reconstruction remained patchy, with newly rebuilt houses standing alongside those still in ruins. Even more disconcerting was the number of strangers in town, most of them poor and living in overcrowded conditions. Stratford's population had grown from just under 1,500 when Shakespeare had been born to upwards of 2,500 in 1599. A quarter of the inhabitants, many of them displaced by the series of bad harvests or by the pace of enclosure, were impoverished. Stratford was struggling, country life a far cry from the pastoral fantasy served up by England's poets and playwrights.

Home for Shakespeare was New Place, an imposing house on the corner of Chapel Street and Chapel Lane, across from the Guild Chapel. It was the second-best house in town, which Shakespeare had bought two years earlier for the considerable sum of £120. New Place was a fifteenth-century, three-storey brick-and-timber building. It was very spacious, with ten rooms warmed by fireplaces, far more than the small family and any servants would have needed. The property also contained two gardens, two orchards and two barns. Shakespeare's recently acquired coat of arms would have been prominently displayed. In putting so much money into a huge home far from where he worked Shakespeare may have been trying to assuage his guilt over living so far away from his wife and daughters. He may have been thinking ahead towards an early retirement. Or perhaps it was simply a good investment, one that few in hard-hit Stratford were in a position to make.

It's impossible to reconstruct what Shakespeare's homecoming would have been like, what being reunited with his wife and daughters after a long absence might have meant to him. He had not lived with Anne since he was in his early twenties. After he was established in London Shakespeare could easily have purchased a home there and moved his family, but chose not to. Anne, now forty-three, had reached middle age sooner than her younger husband, while their teenage daughters Susanna and Judith, sixteen and fourteen, were almost grown up. Given that Shakespeare had only seen the girls at most a few times a year since they were children – and perhaps as few as a dozen or so times in all since he had left for London in the late 1580s, it's hard to imagine that his relationship with them was especially close, even by sixteenth-century standards. Yet the profound interest that Shakespeare shows in his plays in reunited families and his extraordinary insight into the relationship of fathers and daughters in plays from *The Merchant of Venice* and *Lear* to *Pericles* and *The Tempest* – would suggest the very opposite; unless, of course, that writing was compensatory, a chance to create in stories what he had rejected in his life. There's simply no way of knowing how he felt unsaddling at New Place on this or other visits – or how Anne, Susanna and Judith may have felt about his return.

Shakespeare's visits home could not have been relaxing. He couldn't count on getting much writing done. There was much to catch up on, many friends and relations to see, congratulate and condole, ageing parents that he might not see alive again, as well as some pressing legal matters to be looked into. Shakespeare would have found it much less noisy than London, the pace slower, and the food better, especially during the summer.

One of the advantages of returning to Stratford was that he would not have to worry about having a meal prepared; and his gardens and orchards at New Place would have provided vegetables, herbs and fruit, and the local markets cheese and other dairy products. Shakespeare may have ridden back to London a bit heavier than when he had left – or he may have been abstemious at home too.

The Shakespeare that his neighbours saw ride into town was not the 'poet of the heart-robbing line' but a wealthy citizen with one of the most expensive homes in town. It's this Shakespeare whose staid memorial bust still claims a prominent place in Stratford's church. Shakespeare played vastly different roles in London and in Stratford: in his home town he was sought out not for his plays or poems but for loans for business deals; just the previous October (1598) it was his 'loving good friend and countryman' William Shakespeare that Richard Quyney, a leading citizen, tried to contact when he needed to borrow the considerable sum of £30. It's unlikely that he ever had a chance to perform in Stratford for his parents, wife, children and friends, for Puritan-leaning authorities strongly discouraged playing there. Shakespeare was fortunate to have grown up at a time when leading groups such as Leicester's Men, Worcester's Men, Berkeley's Men, and Derby's Men had toured through Stratford. By 1602 the local bailiff had even imposed fines on anyone who permitted playing in town.

Shakespeare was known locally as an investor. Upon taking possession of New Place he had invested heavily in malt, eighty bushels of it, and stored it in his new barns. Malt was derived from barley, an expensive staple crop. It didn't take much labour to turn barley to malt and because of that the only ones to profit handsomely from malting were those wealthy enough to buy and store large amounts of grain. Shakespeare knew that by the time he began hoarding, the Privy Council – responding to terrible harvests and dearth – was trying to end this practice, forbidding the export of grain and ordering that hoarded stock be sold on the open market. The councillors also instructed Justices of the Peace to look into local abuses. Since Stratford's leading citizens were among the worst offenders – and also responsible for enforcing the new rules – little changed. Sick and hungry neighbours grew increasingly 'malcontent' and hoarders of malt were much hated (a Stratford weaver named John Grannams wished see them 'hanged on gibbets at their own doors'). Fortunately for Shakespeare, who was one of the leading offenders, the crisis passed; but he could not have stuffed his barns in 1597 ignorant of the consequences upon the poor of Warwickshire. He was clearly a man comfortable at playing many roles and capable of turning all of them into art. A decade later Shakespeare would begin *Coriolanus* by sympathetically portraying hungry citizens threatening to rise up against those hoarding grain.

Heading home, the irony could not have escaped Shakespeare how closely his journey resembled the experience of his characters. Like Orlando, Celia, Rosalind, Touchstone and the rest, he had left the world of court and city behind and entered Arden. Unlike Touchstone, who complains: 'Ay, now am I in Arden; the more fool I,' Shakespeare knew that the journey to the country was only temporary; in the end, in his comedies as in his life, the lure of the city and court – what Touchstone calls the 'better place' – was too powerful.

Jonson and Dekker and other dramatists who were London born and bred gravitated at this time to plays set in contemporary London. Shakespeare preferred distant lands and times. In *As You Like It* he would offer a more realistic and contemporary setting, but it would be rural, not urban – the Forest of Arden. When

Shakespeare saw that Lodge had set his *Rosalind* in Arden (that is, the French Ardennes, though spelled 'Arden'), the temptation must have been overwhelming to domesticate it to a familiar English landscape, at the same time making it accommodating enough to embrace all kinds of associations with Ardens domestic and foreign, past and present.

The Shakespeares had come from the heart of the old Forest of Arden, villages like Balsall and Baddesley Clinton, Wroxall and Rowington. His mother even bore the name of Arden, and through her he could trace his English roots to a time before the Norman Conquest. Shakespeare's Arden in *As You Like It* is close to home, though not home itself – and he took care to retain some of the more fantastic bits from Lodge – the lions and snakes and palm trees that made clear that this was an imaginary world. As usual, Shakespeare managed to have it both ways; but it's also the closest he would come to exploring the depth of his investment in his native Arden.

Once again, Shakespeare had been born too late. Like the old faith, Arden had been central to the world of his ancestors, the stuff of family legends; yet all that now remained was traces of what had been. Just as the Catholic paintings in Stratford's church and chapel had been whitewashed, the great Forest of Arden had been cut down, pasture and mixed woodland having replaced the endless woods rich in mystery and folklore. Writing about it in *As You Like It* must have stirred conflicting feelings in Shakespeare, for the play, in its disorientating shifts between woodland and pastoral landscapes, juxtaposes the romanticized Arden that stirred his imagination as a child with the realistic Arden that Shakespeare, sharp observer of land and people, witnessed as an adult. This helps explain the radically different Arden settings in the play. Four scenes in the play are set in the woods, the forbidding terrain where Orlando and Adam stumble upon the Duke and his men – the forest of ancient oak, streams, caves and herds of deer, of men dressed as outlaws and 'the old Robin Hood of England' (I, i, 112). Twelve other scenes set in the Forest of Arden offer an alternative landscape, a world of enclosure, of sheep and shepherds, landlords and farmers, landed peasants and the less fortunate wage-earners, where 'green cornfield' and 'acres of the rye' are now established (V, iii, 17, 21). When Oliver seeks Rosalind he does so 'in the purlieus' – Shakespeare here using the technical term for parts of royal forests that were no longer wooded.

His fellow poet and playwright Michael Drayton, another Warwickshire native, gave voice to what it felt like to be born too late to have experienced the forest of old in his topographical poem *Poly-Olbion*. Drayton explains that 'the woodland in Warwickshire' was once 'part of a larger weald or forest called Arden', whose bounds extended from the Severn to the Trent. Drayton is quick to assign blame for the end of Arden, first to overpopulation:

> When Britain first her fields with villages had filled,
> Her people waxing still, and wanting where to build,
> They oft dislodged the hart, and set their houses, where
> He in the broom and brakes had long time made his lair.

Then to greed:

> For, when the world found but the fitness of my soil,
> The gripple wretch began immediately to spoil
> My tall and goodly woods, and did my ground enclose,
> By which, in little time my bounds I came to lose.

Drayton may not have known it, but even by medieval times enclosure had already cleared most of the woods. One reason for these depredations was that Arden had never technically been a forest – and therefore protected under forest law. When the antiquarian John Leland rode through Warwickshire in the 1530s, deforestation was well advanced. He writes that the area north of the Avon is 'much enclosed, plentiful of grass, but no great plenty of corn', a view confirmed in 1586 by William Camden, who observed that the area is woodland, but 'not without pastures, corn fields, and iron mines'. Those iron mines, a sign of early industry, were hungry for fuel. Shakespeare wasn't as sentimental as Drayton, but he shared some of his nostalgia. His portrayal of Arden in *As You Like It* also acknowledges the economic and environmental changes Drayton describes in *Poly-Olbion*. They don't swamp Shakespeare's play, but they can't be ignored either. Perhaps because he saw it every time he passed the dispossessed on his ride home, Shakespeare's work is sensitive to the personal and social cost of enclosure.

When Shakespeare worked through his main source for *As You Like It*, he could easily have represented the shepherd Coridon as Lodge had: a successful tenant farmer who made a living tending to his landlord's sheep and tilling the land adjoining his rented cottage. What we get instead is the grim fate of Corin, unexpected in a comedy, who is so impoverished that he can't even feed or lodge his guests. He apologetically explains that he is 'shepherd to another man / And do not sheer the fleeces that I graze'. It gets worse, for his master's cottage, 'flocks, and bounds of feed / Are now on sale' (II, iv, 74–80). Shakespeare reduces Lodge's tenant farmer to a wage-earner who will be homeless and unemployed as soon as his master can sell off the cottage and the enclosed 'bounds' for a quick profit (III, v, 106). This is no throwaway scene. Shakespeare even names the owner, 'old Carlot', later in the play. He also romanticizes Corin as the epitome of country virtues. As Corin tells Touchstone, when asked whether he likes 'this shepherd's life' (III, ii, 12): 'Sir, I am a true labourer: I earn that I eat, get that I wear, owe no man hate, envy no man's happiness, glad of other men's good, content with my harm, and the greatest of my pride is to see my ewes graze and my lambs suck' (71–5).

Of course the sheep are not his. Celia's offer to buy the farm and mend Corin's wages is all that stands between him and the highway. *As You Like It* quietly but firmly reminded contemporary audiences that the new economy could be ruthless. Shakespeare knew that there were more Corins around than ever, left, as the historian Victor Skipp puts it, 'with no alternative but to take to the road, and ultimately to die on it'. Elizabethans knew what it meant when old Adam staggered onstage at the beginning of Act II, scene vi, exhausted and starving in the Forest of Arden, and told Orlando, 'I can go no further. Oh, I die for food! Here lie I down and measure out my grave' (II, vi, 1–2). The early acts of the play circle back time and again to the problems caused by vagrancy and hunger, including Orlando's angry words when Adam first suggests that they turn itinerant:

> What, wouldst thou have me go and beg my food?
> Or with a base and boist'rous sword enforce
> A thievish living on the common road?
> This I must do or know not what to do.
> (II, iii, 31–4)

Even as some starved, others profited. There's a brief exchange late in the play in which Touchstone addresses William, a young man in his twenties who was born in the forest, and asks him, point blank, 'Art rich?' William, who for a landed Warwickshire peasant has done quite well, admits as much, though in a cautious country way, 'Faith, sir, so-so' (V, i, 24–5). We don't need to see a sly bit of self-parody here in this Arden-bred William to know that another Warwickshireman with this name was also doing 'so-so' – thanks in part to activities like his recent hoarding of malt. Shakespeare understood all too well that there was a profit to be made from economic hardships endured by others. What we are offered in this play, then, is a much grittier comic landscape than Shakespeare had ever offered, one that provides an almost subliminal source of conflict in a play largely devoid of it, and at times casts a shadow over an otherwise relatively sunny comedy. Its quiet recognition of the threat of social dislocation helps explain why at so many points *As You Like It* seems to anticipate the next play Shakespeare set in England, *King Lear*.

Shakespeare's investment in Arden at this time extended beyond the play he was completing this summer. He would have taken advantage of a trip home in late summer to discuss with his father two issues concerning the family's Arden legacy that demanded their immediate attention. The first was the family coat of arms; the other, his mother's Arden inheritance, which his father had mortgaged and lost, and which they were in the final stages of a drawn-out and ultimately unsuccessful attempt to recover. Shakespeare's stake in Arden was real, and personal.

It seems that the family were not satisfied with the coat of arms that they had secured in 1596. Shakespeare and his father now sought more than simply the status of gentlemen; they wanted to incorporate their Arden connection. Whatever strategy he and his father decided upon, Shakespeare was the one who would have to deal directly with the heralds back in London. In November, or a few months after, Shakespeare returned to the College of Arms to plead the case (and to pay, once again, the steep price of twenty or so pounds for the privilege of doing so). In 1596 he and his father had claimed their right to a coat of arms on the grounds that John Shakespeare's own father and grandfather had faithfully and valiantly served King Henry VII and had been rewarded by him. They also noted that John, in taking Mary Arden as his wife, had married the daughter of an esquire.

The 1599 draft rewrites and expands this story. This time, their family service to the crown, which is 'approved' rather than 'valiant', is pushed further back in time, involving John Shakespeare's 'great grandfather and late antecessor'; and the royal largesse to the

Shakespeares, previously left unspecified, is described in a way that emphasizes the family's deep Warwickshire roots: 'lands and tene- ments . . . in those parts of Warwickshire, where they have contin- ued by some descents in good reputation and credit'. This was stretching things, for no grant that appears on the Patent Rolls has ever been traced to a Shakespeare; Shakespeare's ancestors had at best been freeholders or leaseholders.

These changes, however, were incidental to the main reason for the return visit to the heralds in 1599, which was to justify impal- ing the Arden arms alongside those of Shakespeare. Curiously, Mary Arden, mentioned by name in 1596, becomes nameless in the 1599 draft, where what matters is John Shakespeare's relation to Robert Arden, whose daughter he married. It wasn't just plays and sonnets that Shakespeare put his mind to revising. In 1596 he had first described his maternal grandfather as a 'gentleman' before asking the heralds to upgrade that to 'esquire', the rank repeated in 1599. This overlooked the fact that Robert Arden, though finan- cially comfortable, never in his lifetime even claimed the middling status of a yeoman.

The main challenge facing the Shakespeares and, by implica- tion, the heralds, was to which gentle line of Ardens to assign a Shakespeare connection. The absence of documentation was both an advantage and a problem. Had there been no doubt about Robert Arden's relation to those Ardens who bore coats of arms, the Shakespeares would not have had to return to the heralds for an empowering grant. The surviving 1599 draft shows that the her- alds initially decided on (or were persuaded by Shakespeare to assert) an alliance with the ancient line of the Ardens of Park Hall. So they began to draw in the margin of the document a sketch of the Shakespeare arms impaled alongside those of the Park Hall Ardens: 'Ermine, a fess checky or and azure,' a coat ultimately derived from the Beauchamps, Earls of Warwick. But at this point, the heralds had a change of heart. The side of their sketch of the shield showing the arms of the Park Hall Ardens was scratched out, and next to it was sketched in another and less illustrious Arden coat, the so-called 'old coat' with 'Gules, three cross-crosslets fitchées gold, and on a gold chief a martlet gules.'

Alternatively, if the decision to alter the coat of arms at the last moment had been Shakespeare's, it might have been motivated by his desire to put his family at some distance from the Arden line that had been implicated in the failed Catholic assassination attempt on Elizabeth. It's more likely, though, to have been the heralds' decision. They must have been unconvinced that the Shakespeares were connected with even a cadet branch of so ancient a family as the Park Hall Ardens. Still, the draft ultimately allowed that the Shakespeares could join their arms with the 'ancient arms' of Arden. Yet it remains unclear whether the confirmation was complete. If William Shakespeare's Arden-less coat of arms on his monument in Stratford's church and the family coat of arms subsequently used by his daughter Susanna and her husband John Hall are any indication, heraldic authorization was in the end withheld. Regardless of the outcome, the episode points to the depth of Shakespeare's investment – financial as well as emotional – in the Arden legacy. He and his father either knew that what they were telling the heralds was a fiction, or they themselves had come to believe the stories they had been telling of their connection to Warwickshire and to Arden.

The same obsession with an Arden legacy informs their persistence in trying to recover property that Shakespeare's father had lost twenty years earlier. In 1556 Robert Arden had bequeathed property to his youngest daughter Mary in the Arden village of Wilmcote. In 1578, struggling financially, John Shakespeare, who had married Mary Arden, borrowed £40 from Edmund Lambert and mortgaged Mary's house and land as security. This must have seemed a safe bet, for Lambert was his brother-in-law: his wife Joan was Mary's sister and it's likely that Edmund and Joan had stood godfather and godmother to John and Mary's children, who bore their names. But things didn't work out as planned. William Shakespeare was fourteen years old when his father, unable to repay all of the money on time on 29 September 1580, saw his wife's property passed into Lambert's hands. However unjust, that was the law. After Lambert's death, in 1587, the property went to his son John. At this point the Shakespeares seemed ready to cut their losses and, according to their version of what happened, in 1588 they agreed to give up any rights to the property and hand over any title deeds in their possession if John Lambert would compensate them with a cash payment of £20. It seems that some kind of conversation about this took place, but Lambert later denied that an agreement had been reached.

So the matter stood until November 1597, when Shakespeare and his father, having recently received their coat of arms, reversed course. They now wanted back their piece of Arden and sued for its return in Chancery, the court responsible for granting relief for unfair agreements. Once again, Shakespeare had to scramble to revise earlier narratives of what had transpired. His literary skills would have proved useful. The wheels of justice ground slowly, and it wasn't until the summer of 1598 that the court appointed commissioners to look into the facts of the case. Because John Shakespeare had mistakenly filed proceedings with the court twice in the same cause, there were further delays, and it wasn't until late June 1599 that the confusion was straightened out. Between June and October 1599 witnesses for both sides were deposed and depositions prepared and submitted to the court, and evidence shared by the two parties. It would have been critical for William Shakespeare to be on the scene in Stratford at some point during these months to sift through documents, contact potential witnesses and steer the case (we don't know whether his father was literate or whether, given his advanced age, he was physically up to the task). Unfortunately, the depositions each side put together are lost; if they had survived, they could have told us a great deal more about the Shakespeares. It appears that their claim wasn't strong enough, or, alternatively, that they grudgingly came to terms with Lambert, for the case was never heard by the court. Shakespeare and his father had spent an enormous amount of time, money and energy in their attempt to regain this Arden legacy. There's something quite brutal about having lost it on a legal technicality; but the episode, like that of the coat of arms, underscores how much the Arden connection had come to matter.

The Arden of Shakespeare's *As You Like It* and the Arden of his legal and heraldic pursuits have much in common. There's a tension in the work as in the life between the real and the romantic, between the way things once had been and the way that things now stood. Even as we see two versions of the Forest of Arden in the play – the wooded forest of days of yore and the deforested, enclosed and economically fraught one of the present – so too we get two vastly different versions of Shakespeare's Arden legacy. The fantasy of a heroic Shakespearean past, and of a connection to Arden that stretched back to the days when it was indeed a magnificent forest, competed in Shakespeare's mind with the reality that his ancestors on both sides had never been more than husbandmen. One of the most teasingly mysterious things about Shakespeare is his ability to sustain such contradictions; the same writer whose work exposed how embellished historical narratives often were found himself, when it came to his own past, making it up as he went along.

AUTUMN

The husband man doth choose his sowing graine
And makes it cleane before it go to ground
He knowes at length thencrease will quit y paine
the cleaner corne lesse darnell shalbe founde

October
scorpio

Dolose agunt filij iniquitatis

13
Things Dying, Things Newborn

Essex had landed in Ireland on 14 April, joining his troops after a rough passage. Almost three weeks had passed since his inspiring if ominous departure from London. Even before embarking, Essex knew how much was at stake: 'For myself, if things succeed ill in my charge, I am like to be a martyr.' He was worried, too, about what effect 'moist, rotten' Ireland might have upon his 'sad mind' and his 'rheumatic body', prone to the dysentery that had killed his father. What he discovered upon his arrival in Dublin could only have depressed him further.

Almost immediately Essex saw that he had to abandon his long-standing plans to seize the initiative by marching on Tyrone in Ulster. The Irish Council explained that there wouldn't be enough grass for fodder there until June. Nor was there sufficient transport to supply troops heading into Ulster. Essex also had to scrap plans to establish a garrison at Lough Foyle in the north, so

Essex and Tyrone at Bellaclinthe Ford,
Carleton, *Thankfull Rememberance*, 1627

crucial for flanking Tyrone's forces. He lacked sufficient shipping and men to accomplish this and the Privy Council rejected his request for 4,000 reinforcements, encouraging him to make do with what he had.

Essex was surprised by the number of rebels he now faced. Initial reports spoke of Tyrone with 6,000 or 7,000 men near Armagh; O'Donnell, in Connaught, with 4,000 more; and another 4,000 in Munster commanded by the Earl of Desmond. A few days later the Irish Council raised their estimate of enemy combatants to 30,000; the rebels outnumbered Essex's expeditionary force by almost two to one. The Council – motivated by self-interest and fearful of what would happen if the raw English troops were overwhelmed by Tyrone's battled-tested veterans – persuaded Essex to turn his attention first to the south, to suppress the rebellion in Leinster and Munster, a strategy that Elizabeth and her Privy Council reluctantly approved.

Rather than cutting the root of the rebellion in Ulster, Essex was now committed, as he put it, to shaking and sawing its branches in the south and west. The problem was with the metaphor itself: Essex would have been better off taking a torch to the entire tree – branches, trunk, roots and all. A scorched-earth policy, the kind that Edmund Spenser had advocated, would starve the Irish into submission, destroying their crops as well as the trees behind which they hid and fought; but Essex considered a war of attrition dishonourable. 'To speak plainly,' Essex gamely wrote to the Privy Council, 'our numbers are inferior to those which come against us, but our cause is better, our order and discipline stronger; our courage likewise, I doubt not, shall be greater.'

If Essex was unsure of how the war should be waged, he was fully committed to his band of brothers, the gentlemen adventurers who had followed him at their own expense to fight in Ireland. One of his first acts after landing was appointing his close friend the Earl of Southampton as General of the Horse in Ireland, though Elizabeth had warned him not to. Essex stood upon prerogative, however: his commission entitled him 'to make free choice of all officers and commanders of the army' and he would do so. He also made another loyal friend, the Earl of Rutland – who had come to Ireland against the Queen's command – Lieutenant General of the Infantry. Elizabeth responded by calling Rutland home; and she refused to let Essex appoint his father-in-law, Sir Christopher Blount, to the Irish Council. From Essex's perspective, the Queen, unlike her father and grandfather, had no first-hand experience of war and was simply meddling in affairs she knew nothing about. Elizabeth, for her part, feared that such appointments, along with Essex's right to knight those who followed him to Ireland, would bind men more closely to him than to her. She wouldn't stand for that, nor would she tolerate a shadow court in Ireland.

Behind these manoeuvres, behind the entire Irish campaign, was a struggle over a culture of honour. In the early fourteenth century there had been twelve hundred knights in England; by the time Elizabeth became queen that number had been halved through attrition. Midway through her reign the number had been halved again. It was a quietly efficient way for Elizabeth to consolidate power and break the will of an ancient nobility that had periodically risen up against the English monarchy. Since her unflinching response to the Northern Rebellion thirty years earlier the aristocracy had been submissive. By the end of her reign the noblemen who bore the titles that had struck fear into the hearts of monarchs in Shakespeare's history plays – the Percys, Pembrokes, Buckinghams, Westmorelands, Northumberlands and Norfolks – were poor shadows of their grandfathers and great-grandfathers, men whose power had been rooted in land and armed followers. So weakened was the nobility that Shakespeare's depiction of their ancestors' martial exploits in his history plays, while nostalgically recalling the great age of English chivalry, also reminded audiences how far, and how irrevocably, that culture of honour had declined. Essex, who had little land and less money, was more dependent on Elizabeth's largesse than most. He was the last upstart, the last, in the Earl of Northumberland's words, to wear 'the crown of England in his heart'. Even if his ambitions stopped short of the throne, Essex was determined to restore English knighthood in both numbers and prestige.

This explains why he had so coveted the post of Earl Marshal, whose responsibilities included presiding over the court's chivalric activities. Essex refused to see the post as largely ceremonial and set scholars to work delving into the long-forgotten powers of the office, including the responsibility for judging all questions of honour in the realm. And he sought to strengthen his authority by combining this post with that of the office of Constable, which, some believed, carried with it the right to arrest anyone in England, including the monarch. Essex began to sign his letters to the Queen as her 'vassal', bound in feudal traditions of homage and allegiance, rather than her 'servant' ('What I owe as a subject, I know, and what as an Earl, and Marshal of England; to serve as a servant and a slave I know not'). A month before departing for Ireland, at a hearing of the College of Arms held at Essex House, he had publicly declared that England was 'most mighty when the nobility led and commanded in war' and that even as 'God hath tied himself to the honour of men', so 'should the prince do likewise'. 'When nobility is suppressed,' he added, 'all government [is] subverted.'

Essex had taken advantage of the prerogative of command to dub twenty-one knights in the siege of Rouen in 1591, and another sixty-eight in Cadiz, many of whose allegiance to him was now unquestioned. 'Knights be not born,' William Harrison reminded readers in his *Description of England* (1577), not even 'the King'. Essex knighted eighty-one of his followers in Ireland, so many that it was hard to persuade Elizabeth not to revoke some of them.

Sir John Chamberlain spoke for those who saw that this explosion in the number of knights undermined the authority of the monarch and '[drew] the order' of knighthood 'into contempt': 'It [was] noted as a strange thing' that Essex 'in the space of seven or eight years' should 'make more knights than are in all the realm besides.'

The chivalric culture Essex was determined to restore and whose future was at stake in this Irish campaign had its apotheosis in the Order of the Garter, celebrated annually on St George's Day, 23 April. The chance to hold a Garter feast immediately after his arrival in Ireland enabled Essex to showcase the chivalric values he felt were unappreciated in Elizabeth's court, which rewarded 'little men' (a jab here at the diminutive Cecil, who preferred 'ease, pleasure, and profit'). It would be a replay of the famous Garter feast held by the Earl of Leicester in Utrecht in 1586, where, at the fighting at barriers, Essex, at age twenty, had first burst onto the scene, and 'gave all men great hope of his prowess in arms'.

The celebration Essex arranged in Dublin beggared description. Sir Anthony Standen confided to Edward Reynolds, Essex's secretary back in London, that the ceremonies 'on St George's Day passed all the service that I ever saw done to any prince in Christendom'. Standen knew how poorly this would be received at home: 'Though all was to her Majesty's honour, yet what malice may hew out of this, you know.' Another account was provided by the famously blunt Sir James Perrot (who had said of Elizabeth's tendency to pay attention to her skilled soldiers only in time of war, 'Now she is ready to piss herself for fear of the Spaniard, I am again one of her white boys'). As for Essex's show in Dublin, Perrot, who was there, wrote: 'There was not greater state, plenty, and attendance used at that time in the Court of England on the Queen and all her Knights of the Order.' Even Irish writers, who had few good words for the English, conceded that Essex 'displayed a regal pomp the most splendid that any Englishman had ever exhibited in Ireland'. It was high romance, fit to be immortalized by ballad-makers:

In Ireland, St George's Day
Was honoured bravely every way,
By lords and knights in rich array,
As though they had been in England.

The chivalric display in Dublin could not have stood in starker contrast to what was taking place that very day at Windsor, where Elizabeth saw to it that Garter celebrations were muted, owing to the 'sedition and flames of rebellion in Ireland'. Nonetheless, she decided that three knights were to fill the depleted ranks of the Order that day at Windsor: Thomas Scrope; Robert Ratclyffe, the Earl of Sussex; and Henry Brooke, Lord Cobham, deeply despised by Essex and his martial followers (and recently mocked onstage by Shakespeare). It must have struck many on both sides of the Irish Sea that day that England's true knights were with Essex while those rewarded at Windsor were foppish impostors, none more so than Cobham, whose train was called 'the bravest' (in the sense of 'sumptuous', not 'courageous'), and who had spent lavishly on the event. Cobham outfitted his gentlemen followers 'in purple breeches, and white satin doublets and chains of gold', and his 'yeomen in purple cloth breeches, and white fustian doublets, all in blue coats, and faced with white taffeta, and feathers of white and blue'.

It was the kind of performance that interested Shakespeare. Two years earlier, at the previous induction ceremony at Windsor (which fell on or near his thirty-third birthday), Shakespeare had almost certainly been part of the procession of gentlemen retainers following his patron Henry Carey, the Lord Chamberlain, all of them arrayed 'in blue coats faced with orange-coloured taffety, and orange-coloured feathers in their hats'. It may have been the gaudiest costume Shakespeare ever wore. The ceremonies at Windsor, which had brought him into such close proximity to the traditions of English chivalry, made a strong impression on him. They were still on his mind when, not long after, he wrote *The Merry Wives of Windsor*, in which he included an otherwise gratuitous allusion to 'Each fair instalment, coat, and several crest / With loyal blazon' of the Order, and even quoted its motto: *'Honi soit qui mal y pense'* – 'Evil to him who thinks evil' (V, v, 62–8).

Shakespeare's fascination with the Order and with the decline of chivalry in England goes back to the beginning of his career. In *The First Part of Henry the Sixth*, brave Talbot strips the Garter off Sir John Fastolfe, demanding to know if 'such cowards ought to wear / This ornament of knighthood, yea or no?' (IV, i, 28–9). Shakespeare went out of his way here to draw attention to the devaluation of the Order, and the speech that follows, which is not based on anything in his sources, would have resonated with England's martial faction:

> When first this order was ordained, my lords,
> Knights of the Garter were of noble birth,
> Valiant and virtuous, full of haughty courage,
> Such as were grown to credit by the wars.
> (IV, i, 33–6)

Shakespeare's long-standing interest in his history plays in the struggle over chivalric values, coupled with his strenuous efforts in the late 1590s to secure for his family a coat of arms, suggests that he himself was torn by the tension between past and present, between the form and substance of what it meant to bear arms.

As for Elizabeth, when reports trickled back to England of Essex's extravagant celebration, paid for out of her pocket, she responded in characteristic fashion, punishing Essex by giving the juiciest plum of all monopolies in England – the lucrative Mastership of Wards that had enriched Burghley and which she had dangled before Essex for months – to her dutiful bureaucratic servant Sir Robert Cecil.

*

By the time this news reached Ireland in early May, Essex had already marched out of Dublin, leading 4,000 foot soldiers and 500 cavalry against the rebels in Leinster and Munster. His army headed south-west, through Newcastle, Naas, Kilcullen, Athy, Maryborough, Ballyragget, Kilkenny and Clonmel. There were a few skirmishes but no serious battles with the Irish, who preferred to fight on their own terms, frustrating the gentlemen on horse, who were anxious for glory and prone to making foolhardy cavalry charges. One of these adventurers, the young Lord Grey, had to be reined in for his aggressiveness by the Earl of Southampton, a stinging insult that Grey, who packed up and went home, never forgot.

Essex reported to the Privy Council that 'the rebels fight in woods and bogs, where horse are utterly unserviceable; they use the advantage of lightness and swiftness'. And Essex's spies reported that the enemy was deliberately avoiding a fight, relying instead on 'the three furies, Penury, Sickness, and Famine' to wear down the English invaders. There were a few token demonstrations of submission to English authority by rebel leaders and Essex was greeted with orations in towns like Kilkenny and Clonmel, his path strewn with rushes – leading Elizabeth to complain aloud that she was spending a thousand pounds a day so that Essex might 'go in progress'.

The last week of May also witnessed the campaign's first victory, the taking, with artillery, of Castle Cahir, a major rebel stronghold. Elizabeth, when told of this, remained unimpressed with the capture of 'an Irish hold from a rabble of rogues', but it was a fine piece of tactical warfare. The same cannot be said of the disastrous defeat visited that same week upon Sir Henry Harrington's troops at Wicklow. Harrington had been dispatched by Essex to suppress Phelim McFeagh, the O'Tooles and their followers. In a replay of the defeat at Blackwater, command broke down. Outnumbered by the surrounding rebel forces, Harrington struggled to return his forces to Wicklow, five miles or so from where they were encamped. There was apparently collusion between Adam Loftus, who led an Irish company fighting for the English, and the rebel forces. Under attack, the English troops broke and ran, 'possessed with such a fear, that they cast away their arms, and would not strike one blow for their lives'. Nearly half of the English force of 450 men was cut down.

Meanwhile, the main body of Essex's expeditionary force trudged on, reaching as far west as Limerick and Askeaton before doubling back and completing a loop that took them through Mallow, Waterford, Arklow and Wicklow, before they returned, exhausted, to Dublin on 2 July, nearly two months since their departure, a month after the Ulster campaign should have begun. Aside from a few more submissions and orations they had little to show for their efforts, the sea of rebellion simply closing behind them. A disappointed John Harington wrote to a friend in England that in 'all that journey' nothing was 'done greatly worthy of speaking of'. Essex's men, William Camden records, were 'weary, distressed, and their companies incredibly wasted'. The knighting of over a score of gentlemen who had been part of the force no doubt kept other hopeful gallants, though 'lousy as beggars', from heading home. Elizabeth, all too conscious of how news of this ragged campaign was playing both in foreign capitals and in England, was furious, and let Essex know that the people 'groan under the burden of continual levies and impositions, which are occasioned by these late actions'.

Essex, deteriorating mentally and physically, was further disheartened by the news that his daughter Penelope had died in his absence, while his wife, sick and pregnant, feared miscarriage. While recuperating in Dublin, he dealt harshly with the survivors of the defeat at Wicklow. He held a court martial on 11 July, after which Lieutenant Walsh, who served under Captain Loftus, was executed for cowardice. Other officers were cashiered and imprisoned. Every soldier who had fought in that battle was 'condemned to die', then 'most of them pardoned and for example's sake every tenth man only executed'. Decimation – literally killing every tenth man – wasn't English military practice. Essex had come across the idea in a scholarly footnote in the 1598 translation of Tacitus (where he had read that when soldiers had 'thrown away their weapons and run cowardly out of the field' their general would 'put all standard bearers, centurions, etc., to death, and of the common sort every tenth man'). It may have kept other troops from deserting, but it was poorly received at home: John Chamberlain writes that 'My Lord's decimating of Sir Harry Harrington's companies is much descanted of, and not greatly liked here.'

Beyond the confines of the court, news of the Irish campaign remained anecdotal. Deserters returning into England told tall tales of how badly Essex was faring in Ireland. One of them, Harry Davis, a Welshman pressed into service at Windsor, was apprehended and confessed to the local authorities in Rye that the 'Earl of Essex travelling from Waterford to Dumdarricke in a wood was met withal by the wild Irish and set upon, where he lost fifty thousand men and the Earl himself was wounded in the right arm in such sort as he was like to lose his arm.' None of this was true, but in the absence of any official word on the course of the war, news like this – 'Stuffing the ears of men with false reports' (Induction, 8) as Shakespeare had put it in *The Second Part of Henry the Fourth* – was deeply disconcerting and could only erode support for the costly war. Venice's ambassador in London reported home this summer that 'Ireland may well be called the Englishman's grave.'

The conscripted soldiers could hardly be blamed for their low morale. By mid-July only 6,000 of the original 16,000 troops that had sailed for Ireland were fit for battle. Their lot was miserable: food, gunpowder and even their uniforms were deducted from their meagre pay – and, to make matters worse, the lightweight

'English stockings and shoes sent over' were worthless for fighting in bogs, where they quickly shrank. The morale of their general wasn't much better. Essex began to sound increasingly paranoid, convinced that his 'enemies in England, who first procured a cloud of disgrace to overshadow me . . . now in the dark give me wound upon wound'. He complained darkly to the Privy Council: 'I am armed on the breast, but not on the back.' His spirits must have sunk even lower when he received the first of a string of abusive letters from Elizabeth, who ordered him to march on the 'base bush kern' Tyrone in Ulster without further delay.

By the time her letter arrived in Dublin, Essex was already gone, leading a brief foray west into Offaly, at the head of 1,200 foot soldiers and 200 cavalry. Little of substance was accomplished on this ten days' mission, which ended in early August, though much gallantry was demonstrated and thirty more knights were dubbed, including two writers, John Harington and William Cornwallis. Elizabeth wrote again, incensed: 'You have broken the heart of our best troops and weakened your strength upon inferior rebels, and run out the glass of time which can hardly be recovered.' Facing the threat of the Spanish invasion in late July and early August, and fearful that Essex, once reports reached him, would use this as an excuse to abandon Ireland and return home at the head of some of his troops, Elizabeth further eroded their relationship by revising the terms of his commission and forbidding Essex from setting foot in England until she said so.

Essex's campaign was then struck by another blow: on 5 August a large English force under Sir Conyers Clifford was ambushed by O'Donnell's forces in the Curlew Mountains. Of Clifford's 1,500 troops, 241 soldiers (including ten officers) were killed and another couple of hundred wounded, almost a third of the force. Clifford himself was killed and decapitated, his head sent to O'Donnell. John Harington, who survived the encounter, was sure that the English had been bewitched: 'I verily think that the idle faith which possesses the Irishry, concerning magic and witchcraft, seized our men and lost the victory.' He adds that if not for the courage of the gallants on horseback, who 'gave a desperate charge upon the hill, among rocks and bogs, where never horse was seen to charge before', the losses would have been even greater.

Even before news of this latest defeat reached England, Elizabeth had written yet again, pouring salt in Essex's wounds, reminding him of what people would think if he failed to attack Tyrone: 'What despair will this work in our subjects' minds, that had greater hopes; what pride it will raise in the rebels, that had greater fears; and what dishonour it will do us in foreign parts, we had rather you had prevented than we had noted.' She did her own arithmetic and imagined that he could scrape together ten or eleven thousand troops (though in truth he had fewer than half that number at his disposal). Elizabeth saw what she wanted to see: 'We command you no impossibilities.' Essex knew better: 'Those who yesterday I led to the field, fight against me today,' he wrote, 'and those who shot at me today, will come in and fight on my side tomorrow. Such is the nature of this people and of this war.' This was not as he had imagined things would turn out when he proudly rode out of London to the cheers of thousands.

On 14 August Essex wrote home promising: 'Within eight or ten days at the furthest, I hope to be marching.' But marching where? William Camden later wrote that about this time Essex began 'to cast in his mind sinister designs of returning into England with select bands, and reducing his adversaries into his power by armed hand, being persuaded that many would side with him, partly out of love, and partly out of desire of innovation'. Sir Christopher Blount later confessed that 'a few days before the Earl's journey into the North', Essex had discussed with him and Southampton at the Castle in Dublin 'the best manner of going into England'. Essex's plan was to take two or three thousand soldiers with him, land at Milford Haven and drum up support for his cause there. It was a scheme that might have been partly inspired by Shakespeare's *Richard the Third*, where Henry VII, Elizabeth's grandfather, 'with a mighty power landed at Milford' (IV, iv, 532–3) on his way to rescue the nation from despotic rule. Rumours would reach Cecil that Essex had been viewing 'diverse havens' in Wales in anticipation of returning at the head of an army and that it had been preached in Chester that while the war in Ireland was great, 'the greatest was to come'. Blount and Southampton convinced Essex that such a plan would be his ruin and an 'irrecoverable blot' upon his reputation. They urged that if he must go, he should lead a small party of choice men, sufficient to secure him from being seized before he could speak with the Queen.

On 21 August Essex held a council of war at which Southampton and his junior officers pointed out the impracticality, if not the folly, of mounting an assault on Ulster. Morale had plummeted: 'The amazement of our base soldiers upon the late disaster and the fear of a northern journey is such as they disband daily; the Irish go to the rebels by herds . . . and some force themselves to be sick.' Gallants were quietly stealing home. Essex, for his part, was desperate and self-pitying. He wrote to the Queen: 'From a mind delighting in sorrow; from spirits wasted with travail, care, and grief; from a heart torn in pieces with passion; from a man that hates himself and all things that keep him alive, what service can your Majesty reap?' Elizabeth's tirades against Essex were increasingly public. Francis Bacon recorded hearing the Queen rail against Essex at this time, calling his actions in Ireland 'unfortunate, without judgment, contemptuous, and not without some private end of his own'. With her wise old councillor Burghley dead, and the rest of the court badly factionalized, there was nobody left to keep the Queen in check or stop the widening gyre of mutual recrimination.

Faced with Elizabeth's unrelenting criticism, Essex had no choice but to seek out Tyrone, though badly outnumbered. He gathered his few healthy troops – now reduced to 3,200 on foot and 360 cavalry – to face an enemy force over twice that size. The long-awaited campaign into Ulster lasted all of twelve days. It couldn't have lasted much longer than that since the troops could only carry three weeks of supplies with them. Without the pressure of Clifford's forces, Tyrone's men had no fear of being outflanked from either the north or the west. If Essex impetuously drove as far as Cavan, Tyrone's army could slip behind his troops and invade Dublin itself. The skies themselves seemed to conspire against the English attack, for it was 'so monstrous wet as the like hath not been seen'. Tyrone's superior force shadowed Essex's but remained tantalizingly out of reach, refusing to meet the desperate English in the field.

Essex's last hope was to appeal to Tyrone's sense of chivalry. He challenged him to single combat: 'Meet me in the field . . . where we will parley in that fashion which best becometh soldiers.' Tyrone, who was fifty-four, twenty-two years older than Essex, had no interest in such heroics. He had his own plan, one that he hoped would appeal to Essex's chivalric sensibility if not his love of theatre. Though Tyrone clearly had the upper hand, he had nothing to gain from gloating and that had never been his style. He offered to meet Essex to show deference and submit to his authority in form (if not much more than that).

Unable to provoke Tyrone or lure his disciplined soldiers into a fight, Essex finally agreed to meet on his enemy's terms. The place agreed upon was the ford of Bellaclinthe, where, on 7 September, Tyrone submissively rode into the strong current, the waters reaching as high as his horse's belly, while Essex, also on horseback, remained on dry land across from him. It was a remarkable scene. Those watching from a distance recorded how Tyrone 'took off his hat, and, inclining his body, did his duty unto his Lordship with very humble ceremony, continuing the same observancy the whole time of the parley'. Tyrone knew what role he had to play and played it to perfection. They spoke privately for half an hour. What words passed between them went unheard by others. Essex later told Southampton that Tyrone urged him 'to stand for himself and he would join with him', an offer that Essex later said he 'utterly rejected'. Nonetheless, the very act of meeting in private with the rebel leader was foolhardy, a tactical error that Essex would pay for dearly. Rumours quickly circulated. One held that 'Essex will be King of Ireland.' Another, reported to the King of Spain by a Franciscan in Ireland, was that Tyrone 'had almost prevailed upon the Earl of Essex to desert the Queen's cause and join that of your Majesty'. Tyrone of course had much to gain by spinning such tales. He even hinted darkly at a contemplated coup by Essex when he told an English emissary in late September that within two months he 'would see the greatest alteration and the strangest that he could imagine or ever saw in his life'.

After Essex and Tyrone had parleyed, their lieutenants met to confirm the terms of a truce that the two leaders had agreed upon, and on 15 September the terms were drawn up: there was to be a cessation of fighting, to be broken with a fortnight's notice. Little else was ceded by the Irish, who retained the right to 'enjoy what they have now', including the freedom to pass through the country. Even before news of this feeble armistice reached court, Elizabeth had become fed up with Essex's 'impertinent arguments'. She wrote again to Essex in stinging terms and there was talk at court of her replacing him with Lord Mountjoy: 'You had our asking, you had choice of times, you had power and authority more ample than ever any had, or ever shall have. It may well be judged with how little contentment we seek this and other errors. But how should that be hid which is so palpable?' Camden notes that 'with these letters the Lord Deputy was incensed'.

So too was Elizabeth when, on Sunday, 16 September, a Captain Lawson arrived at Nonsuch Palace from Ireland to report on Essex's conference with Tyrone (though not on the terms of the truce). The Swiss tourist Thomas Platter happened to be visiting Nonsuch that day, and from his account it seems that Elizabeth gave nothing away. Platter describes how she appeared 'most lavishly attired in a gown of pure white satin, gold-embroidered, with a whole bird of paradise for panache'. Although 'she was already seventy-four', he adds (though in fact she was only sixty-seven), she was 'very youthful still in appearance, seeming no more than twenty years of age'. A seemingly unruffled Elizabeth played cards with Lord Cobham and the Lord Admiral, read a bit, heard a sermon and had lunch served. Poised and resolute, she was still a force to be reckoned with, and Essex had underestimated her. She gave Captain Lawson a letter to carry back to Essex warning that his actions would prove 'perilous and contemptible', that he had merely patched together a 'hollow peace', and that he had better not pardon Tyrone or agree to terms with him without her written permission: 'To trust this traitor upon oath is to trust a devil upon his religion.'

It is unlikely that Essex ever received this letter. On 24 September he called a meeting of the Irish Council, at which he handed back the sword of state. Determined to leave Ireland and appeal to the Queen in person, Essex took ship with a band of his most loyal supporters, pausing only long enough to knight four more followers 'on the sands' before embarking. It was 'jested at in Ireland', William Udall wrote at the time, that Essex 'made more knights than he killed rebels'. Those who accompanied Essex included the Earl of Southampton, Sir Henry Danvers (who was still recovering from a head wound), Sir Thomas Gerard, Captain Christopher St Lawrence and Sir Henry Wotton. Upon landing in England, Essex dispatched letters to his uncle, Sir William Knollys, that offer some insight into his motives: he was 'resolved with all speed (and your silence) to appear, in the face of my enemies; not trusting afar off to my own innocency, or to the Queen's favour, with whom they have got so much power'.

It's hard to imagine the exhilaration these men experienced to be out of a war zone, back on English soil. They rode post-haste, aided by a full moon, without fear of bogs or ambush, desperate to reach court before their enemies had word of their return. Their pace was blistering and within three days of leaving Dublin the small group approached London. At dawn on the 28th they raced south on the final leg of their journey, to Nonsuch, where the Queen was holding court.

Much of what we know about what happened next comes from the letters that Rowland Whyte, then at court, wrote to Sir Robert Sidney. Whyte only passed along these sensitive reports after Sidney had assured him that he would destroy the letters as soon as he had read them ('Burn my letters,' Whyte wrote, 'else shall I be affrighted to write, the time is now so full of danger'). If Sidney hadn't gone back on his word, a good deal of what next took place would have remained even more mysterious than it is. Whyte writes how Lord Grey, now back from Ireland and still smarting from Southampton's reprimand, learned of the return of Essex's band and raced to Nonsuch to alert the court. Essex's friend Sir Thomas Gerard rode hard and caught up with Grey. The courteous formality of the two men, so recently comrades in arms, barely masks the bitterness of their exchange:

'I pray you,' said Sir Thomas Gerard, 'let my Lord of Essex ride before, that he may bring the first news of his return himself.' 'Doth he desire it?' said my Lord Grey. 'No,' said Sir Thomas, 'nor I think will desire nothing at your hands.' 'Then,' said he, 'I think I have business,' and made greater haste than before, and upon his arrival went straight to Robert Cecil.

After Gerard failed to stop him, Christopher St Lawrence, the bold Irishman, offered to ride ahead and kill Grey and Cecil too, but Essex wouldn't 'assent to it'.

Upon arriving at Nonsuch perhaps a quarter-hour after Grey,

Essex leaped from his horse at the court gate and entered the palace. There was no time to lose. He raced through the presence chamber into the privy chamber, only to discover that, though it was already ten in the morning, the Queen was not yet up and dressed. What followed next was like a scene out of Shakespeare's *Lucrece*:

> Now is he come unto the chamber door
> That shuts him from the heaven of his thought,
> Which with a yielding latch, and with no more,
> Hath barred him from the blessed thing he sought.
>
> (337–40)

Essex burst into the Queen's bedchamber, where he discovered Elizabeth 'newly up, her hair about her face'. ''Tis much wondered at,' Whyte writes with considerable understatement, 'that he went so boldly to her Majesty's presence, she not being ready, and he so full of dirt and mire, that his very face was full of it.' No man had ever entered into her bedchamber in her presence, had seen Elizabeth beside her famous walnut bed, hung with cloth of silver, fringed with gold and silver lace and crowned with ostrich plumes. For the Queen and her women-in-waiting it must have come as an unbelievable shock. It's next to impossible today to grasp how great a taboo Essex had violated. This was England's virgin Queen and her bedchamber was sacrosanct. When Ben Jonson daringly chose to revisit this scene a year later in his play *Cynthia's Revels*, he cast Essex's action as a crime of mythical proportions – like Actaeon, he wrote, seeing the naked Diana:

> Seems it no crime to enter sacred bowers,
> And hallowed places, with impure aspect,
> Most lewdly to pollute? Seems it no crime
> To brave a deity? Let mortals learn
> To make religion of offending heaven.
>
> (V, xi)

As Jonson's play suggests, it was a primal scene, one that left a deep impression at court and on England's writers, including Shakespeare. It may well have informed the play he was now writing, with its fraught closet scene in which a rash Prince Hamlet confronts Queen Gertrude and remonstrates with her there.

In many ways, the encounter proved to be Elizabeth's finest hour. She didn't know if Essex had come at the head of an army, if he had already killed his enemies at court, or even whether she herself was in physical danger. Great actress as she was, she hadn't had time to prepare for the scene, to present herself as a formidable queen. With the advance of years, making herself up for this role had become increasingly time-consuming; Essex's entry had caught her, embarrassingly, in the midst of her preparations. If Elizabeth was rattled, she didn't show it. Essex, reports ran, 'kneeled unto her, kissed her hands and her fair neck, and had some private speech with her, which seemed to give him great contentment'. He had chosen to play the role of the courtier. His words don't survive, but there's a likelihood that his sentiments were mirrored in a sonnet Essex composed about this time, one that translated the disappointments of the courtier into the language of frustrated courtship:

> To plead my faith where faith hath no reward
> To move remorse where favour is not borne,
> To heap complaints which she doth not regard,
> Were fruitless, bootless, vain, and yields but scorn.
> I loved her whom all the world admired,
> I was refused of her that can love none;
> And my vain hopes which far too high aspired,
> Are dead and buried, and for ever gone.
> Forget my name since you have scorned my love,
> And woman-like, do not too late lament;
> Since for your sake I must all mischief prove,
> I none accuse nor nothing do repent.

I was as fond as ever she was fair,
Yet loved I not more than I now despair.

It reveals a great deal about Essex that he not only seems to have believed in such sentiments, but spent his time, as his follower Henry Wotton put it, 'evaporat[ing] his thoughts in a sonnet'.

Elizabeth adapted easily enough to this familiar script. She kept her wits, heard him out, played for time and told Essex to come back after he had cleaned himself up. She might have told him what everyone else already knew: the great age of the disappointed Petrarchan sonneteer was over. Essex, who for the second time this month had badly misread the scene he was playing, left convinced that his charm and chivalric manner had turned back Elizabeth's anger. Delighted with how things were going, he departed 'very pleasant, and thanked God, though he had suffered much trouble and storms abroad, he found a sweet calm at home . . . At eleven he was ready, and went up again to the Queen, and conferred with her till half an hour past twelve.' By that time Elizabeth had got word that Essex had returned with only a handful of supporters and that her court and kingdom were safe.

When Essex was invited back to the Queen's presence, he 'found her much changed in that small time, for she began to call him to question for his return and was not satisfied in the manner of his coming away and leaving things at so great a hazard'. Essex was dismissed and told to await her instructions. He would never set eyes on the Queen again. From that moment, at least in England, it's fair to say that chivalry was dead.

Even as Essex and his cohort were racing home from Ireland on 24 September on their way to Nonsuch, the cream of London's merchant class were assembling at Founders' Hall, on Lothbury Street, south of Moorgate. Over a hundred of them – from Lord Mayor Soame and leading aldermen to prosperous drapers and grocers – had convened two days earlier to form a joint-stock company to which they committed the remarkable sum of £30,000. They were meeting again on the 24th to choose directors and treasurers and draft a petition to the Queen 'for the honour of our native country and for the advancement of trade ... to set forth a voyage this present year to the East Indies'. It was a venture that transformed England as few things ever would. The East India Company was born at this moment, which, as it expanded its markets, geographic range and political, industrial and military might, helped forge a British Empire. It was also a seminal moment in the history of global capitalism.

Except that few, save for a visionary like John Dee, who had coined the phrase 'British Empire' twenty years earlier, could even dream of such a future. History looks very different when read backwards. Until now, efforts to establish England as an imperial power had gone nowhere. The investors gathered at Founders' Hall that day knew all too well that England had failed to plant colonies in America; it couldn't even protect its plantations in Ireland. English venturers had failed to break into the Caribbean slave trade, failed to discover the much sought after northern passage to the East, and failed to establish a direct trade with the East Indies around the Cape of Good Hope. Their success in importing and exporting goods through the Turkey, Venice, Levant, Muscovy and other limited trading companies had been only modestly profitable and restricted to the few members of these companies. And everyone knew that the penny-pinching Queen was not ambitious for empire and was happier signing a peace treaty that would save her money than antagonizing Spain by encroaching on its exclusive trade.

Yet the merchants who gathered to form the East India Company had little choice. Their hand had been forced by the recent and stunning success of the Dutch in penetrating the Eastern trade. Jacob van Neck's envy-inspiring account, immediately translated into English in 1599 – *A True Report of the Gainful, Prosperous and Speedy Voyage to Java in the East Indies, Performed by a Fleet of Eight Ships of Amsterdam* – recounted the get-rich story in detail: the Dutch ships had returned on 19 July 1599, and 'there never arrived in Holland any ships so richly laden'. The haul was staggering: 800 tons of pepper, 200 tons of cloves, and great quantities of nutmeg, cinnamon, and other luxury goods. Dutch merchants had made a 400 per cent return on their investment. The English merchants knew that, even as they were petitioning the Queen, more Dutch ships were outward bound.

This news was potentially ruinous for many of those at Founders' Hall. Until now, luxuries from the East had entered English markets through the Levant trade. Goods such as pepper and other spices were brought overland from south-east Asia to the Middle East and English merchants would transport them home from there through the Mediterranean. Levant Company agents stationed in the Middle East quickly saw that the Dutch venture would put them out of business. Somewhere between a quarter and a third of those who gathered to form the East India Company were affiliated with the Levant Company and had the most to lose. They made no secret in their petition to the Queen that they were responding to 'the success of the voyage performed by the Dutch nation'. They were concerned that 'the Dutchmen prepare for a new voyage' and threw in for good measure an appeal at once nationalist and commercial, that they were 'stirred up with no less affection to advance the trade of their native country than the Dutch merchants'. In return for their huge investment, with no hope of immediate returns (the outbound voyage alone was likely to take over a year), they sought a charter from the Queen guaranteeing a monopoly on trade beyond the Cape of Good Hope for fifteen years; and to forestall any argument that their venture would frustrate Elizabeth's plans for peace with Spain, they drafted a document setting out 'the true limits' of Iberian 'conquest and jurisdiction', to reassure her that the Spanish had no legal grounds for complaint.

The London merchants knew that they were in an unusually strong position with the Queen and Privy Council. After all, they had twice come to the rescue of the Crown this year, first when providing loans for the Irish campaign and then again, in July and August, when they had provided substantial financial and military support in defending London against the threatened Spanish invasion. Their generosity during this false alarm (self-interest notwithstanding) had no doubt done much to erase hard feelings about rich merchants that the Privy Council had hauled in for refusing to pay the forced loan (like Augustine Skinner, now no longer pleading poverty but one of the original subscribers to the East India venture). What they didn't know was that the Queen, wary of Essex and his militant supporters, needed the City on her side in case of armed rebellion.

The timing was right for London's merchants to ask for something in return from the Queen. To send ships around the Cape of Good Hope was a daunting enterprise (and, in fact, the first expedition, which after a series of delays finally sailed in 1601, cost more than twice the £30,000 that had been committed). It required not just capital, but skilled commanders, ships of adequate tonnage capable of making the long voyage and fending off privateers, maps and knowledge of the regions, and a demand for these luxury items at home; and since this venture wasn't about trading goods (for there wasn't much of a market in the sweltering East Indies for heavy cloth, England's main export), large amounts of gold and silver had to be available for export to purchase foreign commodities. In all these respects, England had reached, and passed, the tipping point. Drake and other naval heroes had made their fame and fortune by privateering – glorified purse-snatching. What was needed now was long-term investment in a venture that required patience and capital and cool heads – things for which merchants, not courtiers, were famous.

Because of the vast expense and because 'the trade of the Indies' was 'so far remote from hence', the organizers of the East Indies subscription understood that only a 'joint and a united stock' would work – that the circle of investors had to be widened well beyond the scope of those who were already members of the Levant or other exclusive trading companies. It's notable, though, that the initial subscription to the East India Company failed to include a single nobleman; there was as yet no overlap between Elizabethan knight adventurers seeking glory in Ireland and the stay-at-home merchant adventurers in search of profits. Until now, aristocrats who invested in shipping had done so in semi-military operations, like the privateering Earl of Cumberland, who personally led six of the eleven voyages he financed between 1586 and 1598. The problem was that these expeditions were hit-or-miss affairs, more likely to bring glory than profits (Cumberland himself complained that in the end all he had done was 'thrown his land into the sea'). It couldn't be managed alone.

Collective will was needed too, and this was stiffened by the propagandistic efforts of men like Richard Hakluyt, who attended the organizational meetings of the East India Company this autumn and who was handsomely rewarded by the company with a gift of £10, in addition to the thirty shillings he received for providing maps. Hakluyt is best known as the author of the massive three-volume *Principal Navigations, Voyages, Traffics, and Discoveries of the English Nation*, a million-and-a-half-word epic of English voyages of exploration, which appeared in successive folio volumes in 1598, 1599 and 1600. In the autumn of 1599 he was feverishly completing the second volume, whose dedication to Robert Cecil he finished on 24 October, and which focused on voyages 'to and beyond the East India'.

His preface to that volume now seems innocuous but at the time was radical: Hakluyt describes London's merchants as England's true 'adventurers' and criticizes the gentry, who 'now too much consume their time and patrimony'. He hopes that England's knight adventurers 'will do much more' when 'they are like to have less employment than now they have', preoccupied as they are in 'our neighbour wars' in Ireland and the Low Countries. This is a role reversal of staggering proportions: true adventure now consisted in pursuing national glory through trade and empire, not through a culture of honour. Writing after Essex's ill-fated return, Hakluyt saw which way contemporary winds were blowing. His first volume, published in 1598, had advertised on its title page Essex's exploits in the Cadiz campaign of 1596, and the volume had even culminated with a lively account of that enterprise, including a list of those knighted in the campaign. When, in late 1599, a second edition of this volume was published, Hakluyt cut the Cadiz chapter and erased from the title page any reference to Essex's heroic (and unprofitable) actions there.

The death of chivalry coincided with the birth of empire. Hakluyt wasn't alone in seeing the writing on the wall: roughly a fifth of the men knighted by Essex in Ireland, including his most loyal supporters the Earls of Southampton and Monteagle, would go on to become members of the investor class, belatedly elbowing their way into one or another trading venture. The knight adventurers found themselves playing an uncharacteristically subordinate role. When, for example, Lord Treasurer Buckhurst tried pressuring the East India Company to appoint Sir Edward Michelbourne, one of Essex's knights, to be a commander on their first voyage, the merchants demurred, explaining that they had no intention of employing a gentleman in a position of authority – they didn't want a hot-headed knight ruining trade by wrangling with the Portuguese in the East Indies. From now on, merchant adventurers were in charge.

Shakespeare, almost surely at work on *Hamlet* by this time, wasn't among those gathered in Founders' Hall that September day. If he didn't have enough ready money on hand after the building of the Globe, he certainly would within a year or two; but his name never appears in the rolls of joint-stock company investors: he preferred to invest his wealth in English property (or products like malt) rather than in speculative voyages abroad. Yet Shakespeare played his part indirectly: one of the items carried aboard an early East India Company voyage was a copy of *Hamlet*. In 1607 William Keeling, captain of the *Dragon*, and his crew were bound, along with the *Hector* and the *Consent*, for the East Indies. In early September of that year, while the ships were off Sierra Leone, Keeling notes in his ship's log that he ordered his men to perform *'The Tragedy of Hamlet'*. Six months later they gave a repeat performance when Captain Hawkins of the *Hector* came aboard. Keeling explains that he 'had *Hamlet* acted' for practical rather than artistic reasons: 'to keep my people from idleness and unlawful games, or sleep'. Shakespeare's play had quickly become part of the cultural transformations it was itself reckoning with.

It's not that Shakespeare wasn't interested in adventuring and trade – *The Merchant of Venice*, *Othello*, *Pericles*, and *The Tempest* all testify to his fascination with foreign trade, conquest and exploration; but he didn't follow the lead of other playwrights whose plays celebrated the achievements of London's merchants. Shakespeare's choice of subject matter suggests that from his early twenties, and perhaps from his childhood, he was the kind of writer who dreamed and wrote of kings and queens, war and empire, heroism and nobility, and stranger shores. While there were merchants and ordinary men and women in his plays, neither they, nor London itself, were ever at the heart of it.

Shakespeare also knew that the word 'adventurer' cut two ways and employed it in both senses. Hamlet, for example, when speaking of the Players, describes how 'the adventurous knight shall use his foil and target' (II, ii, 320–21). Romeo, on the other hand, as befits a merchant's son, tells Juliet:

were thou as far
As that vast shore washed with the farthest sea,
I should adventure for such merchandise.
    (II, ii, 82–4)

That Shakespeare was alert to the decline of chivalry is clear enough by the time that he wrote *Troilus and Cressida*, not long after *Hamlet*, with its trenchant contrast between its Prologue's parody of epic language – 'princes orgulous' with 'high blood chafed' arriving in Troy on 'deep-drawing barks' that 'disgorge / Their warlike freightage' (Prologue 1–13) – and the egotism, vanity and brutality that mark the behaviour of the Greek heroes. Shakespeare exposes the seamier side of Homer's heroic story, emphasizing the more sordid and rapacious aspects of the Trojan campaign. Only a writer who had partly believed in the possibility of heroism could have turned so sharply against it, and the bitterness of this repudiation sours the play and diminishes it. Had Shakespeare's late and collaborative play *Cardenio* survived (it was written around 1612 and performed at court not long after), we would probably have an even sharper sense of this disenchantment, for that play almost surely took its plot from the story of Cardenio and Lucinda in *Don Quixote*, Cervantes' masterly send-up of knight-errantry, recently translated into English. Shakespeare would continue to write about heroes like Othello, Antony, and Coriolanus – though each of these tragic figures finds himself crushed by a world too small to accommodate his heroic greatness. Coriolanus offers the finest expression of this when he turns his back on Rome and declares, 'There is a world elsewhere' (III, iii, 145); the punishing ending of *Coriolanus* shows him how wrong he was.

Hamlet, born at the crossroads of the death of chivalry and the birth of globalization, is marked by these forces, but, unlike the caustic *Troilus and Cressida*, not deformed by them. They cast a shadow over the play, though, and certainly inform its reflections on the possibility of heroic action. They also reinforce the play's nostalgia: there's a sense in *Hamlet* no less than in the culture at large of a sea-change, of a world that is dead but not yet buried. The ghost of Hamlet's father, who returns from Purgatory in the play's opening scene, not only evokes a lost Catholic past, then, but is also a ghostly relic of a chivalric age. The distance between this past and the present is underscored by the Ghost's martial appearance. He enters dressed exactly as he was when, as a young man, he had defeated his Norwegian rival on the battlefield: 'Such was the very armour he had on, / When he the ambitious Norway combated' (I, i, 60–61). We see Hamlet's father not as he died but as he heroically fought thirty years earlier. By 1599 such dress was an anachronism; only on Accession Day did knights still dress in otherwise rusting armour.

Shakespeare goes to considerable lengths to paint a verbal portrait of Hamlet's father's heroic encounter, a world of heraldic law and mortal combat, of armoured men wielding broadswords, fighting to the death:

> Our last king,
> Whose image even but now appeared to us,
> Was as you know by Fortinbras of Norway,
> Thereto pricked on by a most emulate pride,
> Dared to the combat; in which our valiant Hamlet,
> (For so this side of our known world esteemed him)
> Did slay this Fortinbras, who by a sealed compact
> Well ratified by law and heraldy
> Did forfeit (with his life) all these his lands
> Which he stood seized of, to the conqueror;
> Against the which a moiety competent
> Was gaged by our King, which had return
> To the inheritance of Fortinbras,
> Had he been vanquisher; as by the same co-mart
> And carriage of the article design,
> His fell to Hamlet.
> (I, i, 80–95)

Hamlet ends with another celebrated encounter; but this fight, which also takes the lives of Claudius, Gertrude, Laertes and Hamlet himself – couldn't be more different from the one Horatio describes at the play's outset. It's a duel, but not quite even that – nothing more than a fencing match, fought with blunted weapons. Shakespeare's contemporaries would have been more attuned than we are to the difference between old and new ways of fighting and what kind of world-view each embodied. It was only in the second half of the sixteenth century that the rapier replaced the heavy sword as the weapon of choice, and it wasn't really until the 1580s that the rapier and dagger, Laertes' preferred weapons, became popular in England.

A book that laments this change, and which Shakespeare drew on when writing *Hamlet*, was George Silver's *Paradoxes of Defence*, dedicated to Essex and published in early 1599. In it, Silver is nostalgic for the lost world epitomized by the kind of combat old Hamlet and Fortinbras had engaged in: 'Our forefathers were wise, though our age account them foolish, valiant though we repute them cowards: they found out the true defence for their bodies in short weapons by their wisdom, they defended themselves and subdued their enemies, with those weapons with their valour.' Silver adds: 'We, like degenerate sons, have forsaken our forefathers' virtues with their weapons and have lusted like men sick of a strange ague, after the strange vices and devices of Italian, French, and Spanish fencers.' Notably, it's a Frenchman's praise of Laertes' swordsmanship that gives Claudius the idea of having Laertes fence with Hamlet.

As recently as *As You Like It*, Shakespeare had lampooned the culture of the challenge in Touchstone's comic routine about how to quarrel without ever coming to blows: 'I have had four quarrels and like to have fought one' (V, iv, 46). In *Hamlet*, we get a different version of Touchstone's 'Retort Courteous' in the affected language Osric uses to describe the impending fencing match – so that

Hamlet is told that his rival, Laertes, is 'full of most excellent differences, of very soft society, and great showing; indeed, to speak
feelingly of him, he is the card or calendar of gentry'. Chivalry and
honour are reduced in the Danish court to jargon and an elaborate
bet: Hamlet is told that a Frenchified Laertes has wagered 'six
Barbary horses against six French swords, their assigns, and three
liberal-conceited carriages – that's the French bet against the
Danish' (V, ii, 160–64). Acting as if one still lived in the world of
Hamlet's heroic father – where it was possible to win fame through
martial feats – was no longer possible; but how to act in the world
that had replaced it was not yet clear, and part of Hamlet's dilemma.

The gap between exploits in the field and merely playing soldiers would also have been unmistakable to Elizabethans at this
year's annual Accession Day joust, held once again at Whitehall in
November. Those who had fought in Ireland from the beginning
to the end of the campaign, some bearing the scars of battle, were
excluded from joining the lists this year, including Essex himself,
who a year earlier had been chief challenger. Only two men who
had served in Ireland (and who had returned by mid-summer)
were among the combatants at Whitehall and both had jousted
the previous year: Essex's sworn enemy, Lord Grey, and Henry
Carey, now Sir Henry, who had also been knighted by Essex in
Ireland and who remained devoted to him. Their non-fatal
encounter – for Grey and Carey were paired with each other in the
tilts – would no doubt have been closely watched by friend and foe
alike in the crowd outside Whitehall. But what, in the end, 'was
most memorable' about the tournament, according to Rowland
Whyte, speaks worlds about how martial display had become sub-
ordinated to theatre and conspicuous display: a minor court figure,
Lord Compton, had appeared 'like a fisherman, with six men clad
in motley, his caparisons all of net, having caught a frog'. To those
in the crowd returning from the wars – officers and soldiers alike –
this Accession Day show must have confirmed for them, if further

proof was needed, that things had degenerated, that the world had changed, and changed quickly.

In *Hamlet*, Shakespeare once again found himself drawn to the epochal, to moments of profound shifts, of endings that were also beginnings. It was such a rupture that he had in mind when he wrote in *The Winter's Tale* of 'Heavy matters, heavy matters! . . . Thou met'st with things dying, I with things newborn' (III, iii, 109–11). Born into a world in which the old religion had been replaced by the new and, like everybody else, living in nervous anticipation of the imminent end of Elizabeth's reign and the Tudor dynasty, Shakespeare's sensitivity to moments of epochal change was both extraordinary and understandable. In *Hamlet* he perfectly captures such a moment, conveying what it means to live in the bewildering space between familiar past and murky future.

As long as Essex's fate remained unresolved, nothing was resolved: 'All men's eyes and ears,' Rowland Whyte writes, 'are open to what it will please her Majesty to determine.' Until Elizabeth made up her mind, Essex remained under house arrest, cut off from his friends and even his newly delivered wife. Yet it wasn't entirely clear what, if anything, Essex had done wrong. Many outside the orbit of the court were confused. One of them, the aged poet Thomas Churchyard, who had celebrated Essex's departure and had been labouring in his absence on a companion poem honouring his return, entered 'The Welcome Home of the Earl of Essex' in the Stationers' Register on 1 October. His ill-timed poem was never printed and the manuscript almost surely consigned to the dust-heap.

Adding to the confusion and tension in the city, Essex's gallant followers were abandoning Ireland and flooding London: 'This town is full of them, to the great discontentment of her Majesty.' The public theatres appear to have been one of their haunts and Shakespeare probably spotted at the Globe some of these gentlemen volunteers, for according to Rowland Whyte, 'Lord Southampton and Lord Rutland came not to Court . . . they pass away the time in London merely in going to plays every day.'

We don't know what old plays they might have seen at the Globe in October or early November. It would turn out to have been a dangerous coincidence had the Chamberlain's Men staged Shakespeare's *Third Part of Henry the Sixth*, which included a scene in which supporters of Edward, who was under house arrest, succeed in a daring rescue attempt 'to set him free from his captivity' (IV, v, 12). For in early November Essex's friends, fearing that he was to be delivered to the Tower of London, contemplated a similar scheme. According to Sir Charles Danvers, the plan, spearheaded by Essex's close friends Southampton and Mountjoy, was 'either by procuring him means to escape privately into France, or by the assistance of his friends into Wales, or by possessing the Court with his friends to bring himself again to her Majesty's presence'. This last and violent act would have been treasonous.

Danvers adds that these ideas had been 'rather thought upon, than ever well digested', until around mid-November, when he met with Southampton, his brother Henry Danvers and Mountjoy, and Essex's friends resolved that if he were in danger of being carried to the Tower, the best plan was 'to make a private escape'. Somehow Southampton got this message through to Essex, offering that he and Henry Danvers go into exile with him; and Danvers said that if they chose to leave him behind, he would 'sell all that [he] had, to [his] shirt', to maintain Essex abroad. Essex, though, categorically refused to flee, saying that 'if they could think of no better a course for him than a poor flight, he would rather run any danger than lead the life of a fugitive'. Southampton later remembered things a bit differently, and claimed to have opposed the plot and stopped it 'not three hours before it should have been attempted'.

Even some of Essex's more loyal supporters found the recent turn of events terrifying and thought Essex himself mad. John Harington – now Sir John – who had just a few months earlier written how he had been 'summoned by honour to this Irish action', now saw things differently: 'Ambition thwarted in its career, doth speedily lead on to madness. Herein I am strengthened by what I learn in my Lord of Essex, who shifteth from sorrow and repentance to rage and rebellion so suddenly, as well proveth him devoid of good reason or right mind.' In their last conversation back in Ireland, Harington adds, '[Essex] uttered strange words bordering on such strange designs, that made me hasten forth and leave his presence. Thank heaven! I am safe at home, and if I go in such troubles again, I deserve the gallows for a meddling fool.'

Politically, then, the autumn of 1599 proved not much less unsettling than the summer of the 'Invisible Armada' had been. Essex was disgraced, but what was to be done with him, and what 'strange designs' might he and his desperate faction undertake – or lure the King of Scots into joining? The political uncertainty that autumn was the stuff of Shakespearean drama: libels posted in the streets and scrawled on the walls at court, censorship, surveillance, intercepted letters and wild rumours. If the testimony of Francis Bacon is to be believed, the politics and libels reached the playhouses: 'About that time there did fly about in London streets and theatres, diverse seditious libels, and Paul's and ordinaries were full of bold and factious discourses, whereby not only many of her Majesty's faithful and zealous councillors and servants were taxed, but withal the hard estate of Ireland was imputed to any thing rather than unto the true cause (the Earl's defaults).'

Others, like Fulke Greville, were convinced that these libels were circulated not by Essex's supporters but by his enemies, a Machiavellian move intended to further discredit Essex:

His enemies took audacity to cast libels abroad in his name against the state, made by themselves; set paper upon posts, to bring his innocent friends in question. His power, by Jesuitical craft of rumour, they made infinite; and his ambition, more than equal to it. His letters to private men were read openly, by the piercing eye of an attorney's office, which warrants the construction of every line in the worst sense against the writer.

Who then was responsible in late December, when, Rowland Whyte reports, it was discovered: 'At court upon the very white walls, much villainy hath been written against Sir Robert Cecil'?

As the year came to a close, the Essex faction grew increasingly desperate. With Essex unwilling to go into exile, there was one card left to play, the Scottish one. Some time over the past summer Essex's friend Lord Mountjoy had sent Henry Lee to the King of Scots to reassure him that despite rumours to the contrary, Essex had no personal designs upon the throne of England – and in fact 'would endure no succession' but James's. Around Christmas time 1599 (a date later confirmed by Henry Cuffe, Essex's secretary), a new plan was hatched. After being chosen by Elizabeth to succeed Essex as Lord Lieutenant in Ireland, Mountjoy sent Henry Lee back to Scotland, this time to say that if the King of Scots

would enter into the cause at that time, my Lord Mountjoy would leave the kingdom of Ireland defensively guarded, and with four or five thousand men assist that enterprise which, with the party that my Lord of Essex would be able to make, were thought sufficient to bring that to pass which was intended –

that is, the rehabilitation of Essex, the downfall of his rivals at court, and the assurance of James's succession in England. Southampton also wrote to James committing himself to the plan.

Essex's friends were counting on the King of Scots' impatience to claim the English throne. It wasn't clear to Sir Charles Danvers (who later confessed details of this plot) whether James would actually enter hostilely into England – nor is it clear how the Scottish King treated this overture. Still, the combined threat of a foreign army making manoeuvres on the English border, combined with an insurrection by English troops landed in Wales and a local uprising in London would have been Elizabeth's and Cecil's worst nightmare. By the time that Lee – whose activities were closely monitored – returned from Scotland, Mountjoy had already shipped off to Ireland. Lee was committed by the authorities to prison in the Gatehouse. Essex himself didn't lose hope in this scheme, even sending Southampton to Mountjoy in Ireland 'to move him to bring over those former intended forces into Wales', and from there 'to proceed to the accomplishment of the former design'. Southampton said that Danvers was convinced that the forces Mountjoy would bring from Ireland were sufficient – they didn't need to count on the equivocating James. Mountjoy at this point refused, telling Southampton to drop the idea; with James remaining uncommitted to the plan, it was no longer about the succession, merely Essex's private ambition.

It is extremely unlikely that more than a handful of conspirators knew anything about this plot at the time, or even later, when it was confessed to the authorities – so the fact that *Hamlet* contains both an abortive coup (by Laertes' faction, who burst in on Claudius) and a neighbouring foreign prince at the head of an army (led by Fortinbras, who claims the Danish throne in the end) is sheer coincidence; but it was a time when such things could be imagined – and by some even plotted. *Hamlet*, composed during these months, feels indelibly stamped by the deeply unsettling mood of the time. The play offered no temporary respite; the atmosphere in which Elizabethans found themselves at performances was uncomfortably familiar. Shakespeare was as good as his word in *Hamlet* that the 'purpose of playing' was to show 'the very age and body of the time his form and pressure' (III, ii, 20–24). An anxious Rowland Whyte could have easily been speaking of Claudius' court when he wrote to Sir Robert Sidney this autumn: 'There is such observing and prying into men's actions that I hold them happy and blessed that live away.' 'As God help me,' Whyte warns, 'it is a very dangerous time here.'

14
Essays and Soliloquies

In terms of plot *Hamlet* is Shakespeare's least original play. He lifted the story from a now lost revenge tragedy of the 1580s, also called *Hamlet*, which by the end of that decade was already feeling shopworn. In 1589, in an attack on Elizabethan tragedies that overindulged in Senecan rant, Thomas Nashe singled out *Hamlet* as a notable offender – 'English Seneca read by candlelight yields many good sentences, as "Blood is a beggar" and so forth, and if you entreat him fair in a frosty morning he will afford you whole *Hamlets*, I should say handfuls, of tragical speeches.' Nashe also hints that Thomas Kyd, author of the wildly popular revenge play *The Spanish Tragedy*, had written *Hamlet* as well.

This *Hamlet* was on the boards, then, when Shakespeare first arrived in London. He would get to know it intimately, for by the mid-1590s the play had entered the repertory of the newly formed Chamberlain's Men. On 9 June 1594 Shakespeare, Burbage and

Detail of the title page of William Cornwallis's *Essayes*

Kemp were probably in the cast that performed it at Newington Butts, a theatre located a mile south of London Bridge, which the Chamberlain's Men were temporarily sharing with their rivals, the Admiral's Men. If box-office receipts are any indication, the play continued to show its age: fewer customers paid to see *Hamlet* than to see other old revenge plays staged the previous week, Shakespeare's own *Titus Andronicus* and Marlowe's *The Jew of Malta*. When the Chamberlain's Men moved to the Theatre, they brought the play with them. By now the Ghost's haunting cry for revenge had become a byword. Three years before Shakespeare sat down to write his own *Hamlet*, Thomas Lodge spoke familiarly of one who 'walks for the most part in black under the cover of gravity, and looks as pale as the vizard of the Ghost who cried so miserably at the Theatre like an oyster-wife, "Hamlet, revenge!"' Shakespeare would have had many years to reflect upon what he might do with the old play.

Long before this *Hamlet* was staged, the contours of the story were fixed, having been in place since the twelfth century, when Saxo Grammaticus wrote of the legendary Danish revenger Amleth. His saga was printed in Latin in 1514. Little in it is unfamiliar to those who know the plot of Shakespeare's play. His uncle kills Amleth's father (after he has defeated the King of Norway in single combat) and then marries Amleth's mother. The murder is no secret and to avert suspicion about his plans to avenge his father's death, young Amleth acts mad and speaks nonsense. A beautiful young woman is sent to discover his intentions. Later, while speaking with his mother in her chamber, Amleth is spied on by the king's adviser – whom he kills and dismembers. His uncle then packs Amleth off to Britain to have him executed, accompanied by two retainers, but Amleth intercepts their instructions and substitutes their names for his own. He returns to Denmark and avenges his father's death by killing his uncle. In Saxo's version Amleth survives and is made king. The codes of honour and revenge are clear and Amleth triumphs because of his patience, his intelligence and his ability to act decisively when he sees his chance.

Standing between Saxo's story and the old play of *Hamlet* is a French retelling by François de Belleforest, the long-winded *Histoires Tragiques*, first published in 1570. Shakespeare may not have read Saxo, but he was familiar with Belleforest, who introduced a few new wrinkles. The most notable is the change in Hamlet's mother's part. In Belleforest, she has an adulterous affair with her brother-in-law before he murders her husband. Later, she is converted to Hamlet's cause, keeps his secret and supports him in his efforts to regain the throne. Belleforest also speaks of the young revenger as melancholy. The Ghost, the play-within-a-play, the feigned madness, and the hero's death – familiar features of the revenge drama of the late 1580s – are all likely to have been introduced by the anonymous author of the lost Elizabethan *Hamlet*. Of all the characters only Fortinbras, who threatens invasion at the outset and succeeds to the throne at the end, is probably Shakespeare's invention.

There are many ways of being original. Inventing a plot from scratch is only one of them and never held much appeal for Shakespeare. Aside from the soliloquies, much of Shakespeare's creativity went into the play's verbal texture. In writing *Hamlet* Shakespeare found himself using and inventing more words than he had ever done before. His vocabulary, even when compared to those of other great dramatists, was already exceptional. The roughly 4,000 lines in the play ended up requiring nearly the same number of different words (for comparison's sake, Marlowe's *Doctor Faustus* and *The Jew of Malta* each use only about half that number). Even the 14,000 or so different words or compounds that Shakespeare had already employed in his plays (by the end of his career that figure would reach about 18,000) proved insufficient. According to Alfred Hart, who painstakingly counted when and how Shakespeare introduced each word into his work, he introduced around 600 words in *Hamlet* that he had never used before, two-thirds of which he would never use again. This is an extraordinary number (*King Lear*, with 350, is the only one that comes close; in the spare *Julius Caesar* only seventy words appear that Shakespeare had not previously used). *Hamlet*, then, didn't sound like anything playgoers had ever heard before and must at times have been taxing to follow, for by Hart's count there are 170 words or phrases that Shakespeare coined or used in new ways while writing the play.

It isn't just the words he chose but how he used them that makes the language of *Hamlet* so challenging. Shakespeare clearly wanted audiences to work hard and one of the ways he made them do so was by employing an odd verbal trick called hendiadys. Though the term may be strange, examples of it – 'law and order', 'house and home', or the Shakespearean 'sound and fury' – are familiar enough. Hendiadys literally means 'one by means of two', a single idea conveyed through a pairing of nouns linked by 'and'. When conjoined in this way, the nouns begin to oscillate, seeming to qualify each other as much as the term each individually modifies. Whether he is exclaiming 'Angels and ministers of grace defend us' (I, iv, 39), declaring that actors are 'the abstract and brief chronicles of the time' (II, ii, 524), speaking of 'the book and volume of my brain' (I. v, 103), or complaining of 'a fantasy and trick of fame' (IV, iv, 61), Hamlet often speaks in this way. The more you think about examples of hendiadys, the more they induce a kind of mental vertigo. Take for example Hamlet's description of 'the book and volume of my brain'. It's easy to get the gist of what he's saying and the phrase would pass unremarked in the course of a performance; but does he mean 'the book-like volume' of my mind? or 'the big book of my mind'? Part of the problem here is that the words bleed into each other – 'volume', of course, is another word for 'book' but also means 'space'. The destabilizing effect of how these words play off each other is slightly and temporarily unnerving. It's only on reflection – which is, of course, Hamlet's problem – that we trip.

It's very hard to write in hendiadys; almost no other English writer did so very often before or after Shakespeare – nor did he much before 1599. Something happened in that year – beginning with *Henry the Fifth* and *As You Like It* and continuing for five years or so past *Hamlet* through the great run of plays that included *Othello*, *Measure for Measure*, *King Lear*, and *Macbeth*, after which hendiadys pretty much disappears again – that led Shakespeare to invoke this figure almost compulsively. But nowhere is its presence felt more than in *Hamlet*, where there are sixty-six examples, or one every sixty lines – and that's counting conservatively. *Othello*, with twenty-eight, has the next highest count. There's a kind of collective desperation to all the hendiadys in *Hamlet* – a striving for meaning that both recedes and multiplies as well as an acknowledgement of how necessary and impossible it is to suture things together – that suits the mood of the play perfectly.

What the Chamberlain's Men did to the wooden frame of the Theatre, Shakespeare did to the old play of *Hamlet*: he tore it from its familiar moorings, salvaged its structure and reassembled something new. By wrenching this increasingly outdated revenge play into the present, Shakespeare forced his contemporaries to experience what he felt and what his play registers so profoundly: the world had changed. Old certainties were gone, even if new ones had not yet taken hold. The most convincing way of showing this was to ask playgoers to keep both plays in mind at once, to experience a new *Hamlet* while memories of the old one, ghost-like, still lingered. Audiences at the Globe soon found themselves, like Hamlet, straddling worlds and struggling to reconcile past and present. There was an added benefit, having to do with the play's difficulty: familiarity with the plot allowed playgoers to lose themselves in the complexity of thought and the inwardness of the characters without losing track of the action.

The desire to mark the end of one kind of drama and the beginning of another carried over into the internal dynamics of Shakespeare's playing company. Spectators at this *Hamlet* wouldn't be distracted by a clown. Tellingly, when 'the tragedians of the city' (II, ii, 328) arrive at Elsinore they are without a clown; even after his departure from the company Kemp was still on Shakespeare's mind. And Hamlet cannot resist a gratuitous attack on improvisational clowning:

> And let those that play your clowns speak no more than is set down for them; for there be of them that will themselves laugh to set on some quantity of barren spectators to laugh too, though in the meantime some necessary question of the play then to be considered. That's villainous, and shows a most pitiful ambition in the fool that uses it.
>
> (III, ii, 38–45)

While these are Hamlet's words, judging by the company's recent history, Shakespeare's own view was probably not much different. Shakespeare made sure that in *Hamlet* the last laugh would be on the Kemp-like clown – and he did so by dividing up his role between the new, clownish fool (Robert Armin, who played the Gravedigger) and, surprisingly, the tragic protagonist himself, played by Richard Burbage. In his verbal sparring, his intimate relationship with the audience, his distracting and obscene behaviour at the performance of 'The Mousetrap' (where he cracks sexual jokes at Ophelia's expense and calls himself her 'only jig-maker'), and his 'antic' performance for much of the play, Hamlet appropriates much of the traditional comic part.

Only after Hamlet has stopped clowning does Shakespeare introduce Armin, creating for him a role that made much of his singing (he breaks into song four times) as well as his celebrated repartee. And in the Gravedigger's recollection of Yorick – 'This same skull, sir, was, sir, Yorick's skull, the King's jester' (V, i, 180–81) – Shakespeare also allows Armin a private tribute to Richard Tarleton, the first of the great Elizabethan clowns, who had reputedly chosen the young Armin as his successor. Armin understood what was expected of him. As Gravedigger, he never competes with Hamlet for our affection.

The eighteenth-century biographer Nicholas Rowe reported that the only role he was able to learn that Shakespeare played was 'the Ghost in his own *Hamlet*'. So that when the Ghost tells Hamlet, 'Remember me,' it is likely to have been Shakespeare himself who spoke these words to Richard Burbage. Burbage would remember. His success was closely tied to Shakespeare's. At the beginning of the 1590s he had not yet come into his own and was still being cast in messenger parts. Within a few years, Shakespeare would fashion breakthrough roles for him in Richard III and Romeo, but it was Hamlet that defined Burbage's greatness for contemporaries. An anonymous eulogist, recalling Burbage shortly after his death in 1619, remembers his finest roles (Hamlet foremost) and speaks with particular fondness of the scene in which Burbage, as Hamlet, leaped into Ophelia's grave (unless, that is, the passage describes Burbage's Romeo):

> young Hamlet, old Hieronimo,
> Kind Lear, the grieved Moor, and more beside
> That lived in him have now for ever died.
> Oft have I seen him leap into the grave,
> Suiting the person which he seemed to have
> Of a sad lover with so true an eye
> That there, I would have sworn, he meant to die.

The eulogist's description of Burbage's style closely corresponds to what Burbage – as Hamlet – himself recommends to the Players: 'Suit the action to the word, the word to the action,' and 'you must acquire and beget a temperance that may give it smoothness' (III, ii, 7–8, 17–18):

How did his speech become him, and his pace,
Suit with his speech, and every action grace
Them both alike, whilst not a word did fall
Without just weight, to ballast it withal.

Shakespeare also wrote Burbage's response to 'Remember me,' lines
that double as a private reflection on what the two men hoped to
create together at the new playhouse:

Remember thee,
Ay, thou poor ghost, whiles memory holds a seat
In this distracted globe.
(I, v, 95–7)

Shakespeare's break with the past was tempered by the ambivalence that had characterized his responses to the death of chivalry,
the loss of Arden and the fading of Catholicism. Even as he was
rendering the old style of revenge play obsolete, Shakespeare
found room in the play for a last nostalgic glance at it in the dramatic speech that Hamlet says he 'chiefly loved' (II, ii, 446). The
old-fashioned speech describes how Achilles' son Pyrrhus kills a
king and unhesitatingly avenges his father's death. Hamlet knows
the lines by heart and recites them excitedly:

The rugged Pyrrhus, he whose sable arms,
Black as his purpose, did the night resemble
When he lay couched in th'ominous horse,
Hath now this dread and black complexion smeared
With heraldry more dismal. Head to foot
Now is he total gules, horridly tricked
With blood of fathers, mothers, daughters, sons,
Baked and impasted with the parching streets,
That lend a tyrannous and a damned light
To their lord's murder. Roasted in wrath and fire,
And thus o'ersized with coagulate gore,
With eyes like carbuncles, the hellish Pyrrhus

Old grandsire Priam seeks.
  (II, ii, 452–64)

By the end of the seventeenth century admirers of Shakespeare no longer understood what he was doing here and decided that he was either writing quite badly or lazily recycling old material. The dramatist John Dryden's verdict was harsh: 'Would not a man have thought that the poet had been bound prentice to a wheelwright for his first rant?' A generation or so later, Alexander Pope floated the idea that Hamlet 'seems to commend this play to expose the bombast of it' – but even he wasn't convinced that Shakespeare had written the speech. Not until the late eighteenth century did Edmond Malone first suggest that Shakespeare was trying to sound old-fashioned. You can feel in these lines the hold that this kind of revenge drama once had on Shakespeare as well as his appreciation of a moral clarity that was no longer credible. It's one of the keys to understanding what makes *Hamlet* so distinctive: even as he paints over an earlier work of art, Shakespeare allows traces of what's been whitewashed to remain visible.

In the closing years of Elizabeth's reign, as in the play, heroic action had become increasingly hard to believe in. And things probably seemed worse than they actually were when Shakespeare was writing *Hamlet* in the autumn of 1599. Londoners, barely recovered from the murky armada threat and Essex's ill-fated expedition, felt this plainly enough by mid-November, as noted earlier, when the preacher who had dared to speak 'of the misgovernment in Ireland' in 'open pulpit' before thousands of spectators at St Paul's was silenced. Many thousands more saw it at Whitehall's tiltyard later that week, where the exclusion of Essex and his Irish knights made this celebration of martial valour seem more artificial than the pasteboard shields the knights carried to the tilt. Shakespeare and others in the capital would have found the degree to which politics was being played out in public unprecedented. So 'many scandalous libels' began circulating in 'the court, city and country' this autumn that the government felt forced to counter by publicly embarrassing Essex in open hearings of the Star Chamber. Francis Woodward couldn't believe it and went to see for himself. He writes to Robert Sidney of the 'throng and press' of Londoners who elbowed him at these proceedings, a crowd 'so mighty that I was driven so far back that I could not hear what they said'. Henry Wotton, who had followed Essex to Ireland and served as his secretary, wrote to his friend John Donne in London that while it was true that Ireland suffered from 'ill affections and ill corruptions', the English court was suffering from 'a stronger disease'. 'Courts', he bitterly concluded, 'are upon earth the vainest places.' That's as much as Wotton dared put on paper: 'I will say no more, and yet peradventure I have said a great deal unto you.' Shakespeare, like many others unsettled by the political climate this autumn, probably shared Rowland Whyte's sense that 'it is a world to be, to see the humours of the time'. It was one thing for Shakespeare to have reflected upon the limits of heroic action and the culture of honour in *Henry the Fifth* and *Julius Caesar* earlier in the year – plays that couldn't and wouldn't be chosen to be performed at court this Christmas for that very reason. It was all the more striking that he would choose such a moment to update a story of a corrupt court (before whom a seditious play is performed), problematic succession, the threat of invasion, and the dangers of a coup.

'Now I am alone,' Hamlet says with relief, after Rosencrantz and Guildenstern, the Players and Polonius leave him in Act II. But he's not: we are still there to hear him 'unpack [his] heart with words' (II, ii, 586) in a way that no character in literature had done before. One of the mysteries of *Hamlet* is how Shakespeare, who a half-year earlier hadn't quite been able to manage it in *Julius Caesar*, discovered how to write such compelling soliloquies:

327

O, that this too too sallied flesh would melt,
Thaw, and resolve itself into a dew,
Or that the Everlasting had not fixed
His canon 'gainst self-slaughter. O God, God,
How weary, stale, flat, and unprofitable
Seem to me all the uses of this world!
Fie on 't, ah fie, 'tis an unweeded garden
That grows to seed; things rank and gross in nature
Possess it merely.
      (I, ii, 129–37)

The sense of inwardness that Shakespeare creates by allowing us to hear a character as intelligent as Hamlet wrestle with his thoughts is something that no dramatist had yet achieved. He had written memorable soliloquies from early on in his career, but powerful as these were, even they fall far short of the intense self-awareness we find in Hamlet's. The breakthrough is one that Shakespeare might have arrived at sooner or later, but it was given tremendous impetus at the time that he was writing *Hamlet* by his interest in a new literary form: the essay.

English writers did not discover Montaigne until the late 1590s. In his late thirties, Montaigne had withdrawn from a world torn by religious wars to read, reflect and write – and had taken the unprecedented step of making himself his subject in a new literary form, the personal essay. The first two volumes of Montaigne's *Essays* were published in France in 1580. Shakespeare could easily have turned to the essay at earlier points in his career – his French was good enough to read Montaigne in the original – but he didn't. Only at the end of the century, a cultural moment marked by a high degree of scepticism and a deepening interest in how subjective experience could be expressed, did Montaigne begin to speak to Shakespeare and other English writers with great immediacy.

The experience of William Cornwallis, the first Englishman to follow closely in Montaigne's footsteps, suggests not only why conditions were ripe but also what attracted Shakespeare to the essay and how it helped trigger such a change in his soliloquies. At the age of twenty-one Cornwallis volunteered to fight under Essex in Ireland. He was knighted during the campaign and returned home in the autumn of 1599 world-weary and broke. He turned to writing. A few years earlier he might have found an outlet composing sonnets. Even a year earlier, before the Bishops' Ban, Cornwallis might have gravitated to satire. Instead, by late 1599 he began writing essays. It's hard now to imagine a time when essays, like diaries, didn't exist, when the self was not explored in these ways; but in 1600, when a collection of Cornwallis's first twenty-five essays appeared in print (another twenty-four came out a year later), even the word 'essay' was unfamiliar. Cornwallis freely acknowledges his debt to Montaigne's *Essays*, though he admits that his French was so poor he relied on an unnamed translator. He had several to choose from. It might have been John Florio, whose unsurpassed translation, published in 1603, was already under way by 1598. More likely it was a competitor, one of the 'seven or eight of great wit' who Florio claims tried (and failed) to complete a translation. Florio's assertion – and there is no reason to doubt it – suggests that there was a rush to translate Montaigne at this time.

As it turned out, the English reading public wasn't quite ready for the personal essay. With the exception of a half-dozen or so other essay collections published in the early seventeenth century, the experiment fizzled and essay writing was not to be taken up again in any significant way until the eighteenth century. Because Cornwallis's *Essays* remain virtually unread today, a few examples are worth sharing. If his words sound like something Hamlet might have said, it's because they share with the soliloquies a sense of a mind overwhelmed by conflicts that cannot be resolved. Again and again Cornwallis identifies these obstacles and just as often speaks of his frustration that he cannot reconcile competing claims:

Anger is the mother of injustice, and yet justice must lackey on her errands, fight battles, and give her the victory. I cannot reconcile these together, but even in the behalf of truth and mercy, I will combat against a received tradition. I think nothing but murder should be punished.

(from 'Of Patience')

About nothing do I suffer greater conflicts in myself than about enduring wrongs.

(from 'Of Patience')

There have been great contentions about my mind and my body about this argument of life. They are both very obstinate in their desires, and I cannot blame them, for which soever prevails deprives the other of the greatest authority. My soul extols contemplation and persuades me that way; my body understands not that language but is all for action. He tells me that it is unproper, being of the world not to love so, and that I am born to my country, to whom, embracing this contemplative life, I am unprofitable. The other wants not reasons forcible and celestial. It hath been my continual labour to work a reconciliation between them, for I could not perfect any course by reason of this division. Earth and Heaven cannot be made one; therefore, impossible to join them together.

(from 'Of Life')

He that says of me only, 'He lives well,' speaks too sparingly of me, for I live to better my mind and cure my body of his innate diseases. I must choose the active course; my birth commands me to that.

(from 'Of Life and the Fashions of Life')

It is the mind that can distil the whole world, all ages, all acts, all human knowledges within the little, little compass of a brain; and yet with the force of that little treasure command, dispose, censure, and determine states, actions, kingdoms, war, overthrows, and all the acts and actors busied upon our human theatre.

(from 'Of Advice')

Copies of his essays were passed from hand to hand and Cornwallis probably read his work aloud to admirers, much as Shakespeare had shared his sonnets with his 'private friends'. Most of

Cornwallis's essays are under 2,000 words long, an ideal length to recite. The 1600 edition was small enough to fit in a palm or slip into a pocket, so that readers could carry the essays around and reflect on their ideas.

Cornwallis likened his essays to a kind of sketch, akin to 'a scrivener trying his pen before he ingrosseth his work' – the kind of essay-writing that Dr Johnson would later define as 'a loose sally of the mind, an irregular indigested piece'. In this respect, his essays mark a leap forward from the ten Francis Bacon published in 1597, the first in English. Though Bacon borrowed Montaigne's title (he had probably been introduced to the Frenchman's work through his brother Anthony Bacon, who had corresponded with Montaigne), his early essays are typically impersonal and aphoristic. While they are sharply drawn, Bacon's early essays aren't especially personal, nor do they exhibit the play of mind or the improvisational qualities of Cornwallis, let alone Montaigne – and wouldn't, until, over the next several decades, Bacon radically changed his approach and overhauled them. Until that point, if he hadn't called them essays, we probably wouldn't either.

Ironic, self-critical, conversational, Cornwallis's essays have a strongly autobiographical tilt, even when they rely on generalizations to render heartfelt feelings. The disillusioning Irish campaign and the dark politics at court that autumn hang like a cloud over his thoughts. He may have sailed for Ireland with great assurance, but, as with John Harington and other veterans of the campaign, upon his return a healthy scepticism was in order. I dwell at such length on this largely forgotten writer to emphasize that Shakespeare didn't invent a new sensibility in *Hamlet*; rather, he gave voice to what he and others saw and felt around them – which is why *Hamlet* resonated so powerfully with audiences from the moment it was first staged.

Cornwallis's loss of bearings is painfully realized in moments like the conclusion to the essay 'Of Resolution', where he writes: 'I am myself still, though the world were turned with the wrong side out.' Observations like this suggest the strength of the affinity between the new sensibility that Cornwallis struggles to articulate and the kind that Shakespeare fully realizes in Hamlet's soliloquies. These soliloquies, which are not even hinted at in Shakespeare's sources, aren't needed to advance the story. If anything, like the Choruses to *Henry the Fifth*, they compete with and retard the action. But they define the play. Tempting as it is to imagine that Shakespeare came across Cornwallis's essays before writing *Hamlet*, it's unlikely: they were writing at the same time. At best, Shakespeare might have heard about them or seen a few that were in circulation.

If a newcomer like Cornwallis had access to Montaigne in 1599, even in translation, Shakespeare, who seems to have been able to get his hands on all kinds of work in manuscript, could easily have come across essays by Montaigne or his imitators. He had surely looked into Montaigne by the time that he wrote *Hamlet* – the intuition of critics stretching back to the 1830s on this question should be trusted – but he didn't need to paraphrase him or pillage his essays for ideas. Nor did he need to read that 'the taste of goods or evils doth greatly depend on the opinion we have of them' in order to write 'there is nothing either good or bad, but thinking makes it so' (II, ii, 250). There was more than enough scepticism and uncertainty to go round in England in the final years of Elizabeth's reign, and in 1599 in particular; it did not have to be imported from France.

Shakespeare cared less about appropriating Montaigne's language or philosophy than about exploring how essays – with their assertions, contradictions, reversals and abrupt shifts in subject matter and even confidence – captured a mind at work ('It is myself I portray,' Montaigne famously declared). Other dramatists, including John Webster and John Marston, soon turned their attention to the essay as well. The extent of Montaigne's influence in the early years of the seventeenth century was so great that Ben Jonson has a character in *Volpone* joke that English writers were stealing from a popular poet 'Almost as much as from Montaigne' (III, iv, 87–90).

Like sonnets and plays, essays straddled the spoken and the written, existing somewhere between private meditations and performance scripts. In redefining the relationship between speaker and audience, the essay also suggested to Shakespeare an intimacy between speaker and hearer that no other form, not even the sonnet, offered – except, perhaps, the soliloquy. Probably more than any other character in literature, Hamlet needs to talk; but there is nobody in whom he can confide. When Marlowe and Jonson were confronted with this problem, each provided straight-men with whom their heroes could banter (Marlowe's Barabas has his Ithamore and Faustus his Mephostophiles, while Jonson's Volpone has his Mosca, Subtle his Face, and so on). In contrast, be it Brutus or Henry V, Shakespeare's heroes are loners. Hamlet is an extreme case. His old friends Rosencrantz and Guildenstern are spies and viewed with suspicion. Horatio is deeply loyal but likes the sound of his own words a bit too much and never seems to understand him (you can sense Hamlet's exasperation with his friend when he tells him: 'There are more things in heaven and earth, Horatio, / Than are dreamt of in your philosophy' (I, v, 166–7). Given Gertrude's dependence on Claudius, she cannot be trusted either; and there's no hope of unburdening himself to his terrifying father, back from Purgatory.

Hamlet's relationship with Ophelia is more complicated. There was a time before the action of the play begins when he confided in her; his bundle of love letters to her testifies to that. But Shakespeare undermines this trust by almost cruelly introducing one of these intimate letters into the play – with its hyperbolic address to 'the celestial and my soul's idol, the most beautified Ophelia' – and, to make matters worse, has Polonius read it aloud:

Doubt that the stars are fire,
Doubt that the sun doth move,
Doubt truth to be a liar,
But never doubt I love.
  (II, ii, 116–19)

It's mortifying to hear this lame verse recited and it underscores the dangers of baring one's soul, because Ophelia, in 'duty and obedience' (II, ii, 107), has betrayed Hamlet by turning these letters over to her father. As John Harington, sensitive to surveillance, wrote at the time: 'Who will write, when his letters shall be opened by the way and construed at pleasure, or rather displeasure?'

The scene returns us to the world of *As You Like It*, where an immature Orlando first finds an outlet in wretched poetry. Like Orlando, 'young Hamlet' (I, i, 170), as he's called early on in the play, grows out of it. We're offered a brief and uncomfortable glimpse of a Hamlet who has not yet been shocked into complexity – and the soliloquy that shortly follows confirms that a chasm has opened up between the Hamlet who loved Ophelia and the one we now see. The Ptolemaic science on which Hamlet's protestations are grounded, as Shakespeare knew, was already discredited by the Copernican revolution: the stars aren't fire; the sun doesn't revolve around the earth. In such a universe, truth may well turn out to be a liar. Ophelia really does have good grounds to doubt – that is, suspect – that Hamlet never loved her. We can see why Hamlet doesn't want his love letters back – and why he can no longer unburden himself to Ophelia. We are all that's left. Maybe the great secret of the soliloquies is not their inwardness so much as their outwardness, their essay-like capacity to draw us into an intimate relationship with the speaker and see the world through his eyes.

When the dying Hamlet insists that Horatio live on to 'tell my story' (V, ii, 348), Horatio's words underscore much he has failed to grasp about his friend, relative to what we now know:

> So shall you hear
> Of carnal, bloody, and unnatural acts,
> Of accidental judgements, casual slaughters,
> Of deaths put on by cunning and for no cause,
> And, in this upshot, purposes mistook
> Fallen on th' inventors' heads. All this can I
> Truly deliver.
> (V, ii, 380–86)

The same could as easily be said of *Titus Andronicus*. Horatio can be excused for how much he has missed; unlike us, he has not been privy to Hamlet's soliloquies, the part of the play – rather than the 'carnal, bloody, and unnatural acts' one finds in any number of contemporary revenge plays – that has kept it on the boards without interruption for over four hundred years.

The resemblances between the essay and the soliloquy extend beyond the world-weariness or depth of self-revelation found in each. Shakespeare had been struggling for much of the previous decade to find his way into tragedy. Very early on in his career he had grasped how both comedy and history worked; the nine comedies and nine history plays he had written or collaborated on by late 1599 feel like brilliant variations played by a master who deeply understood these forms and was intent on extending the range of possibilities inherent in them. In comparison, tragedy had largely resisted Shakespeare. His sporadic attempts in this vein – the early and melodramatic revenge tragedy *Titus Andronicus* and the love tragedy of *Romeo and Juliet* – though extraordinarily popular, had not led him much closer to the heart of tragedy.

When he returned to the genre for the third time in *Julius Caesar*, Shakespeare found himself on the verge of the kind of drama that would preoccupy him for the next six years. He had glimpsed it in the great pair of soliloquies he had written for Brutus, both the one in which he reflects on how

> Between the acting of a dreadful thing
> And the first motion, all the interim is
> Like a phantasma or a hideous dream ...
> (II, i, 63–4)

and the one that begins:

> It must be by his death. And for my part
> I know no personal cause to spurn at him,
> But for the general. He would be crowned ...
> (II, i, 10–12)

These soliloquies not only allow us to observe a character thinking aloud, but also and crucially enable us to overhear a great moral struggle – precisely what we never heard when Juliet, Richard III or even Falstaff addressed us directly. In *Julius Caesar* Shakespeare had discovered the potential of writing tragedy constructed on the fault line of irresolvable ethical conflict; but after Brutus' early soliloquies he retreated from embodying this conflict within the consciousness of a single protagonist, allowing it instead to play out in the tragic collision of Brutus and Caesar – and in the second half of the play subsumes their conflict within the larger design of a revenge plot in which the conspirators turn against themselves the very swords they used to kill Caesar.

Elizabethan drama had its roots in a morality tradition in which the struggle between the forces of good and evil had been externalized – literally played out by opposing characters onstage. Vestiges of this homiletic tradition are still visible in the appearance of the good and bad angels who vie for the protagonist's soul in Marlowe's *Doctor Faustus*. It's more or less the same structure, though drained of its theological content, that informs plays as diverse as *The Third Part of Henry the Sixth* (with its warring houses of York and Lancaster), *Titus Andronicus* (which can't quite decide if the externalized struggle is between Goths and Romans or warring factions within Rome), and *Romeo and Juliet* (where Montagues and Capulets clash tragically). The plays that Shakespeare worked on in 1599 all show signs of a struggle to move beyond this dynamic, to forge a new kind of drama by resisting the tendency to handle conflict in conventional ways. In *Henry the Fifth*, Shakespeare had broken with the model of his dramatic sources – as well as his own earlier histories – by making the alternation of the Chorus and the action rather than the rivalry of King Henry and the French Dauphin the main source of conflict. And in *As You Like It* he had refused to resort to comedy's traditional blocking figures, locating the obstacle to the love of Orlando and Rosalind not in a parent or rival lover but in Orlando's need to learn what love is.

With *Hamlet*, a play poised midway between a religious past and a secular future, Shakespeare finally found a dramatically compelling way to internalize contesting forces: the essay-like soliloquy proved to be the perfect vehicle for Hamlet's efforts to confront issues that, like Brutus', defied easy resolution. And he further complicated Hamlet's struggle by placing it in a larger world of unresolved post-Reformation social, religious and political conflicts, which is why the play is so often taken as the ultimate expression of its age. As puzzled readers of the play have long acknowledged, we're denied information crucial to understanding whether or how Hamlet should act: is he or his uncle the rightful heir to the Danish throne? Is Gertrude's remarriage too hasty – and is she committing incest by marrying her dead husband's brother? Is Ophelia's death a suicide?

Within this maze, Shakespeare forces Hamlet to wrestle with a series of ethical problems that he must resolve before he can act – and it is this, more than over-intellectualizing (as Coleridge had it) or an Oedipal complex (as Freud urged) that accounts for Hamlet's delay. The soliloquies restlessly return to these conflicts, which climax in 'To be or not to be': in a world that feels so 'weary, stale, flat, and unprofitable', is it better to live or die? And is the fear of what awaits him in the next world enough to offset the urge to commit suicide? Is the Ghost come from Purgatory to warn him or should he see this visitation in a Protestant light (for Protestants didn't believe in Purgatory), as a devil who will exploit his melancholy and who 'Abuses me to damn me'? (II, ii, 603). Is revenge a human or a divine prerogative? Is it right to kill Claudius at his prayers, even if this means sending his shriven soul to heaven? When, if ever, is killing a tyrant justified – and does the failure to do so invite damnation?

In locating the conflict of the play within his protagonist, Shakespeare transformed for ever the traditional revenge play in which that conflict had until now been externalized, fought out between the hero and powerful adversaries, and in which a hero (like the Amleth of Shakespeare's sources) had to delay for practical, self-protective reasons. This was one of the great breakthroughs in his career. Yet in revising his first draft of *Hamlet* – as we shall see in the chapter that follows – Shakespeare discovered that he had pressed his experiment too far and belatedly recognized that there were unforeseen dangers in locating too much of the conflict in Hamlet's consciousness. The lesson learned, Shakespeare revised until he got the balance right. He had at last found a path into tragedy, one that soon led him into the divided souls of Othello and Macbeth. The innovation inspired by the essay-like soliloquy opened the way as well into the world of his dark and brilliant Jacobean problem comedies *Measure for Measure* and *All's Well that End's Well*, which turn not on comedy's familiar obstacles but rather on the wrenching, internalized struggle of characters like Isabella and Bertram.

15
Second Thoughts

Of the many remarkable things about *Hamlet* perhaps the most extraordinary is its length. At roughly 4,000 lines, the Second Quarto – the closest thing we have to what Shakespeare wrote in late 1599 – could not have been performed uncut at the Globe. Nor could his revised version of the play, a couple of hundred lines shorter, which eventually appeared in the First Folio. Though the Elizabethan stage dispensed with time-consuming intermissions and changes in scenery, these versions of *Hamlet* would still have taken four hours to perform; even at top speed, actors couldn't rattle off much more than a thousand lines of verse in an hour. With outdoor performances at the Globe beginning at two in the afternoon and the sun setting in late winter and early autumn around five o'clock, an uncut *Hamlet* staged in February or October would have left the actors stumbling about in the fading light by the Gravedigger scene; the fencing match, fought in the dark, could have been lethal.

Title page, *Hamlet*, 1605

Shakespeare alluded in the Prologue to *Romeo and Juliet* to the 'two hours' traffic of our stage'. Ben Jonson was probably closer to the mark when he spoke in *Bartholomew Fair* of 'two hours and a half, and somewhat more'. By any measure, *Hamlet* uncut was truly, in the play's own words, a 'poem unlimited' (II, ii, 400). After a decade in the theatre Shakespeare knew how long scripts ran and could cut to size when he wanted to: *Julius Caesar* (at 2,500 lines) and *As You Like It* (at 2,800) could have gone from study to stage uncut – as they should have: given the culture of playwriting at this time, there was little to be gained by submitting a play far too long to be performed.

The most tempting explanation for *Hamlet*'s unusual length – that Shakespeare had finally begun to care more about how his words were read than about how they were staged – is implausible. Had Shakespeare suddenly become interested in having a play published, he could have followed the path just taken by Ben Jonson, who had carefully seen *Every Man Out of His Humour* into print. Jonson had indicated on the title page that it contained 'more than hath been publicly spoken or acted' by the Chamberlain's Men in late 1599 and declared himself the play's 'author' – both novel claims. There was a strong market for Jonson's book and the printed version was a best-seller, going through a remarkable three editions in eight months. But Shakespeare neither pressed for the publication of *Hamlet* nor cared much for this kind of literary status. Several years would pass before even an unauthorized, pirated version of *Hamlet* was published.

Shakespeare's early versions of *Hamlet* don't show him to be overly concerned with writing something that could be immediately performed or published. He was letting the writing take him where it would. Alone among contemporary playwrights in 1599, Shakespeare – as shareholder, principal playwright, and part-owner of the theatre in which his plays were staged – had the freedom to do so. But he would never write so long a version of a play again and only *King Lear* would undergo such extensive revision. His fellow sharers may even have given him time off from rehearsing and acting to work on *Hamlet*, for Shakespeare's name is conspicuously absent from the list of those who acted in Jonson's *Every Man Out of His Humour* this autumn, though it was given pride of place among those who had performed *Every Man In His Humour* a year earlier.

The differences between the first and second versions of *Hamlet* reveal a good deal about how Shakespeare wrote and for that reason alone are worth attending to. The revisions also tell a story of Shakespeare's decision to alter the trajectory of the play and shore up the resolve of its hero. Scholars differ on details and some remain committed to radically different accounts of the relationship of the surviving versions of *Hamlet* and of how the play changed. What follows, though necessarily simplified (for to deal with all the vexing issues raised by the play's multiple versions would take volumes), seems to me to be the most plausible and economical reconstruction of what happened.

Shakespeare finished tinkering with his first version of *Hamlet* in the waning months of 1599 but wasn't yet ready to turn it over to his fellow players. When he returned to his finished draft not long after, he revised extensively as he wrote out the play again in a fresh copy. It doesn't appear that he knew in advance what kinds of changes he would make and most of the thousand or so alterations are minor and stylistic. This revised *Hamlet* was still not, as his fellow players might have hoped, a performance-ready script: Shakespeare trimmed only 230 lines (while adding ninety new ones), so that the revisions wouldn't have reduced the playing time by more than ten minutes. Even in this second version he was still letting the work follow its own course. When he was done with the new draft, in the winter of 1600, Shakespeare turned it over to his fellow players; a significant abridgement would still be necessary before it could be performed at the Globe.

Because versions of both Shakespeare's first and second thoughts survive, it's possible to follow the process of revision (while recognizing that some of the changes can be attributed to compositors, bookkeepers, scribes, censors and others through whose hands they passed). Shakespeare tinkered obsessively – far more than his reputation for never blotting a line would suggest. He turned Hamlet's famous cry, 'What's Hecuba to him, or he to her?' into the more sonorous, 'What's Hecuba to him, or he to Hecuba?' (II, ii, 559). He modernized old-fashioned words and simplified obscure ones, so that Gertrude's description of the drowning Ophelia chanting 'snatches of old lauds' is changed to 'snatches of old tunes' (IV, vii, 177) and Ophelia's 'virgin crants' become 'virgin rites' (V, i, 232). There are dozens of similar examples.

Seemingly insignificant changes prove to be consequential. The most famous is the substitution of a single word in the opening line of Hamlet's first soliloquy, which had begun, 'O that this too too sallied flesh would melt.' The second time around this appears as 'too too solid flesh' (I, ii, 129). Hamlet's initial sense of being assaulted or assailed ('sallied' conveys a sense of being sullied or polluted by his mother's infidelity) is replaced by an anguished desire for nothingness that has less to do with his mother's behaviour than with his own inaction.

The smallest of changes complicate Hamlet's character. When an armed Hamlet comes upon Claudius at prayer, Shakespeare first had his hero say: 'Now might I do it, but now a is a-praying.' When he returned to this passage, he substituted the words 'do it pat' for 'do it, but' – so that the line now read: 'Now might I do it pat, now he is praying' (III, iii, 73–4). There is a world of difference. In the earlier version, a more hesitant Hamlet can't take revenge because Claudius is praying. In the revised version a more opportunistic Hamlet can act precisely because he has caught his adversary off guard but won't because to do so would mean sending a shriven Claudius to heaven.

A more striking example of revision occurs early on when Hamlet angrily turns on Ophelia:

I have heard of your paintings well enough. God hath given you one face, and you make yourselves another; you jig and amble, and you list, you nickname God's creatures, and make wantonness ignorance.

When Shakespeare reworked these lines he shifted the grounds of Hamlet's attack and sharpened its staccato rhythm:

I have heard of your prattlings too well enough. God has given you one pace, and you make yourself another; you jig, you amble, and you lisp, and nickname God's creatures, and make your wantonness your ignorance.

(III, i, 141–6)

It's no longer about how Ophelia looks but about how she speaks and moves – prattling and lisping (while 'pace' replaces 'face', connecting up with 'jig' and 'amble').

Shakespeare also caught himself on the verge of incomprehensibility. In the revised text, for example, Claudius straightforwardly brings Act IV, scene i, to an end, saying:

Come, Gertrude, we'll call up our wisest friends
To let them know both what we mean to do
And what's untimely done. O, come away,
My soul is full of discord and dismay.

Had Shakespeare's earlier version not survived we could never have guessed that in the middle of this speech Claudius digressed in an impossibly dense metaphor about how 'slander flies in a line of fire like a cannon-ball':

we'll call up our wisest friends,
And let them know both what we mean to do
And what's untimely done. [So envious slander]
Whose whisper o'er the world's diameter,
As level as the cannon to his blank,
Transports his poisoned shot, may miss our name,

343

And hit the woundless air. O, come away
My soul is full of discord and dismay.
  (IV, i, 38–45)

The sheer number of changes to the earlier version suggests a degree of uncertainty on Shakespeare's part, as if he were not quite as sure as he had been in *Julius Caesar* or *As You Like It* where his characters and plot were heading.

The revisions went smoothly enough until Shakespeare got to Act IV, scene iv, and Hamlet's final soliloquy: 'How all occasions do inform against me / And spur my dull revenge.' Until now the soliloquies had deepened our sense of Hamlet's character while circling around problems whose complexities resisted resolution – though by the end of each Hamlet manages to find a way forward, hopeful that the right course of action will become clearer. As he prepares to depart for England in Act IV, Hamlet comes upon young Fortinbras leading an army through Denmark on the way to Poland, 'to gain a little patch of ground / That hath in it no profit but the name' (IV, iv, 18–19). Except for the play's final moments, this is the only time that we see Fortinbras, though we have heard of him periodically. Horatio tells us in the opening scene that 'young Fortinbras' of 'unimproved mettle, hot and full', is leading an army of 'lawless resolutes' (I, i, 95–8) to regain lands that his father lost to Hamlet's thirty years earlier. Fear of Fortinbras's invasion produces 'this post-haste and rummage in the land' (I, i, 107) and explains why Bernardo and Francisco are standing guard as the play begins. We later learn that Fortinbras's bedridden uncle, the King of Norway, at Claudius' urging, has apparently persuaded him to redirect his attack against the Poles. Fortinbras is Hamlet's foil: a restless young prince chafing under his uncle's authority and eager to avenge his father.

The chance encounter is the turning point of the play, crystallizing for Hamlet the futility of heroic action. Looking on as Fortinbras's troops march off to the wars, Hamlet sees the invisible rot at the heart of this martial display:

This is th' impostume of much wealth and peace
That inward breaks, and shows no cause without
Why the man dies.
   (IV, iv, 27–9)

His words echo a line in Holinshed's *Chronicles* that had stuck
with Shakespeare: 'Sedition', Holinshed had written, 'is the apos-
tume of the realm, which when it breaketh inwardly, putteth the
state in great danger of recovery.' There's no cure for this cancer. It
may well be the darkest moment in the play.

The soliloquy that immediately follows returns to ideas Hamlet
has long wrestled with. Beastliness has been much on his mind,
whether it's that of Pyrrhus, an 'Hyrcanian beast' (II, ii, 451), that
'adulterate beast' Claudius (I, v, 42), or even his mother: 'O God, a
beast that wants discourse of reason / Would have mourned
longer' (I, ii, 150–51). Hamlet now unexpectedly reverses himself.
'Thinking too precisely' is as beastly as acting impulsively:

     What is a man,
If his chief good and market of his time
Be but to sleep and feed? A beast, no more.
   (IV, iv, 33–5)

He can't shake the idea of his own beastliness, which now seems to
him grounded in his cowardly habit of hair-splitting analysis:

     Now whether it be
Bestial oblivion, or some craven scruple
Of thinking too precisely on th'event,
(A thought which quartered hath but one part wisdom,
And ever three parts coward), I do not know
Why yet I live to say 'This thing's to do,'
Sith I have cause, and will, and strength, and means
To do't.
   (IV, iv, 39–46)

Hamlet repudiates the very thing that won us over, his refusal to act unthinkingly. He has discovered that he's a beast if he acts and a beast if he doesn't. The example of Fortinbras confirms for him that there can be no right way forward:

> Examples gross as earth exhort me;
> Witness this army of such mass and charge,
> Led by a delicate and tender prince,
> Whose spirit, with divine ambition puffed,
> Makes mouths at the invisible event,
> Exposing what is mortal and unsure,
> To all that fortune, death, and danger dare,
> Even for an eggshell.
>   (IV, iv, 46–53)

It's Hamlet at his most sardonic. Fortinbras is a 'gross' example not only in the sense of 'obvious' but also 'monstrous'. The ironic 'delicate' and 'tender' are the last adjectives the ruthless Fortinbras calls to mind. Fortinbras is 'puffed' with ambition and, child-like, makes 'mouths' or faces at unseen outcomes. He is willing to sacrifice the lives of his followers for nothing, for 'an eggshell' – with the hint here of broken eggshells as empty crowns (an image Shakespeare would develop in *King Lear*).

Hamlet's conclusion has exasperated critics and some have refused to take him at his word, insisting that he means the exact opposite of what he says and that we should take his words 'not to stir' as a double negative: 'not not to stir'. But this is desperate. He concludes that greatness consists not in refraining to act unless the cause is great but in fighting over any imagined slight:

> Rightly to be great,
> Is not to stir without great argument,
> But greatly to find quarrel in a straw
> When honour's at the stake.
>   (IV, iv, 53–6)

It's the discredited argument for a culture of honour left in tatters by the events of the previous year. In the aftermath of Essex's Irish campaign, Elizabethans didn't need to be reminded what an 'army of such mass and charge' leading to the 'imminent death of twenty-thousand men' amounted to. The relentless pursuit of honour can be used to justify anything. Fortinbras is a perfect example, for he is willing to sacrifice his men for a 'fantasy and trick of fame':

> to my shame I see
> The imminent death of twenty thousand men,
> That for a fantasy and trick of fame,
> Go to their graves like beds, fight for a plot
> Whereon the numbers cannot try the cause,
> Which is not tomb enough and continent
> To hide the slain.
> (IV, iv, 59–65)

It's a grim, almost savage soliloquy; and the image of Fortinbras marching through Denmark on his way to slaughter Poles can't help but invite comparison to a scene enacted thirty years earlier when Hamlet's father had taken the same route to the same end. Were his actions against the Poles any less brutal than Fortinbras's – and are we to think that these are the 'foul crimes' (I, v, 12) that still haunt him? Will Fortinbras's costly campaign be recalled in similar heroic language?

'How all occasions' is a fitting culmination to the sequence of soliloquies that preceded it – but only if we want to see the resolution of the play as dark and existential. Hamlet knows that he has to kill Claudius but cannot justify such an action, since the traditional avenger's appeal to honour rings hollow. This bitter and hard-won knowledge serves as a capstone to earlier, anguished soliloquies. Yet, as Shakespeare saw, it derailed the revenge plot. The resolution of the play was now a problem, for it had to be more motivated than the 'accidental judgements' and 'casual slaughters' Horatio describes (V, ii, 361). Yet for a resigned Hamlet

– capable only of bloody 'thoughts' not deeds (IV, iv, 66) – to take revenge after this is to concede that he is no better than Fortinbras. In the final scene, mortally wounded and having killed Claudius, Hamlet hears the 'warlike noise' (V, ii, 349) of Fortinbras's approaching army and declares: 'I do prophesy th'election lights / On Fortinbras; he has my dying voice' (V, ii, 355–6). What could possibly justify Hamlet's urging Fortinbras's succession? These words are either spoken ironically or are the stoical observation of someone who knows that even Alexander the Great and Caesar return to dust. The entry of Fortinbras backed by his lawless troops confirms that there will be no 'election' in Denmark – the country is his for the taking. Hamlet can have no illusions about the fate of Denmark under the rule of an opportunist willing to sacrifice the lives of his own followers. A play that began with hurried defensive preparations to withstand Fortinbras's troops ends with a capitulation to them, the poisoned bodies of the Danish ruling family sprawled on stage, a fitting image of the 'impostume of much wealth and peace, / That inward breaks'.

In allowing his writing to take him where it would in his first draft, Shakespeare had created his greatest protagonist, but the trajectory of Hamlet's soliloquies had left the resolution of the play incoherent and broken too radically from the conventions of the revenge plot that had to sweep both protagonist and play to a satisfying conclusion. Shakespeare now had to choose between the integrity of his character and his plot, and he chose plot. Hamlet's climactic soliloquy had to be cut. When he revised this scene, Shakespeare eliminated the long soliloquy entirely, along with Hamlet's words with Fortinbras's Captain. All that was left to the scene was a perfunctory nine-line exchange between a courteous Fortinbras and the Captain that provided a plausible explanation for why Fortinbras would be in a position to pick up the pieces at the end of the play. One immediate effect of the cut was that in the revised version (in which Hamlet neither sees Fortinbras's army nor speaks of him so trenchantly) the lines in which Hamlet offers Fortinbras his 'dying voice' strike a more upbeat, hopeful note. Their edge is further softened by Shakespeare's decision to return to the opening scene and change Fortinbras's 'lawless resolutes' into the more understandable 'landless' ones – the kind of men, younger sons and gentlemen volunteers, who had sought their fortune in Ireland.

Eliminating Hamlet's soliloquy firmly shifted the play's centre of gravity. Far more weight fell on what was now the play's final soliloquy, immediately preceding Fortinbras's entry. There, Claudius has declared that the only thing that can cure him is 'the present death of Hamlet':

> Do it, England,
> For like the hectic in my blood he rages,
> And thou must cure me.
> (IV, iii, 65–7)

The elimination of Hamlet's words in the following scene turns Claudius into a more formidable adversary as well as one who has the last word until Act V. Shakespeare retreated from locating the conflict within Hamlet's consciousness and reverts at the end to a more conventional (and for the audience more viscerally satisfying) struggle between adversaries.

With Fortinbras's role now diminished to the point where he could no longer serve as Hamlet's opposite, Shakespeare had to go back and turn Laertes into a worthier antagonist and ultimately Hamlet's double. In a clumsy but now necessary addition, Hamlet announces this by regretting to Horatio:

> That to Laertes I forgot myself,
> For by the image of my cause I see
> The portraiture of his.
> (V, ii, 76–8)

349

And in the revised version, Hamlet voluntarily seeks a reconciliation with Laertes (whereas in the earlier version he had only done so at his mother's urging).

Shakespeare still had to find both a new turning point and a rationale for why Hamlet had to kill Claudius. He managed to do both by adding a few key lines to one of Hamlet's speeches in Act V, scene ii. In the earlier version of this scene, Hamlet had launched into another litany of Claudius' crimes –

> Does it not, think thee, stand me now upon?
> He that hath killed my king and whored my mother,
> Popped in between th' election and my hopes,
> Thrown out his angle for my proper life,
> And with such cozenage, is't not perfect conscience?
>   (V, ii, 63–7)

– only to be interrupted in mid-speech by the entrance of a courtier. You can see why Shakespeare cuts him off: in the aftermath of 'How all occasions' Hamlet's complaint seems rhetorical and verges on self-pity. It may be 'perfect conscience' – that is, conform to what is right – but in such a relative world, what difference does that make? When he rewrites this scene, Shakespeare delays the courtier's entrance and extends Hamlet's argument to allow him to build to a new conclusion:

> Does it not, think'st thee, stand me now upon –
> He hath killed my king and whored my mother,
> Popped in between th' election and my hopes,
> Thrown out his angle for my proper life,
> And with such cozenage – is't not perfect conscience
> To quit him with this arm? And is't not to be damned
> To let this canker of our nature come
> In further evil?
>   (V, ii, 63–70)

The additional lines counter Claudius' desire for a 'cure' and restore the metaphor that has been cut about the 'impostume', though it's no longer an undetectable cancer that destroys the state. Now, a cure is possible: this canker – Claudius – can and must be removed; and to fail to remove it is to invite damnation. Salvation, not honour, now justifies the killing of a king. Hamlet realizes that he no longer needs to dread being damned for 'taking arms against the foe', a fear so eloquently expressed in the 'To be or not to be' soliloquy, where he was tormented by 'the dread of something after death' (III, i, 77). The Hamlet of the revised version is no longer adrift, no longer finds himself in a world where action feels arbitrary and meaningless. The change is so deft that it's as if Shakespeare has activated something that has been dormant in the play. Other lines – 'There's a divinity that shapes our ends' (V, ii, 10) and, 'There is special providence in the fall of a sparrow' (V, ii, 219–20), now fall neatly into place and reinforce the argument for salvation through revenge. And this new determination – with its emphasis on salvation – corresponds with Hamlet's words in what is now his final soliloquy, back in Act III, where he commits himself to killing his uncle only when Claudius is 'about some act / That has no relish of salvation in't' (III, iii, 91–2). For most of the revised version, Hamlet is the same reflective, melancholy Dane as he was in the earlier one. It's only near the end that the two Hamlets significantly diverge – each one achieving a different kind of clarity.

Shakespeare was also forced to change Hamlet's unforgettable words as he prepares to fight Laertes. In the earlier version Hamlet's speech served as a coda that echoed the resignation of his famous soliloquy, 'To be or not to be':

If it be, 'tis not to come; if it be not to come, it will be now; if it be not now, yet it will come; the readiness is all, since no man, of aught he leaves, knows what is't to leave betimes. Let be.

(V, ii, 220–24)

Hamlet's emphasis here, as it has been all along in this first version, is on knowing, or rather, on his acceptance of not knowing: you can't regret what you don't know. Samuel Johnson's paraphrase of Hamlet's philosophical resolve is helpful: 'Since no man know aught of the state of life which he leaves, since he cannot judge what other years may produce, why should he be afraid of leaving life behind?'

When he revised these lines, Shakespeare made the last sentence less dispiriting. Hamlet finally has an answer to his persistent fears about the afterlife: 'the readiness is all, since no man has aught of what he leaves. What is't to leave betimes?' (V, ii, 222–4). Now that he is a more committed avenger, Hamlet's calm insistence that there are no easy answers – 'Let be' – must also be eliminated. And while the new Hamlet also acknowledges that death is both certain and inevitable and that it doesn't matter if you die young, he shifts attention away from the impossibility of knowing (which has also dropped out) to the unimportance of having. In this revised version, Hamlet's last piece of advice is that you can't take it with you – 'since no man has aught of what he leaves'. Samuel Johnson summarizes the difference and signals his preference: 'It is more characteristic of Hamlet to think little of leaving because he cannot solve its many mysteries, than because he cannot carry with him his life's goods.' Johnson prefers the Hamlet of the first draft here, the one characterized by a philosophical equanimity in the face of a disappointing world, rather than the one whose revenge is now tied to salvation and a renunciation of worldly things.

As Shakespeare saw (and as editors from the eighteenth century on who are reluctant to part with these and other profound lines that Shakespeare eliminated confirm), the cuts come at a price. The radical argument for a sacred act of violence that underpins the lines

is't not to be damned
To let this canker of our nature come
In further evil?

returns us to the self-justifying fantasy of the conspirators in *Julius Caesar* ('Let's be sacrificers, but not butchers' [II, i, 166]) and more broadly to the language of theologically sanctioned tyrannicide that permeated that play. But in *Julius Caesar* Shakespeare had also shown that while this argument can be justified intellectually, in the real world chaos and blood-letting invariably follow. It didn't help, then, that the earlier version of *Hamlet* had included a long speech by Horatio reminding playgoers how

A little ere the mightiest Julius fell,
The graves stood tenantless, and the sheeted dead
Did squeak and gibber in the Roman streets.
  (I, i, 114–17)

In *Julius Caesar*, fresh in the minds of playgoers at the Globe, Cassius had also seen in these portents 'instruments of fear and warning / Unto some monstrous state' (I, iii, 70–71). Gesturing towards the argument that Hamlet was damned if he didn't kill Claudius was one thing; foregrounding its now disturbing political implications was another: ultimately, killing a bad ruler, though justified, fails to resolve anything. So Shakespeare went back and cut Horatio's speech too. The changes may have temporarily solved Hamlet's problem but not the deeper one, which remains in the play, of what justifies – not just morally but pragmatically – the killing of a bad ruler: when Hamlet finally stabs Claudius, it's easy to forget that in both versions everyone onstage cries out, 'Treason, treason' (V, ii, 323). As Shakespeare's plays from *Henry the Sixth* to *Julius Caesar* had already shown, removing the canker, however necessary, doesn't cure the state, because men who are even more ruthless than their predecessors fill the political vacuum, just as Fortinbras will.

The revised version still had to be shortened for the stage, cut to fewer than 3,000 lines. Whether Shakespeare abridged it himself, left it to others, or collaborated in the effort, we don't know, but this performance version of *Hamlet* was an immediate and unqualified success. Fellow playwrights, who quickly quoted, parodied and shamelessly stole from it, were clearly dazzled. It must have had a great run that first year or two; demand was so great that the Chamberlain's Men, or some part of the company, also took it on the road, performing it by early 1603 in Oxford, Cambridge and probably elsewhere. Since the two universities were not ordinarily on the same touring route, it may have toured more than once at this time. For this itinerant production a new and further abridged version of *Hamlet* was made, though this script too is lost (so that the two most valuable scripts for understanding how *Hamlet* was actually performed no longer exist).

Scholars have been able to reconstruct much of this textual history because in 1603 one or more of those involved in the touring production, including the hired actor who played Marcellus (we know it was this actor because in putting the text together he remembered his own lines a lot better than he did anyone else's) cobbled together from memory a 2,200 line version of the road production and sold it to publishers in London. In the course of three years the play had now gone through five versions, each one shorter than the last. Book buyers coming upon '*The Tragical History of Hamlet Prince of Denmark*, by William Shakespeare' in 1603 would have encountered a mangled version of what they had heard onstage, with some scenes transposed, some characters given names that probably derived from the old and lost *Hamlet* (Polonius is named Corambis and Reynaldo is Montano), and some of the most memorable speeches badly butchered. The opening lines of Hamlet's most famous soliloquy offer a striking example. What audiences had once heard as:

> To be, or not to be, that is the question,
> Whether 'tis nobler in the mind to suffer
> The slings and arrows of outrageous fortune,
> Or to take arms against a sea of troubles,
> And by opposing end them; to die to sleep
> No more, and by a sleep, to say we end
> The heartache and the thousand natural shocks
> That flesh is heir to – 'tis a consummation
> Devoutly to be wished.
>   (III, i, 55–63)

now appeared in print as:

> To be, or not to be. Ay, that's the point.
> To die, to sleep, is that all? Aye, all.
> No, to sleep, to dream, aye, marry, there it goes,
> For in that dream of death, when we awake,
> And borne again before an everlasting judge,
> From whence no passenger ever returned,
> The undiscovered country, at whose sight
> The happy smile, and the accursed damned.
> But for this, the joyful hope of this,
> Who'd bear the scorns and flattery of the world
> Scorned by the right rich, the rich cursed of the poor?

The pirated edition nonetheless proved to be enormously popular, so popular that it was read to shreds: only two copies of this First Quarto survive, each missing a page or two, and the first wasn't rediscovered until 1823.

In response to this unauthorized quarto, in late 1604 the Chamberlain's Men decided to turn over a better version of the play to be published. They could have supplied any one of a number of manuscript versions: a copy of their playhouse prompt book; the longer revised script that was behind it; a better version of the touring text that was behind the First Quarto; or Shakespeare's dark first draft. They chose this first draft – 'newly imprinted and

355

enlarged to almost as much again as it was, according to the true and perfect copy'. Why this draft was chosen is another of the play's mysteries. The company may simply have decided not to release a version of the play that other companies could easily stage. As a sharer, Shakespeare would have had a say in the decision, though we don't know which version he preferred. Even if Shakespeare wanted to see his early draft in print he made no effort to touch it up before it was handed over to the printer – and it was so difficult to decipher that the confused compositors had to check the opening scene against a copy of the bad First Quarto it was intended to replace. There's one more twist: when the time came to publish *Hamlet* in the 1623 Folio, Heminges and Condell broke with their usual practice of printing play texts that were based on good extant quartos: they decided to reject the early version found in the Second Quarto of 1604/5 in favour of the (unpublished) revised one, perhaps because it more closely resembled the acting version with which they were familiar.

Their decision to do so opened up a Pandora's box: editors who could now choose between two good but quite different texts of *Hamlet* were sorely tempted to combine the best of both and few could resist the urge to do so. As a result, since the eighteenth century the play has existed in multiple, hybrid versions – some editors relying more heavily on the Second Quarto, others on the Folio text, and still others promiscuously drawing on both as well as on lines from the First Quarto. One reason why no two readers' or actors' Hamlets are alike is that no two modern versions of *Hamlet* are either. Combining different parts of these texts, editors have cobbled together an incoherent *Hamlet* that Shakespeare neither wrote nor imagined. It's not the excision of motive but its duplication that makes the conflated versions of *Hamlet* that are now taught and staged so puzzling: Hamlet is both resigned and determined, caught between knowing and having, damned if he does and damned if he doesn't kill Claudius. We're left with a

Hamlet who is confused – but not the confusion Shakespeare intended.

Some recent editors have come to regret their decision to fall into line and produce a conflated *Hamlet* they didn't believe in; others have dug in their heels, preferring what's familiar. The only major edition to break with tradition and choose an unconflated text is the Oxford Shakespeare – though its editors went with Shakespeare's revised version rather than his first draft, basing their edition on the Folio text. The long-awaited publication of the new Arden edition of *Hamlet* promises to change this situation. In offering each of the three surviving early versions of *Hamlet* separately, its editors will encourage others to follow their lead. Soon – in a generation or two, I suspect – only scholars interested in the history of the play's reception will still be reading a conflated *Hamlet*.

Changing how we think about Shakespeare's greatest play means revising how we think about Shakespeare. The Romantic myth of literary genius, which has long promoted an effortless and unfathomable Shakespeare, cannot easily accommodate a model of a Shakespeare whose greatness was a product of labour as much as talent. The humbler portrait of Shakespeare presented here is of a writer who knew himself, knew his audience and knew what worked. When Shakespeare saw that he had to wrest his play from where Hamlet had led him, he did so unflinchingly. He didn't write *Hamlet* to please himself. If he had, he would have rested content with the more complicated hero of his first draft. Only an extraordinary writer of the first order could have produced that first draft; and only a greater writer than that could have sacrificed part of that creation to better show 'the very age and body of the time his form and pressure' (III, ii, 23–4). Shakespeare didn't write 'as if from another planet', as Coleridge put it: he wrote for the Globe; it wasn't in his mind's eye, or even on the page, but in that aptly named theatre that his plays came to life and mattered.

357

Ben Jonson, who knew Shakespeare well enough not to under-estimate him as a writer, also knew that part of his greatness was bound up in his gift for second thoughts. Jonson's praise of Shakespeare's craft in the First Folio, largely overlooked today, is worth recalling:

> he
> Who casts to write a living line, must sweat,
> (Such as thine are) and strike the second heat
> Upon the Muses' anvil; turn the same,
> (And himself with it) that he thinks to frame;
> Or for the laurel he may gain a scorn,
> For a good poet's made as well as born.
> And such wert thou.

Like every great writer before or since, Jonson understood that the best poets are both made and born: that all great writing has to be hammered out and all great poets stand or fall by that 'second heat', their laboured revision. In these knotty lines Jonson also hints at the physical toll this process exacts, for when Shakespeare would 'turn' his writing he would turn 'himself with it'. Writing, even for Shakespeare, was a battering experience. Shakespeare's greatness, Jonson tells us, was a result not just of exceptional talent but also of a quarter-century of relentless, driving effort. If we want to see Shakespeare's greatness and his personality illuminat-ed, we need only look at the trail of sparks – still visible in the surviving versions – that flew in the heat of revising *Hamlet*. To see this is also to acknowledge that the *Hamlet* Shakespeare left us was, in the play's own words, 'a thing a little soiled with working' (II, i, 40). This trace of grit and sweat, more than anything else, may help explain why 'Prince Hamlet', in the words of the Elizabethan playgoer Anthony Scoloker, managed then, as it manages now, 'to please all'.

Epilogue

The holiday season at year's end began ominously. On the Sunday before Christmas London was buffeted by south-westerly winds that toppled chimneys, blew lead off church steeples and knocked over trees and barns. A passenger boat heading downriver to Gravesend capsized, drowning most of the thirty men and women aboard. The day after Christmas Shakespeare and his fellow players made their way back to court, now at Richmond, for an evening performance. The Admiral's Men would play there the following night and again at New Year, before it was once more the Chamberlain's Men's turn on Twelfth Night. The Queen, Rowland Whyte reported, 'graced the dancing and plays with her own presence'.

Much had changed since Shakespeare had last visited Richmond on Shrove Tuesday. Essex had been at the height of his popularity, preparing to lead an army to crush Tyrone. He was now under house arrest with little hope of reprieve, humiliated by Star Chamber proceedings against him in late November and in failing

The execution of the Earl of Essex

health. A week earlier, word had circulated in London that Essex was dead and 'the bells tolled for him'. The news was false, but ministers in London read special prayers and politics spilled into the pews: on Christmas Day a parish clerk of St Andrew's in the Wardrobe had asked God to 'Look mercifully . . . upon . . . thy servant the Earl of Essex' and 'in thy good time restore him to his former health', to the 'grief and discomfort of all wicked Edomites that bear ill-will to him'. The authorities found this intolerable. Rowland Whyte, perhaps unconsciously echoing the words describing the fate of the tribunes 'put to silence' in *Julius Caesar*, reported the fall-out: 'Many ministers that made public prayers for [Essex] in their churches are commended to silence; some, indeed, foolishly forgetting themselves, their doubtful speeches tending to sedition.'

Back in February, Tyrone had been braced for an English attack. Now, with Essex and his freshly dubbed knights gone and Lord Mountjoy not yet officially appointed to succeed him, Tyrone gave notice that he was letting the truce expire. It was feared, Fynes Morison wrote, that 'the rebels would presently assault the English Pale', and sure enough, by the end of November rumours reached London that Tyrone 'comes with all his force' and 'that all her Majesty's subjects do leave their houses in the country and retire to the towns'. The 'very heart of the kingdom', Morison wrote, 'now languished under the contagion of rebellion'. Since the previous Christmas several thousand English soldiers had been killed or maimed and tens of thousands of pounds wasted. The English forces still in the field 'were altogether out of heart'. A confident Tyrone, promised support by the Pope and the King of Spain, promoted himself as the champion of 'Irish liberty and Romish religion'. Fresh English troops would have to be conscripted and new subsidies exacted if Mountjoy were to succeed where Essex had failed.

The poet John Donne, who was at court at Richmond for the

Christmas holidays, diagnosed with his usual acuity the extraordinary disjunction between the cheerful mood at court and the sobering reality beyond the palace walls:

The court is not great but full of jollity and revels and plays and as merry as if it were not sick. Her Majesty is well disposed and very gracious in public to my Lord Mountjoy. My Lord of Essex and his train are no more missed here than the angels which were cast down from heaven nor (for anything I see) likelier to return. He withers in his sickness and plods on to his end in the same pace where you left us. The worst accidents of his sickness are that he conspires with it and yet it is not here believed.

They had lived through the fall of angels – though even Donne was unaware that the fallen ones were secretly plotting their return. With his sharp eye for paradox, Donne also marvelled how the court was in denial about how sick it was, even as Essex, who conspired in his own illness, wasn't believed. When John Weever wrote an ironic satire to usher in the new year – 'A Prophesy of This Present Year, 1600', published some months later in his *Faunus and Melliflora* – he began it with an epigraph: 'Who lives past ninety-nine, / Shall afterward speak of a blessed time.' The couplet is purposely ambiguous, leaving it up to the reader to decide whether the time before or after '99 was blessed. Weever's so-called prophecy turns on the joke that everything was fine in England, there was nothing to satirize – all was 'spotless pure' in 'these halcyon times'.

Elizabeth appeared rejuvenated at the year-end festivities, in 'very good health', and spent most of her evenings in the presence chamber watching 'the ladies dance the old and new country dances, with the tabor and pipe'. She may have been amused to see so many of those who were waiting for her to die in ill health themselves: this December the Lord Admiral was sick at Chelsea, the Lord Keeper sick in London, Lord Herbert sick of an ague, Ralegh recovering from one and Essex reportedly at death's door.

She might outlive them all.

A highlight of the holiday season at court was the exchange of gifts on New Year's Day. Courtiers went out of their way to show their devotion to the Queen and each of their gifts was carefully recorded. So, too, were Elizabeth's gifts in return: she rewarded her generous subjects – according to their rank and favour – with gilt plate. Thomas Egerton, the Lord Keeper, was listed first among the gift-givers and sent a gold amulet garnished with rubies and pearls. The Lord Admiral gave a golden necklace adorned with rubies, pearl and topaz. Secretary of State Cecil presented the Queen with seven sprigs of gold decorated with rubies, diamonds and pearls. Scores of lesser gifts followed: some gave gold, others perfumed gloves, and still others clothing (Elizabeth had several thousand outfits in her wardrobe and welcomed more). Francis Bacon presented an embroidered white satin petticoat along with a note wishing the Queen 'that we may continue to reckon on, and ever, your Majesty's happy years of reign; and they that reckon upon any other hopes, I would they might reckon short, and to their cost'. The most spectacular gift of all this New Year was an 'exceedingly rich' one that came, 'as it were, in a cloud, no man knows how'. It was neither 'received nor rejected', and never made it onto the gift-roll. It was offered by Essex and ignored by the Queen.

Sir John Harington wisely shunned the court and sent from his country home a handsome gift to his godmother Elizabeth. A friend reported back to him that his 'present to the Queen was well accepted of; she did much commend your verse, nor did she less praise your prose'. Harington, taking no chances, had also sent along something to eat and that too went over well: 'The Queen hath tasted your dainties and saith you have marvelous skill in cooking of good fruits.' Harington was still recovering from a harrowing interview with Elizabeth after returning from Ireland – which he diplomatically described as 'a full and gracious audience in the withdrawing chamber at Whitehall, where herself being accuser, judge, and witness, I was cleared and graciously dismissed'. Only much later did he confide in a friend what happened: 'I shall never put out of remembrance her Majesty's displeasure. I entered her chamber, but she frowned and said, "What, did the fool [Essex] bring you too? Go back to your business."' 'She chafed much, walked fastly to and from and looked with discomposure in her visage,' and when he kneeled to her, she 'swore "By God's Son, I am no Queen, that man [Essex] is above me; who gave him command to come here so soon?"' His journal of the Irish campaign, which she demanded and he shared, appeased her anger. Harington beat a hasty retreat to his home in Kelston, near Bath – 'I did not stay to be bidden twice, if all the Irish rebels had been at my heels, I should not have had better speed.' We have Harington to thank for one of the most poignant anecdotes about Elizabeth, recorded a year or so later, which captures a moment when life seemed to imitate art, in this case *Hamlet*: 'She walks much in her privy chamber, and stamps with her feet at ill news, and thrusts her rusty sword at times into the arras in great rage.'

Once again, the holiday season provided an opportunity for some of the best plays of the year, vetted by the Master of the Revels, to be staged before Elizabeth. This Christmas Thomas Dekker took the laurels, for he alone had two plays performed at court. Ben Jonson was responsible for another. We don't know if one of Shakespeare's new plays was the fourth and last play staged at Richmond this Christmas. If one was, the likeliest candidate was another comedy, *As You Like It*. Its extensive use of song and its country setting would have made it a good choice for a Christmas performance at rural Richmond, though in truth one of Shakespeare's old plays could have been revived or the Chamberlain's Men might have staged any of the dozen or so lost plays written for them by other hands. But the raw political climate at year's end was ill suited to *Henry the Fifth* and *Julius Caesar*, and *Hamlet* was not yet ready.

Dekker, with his two plays at court, had every right to be proud. It had been a remarkable year for him, the most accomplished he would ever have. It had begun in prison, for he had been arrested in January at the behest of the Chamberlain's Men (perhaps for failing to deliver on a play for which they had paid him). He was bailed by the Admiral's Men and in the next twelve months Dekker wrote or collaborated on a staggering ten plays for them. The Admiral's Men would be performing his popular comedy *The Shoemaker's Holiday* on the evening of 1 January, a play that rewrites *Henry the Fifth* as a rambunctious citizen comedy that glorifies not St Crispian's Day but Shrove Tuesday. Before that, on 27 December, they would perform his *Old Fortunatus*, an old and popular rags-to-riches story that Dekker updated. He had been hard at work on *Fortunatus* two weeks before Christmas, adding material for the royal performance. It now began with a special Prologue, spoken by two old men on their way to court – 'the temple of Eliza' – who look out at the audience and discover Elizabeth herself in the throng:

> Our eyes are dazzled by Eliza's beams,
> See (if at least thou dare see) where she sits:
> This is the great pantheon of our goddess,
> And all those faces which thine eyes thought stars,
> Are nymphs attending on her deity.

The performance at court ended as it began, though with Dekker going even further than others had in celebrating the cult of Elizabeth: in a specially written Epilogue, the actors call for everyone present to kneel before the 'Goddess' Elizabeth.

Ben Jonson, too, had begun the year in fairly desperate straits. It had been a little over a year since he had been convicted of manslaughter and stripped of his worldly goods. After his release from prison, Jonson had recovered his fortunes by writing collaboratively with Dekker and others for the Admiral's Men. By autumn, he had built on that success with the innovative *Every Man Out of His Humour*. The year was ending in triumph for him, for his play was chosen to be performed by the Chamberlain's Men before the Queen. For Jonson's career, no less than for Shakespeare's, 1599 had been pivotal.

Like Dekker, Jonson wrote a special conclusion for the performance at court. He didn't have much choice. In the version first staged at the Globe, *Every Man Out of His Humour* had ended with a boy actor dressed up as Queen Elizabeth, the sight of whom miraculously converts the envious humour-stricken hero of the play, Macilente (the stage direction reads: 'The very wonder of her presence strikes Macilente to the earth, dumb and astonished'). A boy impersonating Elizabeth might be seen as parodic or disrespectful. Even Jonson had to admit that 'many seemed not to relish it' and he was forced to change the ending at the Globe. The possibility of a court performance now offered a third and more fitting way to end the play: Macilente would be transformed by the actual sight of a curative Elizabeth, sitting in the audience. *The Shoemaker's Holiday*, *Old Fortunatus* and *Every Man Out of His Humour* were all rushed into print. Watching their plays performed at court this season, Dekker and Jonson can each be forgiven for imagining himself on the verge of overtaking Shakespeare as the most popular and admired dramatist of the age. For contemporary playwrights, Shakespeare's work had become the mark to aim at and virtually all of Shakespeare's rivals found themselves either imitating his example, repudiating it, or both. In recent months, direct competition with his plays had, if anything, intensified.

Even as his rivals turned to history and romantic comedy, Shakespeare, having virtually exhausted his interest in these genres, had already moved on. One wouldn't know it, however, from what was available in London's bookstalls. For those purchasing plays in the coming year – in which *The Second Part of Henry the Fourth, Henry the Fifth, The Merchant of Venice, A Midsummer Night's Dream*, and *Much Ado about Nothing* were all published for the first time – Shakespeare, whose name was at last regularly appearing on the title pages of his plays, remained the celebrated author of English history and romantic comedy. Neither *Julius Caesar* nor *As You Like It*, both of which were daringly original, would be published for decades; and it's not at all clear whether many contemporaries yet saw in Brutus or Rosalind intimations of a depth and complexity in both language and character until now unavailable (with the exception of Falstaff) even in Shakespearean drama. Once again there was a lag between reputation and accomplishment. For many admirers Shakespeare was still, and would always be, the 'honey-tongued' love poet. Only Shakespeare knew at Richmond this Christmas what others couldn't: he had pushed himself to another creative level this past year and had finished drafting *Hamlet*, a play that was better than anything he had ever written. Through the soliloquy and its internalization of conflict, he had at last found his own way forward.

When Shakespeare was at his most creative he wrote plays in bunches, and when he did so they tended to spill into each other. Though he probably wrote them consecutively, the four plays he had worked on in 1599 overlapped a great deal in his imagination, and the technical innovations in one led to advances in the next. The year that began with *Henry the Fifth* invoking the 'senators of th'antique Rome' (V, Prologue, 26) ended in *Hamlet* with Horatio still hearkening back to the time 'A little ere the mightiest Julius fell' (I, i, 113). That Shakespeare was already thinking ahead to the forest of Arden is evident in Antony's extended metaphor in his funeral oration in *Julius Caesar*:

> Pardon me, Julius! Here wast thou bayed, brave hart,
> Here didst thou fall, and here thy hunters stand,

Signed, in thy spoil, and crimsoned in thy lethe . . .
How like a deer, strucken by many princes,
Dost thou here lie!
   (III, i, 204–10)

And yet when Shakespeare turned to *As You Like It* he couldn't quite forget his recent Roman tragedy. Rosalind can casually remark: 'There was never anything so sudden but the fight of two rams, and Caesar's thrasonical brag of "I came, I saw, I overcame"' (V, ii, 24). When a deer is fatally wounded, it's as if Jaques has recently seen *Julius Caesar*, for he accuses the deer hunters of acting like 'mere usurpers, tyrants' (II, i, 61–2) and later suggests that the deer slayer should be presented 'to the Duke like a Roman conquerer' (IV, ii, 3–5). The melancholy Jaques is a forerunner of Hamlet, though one who has had the misfortune to be put by Shakespeare into a pastoral comedy, where his aloofness and cynicism are mocked rather than rewarded with tragic greatness. With *Hamlet*, the cross-pollination of the plays reaches another level when Polonius unexpectedly tells Hamlet, 'I did enact Julius Caesar. I was killed i'th'Capitol; Brutus killed me' (III, ii, 99). John Heminges, who played older men, probably spoke these lines and also played Caesar. The in-joke, which audiences at the Globe would have shared, is that Richard Burbage, who was playing Hamlet and had played Brutus, was about to stab Heminges again.

The Globe had proved to be critical to Shakespeare's artistic breakthrough. He was the first modern dramatist to develop such an intimate connection to a particular playing space and audience. Had plans to remove the timbers of the Theatre and transport them across the river fallen through, the history of English literature would have looked very different. Until the building of the Globe, playgoers could expect to find more or less the same kinds of drama performed at one public theatre as they could at another. No longer. With the completion of the Globe and the concurrent rise of the boy players, the branding of theatres had begun in earnest, as individual playhouses were increasingly identified with particular kinds of offerings. Having dispensed with raucous jigs and improvisational clowning, the Chamberlain's Men succeeded this year in positioning themselves somewhere between the popular offering of rival adult companies and the more elite offerings of the boys. They could do so only because of the breadth of Shakespeare's appeal – his ability to write plays that were intellectually rigorous and yet pleased all.

Philip Henslowe had been in the business long enough to know that the players at his ageing Rose could not survive such competition – indeed, he may have been shopping around for a site for a new theatre in the northern suburbs for some time and his enquiries may have helped propel the move to Bankside by the Chamberlain's Men rather than the other way around. On 24 December 1599 a lease was taken out on a property on Golding Lane, beyond Cripplegate: it would be the home of the Admiral's Men's new theatre, the Fortune. Two days after Christmas performances at court ended, Peter Street, having finished work on the Globe, was hired to build the new theatre. Physically, the Fortune would resemble the Globe in all respects, except that its exterior frame would be square, not round. Henslowe, who also recognized that his resident company needed to be defined by a house style, decided to appeal to nostalgia, satisfying audiences who preferred the hits of the past. Jigs at the Fortune became so popular that a decade later the authorities had to put a stop to them, for 'by reason of certain lewd jigs, songs, and dances . . . lewd and ill-disposed persons in great multitude do resort thither at the end of every play'. Henslowe also coaxed out of retirement his son-in-law, the tragedian Edward Alleyn, who a decade earlier had made his reputation playing Marlowe's great overreachers. If the Globe would parody Marlowe and reject jigs, the Fortune would revive both.

The fresh start at the Globe had also motivated Shakespeare to challenge both actors and spectators (after 1599 Shakespeare also stopped calling playgoers 'auditors' and switched to 'spectators', perhaps signalling that his was a theatre that would offer more in the way of visual spectacle). He started placing new demands on what he expected from leading players: no boy actor had ever been asked to carry off a role like Rosalind's and even for a star like Burbage the physical and psychic demands of playing Hamlet were daunting. Audiences, too, would be confronted – and rewarded – with more difficult language and more complex characters, and on occasion, with vexing plays like *Troilus and Cressida* and *Timon of Athens* that pushed the edge of experimentation to the breaking point.

The strain of seeing the new theatre up and running, of worrying about its destruction at the hands of Spanish invaders in August, simply of writing and acting and reading as much as he did this year, took its toll. Shakespeare was now midway, as Dante put it, through the journey of life, though his would be cut short at fifty-two. At thirty-five he was also at the midway point in his career, having written or collaborated in over twenty plays with almost that many as yet unwritten. In the charged atmosphere in which *Hamlet* was conceived, Shakespeare might have hoped that the creative rush would carry over into other plays. It didn't. *Hamlet*, in retrospect, faced backwards more than it looked forwards, marking the end of an era and a stage of a career even more than it pointed in new directions. It may simply be that Shakespeare put so much of himself into this capacious play that he was spent. The torrid pace of his play-writing let up. In the three years between the time that *Hamlet* was first staged and the death of Queen Elizabeth, in March 1603, Shakespeare only managed to write *Twelfth Night* and *Troilus and Cressida*, well below his average of two plays a year – and neither of these plays is either anticipated in or echoes those that he wrote in 1599. *Twelfth Night* was a time-tested and accomplished if somewhat formulaic throwback to earlier Shakespearean comedy – and it would be the last of this kind he would write. Compared to *Much Ado* and *As You Like It*, it was safer and less inspired, lacking the sharp wit of Benedict and Beatrice or the dazzling originality of his Arden play. *Troilus* veered in the other direction: it was too unmoored and too bitter. Some scholars remain unconvinced that it was ever staged at the Globe and point to the Epistle to the second printing of the 1609 Quarto, which claims that it was 'never staled with the stage, never clapper-clawed with the palms of the vulgar'. It was not until the accession of James I, in 1603, and the rewarding news that followed – that the Chamberlain's Men would henceforth be known as the King's Men – that Shakespeare produced *Othello* and *Measure for Measure* in quick succession; another two quiet years would pass before his next extraordinary creative moment, in which in just over a year he wrote three of his greatest tragedies: *King Lear*, *Macbeth* and *Antony and Cleopatra*.

While the period immediately after *Hamlet* was a relatively lean one for his dramatic output, it was a rich one for his poetry, for Shakespeare kept writing, turning inwards once again to the lyric as a sounding board and source of inspiration. In 1601 he published the enigmatic poem that now goes by the name 'The Phoenix and Turtle' – the first poetry he had willingly seen into print since 1594. It's an elusive if not evasive poem, one that explores the metaphysical vein popularized by writers like John Donne, even as it hearkens back to older models like Sir Philip Sidney. There's also evidence that Shakespeare returned at this time to writing sonnets, including some of those in the sequence 104–26. He had enough confidence and experience to know that if the great press of plays wasn't there at this time, it would surely return.

Looking back on the year at Christmas time in 1599, Shakespeare must have recognized how much he had thrived on the highly charged political atmosphere of the past twelve months, when the nation had confronted everything from an 'Invisible Armada' and an ill-fated Irish campaign to the banning and burning of books and the silencing of preachers – experiences that had deepened his bond with an audience that had come to depend on the theatre to make sense of the world and had found in Shakespeare its most incisive interpreter. The year may have brought out the best in Shakespeare as an actor, too – unless we read too much into the scanty evidence that suggests that his two most memorable roles were Adam in *As You Like It* and the Ghost in *Hamlet*. At the end of 1598 Shakespeare had asked of his admirers, 'Bate me some and I will pay you some, and, as most debtors do, promise you infinitely.' He had been as good as his word. It would be the most decisive year of his career, one in which he redefined himself and his theatre.

Though his plays would last, the cultural preoccupations that had fuelled the drama of this year would not. When, a few years later, Michael Drayton needed an example of 'incertain times oft varying in their course' and 'how things still unexpectantly have run', England's recent history came immediately to mind. Almost overnight, it seemed, everything familiar to Elizabethans had been upended: 'mine eyes amazedly have seen', Drayton wrote,

> Essex' great fall, Tyrone his peace to gain,
> The quiet end of that long-living Queen,
> This King's fair entrance, and our peace with Spain,
> We and the Dutch at length ourselves to sever.
> (*Idea*, Sonnet 51)

Mountjoy had learned from his predecessor's mistakes and pursued a ruthless campaign of starving the Irish into submission – and Tyrone, with Ireland cruelly brought to its knees, capitulated, though the desire for Irish independence could not be crushed. In February 1601 Essex and his followers, knowing that they would never be restored to favour, belatedly committed themselves to action. The time for military revolt had passed. With that option gone, their alternatives were a palace coup (which meant overwhelming the guards at Whitehall, arresting Essex's enemies at court, and petitioning the Queen) or a London rising supported by the people. Essex, egged on by his more aggressive followers, and counting on a replay of the scene when adoring citizens had swarmed around him as he rode off to Ireland, chose the latter. Seeking inspiration on the eve of the revolt, Essex's supporters paid the Chamberlain's Men to stage Shakespeare's great deposition play, *Richard the Second*. As Essex and his loyal followers marched out of Essex House in the Strand through Ludgate into the City, they called on London's citizens to join them. The crowds that had quickly gathered looked at the unfolding scene in disbelief and decided that it was best to remain spectators. The revolt quickly collapsed. The Chamberlain's Men were called in to explain why they had staged 'the killing of Richard II'; they pleaded ignorance and were fortunate to escape punishment. The ill-conceived rising was Essex's last and greatest miscalculation. Elizabeth didn't flinch and on Ash Wednesday 1601, two years after Lancelot Andrewes's Lenten war sermon at Richmond, a repentant Essex had his head lopped off in the Tower of London. Like his father and grandfather before him, Essex had not made it past thirty-five.

Elizabeth did not long outlive Essex. The report ran that she 'sleepeth not so much by day as she used, neither taketh rest by night. Her delight is to sit in the dark and sometimes with shedding tears to bewail Essex.' The King of Scots' accession to the English throne in March 1603, carefully orchestrated by Cecil, went flawlessly, and for the first time in a half-century England was ruled by a king – and one with sons. Spain would never threaten invasion again.

For the next dozen or so years spectators continued to flock to the Globe to see their world 'perspectively' through Shakespeare's latest plays. His drama continued to register the effects of these seismic changes and anticipate those that would soon throw England into turmoil. Shakespeare died prematurely at age fifty-two, in 1616, so did not live to see the civil war that divided the nation, the public execution of King James's son and heir Charles I, the closing of London's theatres and the destruction of the Globe.

In his letter written from the court at the end of 1599 John Donne concluded witheringly that Essex 'understood not his age' and 'that such men want locks for themselves and keys for others'. The opposite may be said of Shakespeare. He understood his age perfectly, and the depth and profundity of that understanding which continued to draw contemporaries to his plays has ensured that we still read him and see these plays performed today in 'states unborn and accents yet unknown', as he prophetically put it in *Julius Caesar* (III, i, 114). More, perhaps, than any writer before or since, Shakespeare held the keys that opened the hearts and minds of others, even as he kept a lock on what he revealed about himself.

Bibliographical Essay

'He that undertaketh the story of a time, especially of any length,' Francis Bacon warned in his *Advancement of Learning* (London, 1605), 'cannot but meet with many blanks and spaces which he must be forced to fill up out of his own wit and conjecture.' I have often reflected on those words while writing this book; they remind me of how much I owe to the scholars whose work filled in enough blanks and spaces to allow me to undertake the story of a year in Shakespeare's life. What follows is at once an acknowledgement of that debt and a guide for those interested in consulting my sources directly. My model here is Susan Brigden's *New Worlds, Lost Worlds: The Rule of the Tudors, 1485–1603* (London, 2000), the best one-volume history of Tudor England available, whose bibliographical essay is exemplary in addressing the needs of both academic and general readers. Before turning to the specific sources on which I've drawn in individual chapters, it's helpful to list the principal ones for Shakespeare's life, Elizabethan theatre, and sixteenth-century English (and Irish) history. Anyone following in my tracks should turn to these works first.

Principal Sources

SHAKESPEARE'S LIFE

The bare facts of Shakespeare's life have been collected in a few key sources: E. K. Chambers, *William Shakespeare: A Study of Facts and Problems*, 2 vols. (Oxford, 1930) and S. Schoenbaum, *William Shakespeare: A Documentary Life* (Oxford, 1975). J. O. Halliwell-Phillipps, *Outlines of the Life of Shakespeare* (11th impression; London, 1907) is still useful. More

375

recent discoveries can be found in David Thomas, ed., *Shakespeare in the Public Records* (London, 1985); and Robert Bearman, ed., *Shakespeare in the Stratford Records* (Stroud, Gloucestershire, 1994).

Relevant documents about Stratford-upon-Avon in Shakespeare's day can be located through James O. Halliwell, *A Descriptive Calendar of the Ancient Manuscripts and Records in the Possession of the Corporation of Stratford-upon-Avon* (London, 1863). See, too, the five published volumes of the *Minutes and Accounts of the Corporation of Stratford-upon-Avon and Other Records*, vols. 1–4 (Hertford, 1921–30), ed. Richard Savage and E. I. Fripp; and vol. 5 (Hertford, 1990), ed. Levi Fox, which stops at 1598. For Shakespeare in Stratford-upon-Avon and its environs, see: Edgar I. Fripp's several volumes: *Master Richard Quyny, Bailiff of Stratford-upon-Avon and Friend of William Shakespeare* (Oxford, 1924); *Shakespeare's Stratford* (Oxford, 1928); S*hakespeare's Haunts Near Stratford* (Oxford, 1929); and *Shakespeare: Man and Artist*, 2 vols. (Oxford, 1938); Charlotte Carmichael Stopes, *Shakespeare's Warwickshire Contemporaries* (rev. ed., Stratford-upon-Avon, 1907); as well as Mark Eccles's outstanding *Shakespeare in Warwickshire* (Madison, 1961). Two recent and valuable studies are Robert Bearman, ed., *The History of an English Borough: Stratford-upon-Avon 1196–1996* (Stroud, Gloucestershire, 1997); and Jeanne Jones, *Family Life in Shakespeare's England: Stratford-upon-Avon 1570–1630* (Stroud, Gloucestershire, 1996).

I have consulted a number of highly recommended biographies: Peter Thompson, *Shakespeare's Professional Career* (Cambridge, 1992); Park Honan, *Shakespeare: A Life* (Oxford, 1998); Katherine Duncan-Jones, *Ungentle Shakespeare* (London, 2001); Michael Wood, *In Search of Shakespeare* (London, 2003); Anthony Holden, *William Shakespeare: His Life and Work* (London, 1999); and Stanley Wells, *Shakespeare for All Time* (Oxford, 2003). Though not a biography, Jonathan Bate's *The Genius of Shakespeare* (New York, 1998) is also recommended and G. B. Harrison's *Shakespeare at Work, 1592–1603* (London, 1933) is still useful. Frank Kermode offers a brief, useful overview in *The Age of Shakespeare* (New York, 2004). Stephen Greenblatt's *Will in the World* (New York, 2004) only came out as I was making final revisions.

All too little of Shakespeare's London remains. In recreating its topography, I have relied on John Stow, *The Survey of London* (London, 1598;

1603); the latter edition is also available in a modern edition, C. L. Kingsford, ed. (Oxford, 1908; rpt. 1971). Lena Cowen Orlin, ed., *Material London, ca.1600* (Philadelphia, 2000) has also proved useful. I have been greatly aided by a pair of London Topographical Society publications: Adrian Prockter and Robert Taylor, eds., *The A to Z of Elizabethan London* (London, 1979) and Ann Saunders and John Schofield, eds., *Tudor London: A Map and a View* (London, 2001). See, too, Ida Darlington and James Howgego, *Printed Maps of London, circa 1553–1850* (London, 1964; rev. edn, 1979). E. H. Sugden, *A Topographical Dictionary to the Works of Shakespeare and His Fellow Dramatists* (Manchester, 1925) remains indispensable. For the calendar and times of sunrise and sunset I've relied on Gabriel Frend, *An Almanac and Prognostication for This Year of Our Lord Jesus Christ 1599* (London, 1599).

SHAKESPEARE'S PLAYS AND POEMS

Any study of Shakespeare's work begins with editions. The starting point for any researcher – once past the original quartos, octavos and folios – is H. H. Furness's multi-volume Victorian *Variorum Shakespeare*, supplemented by a superb trio of series: the Arden Shakespeare (both Arden 2 and Arden 3), The Oxford Shakespeare, and The New Cambridge Shakespeare. For the four plays Shakespeare was writing in 1599 I've relied heavily on the following editions: for *Henry the Fifth*, ed. Gary Taylor (Oxford, 1982); ed. T. W. Craik (London, 1995); and ed. Andrew Gurr (Cambridge, 1992), as well as Gurr's edition of the 1600 Quarto (Cambridge, 2000). For *Julius Caesar*: ed. H. H. Furness (Philadelphia, 1913); ed. Arthur Humphreys (Oxford, 1984); ed. Marvin Spevack (Cambridge, 1988); and ed. David Daniell (London, 1998). For *As You Like It*: ed. H. H. Furness (Philadelphia, 1890); ed. Agnes Latham (London, 1975); The New Variorum, ed. Richard Knowles (New York, 1977); ed. Alan Brissenden (Oxford, 1993); ed. Michael Hattaway (Cambridge, 2000); and ed. Juliet Dusinberre (London, 2005). And *Hamlet*: ed. H. H. Furness, 2 vols. (Philadelphia, 1877); ed. J. Dover Wilson (2nd ed., Cambridge, 1948); ed. Harold Jenkins (London, 1982); ed. Philip Edwards (Cambridge, 1985); and ed. G. R. Hibbard (Oxford, 1987). The multiple texts of *Hamlet* pose special problems, and, in addition to originals and facsimiles of the 1603, 1604/5, and 1623 texts, I've drawn on Paul Bertram and Bernice W. Kliman, eds., *The Three-Text Hamlet* (New York, 1988); Jesús Tronch-Pérez, ed., *A Synoptic 'Hamlet': A Critical Synoptic Edition of the Second Quarto and First Folio Texts of 'Hamlet'* (Valencia, 2002); Thomas Marc Parrott and Hardin Craig, eds., *The Tragedy of Hamlet: A Critical Edition of the Second Quarto* (Princeton, 1938); and Kathleen O. Irace, ed., *The First Quarto of Hamlet* (Cambridge, 1998). An indispensable account of textual issues, dating and chronology can be found in Stanley Wells and Gary Taylor, with John Jowett and William Montgomery, *William Shakespeare: A Textual Companion* (Oxford, 1987). For Shakespeare's poetry I've relied on Hyder Edwards Rollins's New Variorum edition of *The Poems* (Philadelphia, 1938); Stephen Booth, ed., *Shakespeare's Sonnets* (New Haven, 1977); John Roe, ed., *The Poems* (Cambridge, 1992); G. Blakemore Evans, ed. and Anthony Hecht intro., *The Sonnets* (Cambridge, 1996); Katherine Duncan-Jones, ed., *Shakespeare's Sonnets* (London, 1997), and most of all, Colin Burrow, ed., *The Complete Sonnets and Poems* (Oxford, 2002). I refer to other editions that I've consulted below when dealing with specific issues.

Except for *Hamlet*, quotations from Shakespeare's works are cited from David Bevington, ed., *The Complete Works of Shakespeare* (5th ed., New York, 2004). In the few instances where I disagree with his emendations, I've silently gone back to what appears in the early printed texts. Bevington, like other recent editors, modernizes Shakespeare's spelling and punctuation; I've done the same with Shakespeare's contemporaries throughout the book (and changed Bevington's American spelling and punctuation to British style to be consistent). All quotations from *Hamlet* are from the Second Quarto, unless the Folio or First Quarto texts are specified. Since Bevington reconstructs his *Hamlet* out of multiple texts, for Second Quarto and Folio quotations from the play, I've turned to Jesús Tronch-Pérez's excellent *A Synoptic 'Hamlet': A Critical Synoptic Edition of the Second Quarto and First Folio Texts of 'Hamlet'*, which allows readers to compare the two version in the most accessible way.

I've also relied on a number of valuable resources on Shakespeare's language and sources: Marvin Spevak, ed., *The Harvard Concordance to Shakespeare* (Cambridge, Mass., 1973); Geoffrey Bullough, ed., *Narrative and Dramatic Sources of Shakespeare*, 8 vols. (London, 1957–75); Kenneth

Muir, *Shakespeare's Sources* (London, 1957); and Stuart Gillespie, *Shakespeare's Books: A Dictionary of Shakespeare's Sources* (London, 2001). For the best one-volume resource, see Michael Dobson and Stanley Wells, eds., *The Oxford Companion to Shakespeare* (Oxford, 2001).

SHAKESPEARE ON STAGE AND IN PRINT

I couldn't have written this book without the remarkable scholarship in the past century on Shakespeare's stage. Still unsurpassed is E. K. Chambers, *The Elizabethan Stage*, 4 vols. (Oxford, 1923). I am deeply indebted to R. A. Foakes and R. T. Rickert, eds., *Henslowe's Diary* (London, 1961) for information about the culture of play-writing at the time. Carol Chillington Rutter, ed., *Documents of the Rose Playhouse* (Manchester, 1984) is also useful. Other major sources include: *Annals of English Drama, 975–1700*, eds. Alfred Harbage, S. Schoenbaum, and Sylvia Stoler Wagonheim (3rd edn, New York, 1989); G. E. Bentley, *The Jacobean and Caroline Stage*, 7 vols. (Oxford, 1941–1968); R. A. Foakes, *Illustrations of the English Stage, 1580–1642* (Stanford, 1985); and Herbert Berry, *Shakespeare's Playhouses* (New York, 1987). Relevant documents can also be found in *English Professional Theatre, 1530–1660*, Glynne Wickham, Herbert Berry and William Ingram, eds. (Cambridge, 2000).

I have also consulted Andrew Gurr's influential books: *The Shakespearean Stage 1574–1642* (Cambridge, 1970; 3rd edn, 1992); *Playgoing in Shakespeare's London* (Cambridge, 1987; 2nd edn, 1996); *The Shakespearian Playing Companies* (Oxford, 1996); and *The Shakespeare Company, 1594–1642* (Cambridge, 2004). No less helpful are Bernard Beckerman, *Shakespeare at the Globe 1599–1609* (New York, 1962); Roslyn Lander Knutson, *The Repertory of Shakespeare's Company, 1594–1613* (Fayetteville, 1991) and her *Playing Companies and Commerce in Shakespeare's Time* (Cambridge, 2001); John Astington, *English Court Theatre 1558–1642* (Cambridge, 1999); James P. Bednarz, *Shakespeare & the Poets' War* (New York, 2001); and the many helpful essays collected in John D. Cox and David Scott Kastan, eds., *A New History of Early English Drama* (New York, 1997). For information on boys' companies I've drawn on Michael Shapiro, *Children of the Revels: The Boys' Companies of Shakespeare's Time and Their Plays* (New York, 1977) and Reavley Gair, *The Children of Paul's:*

The Story of a Theatre Company, 1553–1608 (Cambridge, 1982). On Elizabethan *imprese*, tilts and tournaments, I've drawn on Alan Young, *Tudor and Jacobean Tournaments* (London, 1987). And for information about actors on the Elizabethan stage, see Edwin Nungezer's *A Dictionary of Actors* (New Haven, 1929), supplemented by Mark Eccles's four essays on 'Elizabethan Actors' in *Notes and Queries*, vols. 236–8 (1991–3).

Any discussion of Shakespeare in print begins with A. W. Pollard and G. R. Redgrave, eds., *A Short-Title Catalogue of Books Printed in England, Scotland, & Ireland and of English Books Printed Abroad, 1475–1640*, 2 vols. (2nd. edn, rev. London, 1976); Edward Arber, ed., *A Transcript of the Registers of the Company of Stationers of London 1554–1640*, 5 vols. (London, 1875–77); W. W. Greg, *A Companion to Arber. Being a Calendar of Documents in Edward Arber's 'Transcript of the Registers of the Company of Stationers of London'* (Oxford, 1967); and Greg's *A Bibliography of the English Printed Drama to the Restoration* (London, 1939). For important new studies, see Douglas A. Brooks, *From Playhouse to Printing House: Drama and Authorship in Early Modern England* (Cambridge, 2000); David Scott Kastan, *Shakespeare and the Book* (Cambridge, 2001); Andrew Murphy, *Shakespeare in Print: A History and Chronology of Shakespeare Publishing* (Cambridge, 2003); and Lukas Erne, *Shakespeare as Literary Dramatist* (Cambridge, 2003).

ELIZABETHAN LETTERS, JOURNALS AND STATE PAPERS

I have tried throughout to let Elizabethans speak for themselves. An invaluable source, one that I rely on at many points in the book, is *The Letters of John Chamberlain*, ed. Norman E. McClure, 2 vols. (Philadelphia, 1939). I've also had frequent occasion to quote from Sir John Harington's letters, collected in *Nugae Antiquae*, ed. T. Park, 2 vols. (London, 1804) and *The Letters and Epigrams of Sir John Harington*, ed. Norman E. McClure (Philadelphia, 1930). Another excellent contemporary source is the astrologer Simon Forman, especially his unpublished casebooks – Bodleian MS 195 and MS 219. I am deeply grateful to Robyn Adams for locating and transcribing the relevant casebook entries. For more on Forman, see Barbara Traister, *The Notorious Astrological Physician of London: Works and Days of Simon Forman* (Chicago, 2001).

Tourists and ambassadors are a major source of information, and I draw extensively on *Thomas Platter's Travels in England, 1599*, Clare Williams, ed. and trans. (London, 1937) as well as Hans Hecht, ed., *Thomas Platters des Jüngeren Englandfahrt im Jahre 1599* (Halle, 1929). Other insightful travellers include: *Paul Hentzner's Travels in England, During the Reign of Queen Elizabeth*, trans. Horace, late Earl of Orford (London, 1797); *The Diary of Baron Waldstein: A Traveller in Elizabethan England*, G. W. Groos, trans. and ed., (London, 1981); *De Maisse: A Journal of All That was Accomplished by Monsieur De Maisse Ambassador in England from King Henri IV to Queen Elizabeth Anno Domini 1597*, G. B. Harrison and B. A. Jones, trans. and eds., (London, 1931); the diary of Lupold von Wedel in Victor von Klarwill, ed., *Queen Elizabeth and Some Foreigners*, trans. T. H. Nash (London, 1928); and the 'Diary of the Journey of Philip Julius, Duke of Stettin-Pomerania, through England in the Year 1602', eds. Gottfried von Bülow and Wilfred Powell, *Transactions of the Royal Historical Society*, n. s. 6 (1892), 1–67.

Along with other historians of the period, I rely heavily on the collections of Arthur Collins, ed., *Letters and Memorials of State* (London, 1746); Thomas Birch, ed., *Memoirs of the Reign of Queen Elizabeth*, 2 vols. (London, 1754); and Edmund Sawyer, ed., *Memorials of Affairs of State in the Reigns of Q. Elizabeth and K. James I. Collected (Chiefly) from the Original Papers of the Right Honourable Sir Ralph Winwood*, 3 vols. (London 1725). Another important resource is John Nichols, ed., *The Progresses and Public Processions of Queen Elizabeth*, 3 vols. (London, 1823). See too the quirky but rich collection of E. M. Tenison, *Elizabethan England*, 12 vols., especially vol. 10 (1596–1598) and vol. 11 (1599–1601) (Royal Leamington Spa, 1953; 1956).

No history of this year would be possible without the carefully edited calendars of state papers. These, too, constitute a major source for my book and I draw on them freely, especially the *Calendar of State Papers Domestic, Elizabeth, 1598–1601*, ed. Mary Anne Everett Green (London, 1869); *Calendar of the State Papers Relating to Ireland, of the Reign of Elizabeth, 1599, April–1600, February*, ed. Ernest George Atkinson (London, 1899), and *Calendar of the State Papers Relating to Scotland and Mary, Queen of Scots, 1547–1603*, vol. 13, 1597–1603, part 1 (Edinburgh, 1969). I also quote from the *Calendar of State Papers, Colonial: East Indies 1513–1616*, ed. W. Noel Sansbury (London, 1862); *Calendar of Letters and State Papers Relating to English Affairs, Preserved in... the Archives of Simancas,* vol. 4, Elizabeth I, 1587–1603, ed. Martin A. S. Hume (London, 1899); and *Calendar of State Papers and Manuscripts, Relating to English Affairs, Existing in the Archives and Collections of Venice,* vol. 9, 1592–1603, ed. Horatio F. Brown (London, 1897).

Other official correspondence is taken from *Acts of the Privy Council,* vol. 29, 1598–1599, ed. John Roche Dasent (London, 1905). Unfortunately, Privy Council records for the crucial period of 22 April 1599 to 23 January 1600 have not survived. For Scottish affairs, see David Masson, ed., *Register of the Privy Council of Scotland,* vol. 4 (1599–1604) (Edinburgh, 1884). One of my most important sources for government policy is *H.M.C. Calendar of Manuscripts, Salisbury,* part 9, ed. R. A. Roberts (London, 1902). Other family papers include: *Calendar of the Carew Manuscripts, 1589–1600,* ed. J. S. Brewer and William Bullen (London, 1869); *H.M.C. 13th Report, Appendix, Part 4. The Manuscripts of Rye and Hereford Corporations* (London, 1892); *Calendar of the Manuscripts of the Most Honourable the Marquesses of Bath. Vol. 5. Talbot Dudley and Devereux Papers, 1533–1659,* ed. G. Dyfnallt Owen (London, 1980); *Report on the Manuscripts of Lord De L'Isle and Dudley Preserved at Penshurst Place,* vol. 2 (Sidney Papers), ed. C. L. Kingsford (London, 1934), and *The Manuscripts of His Grace The Duke of Rutland Preserved at Belvoir Castle,* vol. 1 (London, 1888). For the Earl of Essex's correspondence, see W. B. Devereux, ed., *Lives and Letters of the Devereux, Earls of Essex,* 2 vols. (London, 1853). And for how England was viewed from abroad, also see *Fugger News-Letters,* trans. Pauline de Chary (London, 1924) and the second series, ed. Victor von Klarwill and trans. L. S. R. Byrne (London, 1926). Royal proclamations are cited from *A Book Containing All Such Proclamations as Were Published during the Reign of the Late Queen Elizabeth,* ed. Humphrey Dyson (London, 1618). And for thumbnail sketches of major figures at court, Sir Robert Naunton's *Fragmenta Regalia: Or Observations on the Late Queen Elizabeth, Her Times, Her Favourites* (London, 1653) is unmatched.

ELIZABETHAN HISTORY

Three contemporary figures loom large here: William Camden, *History of the Princess Elizabeth* (London, 1630); John Speed, *The History of Great*

Britain (London, 1623); and John Stow, *The Annales of England* (London, 1601). Also useful is Thomas Wilson's 'The State of England, anno dom. 1600', ed. F. J. Fisher, in *Camden Miscellany*, Camden Third Series, vol. 52 (London, 1936). For pamphlets, see D. C. Collins, *A Handlist of News Pamphlets 1590–1610* (London, 1941); for woodcuts, see Arthur M. Hind, *Engravings in England in the Sixteenth and Seventeenth Centuries*, 3 vols. (Cambridge, 1952); and for ballads, see Andrew Clark, ed., *The Shirburn Ballads, 1585–1616* (Oxford, 1907).

For politics, economics and foreign affairs, in addition to Brigden's *New Worlds, Lost Worlds*, I've consulted John Guy, ed., *The Reign of Elizabeth I: Court and Culture in the Last Decade* (Cambridge, 1995), as well as his *Tudor England* (Oxford, 1988) and his essay, 'Monarchy and Counsel: Models of the State', in Patrick Collinson, ed., *The Sixteenth Century, 1485–1603* (Oxford, 2002), 113–42; D. M. Palliser, *The Age of Elizabeth: England Under the Later Tudors, 1547–1603* (London, 1983); F. J. Levy, *Tudor Historical Thought* (San Marino, 1967); Penry Williams, *The Later Tudors: England 1547–1603* (Oxford, 1995); Wallace T. MacCaffrey, *Elizabeth I: War and Politics, 1588–1603* (Princeton, 1992); R. B. Wernham, *The Return of the Armadas: The Last Years of the Elizabethan War Against Spain 1595–1603* (Oxford, 1994); *The Making of Elizabethan Foreign Policy, 1558–1603* (Berkeley, 1980); and *After the Armada: Elizabethan England and the Struggle for Western Europe, 1588–1595* (Oxford, 1984); Norman Jones, *The Birth of the Elizabethan Age: England in the 1560s* (Oxford, 1994); and Mervyn James, *Society, Politics and Culture. Studies in Early Modern England* (Cambridge, 1986). Edward P. Cheney, *A History of England: From the Defeat of the Armada to the Death of Elizabeth*, 2 vols. (New York, 1926) is still useful. And for information about who governed England, see Arthur F. Kinney, *Titled Elizabethans: A Directory of Elizabethan State and Church Officers and Knights, with Peers of England, Scotland, and Ireland, 1558–1603* (Hamden, Conn., 1973).

My understanding of the period's social history has been shaped by J. A. Sharpe, *Early Modern England: A Social History* (1987); Lawrence Stone's *The Family, Sex, and Marriage in England, 1500–1800* (New York, 1977) and *The Crisis of the Aristocracy, 1558–1641* (Oxford, 1965); David Cressy, *Birth, Marriage, and Death: Ritual, Religion, and the Life-Cycle in Tudor and Stuart England* (Oxford, 1997); Ian W. Archer, ed., *Religion,*

Politics, and Society in Sixteenth-Century England (Cambridge, 2003); and his *The Pursuit of Stability: Social Relations in London* (Cambridge, 1991); Steve Rappaport, *Worlds within Worlds: The Structure of Life in Sixteenth-Century London* (Cambridge, 1989); Peter Burke, 'Popular Culture in Seventeenth-Century London', in *The London Journal*, 3 (1977), 143–62; A. B. Appleby, *Famine in Tudor and Stuart England* (Stanford, 1978); A. L. Beier, *Masterless Men: The Vagrancy Problem in England 1560–1640* (London, 1985); Martin Ingram, *Church Courts, Sex and Marriage in England, 1570–1640* (Cambridge, 1987); and Paul Slack, *The Impact of Plague on Tudor and Stuart England* (London, 1985). G. B. Harrison, *A Last Elizabethan Journal, Being a Record of Those Things Most Talked of During the Years 1599–1603* (London, 1933) offers a chronological overview.

For post-Reformation religious history, see especially: John Strype, *Annals of the English Reformation*, 4 vols. (Oxford, 1824); Patrick Collinson, *The Elizabethan Puritan Movement* (London, 1963) and his 'William Shakespeare's Religious Inheritance and Environment', in *Elizabethan Essays* (London, 1994); Eamon Duffy, *The Stripping of the Altars: Traditional Religion in England c. 1400–c.1580* (New Haven, 1992); J. J. Scarisbrick, *The Reformation and the English People* (Oxford, 1984); Christopher Haigh, *The English Reformation Revised* (Cambridge 1987); David Cressy, *Bonfires and Bells: National Memory and the Protestant Calendar in Elizabethan and Stuart England* (London, 1989); and Ronald Hutton, *The Rise and Fall of Merry England: The Ritual Year 1400–1700* (Oxford, 1994).

Preface

My account of the sequence and dating of Shakespeare's plays in 1599 draws on the current critical consensus. Though there is not unanimity there is certainly more general agreement about these plays – because more information is available to help in dating – than about most of Shakespeare's works. Everyone agrees that all four plays were written after autumn 1598, when Francis Meres listed most of Shakespeare's extant plays in *Pallidis Tamia: Wit's Treasury* (London, 1598). The allusion to the Earl of Essex in the Chorus to Act V ('the General of our gracious Empress') has led almost all editors to place *Henry the Fifth* in the first half of 1599. Platter saw *Julius Caesar* at the Globe in September 1599, and scholars have concluded that it was written in the spring or summer of that year. Along with *Henry the Fifth* and two plays from 1598 – Ben Jonson's *Every Man In His Humour* and Shakespeare's *Much Ado About Nothing* – *As You Like It* appeared in a special entry in the Register of the Stationers' Company on 4 August 1600 with the instruction 'to be stayed' (delayed, or perhaps even stopped, though there is little consensus about this puzzling document). Some critics date it to early 1599, others to early 1600. The departure of Kemp and arrival of Armin in Shakespeare's company and the appearance in the play of a song that was probably prepared for print in 1599 (during 'vacation time') by the composer Thomas Morley and appeared in 1600 in Morley's *First Book of Ayres* lend support for a date in late 1599, after *Henry the Fifth* and *Julius Caesar*. For the dating of *Hamlet* (at least the early version that was the basis of the Second Quarto) in late 1599, see Harold Jenkins's edition, along with E. A. J. Honigmann, 'The Date of *Hamlet*', *Shakespeare Survey*, 9 (1956), 24–34. More recent support for this position, based on the influence of *Hamlet* on contemporary plays, can be found in Charles Cathcart, '*Hamlet*: Date and Early Afterlife', *Review of English Studies* 52 (2001), 341–59. The chapters that follow will provide more extended support, some of it internal, some historical, some having to do with casting, for the dating and sequence that I offer. It's probable that Shakespeare was thinking about (and perhaps even sketching out) more than one of these plays at the same time, given the extent to which they allude to and are in conversation with each other. For a useful overview of sequence and dating, see Wells and Taylor, *A Textual Companion*.

A word about what constitutes the beginning and ending of a year is also in order. From the late twelfth century until 1752 the civil or legal year in England officially began on Lady Day, 25 March – the day commemorating the Annunciation, nine months before the Nativity. But this was not universally followed: almanacs, for instance, began on 1 January. While some Elizabethan writers and publishers treated 1 January as the start of the New Year, others did not. By 1600 almost all of Europe and even Scotland had switched back to beginning the year on 1 January (only Russia, Tuscany and England and her colonies held out until the eighteenth century).

Dating problems are compounded by another difference between England and most of the Continent, for England did not switch from the Julian to the Gregorian calendar until 1752 – which meant that during Shakespeare's lifetime there was a ten-day difference between the date in, say, France and England. So that when Thomas Platter, who seems to have mistakenly assumed that England was on the Gregorian calendar, recorded that he saw a production of *Julius Caesar* in London on 21 September 1599, the actual date in England was 11 September. I have silently adjusted this and other instances to conform to what the date would have been in Shakespeare's England. Needless to say, legal dating overlaid other calendrical rhythms: the four seasons, the church year, the court calendar, the theatrical seasons, the regnal year, the schedule of the law courts and, most of all, the cycle of the agricultural year. These, in turn, competed with personal ones (birthdays, deaths of loved ones, various anniversaries, and so on).

For a devastating critique of biographies that read a romanticized version of the life into the work (from which I've drawn my quotations from Coleridge and Delius, the unnamed nineteenth-century author), see C. J. Sisson, 'The Mythical Sorrows of Shakespeare', Annual Shakespeare Lecture of the British Academy, 1934, from the *Proceeding of the British Academy*, vol. 20 (London, 1934); and for a companion piece that exposes romanticizing tendencies in discussions of possible portraits of Shakespeare, see Stephen Orgel's 'History and Biography' in his *Imagining Shakespeare: A History of Texts and Visions* (New York, 2003), 65–84. I've consulted Edmond Malone's 'An Attempt to Ascertain the Order in Which the Plays of Shakespeare Were Written', first published in 1778, in the version published in the first volume of his edition of *The Plays and Poems of William Shakespeare*, 16 vols. (Dublin, 1794).

For Platter's comment, see *Thomas Platter's Travels in England, 1599*. For the observations of Ben Jonson, John Ward and John Aubrey – and for contemporary allusions throughout – see volume 2 of E. K. Chambers, *William Shakespeare: Facts and Problems*.

Prologue

For the weather and box-office accounts, see Stow, *Annales* and Henslowe's *Diary*. England was colder by a few degrees in Shakespeare's day, experiencing, like much of Europe, what scientists refer to as a 'little ice age'. For accounts of the building of the Globe, see, in addition to Halliwell-Phillipps, *Outlines of the Life of Shakespeare*: Charles W. Wallace, *The First London Theatre: Materials for a History* (Lincoln, Nebraska, 1913); Irwin Smith, 'Theatre into Globe', *Shakespeare Quarterly*, 3 (1952), 113–20; Herbert Berry, ed., *The First Public Playhouse: The Theatre in Shoreditch* (Montreal, 1979); and Charlotte Carmichael Stopes, *Burbage and Shakespeare's Stage* (London, 1913).

On the number of playgoers, see Appendix II to Martin Butler, *Theatre and Crisis, 1632–1642* (Cambridge, 1984). The names of playwrights in Henslowe's records for 1598 (plus Shakespeare's) are corroborated in Francis Meres's *Palladis Tamia* (London, 1598). Among 'the best for tragedy', Meres includes Shakespeare, Drayton, Chapman, Dekker and Jonson; and the 'best for comedy' include Shakespeare, Heywood, Munday, Chapman, Porter, Wilson, Hathaway and Chettle. Meres also praises the Earl of Oxford's comedies; but while there's limited evidence that other aristocrats flirted with play-writing (Fulke Greville wrote sensitive closet drama at this time and the Earl of Derby wrote some comedies in the summer of 1599 for the company he patronized at the Boars' Head Inn), there's no evidence that Oxford, Derby or other noblemen were ever part of what was necessarily a tight-knit group of practising playwrights.

On topicality in Shakespeare's plays, see David Bevington, *Tudor Drama and Politics* (Cambridge, Mass., 1968); Robert J. Fehrenbach, 'When Lord Cobham and Edmund Tilney "were att odds": Oldcastle, Falstaff, and the Date of *1 Henry IV*', *Shakespeare Studies*, 9 (1986), 87–102; Barbara Freedman, 'Shakespearean Chronology, Ideological Complicity, and Floating Texts: Something is Rotten in Windsor', *Shakespeare Quarterly*, 45 (1994), 190–210; and Gary Taylor, 'William Shakespeare, Richard James and the House of Cobham', *Review of English Studies*, 38 (1987), 334–54. For more on Cobham, see especially David McKeen, A *Memory of Honour: The Life of William Brook, Lord Cobham*, 2 vols. (Salzburg, 1986); Paul Whitefield White, 'Shakespeare, the Cobhams, and the Dynamics of Theatrical Patronage', in *Shakespeare and Theatrical Patronage in Early Modern England*, ed. Paul Whitefield White and Suzanne R. Westfall (Cambridge, 2002), 64–89; and James P. Bednarz, 'Biographical Politics: Shakespeare, Jonson, and the Oldcastle Controversy', in *Ben Jonson Journal*, 11 (2004), 1–20.

The standard authorities on Elizabethan censorship are Richard Dutton's two books, *Mastering the Revels: The Regulation and Censorship of English Renaissance Drama* (Iowa City, 1991), and *Licensing, Censorship, and Authorship in Early Modern England* (New York, 2000); and Janet Clare, *'Art made tongue-tied by authority': Elizabethan and Jacobean Dramatic Censorship* (Manchester, 1990). See too, Andrew Hadfield, ed., *Literature and Censorship in Renaissance England* (New York, 2001).

On Shakespeare and patronage, in addition to the many fine essays in *Shakespeare and Theatrical Patronage in Early Modern England*, ed. Paul Whitefield White and Suzanne R. Westfall, see Peter Davison, 'Commerce and Patronage: The Lord Chamberlain's Men's Tour of 1597', in Grace Ioppolo, ed., *Shakespeare Performed: Essays in Honour of R. A. Foakes* (Newark, 2000), 56–71; Charlotte Carmichael Stopes, *The Life of Henry, Third Earl of Southampton, Shakespeare's Patron* (Cambridge, 1922); and G. P. V. Akrigg, *Shakespeare and the Earl of Southampton* (London, 1968). On the Shakespeare coat of arms, see C. W. Scott-Giles, *Shakespeare's Heraldry* (London, 1950), Chambers, *Facts and Problems*, as well as Katherine Duncan-Jones, *Ungentle Shakespeare*. On the playwrights and their collaboration, in addition to Henslowe's *Diary* and Rutter's *Documents of the Rose Playhouse*, see: J. M. Nosworthy, 'Notes on Henry Porter', *Modern Language Review*, 35 (1940), 517–21; and Leslie Hotson, 'The Adventure of the Single Rapier', *Atlantic Monthly*, 148 (1931), 26–31. On Philip Henslowe, see Bernard Beckerman, 'Philip Henslowe', in Joseph W. Donohue Jr., ed., *The Theatrical Manager in England and America*. (Princeton, 1971), as well as S. P. Cerasano, 'The Patronage Network of Philip Henslowe and Edward Alleyn', *Medieval and Renaissance Drama in England* 13 (2000), 82–92.

1 A Battle of Wills

For Whitehall Palace's architecture and treasures, I have drawn on the detailed accounts of Platter, Hentzner, Waldheim and other foreign tourists, as well as Simon Thurley, *Whitehall Palace: An Architectural History of the Royal Apartments, 1240–1698* (New Haven, 1999) and his *The Royal Palaces of Tudor England* (New Haven, 1993); Ian Dunlop, *The Palaces and Progresses of Elizabeth I* (London, 1962); Sir Oliver Millar, *The*

Inventories and Valuations of the King's Goods 1649–51 (London, 1972) and his *Tudor, Stuart, and Early Georgian Pictures in the Collection of H.M. the Queen* (London, 1963); G. S. Dugdale, *Whitehall through the Centuries* (London, 1950); The London County Council *Survey of London*, The Parish of St Margaret, Westminster – Part II, vol. 1, Neighbourhood of Whitehall (London, 1930); and Henry Glapthorne's little known but wonderful *White-Hall: A Poem* (London, 1643). On Elizabeth's movement from palace to palace, see Nichols, ed., *The Progresses and Public Processions of Queen Elizabeth*, as well as John Astington, *English Court Theatre* and Mary Hill Cole, *The Portable Queen: Elizabeth I and the Politics of Ceremony* (Amherst, 1999).

For Shakespeare's relationship with Kemp, I draw heavily on David Wiles, *Shakespeare's Clown: Actor and Text in the Elizabethan Playhouse* (Cambridge, 1987). See too Kemp's own *Kemp's Nine Days Wonder: Performed in a Dance from London to Norwich* (London, 1600); as well as H. D. Gray, 'The Roles of William Kemp', *Modern Language Review*, 25 (1930), 261–73; Joseph Allen Bryant, Jr., 'Shakespeare's Falstaff and the Mantle of Dick Tarlton', *Studies in Philology*, 51 (1954), 149–62; George Walton Williams, 'The Text of *2 Henry IV*: Facts and Problems', *Shakespeare Studies*, 9 (1976), 173–82; John Dover Wilson, *The Fortunes of Falstaff* (Cambridge, 1943); and Leslie Hotson, *Shakespeare's Sonnets Dated and Other Essays* (New York, 1949). For the jig, see Charles R. Baskervill, *The Elizabethan Jig* (Chicago, 1929). For the reference to the chanting of Kemp's jig, see Satire 5 in Everard Guilpin, *Skialetheia* (1598), ed. D. Allen Carroll (Chapel Hill, 1974). See, too, Melissa D. Aaron, 'The Globe and *Henry V* as Business Document', *Studies in English Literature*, 40 (2000), 277–92. For the anecdote about Shakespeare, Burbage and the citizen's wife, see *The Diary of John Manningham*, Robert Parker Sorlein, ed. (Hanover, New Hampshire, 1976).

For the revised epilogue to the *Second Part of Henry the Fourth*, I've consulted A. R. Humphries, ed., *The Second Part of King Henry IV* (London, 1966); Giorgio Melchiori, *The Second Part of King Henry IV* (Cambridge, 1989); René Weis, *Henry IV, Part 2* (Oxford, 1998); and Matthias A. Shaaber, ed., *A New Variorum Edition of Shakespeare: The Second Part of Henry the Fourth* (Philadelphia, 1940). Despite the long-standing editorial consensus that the epilogue as printed contains either two or three distinct speeches (and the suggestion by older editors that one of the speakers was Shakespeare himself), critics and biographers of Shakespeare have ignored its significance.

2 A Great Blow in Ireland

For Essex's Apology, see Robert Devereux, Second Earl of Essex, *An Apology of the Earl of Essex ... Penned by Himself, in Anno 1598* (London, 1603). For Essex's poetry, see Steven W. May, *The Elizabethan Courtier Poets: The Poems and Their Contexts* (Columbia, 1991) as well as his 'The Poems of Edward DeVere, Seventeenth Earl of Oxford, and of Robert Devereux, Second Earl of Essex', *Studies in Philology* (1980). The standard work on Essex at court is Paul E. J. Hammer, *The Polarization of Elizabethan Politics: The Political Career of Robert Devereux, 2nd Earl of Essex, 1585–1597* (Cambridge, 1999). Older biographical accounts of Essex include E. A. Abbott, *Bacon and Essex* (London 1877); G. B. Harrison, *The Life and Death of Robert Devereux, Earl of Essex* (New York, 1937); Robert Lacey, *Robert, Earl of Essex* (New York, 1971); and Lacey Baldwin Smith, *Treason in Tudor England* (London, 1986). Lytton Strachey's wonderfully engaging though dated *Elizabeth and Essex* (London, 1928) is still worth reading.

For the life of Elizabeth I, I have drawn on Carole Levin, *'The Heart and Stomach of a King': Elizabeth I and the Politics of Sex and Power* (Philadelphia, 1994); Susan Frye, *Elizabeth I: The Competition for Representation* (Oxford, 1993); Clark Hulse, *Elizabeth I: Ruler and Legend* (Urbana, 2003); Georgianna Ziegler, ed., *Elizabeth I: Then and Now* (Washington, DC, 2003); David Loades, *Elizabeth I* (London, 2003); Alison Plowden, *Elizabeth Regina: The Age of Triumph, 1588–1603* (London, 1980); and Julia M. Walker, ed., *Dissing Elizabeth: Negative Representations of Gloriana* (Durham, 1998). For her writings, see *Elizabeth I, Collected Works*, eds. Leah S. Marcus, Janel Mueller, and Mary Beth Rose (Chicago, 2000) and G. B. Harrison, ed., *The Letters of Queen Elizabeth I* (Westport, Conn., 1981).

For the careers of Burghley and his son Robert Cecil, see Conyers Read, *Lord Burghley and Queen Elizabeth* (New York, 1960) and his *Mr. Secretary Cecil and Queen Elizabeth* (New York, 1955), as well as Michael

A. R. Graves, *Burghley: William Cecil, Lord Burghley* (London, 1998). And for the Lord Admiral's life, see Robert W. Kenny, *Elizabeth's Admiral: The Political Career of Charles Howard, Earl of Nottingham 1536-1624* (Baltimore, 1970).

The literature on Elizabethan Ireland is vast. For contemporary accounts on which I draw, in addition to Acts of the Privy Council and various State Papers for England and Ireland, see: Sir James Perrott, *The Chronicle of Ireland 1584-1608*, ed. Herbert Wood (Dublin, 1933); Fynes Morison, *An Itinerary* (London, 1617; rpt., 4 vols., Glasgow, 1907); William Farmer, 'Annals of Ireland from the Year 1594 to 1613', ed. C. Litton Falkiner, *English Historical Review*, 22 (1907), 104-30; 527-52; Robert Payne, *A Brief Description of Ireland* (1589), rpt. in *Irish Archeological Society*, 1 (1841), 1-14; John Dimmok, *A Treatice of Ireland*, transcribed by J. C. Halliwell, ed. Richard Butler, *Irish Archeological Society*, (Dublin, 1842), 1-90; Anon., *The Supplication of the Blood of the English Most Lamentably Murdered in Ireland* (1598), ed. Willy Maley, *Analecta Hibernica*, 36 (1994), 3-91; vol. 6 of John O'Donovan, ed., *Annals of the Kingdom of Ireland by the Four Masters* (Dublin,1856; 3rd edn, rpt. 1990); M. J. Byrne, trans., *The Irish War of Defence 1598-1600: Extracts from the 'De Hibernia Insula Commenatarius' of Peter Lombard, Archbishop of Armagh* (Cork, 1930); M. J. Byrne, ed. and trans., *Ireland Under Elizabeth: Chapters Towards a History of Ireland in the Reign of Elizabeth. Being a Portion by Don Philip O'Sullivan Bear* (Dublin, 1903); and Thomas Gainsford, *The True and Exemplary and Remarkable Life of the Earle of Tirone* (London, 1619).

For modern discussions of Elizabethan Ireland, see David B. Quinn's *The Elizabethans and the Irish* (Ithaca, 1966) as well as his '"A Discourse on Ireland" (circa 1599): A Sidelight on English Colonial Policy', *Proceedings of the Royal Irish Academy*, 47 (1942): 151-66; Alfred O'Rahilly, *The Massacre at Smerwick (1580)* (Cork, 1938); Nicholas Canny, *Making Ireland British 1580-1650* (Oxford, 2001); John McGurk, *The Elizabethan Conquest of Ireland: The 1590s Crisis* (Manchester, 1997); Lindsay Boynton, *The Elizabethan Militia: 1558-1638* (London, 1967); Anthony J. Sheehan, 'The Overthrow of the Plantation of Munster in October 1598', *The Irish Sword*, 15 (1982-3), 11-22; Richard Bagwell, *Ireland under the Tudors* (London, 1890); Andrew Hadfield, '"The Naked and the Dead": Elizabethan Perceptions of Ireland', in *Travel and Drama in Shakespeare's Time*, ed.

Jean-Pierre Maquerlot and Michèle Willems (Cambridge, 1996), 32–54; and Brendan Bradshaw, Andrew Hadfield and Willy Maley, eds., *Representing Ireland: Literature and the Origins of Conflict, 1534–1660* (Cambridge, 1993).

For the military background of Essex's campaign, see especially L. W. Henry, 'Contemporary Sources for Essex's Lieutenancy in Ireland, 1599', *Irish Historical Studies*, 11 (1958-59), 8–17; Cyril Falls, *Elizabeth's Irish Wars* (London, 1950); C. G. Cruickshank, *Elizabeth's Army* (2nd edn, Oxford, 1966); Hiram Morgan, *Tyrone's Rebellion: The Outbreak of the Nine Years War in Tudor Ireland* (Suffolk, 1993); G. A. Hayes-McCoy, 'The Army of Ulster, 1593–1601', *The Irish Sword*, 1 (1949–53), 105–17; and Paul E. J. Hammer, *Elizabeth's Wars: War, Government and Society in Tudor England, 1544–1604* (New York, 2003). For military conscription from the public playhouses in 1602, see Isaac Herbert Jeayes, ed., *The Letters of Philip Gawdy* (London, 1906).

3 Burial at Westminster

For Westminster Abbey itself and Henry V's tomb, see Arthur Penrhyn Stanley, *Historical Memorials of Westminster Abbey*, 2 vols. (5th edn, New York, 1882); Lawrence E. Tanner, *The History and Treasures of Westminster Abbey* (London, 1953); and James Hamilton Wylie, *The Reign of Henry the Fifth*, 2 vols. (Cambridge, 1919).

On Edmund Spenser's life, his writings about Ireland, and his death and funeral in London, see: *The Works of Edmund Spenser: A Variorum Edition*, ed. Edwin Greenlaw, Charles Grosvenor Osgood, Frederick Morgan Padelford and Ray Heffner, 11 vols. (Baltimore, 1932–49); Edmund Spenser, *A View of the State of Ireland*, eds. Andrew Hadfield and Willy Maley (Oxford, 1997); Alexander C. Judson, *The Life of Edmund Spenser* (Baltimore, 1945); Richard Rambuss, 'Spenser's Lives, Spenser's Careers', in *Spenser's Life and the Subject of Biography*, eds. Judith H. Anderson, Donald Cheney, and David A. Richardson (Amherst, 1996), 1–17; Willy Maley, *A Spenser Chronology* (London, 1994) and his *Salvaging Spenser: Colonialism, Culture and Identity* (New York, 1997); Andrew Hadfield, *Edmund Spenser's Irish Experience: Wilde Fruit and Salvage Soyl* (Oxford, 1997); A. C. Hamilton, ed., *The Spenser Encyclopedia*

(Toronto, 1990); Herbert Berry and E. K. Timings, 'Spenser's Pension', *Review of English Studies*, n.s. 2 (1960), 254–9; Roderick L. Eagle, 'The Search for Spenser's Grave', *Notes & Queries*, 201 (1956), 282–3; Lisa Jardine, 'Encountering Ireland: Gabriel Harvey, Edmund Spenser, and English Colonial Adventures', in *Representing Ireland*, 60–75; and William Wells, ed., *Spenser Allusions in the Sixteenth and Seventeenth Centuries*, compiled by Ray Heffner, Dorothy E. Mason, and Frederick M. Padelford (Chapel Hill, 1972).

For Shakespeare's relation to Spenser, see vol. 2 of Edmond Malone, *The Plays and Poems of William Shakespeare* (London, 1821); the entry in *The Spenser Encyclopedia*; James P. Bednarz, 'Imitations of Spenser in *A Midsummer Night's Dream*', *Renaissance Drama*, 14 (1983), 79–102; and Patrick Cheney, 'Shakespeare's Sonnet 106, Spenser's National Epic, and Counter-Petrarchism', *English Literary History*, 31 (2001), 331–64. Christopher Highley, *Shakespeare, Spenser, and the Crisis in Ireland* (Cambridge, 1997) and David J. Baker, *Between Nations: Shakespeare, Spenser, Marvell, and the Question of Britain* (Stanford, 1997) are also helpful.

4 A Sermon at Richmond

For Richmond Palace, in addition to traveller accounts, I have drawn on Simon Thurley, *The Royal Palaces of Tudor England*; Ian Dunlop, *Palaces and Progresses of Elizabeth I*; and Stephen Pasmore's Richmond Local Historical Society Paper, *The Life and Times of Queen Elizabeth I at Richmond Palace* (London, 1992).

For the epilogue itself, see William A. Ringler and Steven W. May, 'An Epilogue Possibly by Shakespeare', *Modern Philology*, 70 (1972), 138–9. It was discovered in 1972, when Steven May came upon it in the commonplace book of Henry Stanford, who served the Lord Chamberlain. See, too, Steven W. May, ed., *Henry Stanford's Anthology* (New York, 1988); and Juliet Dusinberre, 'Pancakes and a Date for *As You Like It*', *Shakespeare Quarterly*, 54 (2003), 371–405. On Elizabethan dramatic prologues and epilogues, see Tiffany Stern, '"A small-beer-health to his second day": Playwrights, Prologues, and First Performances in the Early Modern Theater,' *Studies in Philology*, 101 (2004), 172–99.

On transportation from Richmond to London: the experience of

Thomas Platter, who visited Richmond with some friends in October 1599, showed that it was possible to return in an afternoon. Platter's party had arrived at Richmond by coach. Platter writes that his party was 'invited to lunch at court. But we were afraid we should be kept too long and unable to return to London the same day as we desired, we made our excuses and took our lunch in the village in an inn. After the meal we returned by coach quietly back to London to our former hostelry.' It would not have taken any longer for Shakespeare and his fellow shareholders to return to London in the afternoon.

On Lancelot Andrewes, see his *Ninety-Six Sermons* (London, 1629); vol. II of J. P. Wilson and James Bliss, *The Works of Lancelot Andrewes* II vols. (London, 1841–54); F. O. White, *Lives of the Elizabethan Bishops* (London, 1898); and Paul A. Welsby, *Lancelot Andrewes, 1555–1626* (London, 1958). On preaching at court, including Rudd's sermons to Elizabeth, see Peter E. McCullough's excellent *Sermons at Court: Politics and Religion in Elizabethan and Jacobean Preaching* (Cambridge, 1998).

5 Band of Brothers

For the practice of affixing playbills to posts, see the Prologue to *A Warning for Fair Women* (London, 1599). For how plays were advertised, see Tiffany Stern's forthcoming *The Fragmented Playtext in Shakespearean England*. For the text and a discussion of Shakespeare's debt to the anonymous *The Famous Victories of Henry the Fifth*, see Peter Corbin and Douglas Sedge, eds., *The Oldcastle Controversy: 'Sir John Oldcastle, Part I' and 'The Famous Victories of Henry V'* (Manchester, 1991).

For Shakespeare's *Henry the Fifth* and Ireland, see, in addition to Gary Taylor's edition of the play: Andrew Murphy, 'Shakespeare's Irish History', *Literature and History*, 5 (1996), 38–59; D. Plunckett Barton, *Links Between Ireland and Shakespeare* (Dublin, 1919); Joel B. Altman, '"Vile Participation": The Amplification of Violence in the Theatre of *Henry V*', *Shakespeare Quarterly*, 42 (1991), 1–32; Michael Neill, 'Broken English and Broken Irish: Nation, Language, and the Optic of Power in Shakespeare's Histories', in *Putting History to the Question* (New York, 2000), 339–72; Nick de Somogyi, *Shakespeare's Theatre of War* (Aldershot, 1998); Charles Edelman, *Shakespeare's Military Language: A Dictionary* (London, 2000);

Anthony Dawson, 'The Arithmetic of Memory: Shakespeare's Theatre and the National Past', *Shakespeare Survey*, 52 (1999), 54–67; Jonathan Baldo, 'Wars of Memory in *Henry V*, *Shakespeare Quarterly*, 47 (1996), 132–59; Harold H. Davis, 'The Military Career of Thomas North', *Huntington Library Quarterly*, 12 (1949), 315–21; Paul A. Jorgensen, *Shakespeare's Military World* (Berkeley, 1956); Mark Thornton Burnett and Ramona Wray's collection, *Shakespeare and Ireland: History, Politics, Culture* (Basingstoke, 1997), especially Andrew Murphy, ""Tish Ill Done",: *Henry the Fifth* and the Politics of Editing', 213–34. And for 'Calen o Custore me', see Clement Robinson, *A Handful of Pleasant Delights* (London, 1584). On textual issues and censorship, see Annabel Patterson, 'Back by Popular Demand: The Two Versions of *Henry V*, *Renaissance Drama*, 19 (1988), 29–62. See, too, John Norden, *A Prayer for the Prosperous Proceedings and Good Success of the Earle of Essex and His Companies, in Their Present Expedition in Ireland against Tyrone* (London, 1599); and for John Florio's dictionary entry, see his *Queen Anne's New World of Words* (London, 1611).

The story of Lewis Gilbert, who returned maimed from the Irish wars, is summarized in James O. Halliwell, *A Descriptive Calendar of the Ancient Manuscripts and Records in the Possession of the Corporation of Stratford-upon-Avon*. Additional records detailing his fate can be found in the Stratford Archives: BRU 15/12 and BRU 15/5.

6 The Globe Rises

For Southwark and the liberties in Shakespeare's day, in addition to Stow's *Survey of London*, see: H. E. Malden, ed., *The Victoria History of the Counties of England: Surrey*, vol. 4 (London, 1912); Steven Mullaney, *The Place of the Stage* (Chicago, 1988); Jeremy Boulton, *Neighbourhood and Society: A London Suburb in the Seventeenth Century* (Cambridge, 1987); and David J. Johnson, *Southwark and the City* (London, 1969). For Shakespeare's move to Bankside, see Chambers, *Facts and Problems* and Michael Wood, *In Search of Shakespeare*. There's a possibility that Shakespeare may have lived further west on Bankside at some point after 1596, perhaps near Paris Garden, or if a lost document viewed by Malone is right, near the Bear Garden; if so, it would have meant a considerable commute to the Theatre.

On the location and archaeology of the Globe, see: W. W. Braines, *The Site of the Globe Playhouse, Southwark* (2nd edn, London, 1924); Sir Howard Roberts and Walter H. Godfrey, eds., *Survey of London: Bankside*, vol. 22 (London, 1950). Simon Blatherwick and Andrew Gurr, 'Shakespeare's Factory: Archaeological Evaluations on the Site of the Globe Theatre at 1/15 Anchor Terrace, Southwark Bridge Road, Southwark', *Antiquity*, 66 (1992), 315–33; along with Blatherwick's three subsequent articles, 'The Archaeological Evaluation of the Globe Playhouse', in J. R. Mulryne and Margaret Shewring, eds., *Shakespeare's Globe Rebuilt* (Cambridge, 1997), 67–80; 'Archaeology Update: Four Playhouses and the Bear Garden', *Shakespeare Studies*, 30 (2002), 74–83; and 'The Archaeology of Entertainment: London's Tudor and Stuart Playhouses', in *London Under Ground: The Archaeology of a City*, ed. I. Haynes, H. Sheldon and L. Hannigan (Oxford, 2000), 252–71. On the Bankside communities near the theatres, see William Ingram, '"Neere the Playe House": The Swan Theatre and Community Blight', in *Renaissance Drama*, n.s. 4 (1971), 53–68, as well as his 'The Globe Playhouse and Its Neighbours in 1600', *Essays in Theatre*, 2 (1984), 63–72.

On the Globe's design, the study of which has first been driven by plans to build a replica on Bankside and then by the recent rediscovery of the foundations of the Rose and the Globe, see: John Cranford Adams, *The Globe Playhouse: Its Design and Equipment* (Cambridge, Mass., 1942); John Orrell, *The Human Stage: English Theatre Design, 1567–1640* (Cambridge, 1988); *The Design of the Globe*, ed. Andrew Gurr, Ronnie Mulryne and Margaret Shewring (International Globe Centre, 1993); J. R. Mulryne and Margaret Shewring, eds., *Shakespeare's Globe Rebuilt* (Cambridge, 1997); Franklin J. Hildy, '"If You Build It They Will Come": The Reconstruction of Shakespeare's Globe Gets Underway on the Bankside in London', *Shakespeare Bulletin*, 10 (1992), 5–9; and Gabriel Egan, 'Reconstructions of the Globe: A Retrospective', *Shakespeare Survey*, 52 (1999), 1–16. John Gleason's 'New Questions about the Globe', *Times Literary Supplement* (26 September 2003), 15, draws on new scientific data to revise earlier claims about the dimensions of the Globe. For a speculative account of when the Globe opened, see Steve Sohmer, *Shakespeare's Mystery Play: The Opening of the Globe Theatre, 1599* (Manchester, 1999).

On how the Globe was constructed, see Balthazar Gerbier, *Counsel and Advise to All Builders* (London, 1663), a richly informative account of early modern building practices; Irwin Smith, 'Theatre into Globe'; John Orrell, 'Building the Fortune', *Shakespeare Quarterly*, 44 (1993), 127–44; and Mary Edmond, 'Peter Street, 1553–1609: Builder of Playhouses', *Shakespeare Survey*, 45 (1992), 101–14. For John Wolfe's plans to build a theatre, see *Middlesex County Records*, ed. John Cordy Jeaffreson, vol.1 (London, 1878).

7 Book Burning

In addition to Dutton's essay on Hayward in *Licensing, Censorship, and Authorship in Early Modern England* (and Dutton and Clare's work on censorship in general), see, for the Bishops' Ban in particular, Richard A. McCabe, 'Elizabethan Satire and the Bishops' Ban of 1599', in *Yearbook of English Studies*, 11 (1981), 188–93 and Linda Boose, 'The 1599 Bishops' Ban, Elizabethan Pornography, and the Sexualization of the Jacobean State', in Richard Burt and John Michael Archer, eds., *Enclosure Acts: Sexuality, Property, and Culture in Early Modern England* (Ithaca, 1994), 185–200. For censorship this year, also see James R. Siemon, '"Word Itself against the Word": Close Readings after Voloshinov', in *Shakespeare Reread: The Texts in New Contexts*, ed. Russ McDonald (Ithaca, 1993), 226–58; and Ernest Kuhl, 'The Stationers' Company and Censorship 1599–1601', *The Library*, 4th series, vol. 9 (1928–9), 388–94.

Any study of Hayward's *History* begins with the outstanding edition of John Manning, ed., *The First and Second Parts of John Hayward's The Life and Raigne of King Henrie IIII*, Camden Fourth Series, vol. 42 (London, 1991). Hayward has attracted a good deal of criticism, including Cyndia Susan Clegg, *Press Censorship in Elizabethan England* (Cambridge, 1997); and her subsequent 'Archival Poetics and the Politics of Literature: Essex and Hayward Revisited', *Studies in the Literary Imagination*, 32 (1999), 115–32; G. B. Harrison, 'Books and Readers', *The Library*, 4th series, xiv (1933), 1–33; and Blair Worden, 'Which Play Was Performed at the Globe Theatre on 7 February 1601?', *London Review of Books*, 10 July 2003, 22–4. In addition, see: David Wootton, 'Francis Bacon: Your Flexible Friend', in *The World of the Favourite*, ed. J. H. Elliott and L. W. B. Brockliss (New Haven, 1999), esp. 193–6; Margaret Dowling, 'Sir John Hayward's

1599

Troubles over His *Life of Henry IV*, *The Library*, 4th series, 11 (1930), 212–24; Rebecca Lemon, 'The Faulty Verdict in "The Crown v. John Hayward"', *Studies in English Literature*, 41 (2001), 109–32; Howard Erskine-Hill, *Poetry and the Realm of Politics: Shakespeare to Dryden* (Oxford, 1996); and Arthur Kinney, 'Essex and Shakespeare versus Hayward', *Shakespeare Quarterly*, 44 (1993), 464–6. For what ordinary Elizabethans (at least those who got into trouble) said about Elizabeth, see J. S. Cockburn's edited volumes of *Calendar of Assize Records* (London, 1975–80) for Essex, Kent, Sussex, Surrey and Hertfordshire indictments.

For Hayward's politics and the related issue of his use of Tacitus, see F. J. Levy, 'Hayward, Daniel, and the Beginnings of Politic History in England', *Huntington Library Quarterly*, 50 (1987), 1–37; E. B. Benjamin, 'Sir John Hayward and Tacitus', *Review of English Studies*, n.s. 8 (1957), 275–6; L. Goldberg, 'Sir John Hayward, "Politic" Historian', *Review of English Studies*, n.s. 6 (1955), 233–44; David Womersley, 'Sir Henry Savile's Translation of Tacitus and the Political Interpretation of Elizabethan Texts', *Review of English Studies*, n.s. 57 (1991), 313–42; J. H. M. Salmon, 'Seneca and Tacitus in Jacobean England', in Linda L. Peck, ed., *The Mental World of the Jacobean Court* (Cambridge 1991), 169–88; and Malcolm Smuts, 'Court Centered Politics and the Uses of Roman Historians, c.1590–1630', in *Culture and Politics in Early Stuart England*, ed. Kevin Sharp and Peter Lake (New York, 1994), 21–43. On Tacitus in England, see the two early translations: Henry Savile, trans., *The End of Nero and the Beginning of Galba: Four Books of the Histories of Tacitus* (Oxford, 1591); and Richard Grenewey, trans., *The Annals of Cornelius Tacitus* (London, 1598), where the footnote that Essex read on decimation can be found. On Essex's attraction to Tacitus, see Paul E. J. Hammer, *The Polarization of Elizabethan Politics*. For Shakespeare's interest in Tacitus, see D. J. Womersley, '*3 Henry VI*: Shakespeare, Tacitus, and Parricide', *Notes & Queries*, 32 (1985), 468–73; and George R. Price, '*Henry V* and *Germanicus*', *Shakespeare Quarterly*, 12 (1961), 57–60. For Cornwallis, see William Cornwallis, *Essayes* (1600); rpt. Don Cameron Allen, ed., *Essayes*, by Sir William Cornwallis, the Younger (Baltimore, 1946). And for Jonson on Tacitus, see vol. 1 of *Ben Jonson*, eds. C. H. Herford and Percy and Evelyn Simpson, 11 vols., (Oxford, 1926–52).

Francis Bacon's insights and actions in 1599 can be found in vol. 2 of

398

James Spedding, *The Letters and the Life of Francis Bacon* (London, 1862). For Bacon's character sketch of Julius Caesar, see '*Imago Civilis Julii Caesaris*', along with an English translation, in vol. 6 of *The Works of Francis Bacon*, eds. James Spedding, Robert Leslie Ellis and Douglas Denon Heath (London, 1890). See also: Lisa Jardine and Alan Stewart, *Hostage to Fortune: The Troubled Life of Francis Bacon* (New York, 1999); Fritz Levy, 'Francis Bacon and the Style of Politics', in Arthur Kinney and Dan S. Collins, eds., *Renaissance Historicism: Selections from English Literary Renaissance* (Amherst, 1987), 150–53; and Abbott, *Bacon and Essex*.

For Shakespeare's use of Plutarch, see, in addition to Thomas North's translation, *The Lives of the Noble Grecians and Romans* (London, 1579; 1595): Martha Hale Shackford, *Plutarch in Renaissance England* (n.p., 1929); Christopher Pelling, 'Plutarch on Caesar's Fall', in *Plutarch and His Intellectual World*, ed. Judith Mossman (London, 1997), 215–32; and Judith Mossman, '*Henry V* and Plutarch's *Alexander*', *Shakespeare Quarterly*, 45 (1994), 57–73. For Elizabeth's translation of Plutarch, see Caroline Pemberton, ed., *Queen Elizabeth's Englishings* (London, 1899). For Shakespeare's connection with Richard Field, see A. E. M. Kirkwood, 'Richard Field, Printer, 1589–1624', *The Library*, 12 (1931), 1–35, as well as Duncan-Jones, *Ungentle Shakespeare*.

8 'Is this a holiday?'

On the Guild Chapel and the Stratford of Shakespeare's childhood, see Sidney Lee, *Stratford-Upon-Avon from Earliest Times to the Death of Shakespeare* (London, rev. ed., 1907); Robert B. Wheler, *History and Antiquities of Stratford Upon Avon* (Stratford-upon-Avon, 1806); Levi Fox, *The Borough Town of Stratford-upon-Avon* (Stratford-upon-Avon, 1953); J. Harvey Bloom, *Shakespeare's Church, Otherwise the Collegiate Church of the Holy Trinity of Stratford-upon-Avon* (London, 1902); L. F. Salzman, ed., *The Victoria History of the County of Warwick*, vol. 3 (London, 1945), and Christopher Dyer, 'Medieval Stratford: A Successful Small Town', in Bearman, ed., *The History of an English Borough*. For a record of the ordering of the replacement of the stained glass with clear glass, see Richard Savage et al., eds., *Minutes and Accounts of the Corporation of Stratford*. The paintings of the Guild Chapel are discussed in

Thomas Fisher, *Series of Antient [sic] Allegorical, Historical, and Legendary Paintings, in Fresco: Discovered, in the Summer of 1804, on the Walls of the Chapel of the Trinity... at Stratford-Upon-Avon* (London, 1836) and more recently in Clifford Davidson's helpful *The Guild Chapel Wall Paintings at Stratford-upon-Avon* (New York, 1988). A broader discussion of the destruction of images in post-Reformation England can be found in John Phillips, *The Reformation of Images: Destruction of Art in England, 1535–1660* (Berkeley, 1973); Margaret Aston, *England's Iconoclasts. Vol I. Laws Against Images* (Oxford, 1988); and Richard Marks, *Stained Glass in England during the Middle Ages* (Toronto, 1993). For the importance of St George, see G. J. Marcus, *Saint George of England* (London, 1929).

On holiday and its changing meaning in post-Reformation England, in addition to the important work of David Cressy, *Bonfires and Bells*, and Ronald Hutton, *The Rise and Fall of Merry England*, see: Barnaby Googe, *The Popish Kingdome* (London, 1570), ed. Robert Charles Hope (London, 1880); and J. B., *A Treatise with a Kalendar, and the Proofs Thereof* (London, 1598). For the ways in which Shakespeare engages holiday in his plays, see the seminal work of C. L. Barber, *Shakespeare's Festive Comedy* (Princeton, 1959) and François Laroque, *Shakespeare's Festive World: Elizabethan Seasonal Entertainment and the Professional Stage*, trans. Janet Lloyd (Cambridge, 1991). For holiday and dress codes, see N. B. Harte, 'State Control of Dress and Social Change', in *Trade Government and Economy in Pre-Industrial England. Essays Presented to F. J. Fisher*, eds. D. C. Coleman and A. H. John (London, 1976), 132–65; and Wilfred Hooper, 'The Tudor Sumptuary Laws', *English Historical Review*, 30 (1915), 433–49. For an illuminating recent study, see Alison A. Chapman, 'Whose Saint Crispin's Day Is It?: Shoemaking, Holiday Making, and the Politics of Memory in Early Modern England', *Renaissance Quarterly*, 54 (2001), 1467–94. On the broader issues of Shakespeare and memorialization in 1599, see Anthony B. Dawson, 'The Arithmetic of Memory: Shakespeare's Theatre and the National Past', *Shakespeare Survey*, 52 (1999), 54–67. And for the ways in which Elizabethan drama engaged post-Reformation issues, see Louis Montrose, *The Purpose of Playing: Shakespeare and the Cultural Politics of the Elizabethan Theatre* (Chicago, 1996); and Jeffrey Knapp, *Shakespeare's Tribe: Church, Nation, and Theatre in Renaissance England* (Chicago, 2002).

On the Elizabethan triumph, I have drawn on Gordon Kipling, 'Triumphal Drama: Form in English Civic Pageantry', *Renaissance Drama*, n.s. 8 (1977), 37–56; Anthony Miller, *Roman Triumphs and Early Modern English Culture* (London, 2001); and for the triumph of Henry V, see James Hamilton Wylie, *The Reign of Henry the Fifth*; *The Great Chronicle of London*, eds. A. H. Thomas and I. D. Thornley (London, 1938) and *The Anglia Historia of Polydore Virgil, 1485–1537*, ed. Denys Hay, Camden Society, 3rd series (London, 1950).

On the controversy swirling around Accession Day, in addition to Cressy, *Bonfires and Bells*, see: Roy Strong, 'The Popular Celebration of the Accession Day of Queen Elizabeth I', *Journal of the Warburg and Courtauld Institutes*, 21 (1958), 86–103; as well as his *The Cult of Elizabeth: Elizabethan Portraiture and Pageantry* (London, 1977), along with Frances Yates, *Astrea: The Imperial Theme in the Sixteenth Century* (London, 1975). For contemporary sources, see Thomas Holland, *A Sermon Preached at Paules in London the 17. of November Ann. Dom. 1599* (Oxford, 1601); as well as Edmund Bunny, *Certain Prayers and Other Godly Exercises for the Seventeenth of November* (London, 1585); Thomas Bentley, *The Monument of Matrones* (London, 1582); John Prime, *A Sermon Briefly Comparing the Estate of King Solomon and his Subjectes Together with the Condition of Queen Elizabeth and her People* (Oxford, 1585); and Thomas Bilson, *The True Difference between Christian Subjection and Unchristian Rebellion* (Oxford, 1585). For Sanders' critique, see Nicholas Sanders, *A Treatise of the Images of Christ and His Saints* (Louvain, 1567); Nicholas Sanders, *The Rise and Growth of the Anglican Schism* (Cologne, 1585), trans. and ed. David Lewis (London, 1877), and T. Veech, *Dr. Nicholas Sanders and the English Reformation* (Louvain, 1935). For Robert Wright's story, see *Historical Manuscript Collection Report*, 8: 2, 27 and Strype, *Annals of the Reformation*. And on Elizabeth as goddess, in addition to Sir John Davies, *Hymnes, of Astraea, in Acrostic Verse* (London, 1599), see Helen Hackett: *Virgin Mother, Maiden Queen: Elizabeth I and the Cult of the Virgin Mary* (Basingstroke, 1995). For the timing of the Oxfordshire rising of 1596, see John Walter, '"Rising of the People?" The Oxfordshire Rising of 1596', *Past and Present*, 107 (1985), 90–143.

On representations of Elizabeth, see Roy Strong, *Portraits of Queen Elizabeth* (Oxford, 1963), *The Cult of Elizabeth: Elizabethan Portraiture and Pageantry* (London, 1977) and *Artists of the Tudor Court: The Portrait Miniature Rediscovered 1520–1620* (London, 1983); along with 'The Character of Queen Elizabeth', by Edmund Bohun, in vol. 2 of Nichols, *Progresses of Elizabeth*. Janet Arnold's richly illustrated *Queen Elizabeth's Wardrobe Unlock'd* (Leeds, 1988) contains a wealth of information. And on iconography and iconoclasm, see Michael O'Connell, in 'The Idolatrous Eye: Iconoclasm, Anti-Theatricalism, and the Image of the Elizabethan Theatre', *English Literary History*, 52 (1985), 279–310; and John N. King, *Tudor Royal Iconography: Literature and Art in an Age of Religious Crisis* (Princeton, 1989). On Paul's Cross sermons, see Millar MacClure, *The Paul's Cross Sermons 1534–1642* (Toronto, 1958); Arnold Hunt, 'Tuning the Pulpits: the Religious Context of the Essex Revolt', in Lori Anne Ferrell and Peter McCullough, eds., *The English Sermon Revised: Religion, Literature and History 1600–1750* (Manchester, 2000), 86–114; and McCullough's *Sermons at Court*.

The definitive account of Squires's attempt on Elizabeth's life can be found in Arthur Freeman, *Elizabeth's Misfits* (New York, 1978). For Ralegh's letter about assassination, see Agnes Latham and Joyce Youings, eds., *The Letters of Sir Walter Ralegh* (Exeter, 1999). For the debate over assassination, see Robert Miola, *'Julius Caesar* and the Tyrannicide Debate', *Renaissance Quarterly*, 38 (1985), 271–89; see, too, Rebecca W. Bushnell, *Tragedies of Tyrants: Political Thought and Theatre in the English Renaissance* (Ithaca, 1990). On the matter of succession, in addition to Thomas Wilson's 'The State of England', see Peter Wentworth, *A Pithie Exhortation to Her Majestie for Establishing Her Successor to the Crowne* (Edinburgh, 1598) and Sir John Harington, *A Tract on the Succession to the Crown* (1602), ed. Clements R. Markham (London, 1880).

For depictions of Julius Caesar in Elizabethan England, see the various travel narratives of Platter, Hentzner and others. See, too, Ernest Law, *The History of Hampton Court Palace*, 3 vols. (2nd edn, London, 1890); 'Inventory of the Pictures in Hampton Court Viewed and Appraised the 3rd, 4th, and 5th of October 1649', in Oliver Millar, ed., *The Inventories and Valuation of the King's Goods 1649–51* in *The Walpole Society*, 43 (1972); and George Wingfield Digby, *Victoria and Albert Museum: The Tapestry Collection, Medieval and Renaissance* (London, 1980). More generally, see Lucy Gent, ed., *Albion's Classicism: The Visual Arts in*

Britain, 1550–1660 (New Haven, 1995). And for Shakespeare and Rome more generally, see John W. Velz, 'The Ancient World in Shakespeare: Authenticity or Anachronism? A Retrospect', *Shakespeare Survey*, 31 (1978), 1–12; Terence Spencer, 'Shakespeare and the Elizabethan Romans', *Shakespeare Survey*, 10 (1957), 27–38; and G. K. Hunter, 'A Roman Thought: Renaissance Attitudes to History Exemplified in Shakespeare and Jonson', in Brian S. Lee, ed., *An English Miscellany: Papers Presented to W. S. Mackie* (Capetown, 1977), 93–118.

For criticism on *Julius Caesar* to which I'm especially indebted, see Mark Rose, 'Conjuring Caesar: Ceremony, History, and Authority in 1599', in *True and Maimed Rites: Ritual and Anti-Ritual in Shakespeare and His Age*, eds. Linda Woodbridge and Edward Berry (Urbana, 1992), 256–69; Naomi Conn Liebler, '"Thou Bleeding Piece of Earth": The Ritual Ground of *Julius Caesar*', *Shakespeare Studies*, 14 (1981), 175–96; J. Dover Wilson, 'Ben Jonson and *Julius Caesar*', *Shakespeare Survey*, 2 (1949), 36–43; Wayne Rebhorn, 'The Crisis of the Aristocracy in *Julius Caesar*', *Renaissance Quarterly*, 43 (1990), 78–109; David Kaula, '"Let Us Be Sacrificers": Religious Motifs in *Julius Caesar*', *Shakespeare Studies*, 14 (1981), 197–214; and Ian Donaldson, '"Miscontruing Everything": *Julius Caesar* and *Sejanus*', in Grace Ioppolo, ed., *Shakespeare Performed*, 88–107. Richard Wilson has done important work on the play in his 'A Brute Part: Julius Caesar and the Rites of Violence', *Cahiers Elisabethains*, 50 (1996), 19–32; *Will Power: Essays on Shakespearean Authority* (Detroit, 1993); *Shakespeare: Julius Caesar*, Penguin Critical Studies (London, 1992) and the introduction to his edition of *Julius Caesar. New Casebooks* (New York, 2002). For the play in performance, see John Ripley, *Julius Caesar on Stage in England and America, 1599–1973* (Cambridge, 1980).

9 The Invisible Armada

I have reconstructed the story of the 'Invisible Armada' from various State Papers (the Acts of the Privy Council are lost for this period). The phrase itself is found in Francis Bacon's annotations to Camden's *Annals*, found in vol. 6 of *The Works of Francis Bacon*, eds. James Spedding, Robert Leslie Ellis and Douglas Denon Heath. An invaluable source has been British Library Harl. MS. 168, which documents how 'Upon advertisement and intelligence that the King of Spain made great preparations both of ships and galleys and of great forces to employ the same against this her Majesty's kingdom, there were diverse orders, letters, and directions given for putting the forces of the realm in readiness, and for other necessary preparations, for defence of the same, which are entered hereafter in this book, viz., 1599.' I've also drawn on J. H. Leslie, ed., 'A Survey, Or Muster, of the Armed and Trayned Companies in London, 1588 and 1599', *Journal of the Society for Army Historical Research*, 4 (1925), 62–71. See, too, Wernham, *The Return of the Armadas*; Julian S. Corbett, *The Successors of Drake* (London, 1900); and Lindsay Boynton, *The Elizabethan Militia*. There has been little treatment of its impact upon the stage, though see Charles W. Crupi, 'Ideological Contradictions in Part 1 of Heywood's *Edward IV*: "Our Musicke Runs . . . Much upon Discords"', *Medieval and Renaissance Drama in England*, 7 (1995), 224–56. For the smuggled Spanish proclamation, see *Bibliotheca Lindesiana, A Bibliography of Royal Proclamations of the Tudor and Stuart Sovereigns*, vol. 1 (Oxford, 1910). On the lost play of *Turnhout*, in addition to Whyte's letters (in *H.M.C. L'Isle and Dudley*), see Millicent V. Hay, *The Life of Robert Sidney* (Washington, DC, 1984); and *A True Discourse of the Overthrow Given to the Common Enemy at Turnhaut* (London, 1597).

10 The Passionate Pilgrim

For the history of the text of *The Passionate Pilgrim* I've relied on Joseph Quincy Adams's facsimile edition of the 1599 edition (New York, 1939) as well as Colin Burrow's discussion in his Oxford edition. There is an outside possibility that the first edition of *The Passionate Pilgrim*, for which the title page is missing, came out in late 1598, when Jaggard first set up shop. See too C. H. Hobday, 'Shakespeare's Venus and Adonis Sonnets', *Shakespeare Survey*, 26 (1973), 103–9; and Arthur F. Marotti, 'Shakespeare's Sonnets as Literary Property', in *Soliciting Interpretation: Literary Theory and Seventeenth-Century Poetry*, Elizabeth D. Harvey and Katherine Eisaman Maus, eds. (Chicago, 1990), 143–73. On the poems lifted from *Love's Labour's Lost*, see William C. Carroll, *The Great Feast of Language in 'Love's Labour's Lost'* (Princeton, 1976). And on Shakespeare's poetry in relation to his life, see Colin Burrow, 'Life and Work in Shakespeare's Poems', *Proceedings of the British Academy*, 97 (1998), 15–50.

On Shakespeare's encounter with George Buc, see Alan H. Nelson, 'George Buc, William Shakespeare, and the Folger *George a Greene*', *Shakespeare Quarterly*, 49 (1998), 74–83; and Mark Eccles 'Sir George Buc, Master of the Revels', in *Sir Thomas Lodge and Other Elizabethans*, ed. C. J. Sisson (Cambridge, Mass., 1933), 409–506. For more on Buc's books (including Drummond's and Harrington's collections) see Alan Nelson's website: *http://socrates.berkeley.edu/~ahnelson/BUC/quartos.html*. See also F. J. Furnivall, 'Sir John Harington's Shakespeare Quartos', *Notes and Queries*, 7th series, 9 (1890), 382–3. On London's bookshops, see the remarkable reconstruction offered by Peter W. M. Blayney, *The Bookshops in Paul's Cross Churchyard*, Occasional Papers of the Bibliographic Society, Number 5 (London, 1990).

11 Simple Truth Suppressed

Additional support for the view that that Shakespeare revised 'When my love swears' is the survival of an earlier version of the poem in Folger MS. V.a. 339, fo. 197ᵛ, transcribed around 1630 to 1640, which corresponds closely to the *Passionate Pilgrim* version. On the dating of the sonnets, see A. Kent Hieatt, Charles W. Hieatt and Anne Lake Prescott, 'When did Shakespeare Write Sonnets 1609?', *Studies in Philology*, 88 (1991), 69–109; and Macd. P. Jackson, 'Vocabulary and Chronology: The Case of Shakespeare's Sonnets', *Review of English Studies*, 52 (2001), 59–75. I am deeply indebted to Edward A. Snow, 'Loves of Comfort and Despair: A Reading of Shakespeare's Sonnet 138', *English Literary History*, 47 (1980), 462–83. For the best introduction to Lodge's story, see *Rosalind*, ed. Donald Beecher, (Ottawa, 1997). Frank Kermode's remarks can be found in *Shakespeare's Language* (New York, 2000). For Shakespeare and Marlowe, see James Shapiro, *Rival Playwrights: Marlowe, Jonson, Shakespeare* (New York, 1991).

For Robert Armin's career and writings, see his *Collected Works*, ed. J. P. Feather (New York, 1972); Wiles, *Shakespeare's Clown*; Nora Johnson, *The Actor as Playwright in Early Modern Drama* (Cambridge, 2003); A. K. Gray, 'Robert Armine, the Foole', *Publications of the Modern Language Association*, 42 (1927), 673–85; and C. S. Felver, *Robert Armin, Shakespeare's Fool* (Kent, Ohio, 1961).

On Shakespeare's songs and his collaboration with Morley, see: Thomas Morley, *The First Booke of Ayres or Little Short Songs, to Sing and Play to the Lute, with the Base Viole* (London, 1600); Ernest Brennecke, Jr., 'Shakespeare's Musical Collaboration with Morley', *Publications of the Modern Language Association*, 54 (1939), 139–52; Peter J. Seng, *The Vocal Songs in the Plays of Shakespeare: A Critical History* (Cambridge, Mass., 1967); F. W. Sternfeld, *Music in Shakespearean Tragedy* (London, 1963); and Ross W. Duffin, *Shakespeare's Songbook* (New York, 2004). And on the jig and the dance, see Alan Brissenden, *Shakespeare and the Dance* (Atlantic Heights, New Jersey, 1981).

My thinking about *As You Like It* has been strongly influenced by Marjorie Garber, 'The Education of Orlando', in *Comedy from Shakespeare to Sheridan: Change and Continuity in the English and European Dramatic Tradition*, ed. A. R. Braunmuller and J. C. Bulman (Newark, 1986), 102–112; M. C. Bradbrook, *Shakespeare the Craftsman* (London, 1969); Valerie Traub, *Desire and Anxiety: Circulations of Sexuality in Shakespearean Drama* (New York, 1992); Penny Gay, *William Shakespeare: As You Like It* (Plymouth, 1999); and Louis A. Montrose's essays on the social dynamics of the play: '"The Place of a Brother": *As You Like It* and social change', *Shakespeare Quarterly*, 32 (1981), 28–54; and 'Of Gentlemen and Shepherds: The Politics of Elizabethan Pastoral Form', *English Literary History*, 10 (1983), 415–59. Harold Bloom's account of the character of Rosalind in *Shakespeare: The Invention of the Human* (New York, 1998) is well worth reading. On the mock wedding scene, see Ann Jennalie Cook, *Making a Match: Courtship in Shakespeare and His Society* (Princeton, 1991). And for the sign of the Globe, see Richard Dutton, '*Hamlet*, An Apology for Actors, and the Sign of the Globe', *Shakespeare Survey*, 41 (1988), 35–7.

12 The Forest of Arden

For Shakespeare's family, in addition to Chambers, *Facts and Problems* and the standard biographies, see Charles Isaac Elton, *William Shakespeare: His Family and Friends*, ed. A. Hamilton Thomson (New York, 1904); Joseph William Gray, *Shakespeare's Marriage* (London, 1905); Ivor Brown, *The Women in Shakespeare's Life* (New York, 1969); and Joseph

William Gray, *Shakespeare's Marriage* (London, 1905). For the mustering of his (step) brother-in-law John Hathaway in 1599, see Warwickshire County Record Office, CR1886/2657.

For knowledge of the Stratford carrier William Greenaway, of whom I was ignorant, I am indebted to Prof. Stanley Wells. See, in addition to letters in Fripp's *Quyny*, Stratford Record Office BRU 15/1 (129), and S. Schoenbaum, *Shakespeare's Lives* (Oxford, 1970). For land travel in Shakespeare's England and the route from London to Stratford, see Charles Hughes, 'Land Travel', in *Shakespeare's England: An Account of the Life and Manners of His Age*, ed. Sidney Lee and C. T. Onions, 2 vols. (Oxford, 1916); Joan Parkes, *Travel in England in the Seventeenth Century* (London, 1925); John W. Hales, 'From Stratford to London', in *Notes and Essays on Shakespeare* (London, 1884), first published in *Cornhill Magazine* (June 1877); and the itinerary offered in Russell Fraser, *Young Shakespeare* (New York, 1988).

For conditions within Shakespeare's Stratford, see, in addition to Fripp's work, J. M. Martin, 'A Warwickshire Market Town in Adversity: Stratford-Upon-Avon in the Sixteenth and Seventeenth Centuries', *Midland History*, 7 (1982), 26–41; S. Porter, 'Fires in Stratford-upon-Avon in the Sixteenth and Seventeeth Centuries', *Warwickshire History*, 3 (1276), 97–103; Robert Bearman, 'Stratford's Fires of 1594 and 1595 Revisited', *Midland History*, 25 (2000), 180–90; Anne Hughes, 'Building a Godly Town: Religious and Cultural Division in Stratford-upon-Avon, 1560–1640', and Alan Dyer, 'Crisis and Resolution: Government and Society in Stratford, 1540–1640', both of which appear in Bearman, ed., *The History of an English Borough*. On the broader economic conditions of England in the late 1590s, see R. B. Outhwaite's two essays: 'Dearth, the English Crown and the "Crisis of the 1590s"', in *The European Crisis of the 1590s: Essays in Comparative History*, ed. Peter Clark (London, 1985), 23–43; and 'The Price of Crown Land at the Turn of the Sixteenth Century', *Economic History Review*, 2nd series, 20 (1967), 229–40.

For social and economic conditions in the Forest of Arden in medieval and early modern England, see Andrew Watkins, 'The Woodland Economy of the Forest of Arden in the Later Middle Ages', *Midland History*, 18 (1993), 19–36; and Victor H. T. Skipp's influential work *Crisis and Development: An Ecological Case of the Forest of Arden* (Cambridge, 1978); 'Forest of Arden, 1530–1649', *Agricultural History Review*, 18 (1970), 84–111; and 'Economic and Social Change in the Forest of Arden, 1530–1649', in *Land, Church and People: Essays Presented to Professor H. P. R. Finberg*, ed. Joan Thirsk (Reading, 1970); Brian Short, 'Forests and Wood-Pasture in Lowland England', in Joan Thirsk, ed., *The English Rural Landscape* (Oxford, 2000), 122–49; Andrew McRae, *God Speed the Plough: The Representation of Agrarian England*, 1500–1660 (Cambridge, 1996); Edward Berry, *Shakespeare and the Hunt: A Cultural and Social Study* (Cambridge, 2001); and W. Salt Brassington, *Shakespeare's Homeland: Sketches of Stratford-upon-Avon, the Forest of Arden and the Avon Valley* (London, 1903). See, too, William Harrison, *Description of England* (London, 1577).

A. Stuart Daley has produced a group of essays that have illuminated the social and political realities of *As You Like It*: 'Where are the Woods in *As You Like It?*', *Shakespeare Quarterly*, 34 (1983), 172–80; 'The Dispraise of the Country in *As You Like It*', *Shakespeare Quarterly*, 36 (1985), 300–314; 'The Idea of Hunting in *As You Like It*,' *Shakespeare Studies*, 21 (1993), 72–95; 'Calling and Commonwealth in *As You Like It*: A Late Elizabethan Political Play', *The Upstart Crow*, 14 (1994), 28–46; 'Observations on the Natural Settings and Flora of the Ardens of Lodge and Shakespeare', *English Language Notes*, 22 (1985), 20–29; 'Shakespeare's Corin, Almsgiver and Faithful Feeder', *English Language Notes*, 27 (1990), 4–21; and 'The Tyrant Duke of *As You Like It*: Envious Malice Confronts Honour, Pity, Friendship', *Cahiers Elisabethains*, 34 (1988), 39–51. See, too, Richard Wilson, *Will Power*; Meredith Skura, 'Anthony Munday's "Gentrification" of Robin Hood', *English Literary Renaissance*, 33 (2003), 155–180; and Madeleine Doran, '"Yet I am inland bred"', in James G. Mcmanaway, ed., *Shakespeare 400* (New York, 1964), 99–114. And see Michael Drayton, *Poly-Olbion*, in *Works*, ed. J. William Hebel, vol. 4 (Oxford, 1933).

For Shakespeare's dealing with the College of Arms in 1599, see C.W. Scott-Giles, *Shakespeare's Heraldry*; Chambers, *Facts and Problems*; and Duncan-Jones, *Ungentle Shakespeare*. And for the Arden legacy, see Eric Poole, 'John and Mary Shakespeare and the Astow Cantlow Mortgage', *Cahiers Elisabethains*, 17 (1980), 21–42.

13 Things Dying, Things Newborn

I have reconstructed Essex's campaign in Ireland from State Papers, English and Irish; Cyril Falls, *Elizabeth's Irish Wars*; C. G. Cruickshank, *Elizabeth's Army*; L. W. Henry, 'Contemporary Sources for Essex's Lieutenancy in Ireland, 1599'; Hiram Morgan, *Tyrone's Rebellion*; G. A. Hayes-McCoy, 'The Army of Ulster, 1593–1601', in *The Irish Sword*; E. M. Tenison, *Elizabethan England*; Harington's *Nugae Antiquae*; Paul E. J. Hammer, *Elizabeth's Wars* and his 'The Use of Scholarship: The Secretariat of Robert Devereux, Second Earl of Essex, c.1585–1601', *The English Historical Review*, 109 (1994), 26–51. For Essex's words before the College of Arms, see William Huse Dunham, Jr., 'William Camden's Commonplace Book', *Yale University Library Gazette*, 43 (1969), 139–56; for the ballad celebrating St George's Day in Ireland, see Andrew Clark, ed., *The Shirburn Ballads*; and for Essex's letter to Knollys, see Sir William Sanderson, *Aulicus Coquinariae* (London, 1650).

On John Harington, in addition to his *Nugae Antiquae*, see: R. H. Miller, 'Sir John Harington's Irish Journals', *Studies in Bibliography*, 32 (1979), 179–86; and David M. Gardiner, '"These are Not the Thinges Men Live by Now a Days": Sir John Harington's Visit to the O'Neill, 1599', *Cahiers Elisabethains*, 55 (April 1999), 1–16. For details about Queen Elizabeth's bed, see Roy Strong and Julia Trevelyan Oman, *Elizabeth R* (London, 1971).

On the formation and influence of the East India Company, see: K. N. Chaudhuri, *The English East India Company* (London, 1965); Henry Stevens, *The Dawn of British Trade to the East Indies* (London, 1886); Sir William Foster, *England's Quest of Eastern Trade* (London, 1933); John Bruce, *Annals of the Honourable East India Company*, vol. 1 (London, 1810); and Beckles Willson, *Ledger and Sword: Or, The Honourable Company of Merchants of England Trading to the East Indies (1599–1874)*, 2 vols. (London, 1903). See, too: M. Epstein, *The Early History of the Levant Company* (London, 1908); Nicholas Canny and Alaine Low, eds., *The Oxford History of the British Empire: 1. The Origins of Empire: British Overseas Enterprise to the Close of the Seventeenth Century* (Oxford, 1998); Kenneth R. Andrews, *Trade, Plunder and Settlement: Maritime Enterprise and the Genesis of the British Empire, 1480–1630* (Cambridge, 1984); G. L. Beer,

The Origins of the British Colonial System, 1578–1660 (New York, 1922); and Anthony Farrington, *Trading Places: The East India Company and Asia, 1600–1834* (London, 2002).

On Hakluyt's efforts, see George Bruner Parks, *Richard Hakluyt and the English Voyages* (New York, 1928); and Hakluyt's own *Principal Navigations, Voyages, Traffics, and Discoveries of the English Nation,* 3 vols. (London, 1598–1600). On the participation of the nobility in joint-stock trading companies, see Lawrence Stone, 'The Nobility in Business', in *The Entrepreneur: Papers Presented at the Annual Conference of the Economic History Society* (Cambridge, Mass., 1957), 14–21; and Theodore K. Rabb, *Enterprise and Empire: Merchant and Gentry Investment in the Expansion of England, 1575–1630* (Cambridge, Mass., 1967). I've also drawn on Michael G. Brennan, 'The Literature of Travel', in John Barnard and D. F. McKenzie, eds., *The Cambridge History of the Book in Britain, vol 4: 1557–1695* (Cambridge, 2002), 246–73; William Foster, ed., *The Travels of John Sanderson in the Levant, 1584–1602* (London, 1931); and Sir William Foster, ed., *The Voyages of Sir James Lancaster to Brazil and the East Indies, 1591–1603* (London, 1940). Keeling's account of performances of *Hamlet* at sea can be found in Thomas Rundall, ed., *Narratives of Voyages Towards the North-West . . . With Selections from the Early Records of the Honourable The East India Company* (London, 1849).

On contemporary reflections on the decline of chivalric culture, see George Silver, *Paradoxes of Defence* (London, 1599) and William Segar, *Honour, Military and Civill* (London, 1602). For modern studies, see Mervyn James's important essays on 'English Politics and the Concept of Honour, 1485–1642', and 'At the Crossroads of the Political Culture: The Essex Revolt, 1601', in his *Society, Politics and Culture: Studies in Early Modern England* (Cambridge, 1986), 270–415 and 416–66. I am also indebted to Richard C. McCoy's *The Rites of Knighthood: The Literature and Politics of Elizabethan Chivalry* (Berkeley, 1989) as well as to his earlier essay, '"A Dangerous Image": the Earl of Essex and Elizabethan Chivalry', *Journal of Medieval and Renaissance Studies*, 13 (1983), 313–29. See, too, R. A. Foakes's forthcoming article on the Ghost's armour in *Hamlet*.

Details of Essex's plot to join forces with King James and Mountjoy can be found in *Correspondence of King James VI of Scotland with Sir Robert*

Cecil and Others in England during the Reign of Elizabeth, ed. J. Bruce, Camden Society 78 (London, 1861) along with 'the confessions and other evidence' published in vol. 2 of James Spedding, *The Letters and the Life of Francis Bacon*. For Fulke Greville, see his *Poems and Dramas*, ed. Geoffrey Bullough, 2 vols. (Edinburgh, 1939).

14 Essays and Soliloquies

For Saxo, Belleforest and other sources of *Hamlet*, see Bullough, *Narrative and Dramatic Sources of Shakespeare*. On the play's distinctive vocabulary, see Alfred Hart's pair of essays, 'Vocabularies of Shakespeare's Plays', *Review of English Studies*, 19 (1943), 128–40 and 'The Growth of Shakespeare's Vocabulary', *Review of English Studies*, 19 (1943), 242–54, as well as Frank Kermode, *Shakespeare's Language*. On hendiadys, I am indebted to George T. Wright's authoritative 'Hendiadys and Hamlet', *Publications of the Modern Language Association*, 96 (1981), 168–93, and Frank Kermode's *Shakespeare's Language* and *Pieces of My Mind* (New York, 2003). See Furness's Variorum *Hamlet* for responses to the Player's Speech. For the elegy to Burbage and Burbage's career in general, see Nungezer, *Dictionary of Actors*. For Wotton's letter to Donne, see Logan Pearsall Smith, *The Life and Letters of Sir Henry Wotton*, 2 vols. (Oxford, 1907).

Quotations from Cornwallis's essays are cited from Don Cameron Allen, ed., *Essayes, by Sir William Cornwallis, the Younger*. On Cornwallis and his essays, see Roger E. Bennett, 'Sir William Cornwallis's Use of Montaigne', *Publications of the Modern Language Association*, 48 (1933), 1080–99; Elbert N. S. Thompson, 'The Seventeenth-Century English Essay', *University of Iowa Humanistic Studies*, 3 (1926), especially 3–93; P. B. Whitt, 'New Light on Sir Thomas Cornwallis, the Essayist', *Review of English Studies*, 8 (1932), 155–69; and W. L. MacDonald, 'The Earliest English Essayists', *Englische Studien*, 64 (1929), 20–52. His essays reveal that Cornwallis was a playgoer, and, if anything, Shakespeare had influenced him (though not *Hamlet*, which was staged after Cornwallis's first set of essays was already written). One of Cornwallis's few letters to survive, a verse epistle sent to his 'dear friend' John Donne, speaks of his love of theatre: 'If then for change of hours you seem careless, / Agree with me to lose them at the plays' (*The Poems of John Donne*, Herbert J. C. Grierson, ed., 2 vols. [Oxford 1912], vol. 2, 171–2). Cornwallis mentions the public theatre in his essays and even echoes Shakespeare's recent *Julius Caesar* (and quotes its most famous line) in an account where reading and playgoing recollections blur: 'Caesar is so much beholding to me that I put him on; and all the time I am reading of him, his happiness is mine, his danger is mine. When I am out of my dream with coming to '*Et tu Brute*' I should be very sorry this imagination could last no longer' ('Of Life').

On Montaigne and his influence on *Hamlet*, see Michel Eyquem de Montaigne, *Essays*, trans. John Florio (1603), intro. L. C. Harmer, 3 vols. (1910; London, 1965); Robert Ellrodt, 'Self-Consciousness in Montaigne and Shakespeare', *Shakespeare Survey*, 28 (1975), 37–50; Hugh Grady, *Shakespeare, Machiavelli, and Montaigne* (Oxford, 2002); and Frances A. Yates, *John Florio: The Life of an Italian in Shakespeare's England* (Cambridge, 1934). For Bacon's essays, see Michael Kiernan's excellent introduction to and edition of *Sir Francis Bacon, The Essays or Counsels, Civill and Morall* (Cambridge, Mass., 1985).

15 Second Thoughts

On the rich subject of the textual history of *Hamlet*, in addition to the various editions that I've consulted (cited above, especially Jesús Tronch-Pérez's *Synoptic 'Hamlet'*), see: George Ian Duthie, *The 'Bad' Quarto of Hamlet: A Critical Study Published (Q1, 1603): Origins, Form, Intertextualities* (Newark, 1992); Kathleen O. Irace, ed., *The First Quarto of Hamlet* (Cambridge, 1998); Paul Werstine, 'The Textual Mystery of *Hamlet*', *Shakespeare Quarterly*, 39 (1988), 1–26, and for Shakespeare at work on *Hamlet*, see Barbara Everett, *Young Hamlet: Essays on Shakespeare's Tragedies* (Oxford, 1989) and 'Thinking about *Hamlet*', in the *Times Literary Supplement* (2 September 2004), 19–23. It's possible, though unlikely, that all the touring of *Hamlet* mentioned on the title page of the 1603 First Quarto was crammed into several months in the spring and summer of 1603, following the death of Queen Elizabeth and the outbreak of plague.

On Shakespeare's revision of *Hamlet*, see John Kerrigan, 'Shakespeare as Reviser', in Christopher Ricks, ed., *English Drama to 1710* (London, 1971), 255–75; Werstine, 'The Textual Mystery of *Hamlet*'; Wells and Taylor, *Textual Companion*; Philip Edwards, 'The Tragic Balance in *Hamlet*', *Shakespeare Survey*, 36 (1983), 43–52; David Ward, 'The King and *Hamlet*', *Shakespeare Quarterly*, 43 (1992), 280–302; Giorgio Melchiori, '*Hamlet*: The Acting Version and the Wiser Sort', in *The Hamlet First Published*, 195–210; R. A. Foakes, *Hamlet Versus Lear: Cultural Politics and Shakespeare's Art* (Cambridge,1993); and the editions of Jenkins, Edwards, Tronch-Pérez and Hibbard.

On the special problem of Hamlet's final soliloquy, see Philip C. McGuire, 'Which Fortinbras, Which *Hamlet*?', in Thomas Clayton, ed., *The 'Hamlet' First Published (Q1, 1603)*, 151–78, and Harold Jenkins, 'Fortinbras and Laertes and the Composition of *Hamlet*', in his *Structural Problems in Shakespeare*, ed. Ernst Honigmann (London, 2001). Three centuries would pass before an actor playing Hamlet first recited 'How all occasions do inform against me' onstage. Shakespeare's decision to cut this speech set in motion further cuts by other hands. The First Quarto of *Hamlet* reduced Fortinbras's role in Act 4 to five lines and in the final scene to twenty-two lines. It also eliminated any mention by the dying Hamlet that Fortinbras ought to succeed him. For much of the performance history of *Hamlet*, Fortinbras disappeared completely. Stripping the play of its frame in this way effectively transformed *Hamlet* from a politically fraught drama into a riveting Oedipal one. For better or worse, Shakespeare's revised version had already nudged the play in this direction.

My reading of *Hamlet* is generally indebted to J. Dover Wilson, *What Happens in 'Hamlet'* (Cambridge, 1937); Donald Joseph McGinn, *Shakespeare's Influence on the Drama of His Age, Studied in Hamlet* (New Brunswick, 1938); John Draper, *The Hamlet of Shakespeare's Audience* (1939; New York, 1966); Harley Granville-Barker, *Preface to Hamlet* (1946; New York, 1957); Harry Levin, *The Question of Hamlet* (New York, 1959); Roland Mushat Frye, *The Renaissance Hamlet* (Princeton, 1984); Arthur McGee, *The Elizabethan Hamlet* (New Haven, 1987); Stuart M. Kurland, 'Hamlet and the Scottish Succession?', *Studies in English Literature*, 34 (1992), 279–300; and Ann Thompson, 'The Comedy of *Hamlet, Prince of Denmark*', *Shakespeare Quarterly*, 56 (2003), 93–104. See, too, the essays collected in Mark Thornton Burnett and John Manning, eds., *New Essays on Hamlet* (New York, 1994); David Scott Kastan, ed., *Critical*

Essays on Shakespeare's 'Hamlet' (New York, 1995); and Arthur F. Kinney, ed., *Hamlet: New Critical Essays* (New York, 2002).

Epilogue

The New Year's gift roll for 1598/1599 can be found in the Folger Library (MS Z.d.17). The gift roll for 1599/1600 has been published in vol. 3 of Nichols, ed., *The Progresses and Public Processions of Queen Elizabeth*. Rowland Whyte is the source of my information about Essex's spurned gift. For John Weever's prophecy, see his *Faunus and Melliflora* (London, 1600). For Donne's letter, see Evelyn M. Simpson, *A Study of the Prose Works of John Donne* (Oxford, 1924; 2nd edn, 1948).

On Thomas Dekker's plays this year, see, in addition to Henslowe's *Diary*, R. L. Smallwood and Stanley Wells, eds., *The Shoemaker's Holiday* (Manchester, 1979). On Ben Jonson in 1599 and his revised epilogue to *Every Man Out of His Humour*, see Herford and Simpson's edition of his works; Anne Barton, *Ben Jonson, Dramatist* (Cambridge, 1984); David Riggs, *Ben Jonson: A Life* (Cambridge, Mass., 1989); and Ben Jonson, *Every Man Out of His Humour*, ed. Helen Ostovich (Manchester, 2001). For a discussion of what Dekker and Jonson changed for performances at court, also see Fritz Levy, 'The Theatre and the Court in the 1590s', in John Guy, ed., *The Reign of Elizabeth I*, 74–99. For the argument that Henslowe had been planning to build a theatre in the northern suburbs even before the Chamberlain's Men moved to Southwark, see S. P. Cerasano, 'Edward Alleyn's Retirement 1597–1600', *Medieval and Renaissance Drama in England*, 10 (1998), 99–109. And for an account of Shakespeare's concentrated dramatic output during the Stuart years, see Leeds Barroll, *Politics, Plague, and Shakespeare's Theatre: The Stuart Years* (Ithaca, 1991).

Acknowledgments

I have accumulated many debts while at work on this book. I owe a great deal to James Bednarz, Robert Griffin, Richard McCoy, and Alvin Snider, friends and scholars who read successive drafts, pointed out weaknesses, and challenged me to write a better book. David Kastan, who has deeply shaped my thinking about Shakespeare, patiently discussed every argument and idea in these pages. Reg Foakes and Stanley Wells, whose knowledge of Shakespeare's life and times is formidable, read the penultimate draft and saved me time and again from errors of judgment and fact. David Denby did the same for problems with style. Stephen Greenblatt, Andrew Hadfield, René Weis, and Alan Stewart helped me navigate problems in history and biography. A generation of Columbia undergraduates has taught me a lot about Shakespeare, as have some extraordinary graduate students who have worked with me and have helped out with this book in various ways.

The bibliographical essay at the end of the book indicates how much I owe to fellow scholars of early modern England. I'm especially grateful to the members of the seminar on '1599' that I led at the Shakespeare Society of America in 1991 near the outset of this long journey, as well as to the feedback from participants at the International Shakespeare Association in Stratford-upon-Avon in 2004, near its conclusion. In the interim, I have spent much of my time in archives and am beholding to the expert staff at the

Huntington Library, the Folger Shakespeare Library (especially to Georgianna Ziegler), the British Library, the Cambridge University Library, the Public Records Office, the Bodleian Library, the Columbia University Library, the Dartmouth College Library, the Warwickshire County Record Office, and the Shakespeare Birthplace Trust. Family and friends have offered advice and encouragement – LuAnn Walther, Philippe Cheng, Yair Rosenstock, Bill Monroe, Tom Cartelli, Michael Shapiro, Jill Shapiro, my parents Herbert and Lorraine Shapiro, and my in-laws, Barry and Mary DeCourcey Cregan. I am blessed in my literary agent and graduate school friend, Anne Edelstein, as well as in my remarkable editor at Faber, Julian Loose. Without Mary Cregan and our son Luke this book could not have been written; it is dedicated to them.

I am deeply grateful to the Folger Shakespeare Library for permission to reproduce the illustrations that appear on pages xv, 1, 25, 50, 67, 84, 97, 119, 133, 156, 193, 195, 228, 258, 281, 283, 318; to the Henry E. Huntington Library for those on pages 212 and 339; to the Bodleian Library, Oxford for those on pages 27 and 359; and to the Utrecht University Library for the one on page 121. Illustrations in the plate section are reproduced by kind permission of The Fitzwilliam Museum, University of Cambridge / www.bridgeman.co.uk (1); Woburn Abbey, Bedfordshire / www.bridgeman.co.uk (2); Private Collection, Ken Welsh / www.bridgeman.co.uk (3); Private Collection, Mark Fiennes / www.bridgeman.co.uk (4); Philip Mould, Historical Portraits Ltd, London / www.bridgeman.co.uk (13); Private Collection / www.bridgeman.co.uk (5); The National Portrait Gallery (6, 8); Dulwich Picture Gallery, London / www.bridgeman.co.uk (7); Society of Antiquaries, London / www.bridgeman.co.uk (10); The British Library (11); and The Folger Shakespeare Library (9, 12, 14, 15, 16, 17).

Index

417

at Newington Butts 319
WS's *Hamlet* performed 354
and the breadth of WS's appeal 368
change of name to King's Men 370
Richard the Second performed 372
Chancery 278
Chandos' Men 248
Chapman, George 10, 55, 203
Charles I, King 373
Chaucer, Geoffrey 79, 81, 83, 232, 261
Chettle, Henry 10, 13, 36
Robert the Second, King of Scots (with Dekker
and Jonson) 203
The Stepmother's Tragedy 204
Children of the Chapel 250
children's companies 9, 126, 250–51
Churchyard, Thomas 81, 107–8
'The Fortunate Farewell to the Most Forward
and Noble Earl of Essex' 107
The Scourge of Rebels in Ireland 107
'The Welcome Home of the Earl of Essex' 313
Clifford, Lady Anne 35
Clifford, Sir Conyers 293, 296
Clink prison, Southwark 121
Clonmel 290
Clopton, Hugh 164
Cobham, Henry Brooke, Lord 288, 298
Cobham, William Brooke, Lord 19–20, 21, 36
Coke, Edward 162
Coleridge, Samuel xvi, 256, 357
College of Arms 275, 286
Collier, John Payne 218
Compton, Lord 312
Condell, Henry 7, 356
and the Shakespeare First Folio of 1623 xvi,
356
Connaught 284
Consent (ship) 308
Cooper, Widow 267
Cope, Walter 32–3
Cordale, Francis 195–6
Cork 68, 70
Cornish Rebellion (1549) 170
Cornwallis, Sir William 81, 140, 293, 328–9
Essays 318, 329–32
Court of Requests 126
Cripplegate Ward 202
Cross, Samuel 14
Crown Inn, Oxford 265

Cuffe, Henry 140, 316
Cumberland, Earl of 201–2, 207, 306
Curlew Mountains 293
Curtain Theatre, near Finsbury Field 2, 6, 9, 12,
15–16, 22, 38, 48, 74, 92, 97, 98, 99, 116, 123,
126, 254
Cutwood, Thomas: *Caltha Poetarum* 153

Daniel, Samuel 223
Dante Alighieri 149
Danvers, Sir Charles 314, 316, 317
Danvers, Sir Henry 298, 314
Davenant, William 265
Davies, Sir John 81
Epigrams 153–4
Davis, Harry 292
Day, John 10, 13
Dee, John 303
deforestation 273
Dekker, Thomas 9, 10, 13, 48, 179, 270, 363, 365
Bear a Brain 203
Old Fortunatus 364, 365
Page of Plymouth (with Jonson) 203
Robert the Second, King of Scots (with Chettle
and Jonson)
The Shoemaker's Holiday 364, 365
Derby, William Stanley, sixth Earl of 250
Derby's Men 6, 269
Derricke, John 81
Desmond, Earl of 199, 284
Devereux, Penelope (daughter of the Earl of
Essex) 291
Diana fountain, West Cheap, London 242
Digges, Leonard 192
Discourse of Ireland, A 111–12
Dodington, Lieutenant Edward 197
Donne, John 65, 220, 327, 361, 370, 373
Dover 14
Dowden, Edward 218
Dragon (ship) 308
Drake, Sir Francis 161, 305
Drayton, Michael 10–11, 12, 204, 223, *258*, 273, 371
Poly-Olbion 272
Droeshout, Martin *xv*
Drummond, William 19
Drury, Sir Robert 20
Drury Lane Theatre, London 251–2
Dryden, John 71, 326
Dublin 57, 62, 64, 76, 283, 287, 288, 290, 291, 299